# OCR

# GCSE
# Geography

To Diana

Philip Allan Updates, an imprint of Hodder Education, an Hachette UK company, Market Place, Deddington, Oxfordshire, OX15 0SE

*Orders*
Bookpoint Ltd, 130 Milton Park, Abingdon, Oxfordshire, OX14 4SB
tel: 01235 827720
fax: 01235 400454
e-mail: uk.orders@bookpoint.co.uk
Lines are open 9.00 a.m.–5.00 p.m., Monday to Saturday, with a 24-hour message answering service. You can also order through the Philip Allan Updates website: www.philipallan.co.uk

© Philip Allan Updates, 2006, 2009

First published 2006
Second edition 2009

Impression number   5  4  3  2  1
Year   2014  2013  2012  2011  2010  2009

ISBN 978-0-340-98661-5

All rights reserved; no part of this publication may be reproduced, stored in a retrieval system, or transmitted, in any form or by any means, electronic, mechanical, photocopying, recording or otherwise without either the prior written permission of Philip Allan Updates or a licence permitting restricted copying in the United Kingdom issued by the Copyright Licensing Agency Ltd, Saffron House, 6–10 Kirby Street, London EC1N 8TS.

Ordnance Survey map extracts reproduced by permission of Ordnance Survey © Crown copyright. Licence No 100027418

Cover photograph by Arctic Images

Printed in Italy

Hachette UK's policy is to use papers that are natural, renewable and recyclable products and made from wood grown in sustainable forests. The logging and manufacturing processes are expected to conform to the environmental regulations of the country of origin.

# OCR B GCSE Geography

# Contents

**Introduction** .................................................. v

## Theme 1  Rivers and coasts

### 1 Rivers
| | | |
|---|---|---|
| Part 1 | Hydrology ................................................. | 1 |
| Part 2 | Floods .................................................... | 9 |
| Part 3 | Fluvial landforms and processes ..................... | 16 |

### 2 Coasts
| | | |
|---|---|---|
| Part 1 | Coastal processes and landforms ................... | 27 |
| Part 2 | Coastal management ............................... | 37 |

## Theme 2  Population and settlement

### 3 Population
| | | |
|---|---|---|
| Part 1 | Population structure ................................ | 43 |
| Part 2 | Population change .................................. | 50 |
| Part 3 | Migration ............................................ | 57 |

### 4 Settlement
| | | |
|---|---|---|
| Part 1 | Urban and rural populations ....................... | 63 |
| Part 2 | Land use patterns in cities ......................... | 74 |
| Part 3 | The provision of goods and retail services ........ | 92 |

## Theme 3  Natural hazards

### 5 Tectonic hazards
- Part 1 The distribution and causes of earthquakes and volcanoes ................................ 103
- Part 2 Earthquake and volcanic hazards ................... 109
- Part 3 The impact of earthquakes ......................... 114

### 6 Climatic hazards
- Part 1 Tropical storms ..................................... 123
- Part 2 Droughts ........................................... 130
- Part 3 Case studies of tropical storms and drought ........... 137

## Theme 4  Economic development

### 7 Development and employment
- Part 1 What is development? ............................. 143
- Part 2 Development and international aid ................. 150
- Part 3 Employment structures and patterns ............... 156

### 8 Economic activity
- Part 1 The location of economic activities ................. 161
- Part 2 Multi-national corporations (MNCs) and development .. 173
- Part 3 Economic activities and the physical environment ...... 177

## Geographical enquiry

### 9 Fieldwork investigation in geography
- Part 1 Setting the scene ................................. 198
- Part 2 Method of data collection ......................... 201
- Part 3 Data presentation and analysis ..................... 211
- Part 4 Evaluation and conclusion ......................... 220

## Glossary ................................................. 222

## Index .................................................... 229

# Introduction

This textbook covers the content you need to tackle the written papers (B561 and B563) and the fieldwork enquiry for OCR Specification B GCSE geography. Its four main sections correspond to the four themes that make up the specification:
- Theme 1 Rivers and coasts
- Theme 2 Population and settlement
- Theme 3 Natural hazards
- Theme 4 Economic development

A number of approaches define the OCR (B) specification. Most distinctive is its emphasis on the geographical issues that arise through the interaction of people and the physical environment. Other important themes are the sustainable management of environmental resources, the importance of global information systems (GIS) technologies, and geographical investigative strategies.

The subsections of each chapter start by listing the relevant key ideas from the specification. You should take special note of these: not only do they provide the framework for the detail of each subsection, but they are also the basis for examination questions. The topics covered in the book are approached in two different ways. First, a more general section describes and explains patterns, processes and changes, and the issues that arise from them. Second, there are location-specific case studies. Case studies are vitally important: good exam answers will draw on their specific detail to support more general points. If you learn them and apply them appropriately in the exam, you should do well.

This textbook has a number of other features designed to make learning easier and more effective. Important factual details have been separated from the main text and presented as Factfiles. In addition, each chapter is illustrated with photographs, tables, maps, charts and diagrams. These provide further information and are an integral part of the book. Don't ignore them: they are just as important as the text and should be studied carefully. Chapter 9 is devoted to the fieldwork enquiry and reminds us that fieldwork is an important (and enjoyable) part of the course. This chapter guides you through the skills and methodology you will need to complete a successful fieldwork enquiry.

Numerous activities are interspersed with the text. Their purpose is to:
- encourage you to engage fully with your studies
- test your knowledge and understanding of the topics covered

- help you develop essential skills, such as: map interpretation; data collection, presentation, and analysis; GIS; ICT; and the evaluation of issues
- give you the opportunity to practise examination-style questions

Finally, to do well at GCSE you need a good knowledge of geographical terms. To avoid defining every term within the text, I have included a comprehensive glossary at the back of the book before the index. Where a new term appears in the text for the first time it is emboldened. If you are not sure what a term means, look it up in the glossary. Then make a note of it and its definition (perhaps in the margin of your folder or exercise book) so that you don't forget it.

I hope that you enjoy using this book and that it helps you to make some sense of the complex and changing world we live in. I also hope that it raises awareness of your responsibilities as a global citizen. And, of course, I hope it helps you to do really well in your exams!

Michael Raw
*Ilkley, West Yorkshire*

# Theme 1  Rivers and coasts

# Chapter 1  Rivers

## Part 1 Hydrology

Water is a remarkable substance. It exists at the Earth's surface and in the atmosphere as a liquid (water), a solid (ice) and a gas (water vapour). Its changes of state are well known:
- *evaporation* occurs when liquid water becomes vapour
- *condensation* when vapour turns to water
- *melting* when ice thaws to water
- *freezing* when water becomes ice

> **Key ideas**
> - The **hydrological cycle** is a system comprising stores and flows of water.
> - River basins are systems with inputs, flows, stores and outputs of water and **sediment**.
> - A storm hydrograph describes river flow (discharge) and the response to change.

### The hydrological cycle

Water flows in an unending cycle between the atmosphere, the continents and the oceans. Over thousands of years individual water molecules are recycled over and over again.

This hydrological (or water) cycle is a simple system. It consists of a number of stores (see Table 1.1) linked by transfers of water into and out of store (see Figure 1.1). Evaporation and the **transpiration** of water from plants transport water into the atmosphere. Precipitation, which includes rain and snow, returns water to the Earth's surface. On the surface of the continents, water follows one of three pathways. Most moves over the surface as **runoff** into streams and rivers. Some seeps into the soil and **porous rocks**. The rest collects as snow and ice in **glaciers**.

Within the hydrological cycle, individual water molecules undertake remarkable journeys. Some are transported from the atmosphere to the oceans and continents and back again in just a few days. Other pathways take much longer.

*Table 1.1  Global stores of water*

| Reservoir | Size (km³ × 10,000,000) | % of all water |
|---|---|---|
| Oceans | 1,370 | 97 |
| Polar ice and glaciers | 29 | 2 |
| Groundwater | 9.5 | 0.7 |
| Lakes | 0.125 | 0.01 |
| Soils | 0.065 | 0.005 |
| Atmosphere | 0.013 | 0.001 |
| Rivers | 0.0017 | 0.0001 |
| Living things | 0.0006 | 0.00004 |

# Chapter 1 Rivers

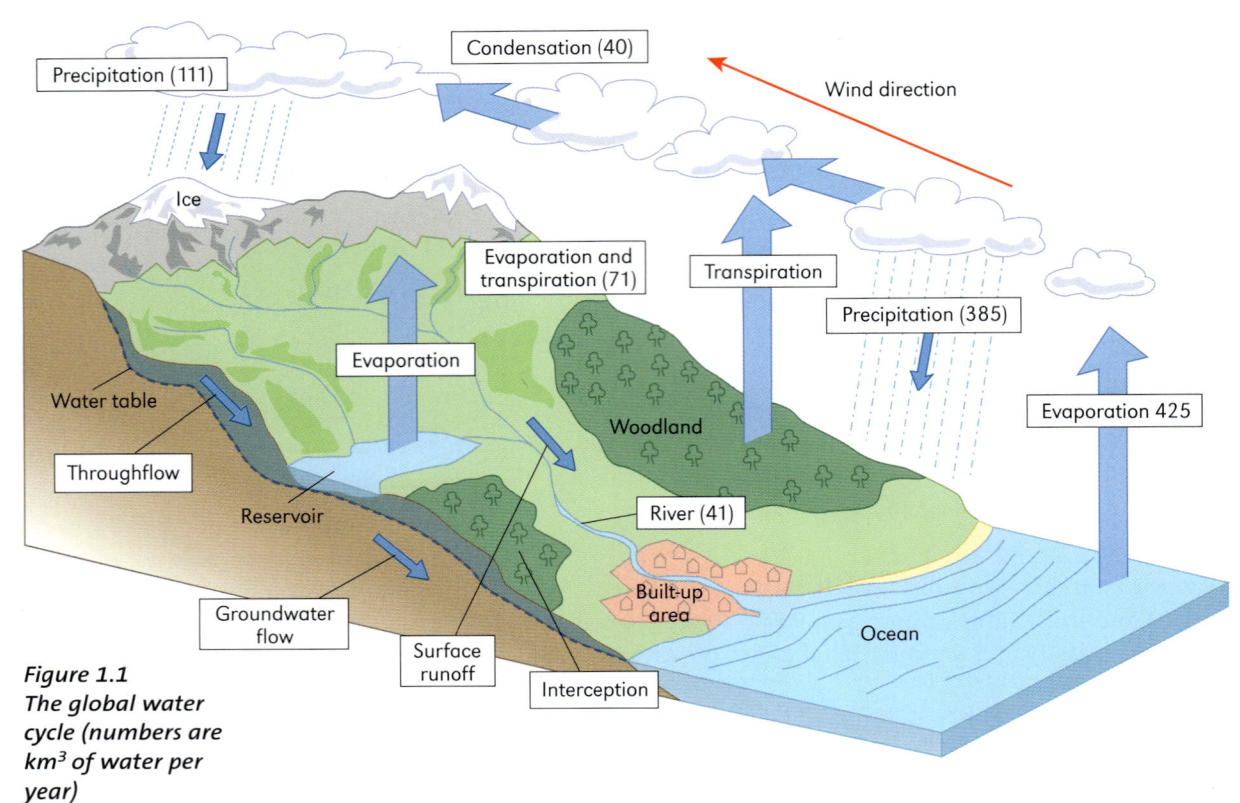

*Figure 1.1 The global water cycle (numbers are km³ of water per year)*

For example, water flowing into porous rocks may be stored for thousands of years (see Table 1.2). But even this water is eventually released and flows into rivers and the oceans.

### Factfile 1.1 Water on the planet

- The oceans and seas are by far the largest stores of water on the planet.
- Water exists as a solid, a liquid and a gas, both at the Earth's surface and in the atmosphere.
- Water circulates between the atmosphere, the oceans and the continents.
- The circulation of water occurs at global, regional and local scales and is known as the hydrological or water cycle.
- The stores in the water cycle are linked by flows such as precipitation, evaporation, transpiration and runoff.

### Activity 1.1

1. Using the data in Table 1.1, draw stacked bar charts to show:
   (a) The global distribution of water between the oceans and the land.
   (b) The size of global fresh water stores.

2. Study Figure 1.1.
   (a) How much water is evaporated from the oceans in a year?
   (b) How much water is evaporated and transpired from the land in a year?

3. More precipitation falls on the continents than is evaporated and transpired from them. Using the evidence of Figure 1.1 only, suggest a reason for this.

Table 1.2 Storage time for water molecules

| Reservoir | Average time spent in store |
|---|---|
| Groundwater (deep) | 10,000 years |
| Groundwater (shallow) | 200 years |
| Lakes | 100 years |
| Glaciers | 40 years |
| Snow cover | 145 days |
| Soil | 70 days |
| Rivers | 15 days |
| Atmosphere | 8 days |
| Puddles | 2 days |
| Vegetation surfaces | 12 hours |

### Activity 1.2

1. Table 1.2 shows the average length of time that individual water molecules are stored in various parts of the water cycle. Estimate the average recycling times of water molecules in the following pathways:
   (a) atmosphere → soil → river → atmosphere
   (b) atmosphere → soil → shallow groundwater → river → atmosphere
   (c) atmosphere → vegetation surface → puddle → river → atmosphere

## People and the global hydrological cycle

Because water is essential to life it has a huge influence on human activities. It is used for drinking, sanitation, manufacturing, **irrigation**, generating electricity and countless other purposes. Almost all of these uses require fresh water, which is drawn from two main sources: first, from surface supplies in rivers and lakes (see Photograph 1.1); and second, from water stored deep underground, in **porous rocks** such as chalk and sandstone.

## Hydrographs

Hydrographs show stream flow over a period of time. Storm hydrographs describe stream flow over just a few hours (see Figure 1.2). Other hydrographs show maximum or average flows per day, over a year or more.

Photograph 1.1 Hayeswater, the Lake District: a natural lake, enlarged by a dam to provide public water supplies

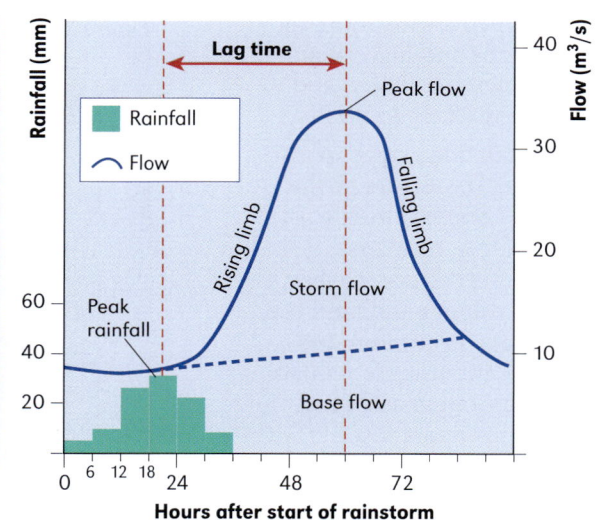

Figure 1.2 A storm hydrograph

# Chapter 1 Rivers

### Storm hydrographs

Storm hydrographs divide stream flow into two parts. **Storm flow** is water from a recent rainfall event. It accounts for the steep rise and fall of the flow curve on the hydrograph (see Figure 1.2). **Base flow** is water that enters streams from storage. Groundwater from porous rocks is the main source of base flow. Unlike storm flow, base flow is constant. It allows streams and rivers to keep flowing even in times of **drought**.

The shape of a storm hydrograph depends on the proportions of storm flow and base flow. This in turn depends on the nature of the drainage basin. For example, are the rocks permeable or impermeable? Are the slopes steep or gentle? Is land use rural or urban? Figures 1.3 and 1.4 show storm hydrographs for two different rivers that experienced the same rainfall event.

## Factfile 1.2 Hydrographs

- Hydrographs show stream flow over a period of time.
- Storm hydrographs show the response of a stream to rainfall over a few hours or a few days.
- Stream flow (or discharge) consists of storm flow and base flow.
- Streams with short lag times and high peak flows are 'flashy' and most likely to flood.
- Peak flows depend on:
  (a) The nature of the drainage basin, e.g. rock type, vegetation cover, slopes and land use.
  (b) The amount and intensity of rainfall.
  (c) Temperature and evaporation.
  (d) Whether the soil is saturated, frozen or dry.

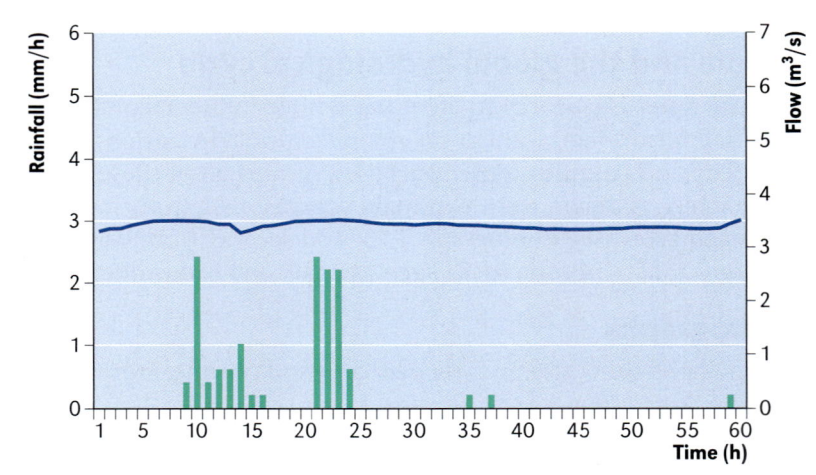

*Figure 1.3 Hydrograph for the River Lambourn, 5–9 January 1993*

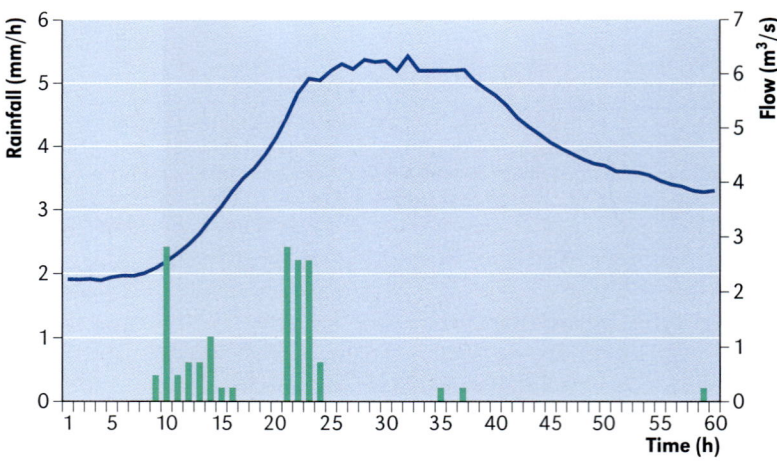

*Figure 1.4 Hydrograph for the River Ock, 5–9 January 1993*

# Theme 1

Streams dominated by storm flow rise and fall quickly and have short **lag times**. This means that there is only a short interval between maximum rainfall and peak flow. Streams with short lag times and high **peak flows** are said to be 'flashy' and often present a serious flood risk.

▶ Photograph 1.2 High Cup Nick, Cumbria: steep slopes and impermeable rock create rapid runoff

Photograph 1.3 Lyon, France: impermeable surfaces such as tiles, concrete and tarmac, and pitched roofs, gutters and drains, are responsible for rapid runoff in cities

Table 1.3 The influence of river basin characteristics on storm hydrographs

| Characteristic | Influence on storm hydrograph |
| --- | --- |
| Rock type | Permeable rocks such as chalk and sandstone absorb rainwater, which they release slowly. The result is long lag times and relatively low peak flows. In other words, the flow is rarely extreme (i.e. very high or very low). In contrast, impermeable rocks like granite and **basalt** cause rapid runoff, resulting in short lag times and high peak flows. |
| Woodland | Well-wooded drainage basins **intercept** rainfall. This slows the movement of water to streams and rivers. Some water stored on leaf surfaces also evaporates. These effects lengthen lag times and reduce peak flows. |
| Slopes | Upland river basins have steep slopes, causing water to run off quickly. Gentle slopes slow the movement of water to streams and rivers. |

## Activity 1.3

The Rivers Ock and Lambourn are tributaries of the River Thames, and lie northwest of London. They are located close together, have similar-sized drainage basins and similar average flows. The main difference between them is rock type. Much of the Ock's drainage basin is impermeable clay. In contrast, most of the Lambourn's drainage basin is chalk, which is porous.

Study Figures 1.3 and 1.4, which show the responses of the Rivers Ock and Lambourn to the same rainfall event from 5 to 9 January 1993.

1. Describe the main features of the two hydrographs.
2. What were (a) the maximum and (b) the minimum flows for the Ock and the Lambourn?
3. Which river is the more 'flashy'? Explain your answer.
4. Explain how rock type has influenced flows on the Rivers Ock and Lambourn.

Rivers and coasts

# Chapter 1 Rivers

## River basins

River (or drainage) basins are areas drained by rivers and their **tributaries** (see Figure 1.5). They are natural systems with inputs, flows, stores and outputs of water and sediment.

## Water transfers in river basins

Within river basins there is a balance between the inputs and outputs of water:

**precipitation = evaporation + transpiration + stream flow +/− storage**

Figure 1.6 shows water transfers in a river basin. Water enters the drainage basin through precipitation. It leaves through evaporation, transpiration from plants, surface **runoff**, **throughflow** and **groundwater flow**. In the short term, some water enters storage. The main stores are permeable rocks, soils, lakes, swamps and vegetation.

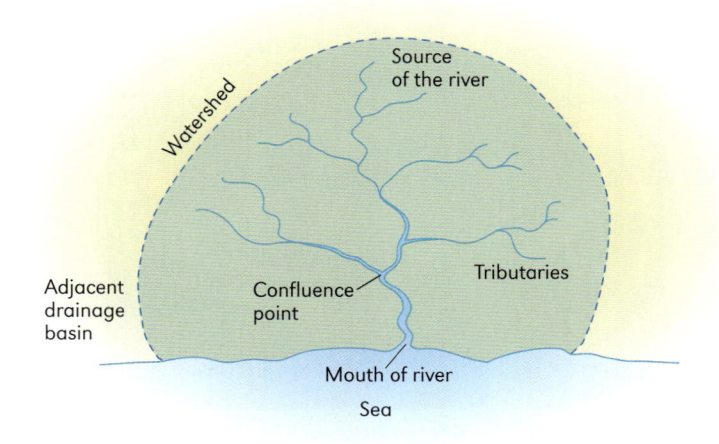

▶ Figure 1.5
A drainage basin

▼ Figure 1.6
The drainage basin as a system

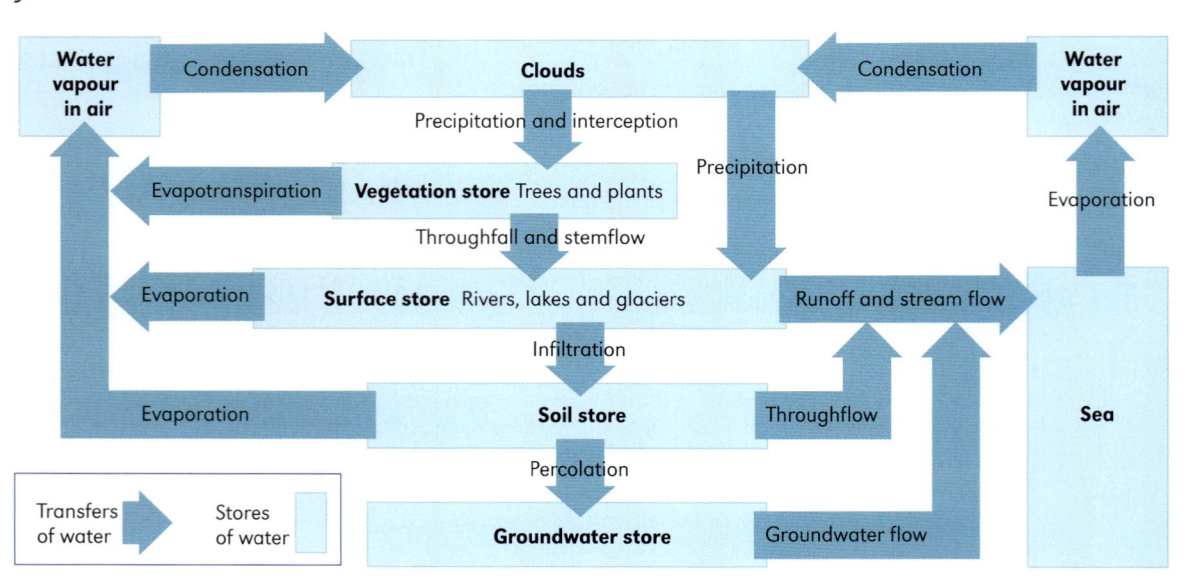

Consider what happens to a typical droplet of water. Once it has left the cloud it may strike the surface vegetation. In other words, it is **intercepted** before either evaporating or dripping to the ground. What happens when it reaches the ground depends on whether the soil is dry, waterlogged or frozen. If it is dry, the droplet seeps into the soil — a process called **infiltration**. If the ground is waterlogged or frozen, water collects in puddles or runs across the surface to join the nearest stream.

Where soils rest on **impermeable rocks** such as clay or granite, water seeps down only as far as the rock layer. It then moves through the soil parallel to the surface, as **throughflow**. However, if the underlying rocks are **permeable** (e.g. chalk or sandstone), the water sinks (or **percolates**) into the rock layer. This water, stored in permeable rocks, is known as **groundwater**. It may take several years for groundwater water to resurface as **springs** or **seepage** areas on hill slopes.

### Activity 1.4

Study Figure 1.7. For each store (A–D):

1. Name one process by which water (a) enters and (b) leaves each store.
2. State whether storage is likely to be short, medium or long term.

*Figure 1.7 Stores of water in drainage basins*

(A) Puddling of water in a field and overland flow

(B) Oak tree in early spring

(C) Fair weather cumulus clouds on a spring day

(D) Rainwater stored on oak leaves

Rivers and coasts

# Chapter 1 Rivers

## Activity 1.5

Study Figure 1.8, which provides information on rock permeability and altitude for three river basins in the UK. The difference between the maximum and minimum altitudes in each drainage basin gives an idea of slope steepness.

1. Which drainage basin appears to have:
   (a) the steepest slopes?
   (b) the gentlest slopes?
2. Which stream is likely to be most dependent on groundwater? Explain your answer.
3. Which drainage basin has:
   (a) the most farmland?
   (b) the most urban land?
   (c) the least woodland?
4. Both the River Wyre and Stevenage Brook have high peak flows and short lag times, but for different reasons. Can you suggest reasons for the differences?
5. The River Inver has a large lake — Loch Assynt — in its drainage basin. What effect do you think this lake will have on the river's storm hydrograph?

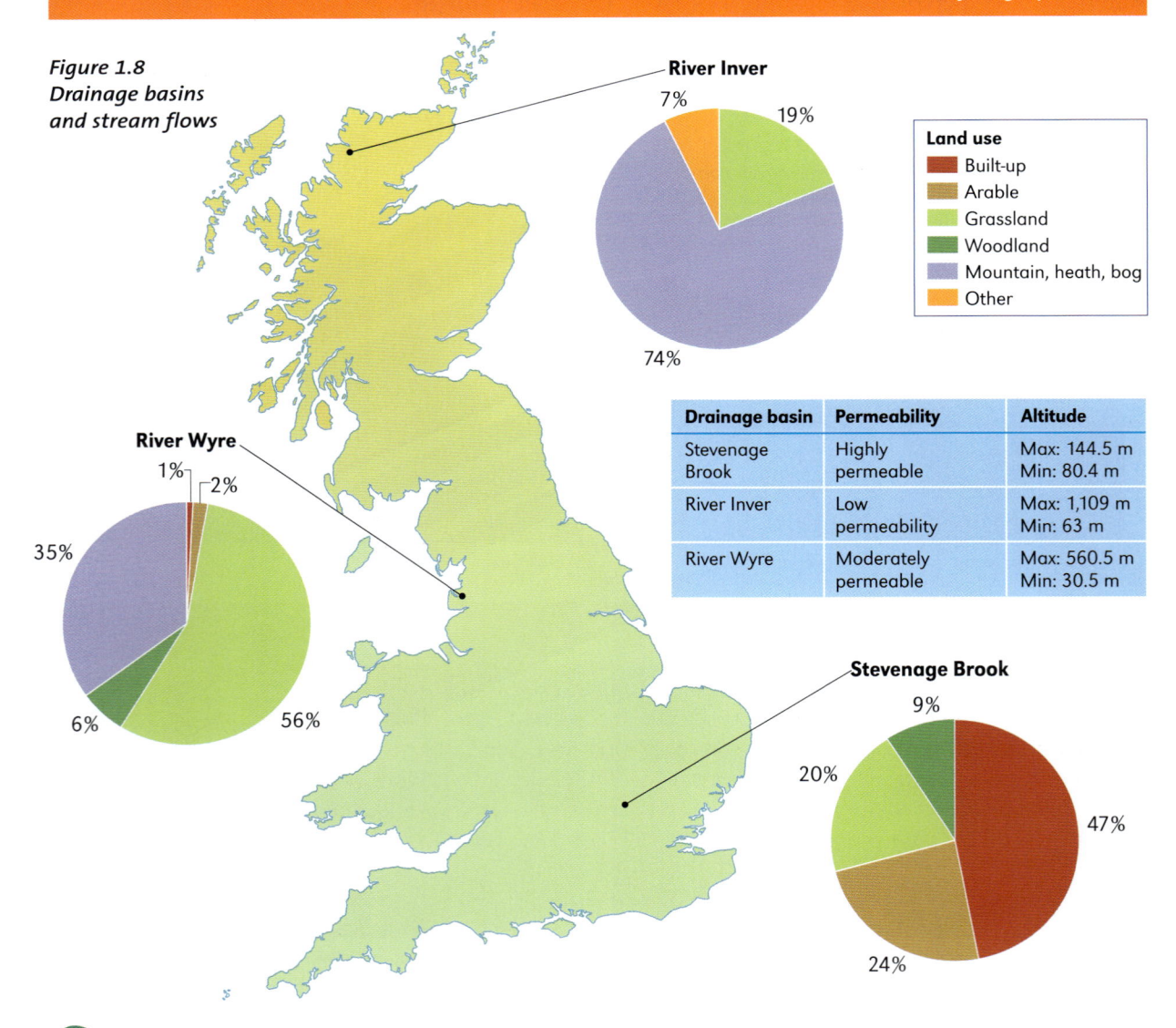

*Figure 1.8 Drainage basins and stream flows*

**River Inver**: 7%, 19%, 74%

**River Wyre**: 1%, 2%, 35%, 6%, 56%

**Stevenage Brook**: 47%, 24%, 20%, 9%

**Land use**
- Built-up
- Arable
- Grassland
- Woodland
- Mountain, heath, bog
- Other

| Drainage basin | Permeability | Altitude |
|---|---|---|
| Stevenage Brook | Highly permeable | Max: 144.5 m<br>Min: 80.4 m |
| River Inver | Low permeability | Max: 1,109 m<br>Min: 63 m |
| River Wyre | Moderately permeable | Max: 560.5 m<br>Min: 30.5 m |

OCR (B) GCSE Geography

## Sediment transfers in river basins

It is easy to overlook the fact that rivers transfer sediments as well as water (see Figure 1.9). Sediments are rock particles produced by weathering and **erosion** (see page 17). Rivers and streams transport these sediments through river basins and ultimately to the sea. Together with water, sediments are the major output from river basins. However, most sediments are not transported *directly* to the sea. Some enter long-term storage in **floodplains**; others are trapped in lakes where they remain for thousands of years. Sediments deposited in river channels form bars, which are temporary stores until they are moved by the next flood event.

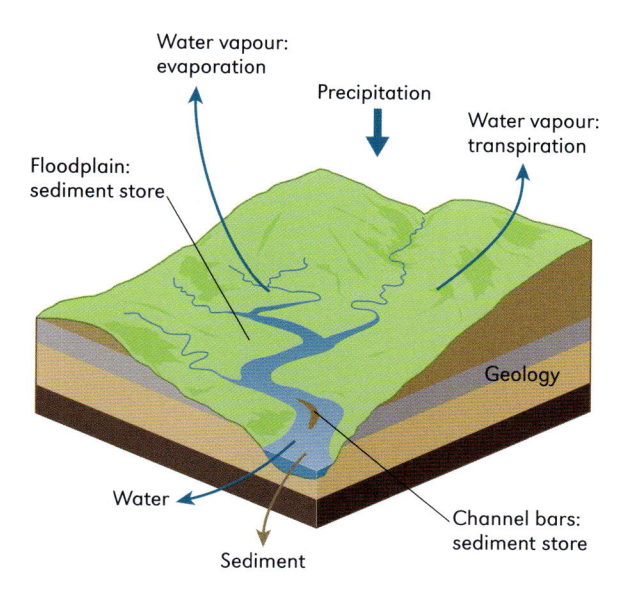

*Figure 1.9 Water and sediment transfers in a river basin*

# Part 2 Floods

Rivers flood when they overtop their banks and spill onto the adjoining valley floor. Flooding is a normal event. Under natural conditions rivers normally flood once or twice a year in the UK. Floods only become **hazards** when they destroy property or cause injury and loss of life. There are concerns that floods seem to be occurring more often and getting bigger. If this is so there are two possible reasons. First, **climate change** caused by **global warming** is resulting in more extreme weather conditions; and second, changes in land use, such as deforestation, **urbanisation** and land drainage, have increased rates of runoff.

### Key ideas

- Flooding may result from physical processes and/or human activities.
- The impact of flooding varies between areas, and especially between **LEDCs** and **MEDCs**.
- Some strategies for flood management are more **sustainable** than others.

A number of management strategies are used to tackle the flood problem. The most costly involve building control structures, such as dams, **flood embankments (levées)**, **sluice gates** and **relief channels** (see Table 1.4, page 11 and Figure 1.10). A cheaper and more sustainable alternative is to work with nature. This could, for example, mean replacing farmland with forests in the headwaters regions, and preserving **wetlands** (important water stores) on floodplains. Other approaches include: better flood warnings (see Figure 1.11); encouraging people in flood-risk areas to take out flood insurance; and stricter planning controls to stop houses, offices and factories being built on floodplains.

# Chapter 1 Rivers

▶ Figure 1.10 Types of flood management

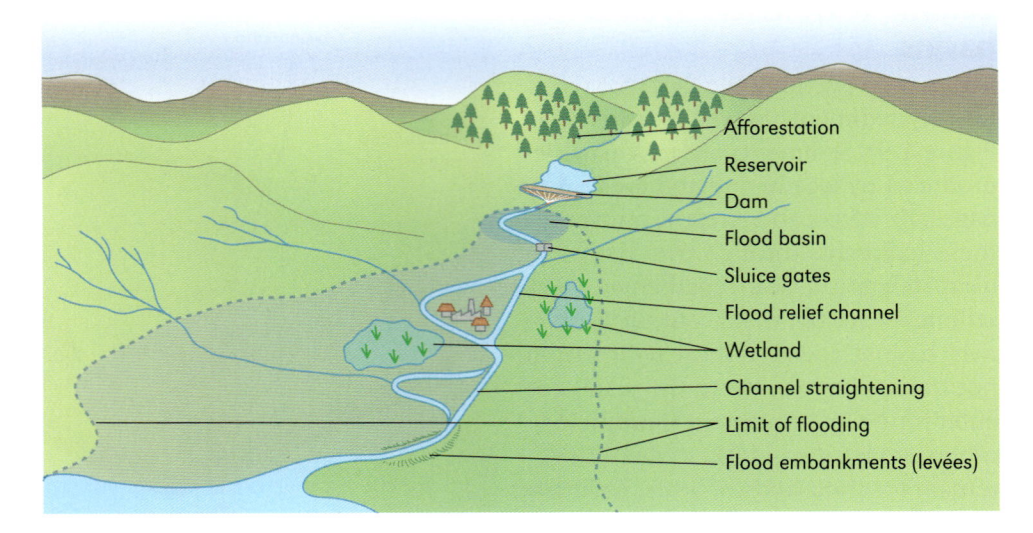

Labels: Afforestation, Reservoir, Dam, Flood basin, Sluice gates, Flood relief channel, Wetland, Channel straightening, Limit of flooding, Flood embankments (levées)

## Factfile 1.3 River floods

- The physical causes of floods are excessive rain and rapid runoff.
- There are two types of flood: flash floods, which are unpredictable, occur quickly and without warning; and slow floods associated with a steady rise in river levels over several days.
- Because of their longer time scale, slow floods are easier to manage (e.g. by issuing flood warnings) than flash floods.
- A variety of hard engineering structures, such as dams, levées and relief channels, provide protection against flooding.
- Alternative flood protection strategies to include afforestation, land-use control on floodplains, early warnings, education and insurance.

**Flood Watch:** There is the possibility of some flooding. Keep a close eye on local radio or television reports. Alert your neighbours and watch water levels.

**Flood Warning:** Flooding is expected and will cause disruption. Move valuables to safety. Turn off gas and electricity. Be ready to evacuate your home. Put sandbags or floodboards in place to protect your home.

**Severe Flood Warning:** Serious flooding is expected with imminent danger to life and property. Prepare for gas, electricity, water and telephone services to be lost. Keep calm and reassure others. Cooperate with the emergency services.

**All Clear:** Flood water levels are going down and no flood watches or flood warnings are in force any longer. You can check it is safe to return home.

Figure 1.11 The flood warning system in the UK

## Activity 1.6

Log on to the Environment Agency's (EA) flood website: www.environment-agency.gov.uk/subjects/flood/floodwarning

1. Find out if any flood warnings are currently in operation in your home region. If warnings have been issued, list them and the status of the flood alert.
2. Find out how many flood warnings are currently in operation by region in the UK.
3. Find out if your local area is at risk of flooding by entering the name of your town or home postcode on the website.
4. What advice does the EA give to the public on personal safety and preparation for floods?

*Table 1.4 Flood control through engineering*

| Flood embankments (levées) | Raising the level of riverbanks keeps floodwaters in the river channel and protects floodplain communities. However, levées can raise flood levels, and if levées fail, floods can be even more damaging. |
|---|---|
| Dams | Dams create reservoirs, which store floodwaters and protect places downstream. The floodwaters can then be released gradually. The disadvantages of dams are:<br>(a) they are expensive to build<br>(b) the reservoirs flood valleys, causing environmental damage |
| Sluice gates and flood basins | Sluice gates are built into the riverbed and are raised when there is a serious flood risk. Floodwaters are diverted into temporary storage basins on the floodplain. |
| Flood relief channels | Flood relief channels give protection by diverting part of the flow to an artificial channel, thereby lowering water levels in the main channel. Although flood relief channels protect individual settlements, they do not prevent flooding further downstream. |
| Channel straightening | Straightening river channels by removing **meanders** increases the gradient of the channel and speeds the flow of water. |

## Case study: The Boscastle floods

On 16 August 2004 a flash flood devastated the picturesque village of Boscastle on the north Cornish coast (see Figure 1.12). Without warning, a 3-metre wall of water swept down the Valency River. It carried trees, cars and other debris through the village (see Photograph 1.4). At its peak, the flood reached 140 m$^3$/s at Boscastle. This compares with average flows of just 0.5 m$^3$/s.

Around 1,000 residents and visitors were affected. Forty-two properties were flooded and four completely demolished. Over 80 cars were wrecked and four footbridges across the Valency River were destroyed. The rapid response of the emergency services prevented any deaths. Helicopters airlifted 100 people to safety (Figure 1.13).

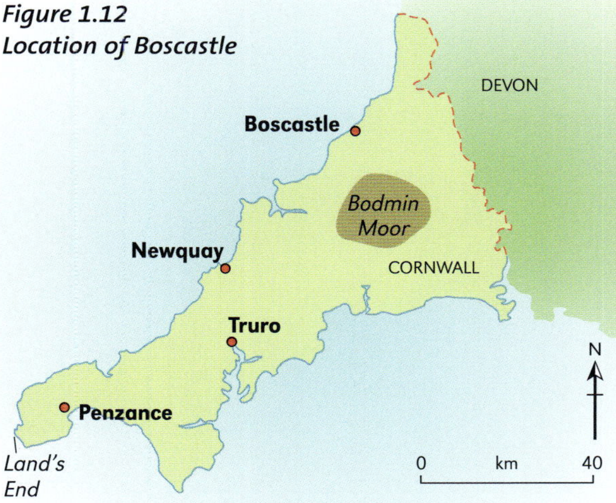

*Figure 1.12 Location of Boscastle*

### 'Cars, trees, everything floating down the road — it was terrifying'

*By Sam Jones*

It was at the bottom of Boscastle near the harbour where devastation was most spectacular; there a huge section of road leading across a river bridge was torn away by the water.

Uprooted trees were piled up to 9 metres high against houses and strewn across the road. Shops that took the full force of the water had their window glass ripped out…The end of one building near the harbour had been completely swept away by the force of the water.

Outside a row of cottages just metres from the river's edge two or three cars had been tossed against the side of the walls and one of them was upside down.

Buildings less than 100 metres from them had been battered by the full force of the water and rubble, debris, vegetation, tree trunks and branches were piled up against the walls.

Source: the *Guardian*, 17 August 2004

*Figure 1.13*

# Chapter 1 Rivers

## Physical and human causes of flooding

Several factors contributed to the Boscastle floods. The most important of these was torrential rain — 200 mm fell in a single day, most of it during a 5-hour spell. It was caused by warm, moist air from the Atlantic Ocean moving inland. This air, pushed up by the high ground of Bodmin Moor, formed convective clouds up to 12 km thick. These huge, slow-moving clouds produced enormous amounts of rain — up to 25 mm in 15 minutes.

Other physical factors responsible for the flood included: the steep slopes in the river basin, which caused water to move quickly into the Valency River and its tributaries (see Figure 1.14); the largely impermeable geology of the basin, made up of clay and shale; and the intensity of the rain which meant that interception was low and little water entered the soil.

But human factors also contributed to the disaster. Building on the Valency's floodplain in Boscastle exposed many houses to the direct path of the floodwaters. In addition, several narrow bridges trapped trees swept down by the floodwaters, causing the waters to pond and flood adjacent properties.

*Photograph 1.4 Helicopters winching people to safety during the Boscastle floods*

*Figure 1.14 Drainage basin of the Valency River*

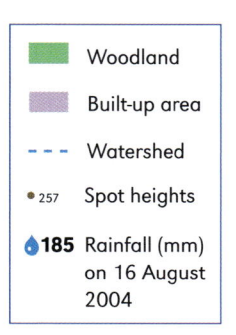

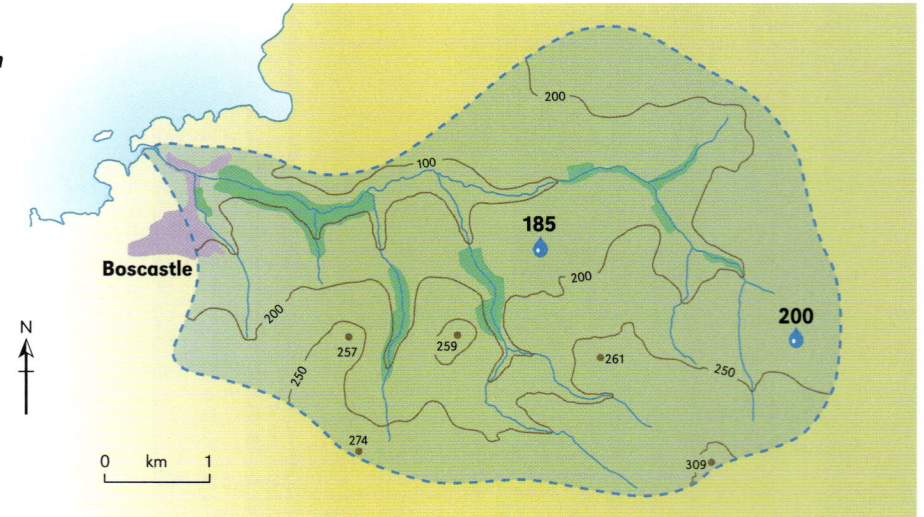

OCR (B) GCSE Geography

# Theme 1

## Flood management

It has been estimated that a flood similar to the one in Boscastle might occur on average once every 400 years. The flood was therefore an extreme event. Even so, a flood management plan is being implemented to prevent a repeat of the disaster. The scheme allows homeowners and businesses whose properties were damaged to rebuild with the confidence that they will be protected in future.

### Activity 1.7

Study Figure 1.14, which shows the drainage basin of the Valency River.

1. What are the highest and lowest altitudes in the Valency catchment?
2. What is the approximate area of the catchment in km²?
3. Complete Table 1.5

*Table 1.5 Effects of features of the Valency catchment on lag time and peak flow*

| Factor | Description | Effect on lag time and peak flow |
|---|---|---|
| Relief (slopes and altitude) | | |
| Woodland cover | | |
| Rock type (permeability) | | |

## Case study: The Koshi River floods, Bihar

On 18 August 2008, the Koshi (or Kosi) River broke through its flood embankments (levées) in Bihar state in northern India, and without warning shifted its main channel to an old one last occupied 200 years ago (see Photograph 1.5). When the river changed channels it hit an area not used to flooding and where the people were totally unprepared. The result was a major flood disaster. At least 3,000 people died, 250,000 homes were destroyed and numerous villages drowned. Overall one million people were forced from their homes. Over the past 250 years the Koshi River has shifted its main channel abruptly in this way a dozen times.

### Causes of flooding

Physical factors contributed to the Koshi floods. Discharge levels were certainly high (though not exceptional) due to the melting of snow and glaciers in the Himalayas and the monsoon rains. Also, the Koshi River has a relatively short, steep course. This, combined with its high discharge, gives it ample power to erode its bed and banks. One other physical factor played a part in the floods: the river's large **sediment load**. Much of this sediment is deposited in the river, elevating the river bed

### Factfile 1.4 The Koshi River

- The Koshi River basin, a major tributary of the Ganges River, covers 69,000 km² — an area roughly the size of Scotland (see Figure 1.15).
- The Koshi River has its source in the Himalayas in Nepal: much of its flow is meltwater from glaciers.
- During the summer the river is swollen by the monsoon rains (as well meltwater).
- The Koshi River has flooded disastrously on many occasions and caused great suffering. In India it is known as 'the sorrow of Bihar'.
- As the Koshi leaves the mountains it flows across the plains of Bihar, which are low lying, and at high risk from flooding.

Rivers and coasts

Chapter 1 Rivers

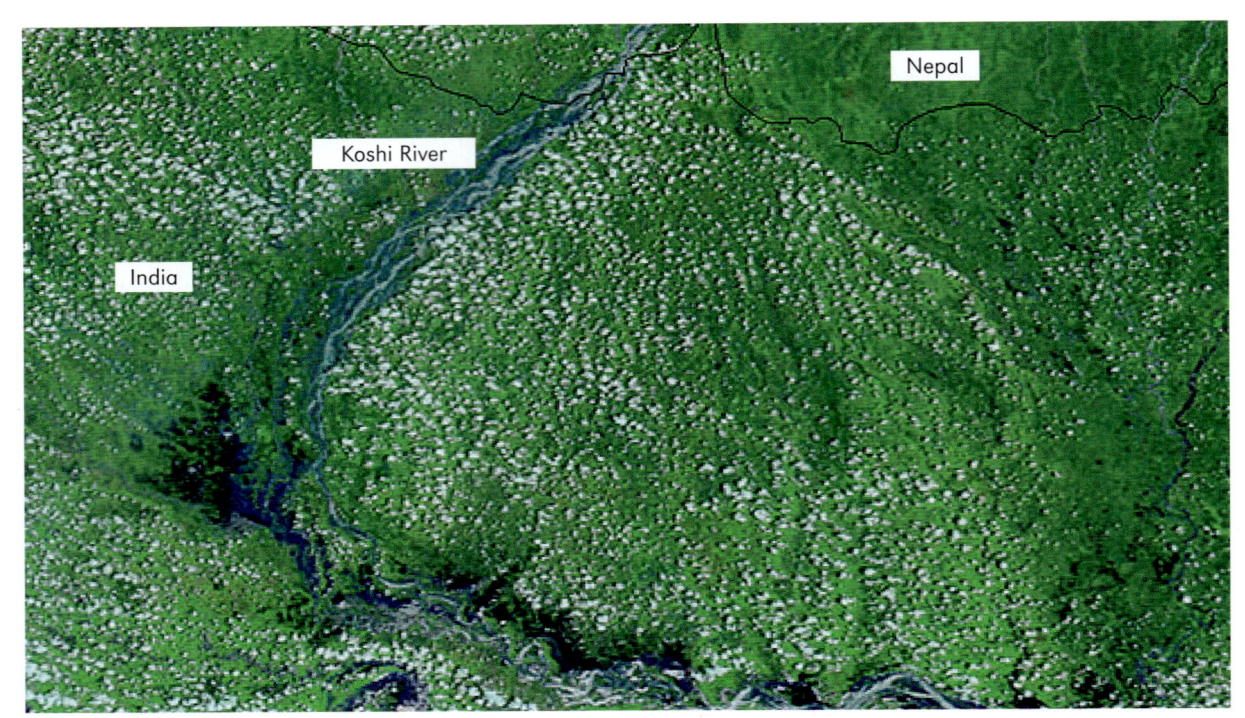

8 August 2008

24 August 2008

Photograph 1.5 Satellite images of the Koshi floods

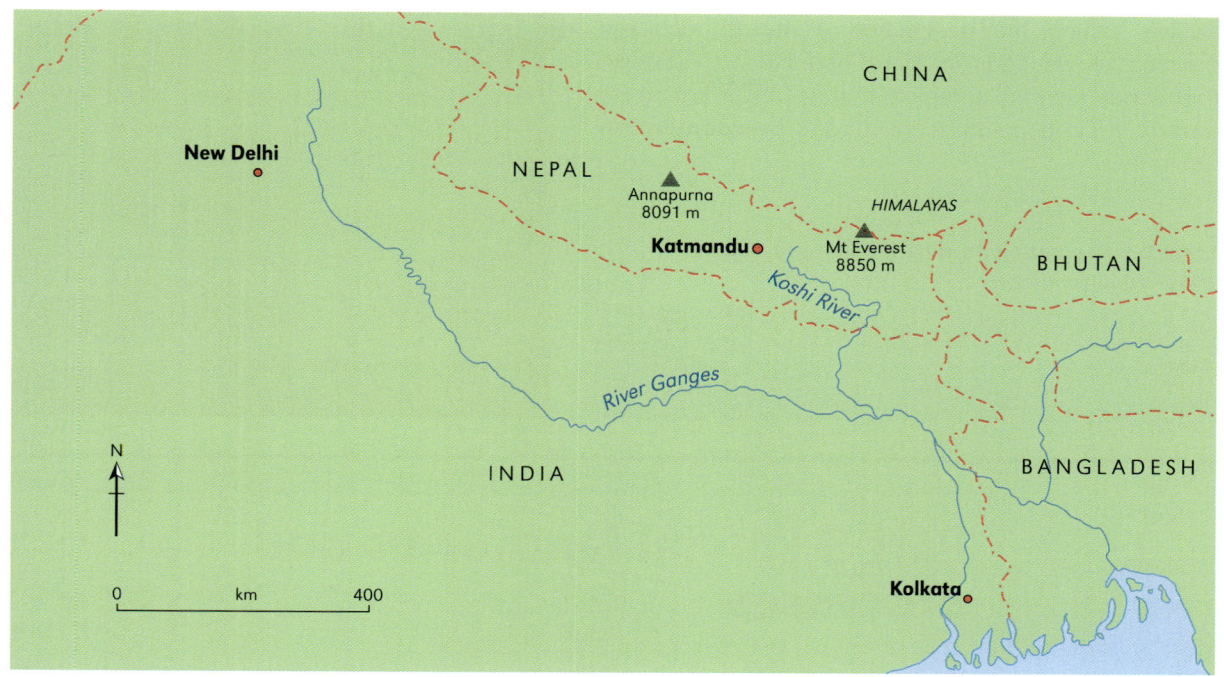

*Figure 1.15 Location of the Koshi River, India*

above the surrounding floodplain and reducing the size of the channel. This results in a greatly increased flood risk.

Human factors also played an important part in the floods:
- Soil erosion caused by deforestation and poor farming techniques (which in turn are driven by poverty and rapid population growth) has increased the Koshi's sediment load and the build-up of sediment in the channel.
- River engineering — many experts believe that the levée system, designed to keep the river within its channel, has made flooding worse. Confined by the levées, the river flows faster, increasing its erosion potential. If the levées are breached the fast-flowing floodwaters are deadly.
- Levées isolate the river from its floodplain, preventing floodwaters escaping upstream, which would normally reduce river levels downstream.
- Levées prevent floodwater from flowing back into the river.
- The levées were poorly maintained.

Ironically, the levées, designed to protect people and property, were a key factor that contributed to the flood disaster.

## Responses to the flood disaster

The emergency relief effort, hampered by damage to roads, railways, electricity lines and other essential **infrastructure**, was slow. One thousand temporary camps were eventually set up to shelter survivors, but aid workers complained about shortages of drinking water, food, blankets and medicines. Food drops were made to survivors, though food relief often failed to reach those in most need. Non-governmental organisations (NGOs) like the Red Cross were involved in search and rescue missions by boat, evacuation, setting up relief camps and providing food, sanitation and healthcare. The threat of disease such as diarrhoea and cholera was ever-present in the overcrowded unsanitary camps.

The long-term response to reduce the flood risk in future is not to strengthen and build more levées. A more sustainable approach is needed. This will

# Chapter 1 Rivers

involve halting the destruction of forests and the draining of wetlands in Bihar and Nepal. However, this is not easy in a region that suffers from acute poverty, rapid population growth and **overpopulation** (Table 1.6).

*Table 1.6 Population growth in Bihar and Nepal: 1981–2001 (million)*

|       | 1981  | 1991  | 2001  |
|-------|-------|-------|-------|
| Bihar | 58.52 | 67.56 | 82.88 |
| Nepal | 15.40 | 19.82 | 25.28 |

> **Activity 1.8**
>
> Study the satellite images (see Photograph 1.5) of northern Bihar and the Koshi River before and after the floods on 18 August 2008. Use the scale to answer the following questions.
>
> 1. How big is the area (in km$^2$) occupied by the old channel reoccupied by the Koshi River?
> 2. How far is the old channel from the modern channel abandoned on 18 August?

# Part 3 Fluvial landforms and processes

## Weathering processes

Rocks found at or near the Earth's surface are affected by changes in heat and moisture. These changes slowly cause the rocks to break down by a process known as weathering. Physical weathering results in rocks simply breaking up into smaller fragments. On the other hand, chemical weathering causes breakdown by altering the minerals in rocks.

### Physical weathering

In high latitude areas like the British Isles, frost action or freeze–thaw is the most common type of physical weathering. It works like this. Rainwater runs into cracks (or joints) in rocks and if the temperature then drops below zero it freezes and turns to ice. On freezing, water expands its volume by 9%. If confined in a narrow crack, the force exerted by the freezing process can split apart even the hardest rocks.

Where rocks crop out in river valleys freeze–thaw weathering creates accumulations of rock particles. Slowly the particles move downslope under the pull of gravity until they are fed into streams and rivers and form part of the sediment load (see Photograph 1.6).

### Chemical weathering

Chemical weathering covers a wide range of complex chemical reactions that alter rock minerals and cause rocks to disintegrate. **Solution** is one of the most common chemical weathering

> **Key ideas**
>
> - The main processes responsible for the formation of fluvial landforms are weathering, erosion, transport and deposition.
> - Fluvial landforms are also influenced by geology.
> - The main fluvial landforms are meanders, **interlocking spurs**, floodplains, river cliffs, valleys and waterfalls.

▲ Photograph 1.6 Weathered rock particles feeding into a stream (bottom right) in a steep Lakeland valley

processes. It occurs when calcium carbonate dissolves in acidic rainwater containing carbon dioxide. The processes is widespread in areas of limestone rocks like the Yorkshire Dales. The streams and rivers that drain such areas literally carry away the limestone in solution.

## Fluvial processes

Rivers do three things:
- erode the land
- transport eroded and weathered rock particles (**sediment**)
- deposit this sediment elsewhere

In this way rivers change the landscape and create distinctive landforms such as valleys and floodplains.

### Erosion

River **erosion** describes the wearing away of land in contact with flowing water. This erosion is concentrated in the channel bed and banks, and in places where the channel meets the valley sides. There are three processes of river erosion: abrasion, **attrition** and **hydraulic action**. They are defined in Table 1.7.

Table 1.7 Processes of river erosion

| Process | Description |
| --- | --- |
| Abrasion | Abrasion is the grinding effect of coarse rock particles, such as cobbles and gravels, which roll and slide along the river bed at high flow. |
| Attrition | Attrition is the gradual wearing down of coarse rock particles through abrasion and collision. Because of attrition, rock particles get smaller and more rounded with distance downstream. |
| Hydraulic action | Hydraulic action is the force of running water. It can dislodge particles of sand and gravel from riverbanks. Water can also get into cracks in silty riverbanks, trapping bubbles of air, which explode and weaken bank material. |

Rivers and coasts

# Chapter 1 Rivers

*Table 1.8 Processes of river transport*

| Load type | Description |
|---|---|
| Bedload | The largest rock particles dragged along the river channel at high flow form the bedload. A lot of energy is needed to get bedload particles moving. |
| Suspended load | Fine particles, such as clay and silt, are carried by the water in suspension. The suspended **load** gives rivers their muddy appearance at high flow. |
| Solution load | Rocks such as chalk and limestone are dissolved in river water. This part of the load is transported all year round. It does not depend on river energy. |

### Factfile 1.5 Weathering, fluvial processes and landforms

- Weathering processes break down rocks at or near the surface.
- The rock debris produced by weathering is slowly fed into streams and rivers.
- Rivers erode the land, transport eroded rock particles, and deposit these particles elsewhere.
- The processes of erosion, transport and deposition create distinctive landforms.
- River erosion is the dominant process in the uplands, producing **V-shaped valleys**, **interlocking spurs** and **waterfalls**.
- River deposition is more important in the lowlands, and creates landforms such as floodplains, meanders and river cliffs.

## Transport

Rivers transport rock particles (sediment) they have eroded or which have been fed to the river by **weathering**. The sediment carried by the river is known as the **load**. The river's load divides into three types: **bedload**, **suspended load** and **solution load** (see Table 1.8). Most transport occurs just once or twice a year, when the river is at high flow and has lots of energy.

## Deposition

After peak flow, energy levels in rivers start to decline. When the river no longer has sufficient energy to carry its load, deposition takes place. The heaviest particles — bedload — are deposited first, and may only be carried short distances. The finer material that forms the suspended load may be transported long distances, even at low energy levels.

Deposition occurs in two places: within the river channel and across the valley floor. Channel deposits are bars of sediment ranging in size from sand to cobbles. Meanwhile, in times of flood, fine sediments, which form the suspended load, are deposited across the entire valley floor.

## Case study: The River Wharfe

The River Wharfe rises in the Yorkshire Dales in the central Pennines. Its source is in boggy hill slopes up to 700 m above sea level. From there it flows eastwards to join the River Ouse, which in turn drains into the Humber Estuary and into the North Sea (see Figure 1.16). As it flows from upland to lowland, the Wharfe erodes the land, and transports and deposits sediment. In doing so it creates distinctive landforms.

### Fluvial landforms in the uplands

The upland area of the Wharfe basin is steep and drained by many small, fast-flowing tributary streams. Because of their steep gradients, tributaries like Buckden Beck (Figure 1.17) have lots of energy for erosion. As a result they create a number of landforms, which include V-shaped valleys, interlocking spurs and **waterfalls**.

# Theme 1

## Factfile 1.6 River Wharfe

- The River Wharfe drains an area of 850 km² in the Yorkshire Dales and Vale of York.
- The highest point in the Wharfe basin is 704 m.
- Most of the river's **headwaters** are moorland 400 m above sea level. They receive more than 1,500 mm of rainfall per year.
- Most of the river basin comprises limestone, sandstone and shale rocks.
- Most of the lower part of the basin is agricultural land.
- Large amounts of water are taken from the river and its tributaries for domestic supply to Leeds and Bradford.

Table 1.9 Describing upland rivers and river valleys from OS maps

(1) What are the maximum and minimum heights of the river's course?
(2) What is the approximate gradient of the river?
(3) Are there any waterfalls along the river's course?
(4) Is the river's course straight or meandering?
(5) How steep are the valley slopes?
(6) How wide is the valley floor?
(7) What is the shape of the valley in cross-section?
(8) Are there any interlocking spurs (visible on 1:25,000 maps only)?

Table 1.10 Describing lowland rivers and river valleys from OS maps

(1) What is the average gradient of the river's course?
(2) Is the river straight or meandering?
(3) How wide is the valley floor?
(4) Are there any abandoned meanders (oxbow lakes)?
(5) Is there a floodplain?
(6) Does the meander belt stretch from one side of the floodplain to the other?
(7) Is the valley straight?
(8) What is the shape of the valley in cross-section?
(9) Is there evidence of flood control works such as levées (flood embankments) or river straightening?

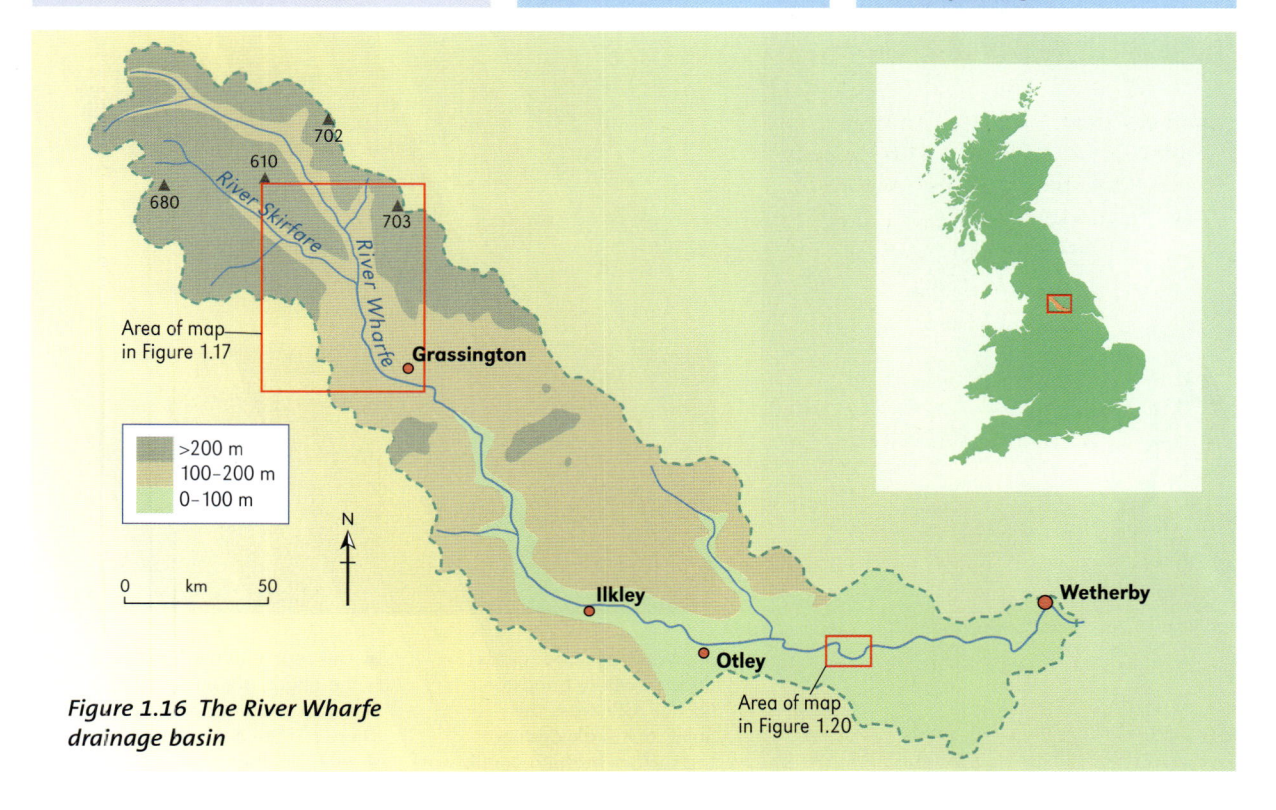

Figure 1.16 The River Wharfe drainage basin

Rivers and coasts

# Chapter 1 Rivers

**Figure 1.17 Upland and river landforms: the headwaters of the River Wharf**

In the uplands coarse bedload is fed into the stream from surrounding valley slopes by weathering and gravity. Transport of bedload erodes the channel and valley by abrasion.

◀ Waterfalls and rapids develop where bands of harder rock cross the river. Solid rock is always near the surface in the uplands.

▲ The source of the River Wharfe is the boggy areas of the central Pennines, 600 m above sea level. There rainfall averages more than 1,500 mm per year.

# Theme 1

▲ Upland valleys such as Buckden Beck are V-shaped in cross-section. Streams erode vertically. Rocky valley walls make it difficult for streams to widen their valleys by eroding sideways. Valley slopes are lowered by weathering and landslides. Where stream channels meander, vertical erosion leads to the formation of interlocking spurs.

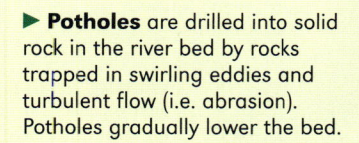

▶ **Potholes** are drilled into solid rock in the river bed by rocks trapped in swirling eddies and turbulent flow (i.e. abrasion). Potholes gradually lower the bed.

◀ Steep **long profile** of Buckden Beck in Upper Wharfedale.

Rivers and coasts

# Chapter 1 Rivers

Figure 1.18 The formation of V-shaped valleys and interlocking spurs

## Activity 1.9

1. Using the questions in Tables 1.9 and 1.10 and the OS map extract in Figure 1.17 describe the main features of:
   (a) Buckden Beck and its valley
   (b) the River Wharfe and its valley

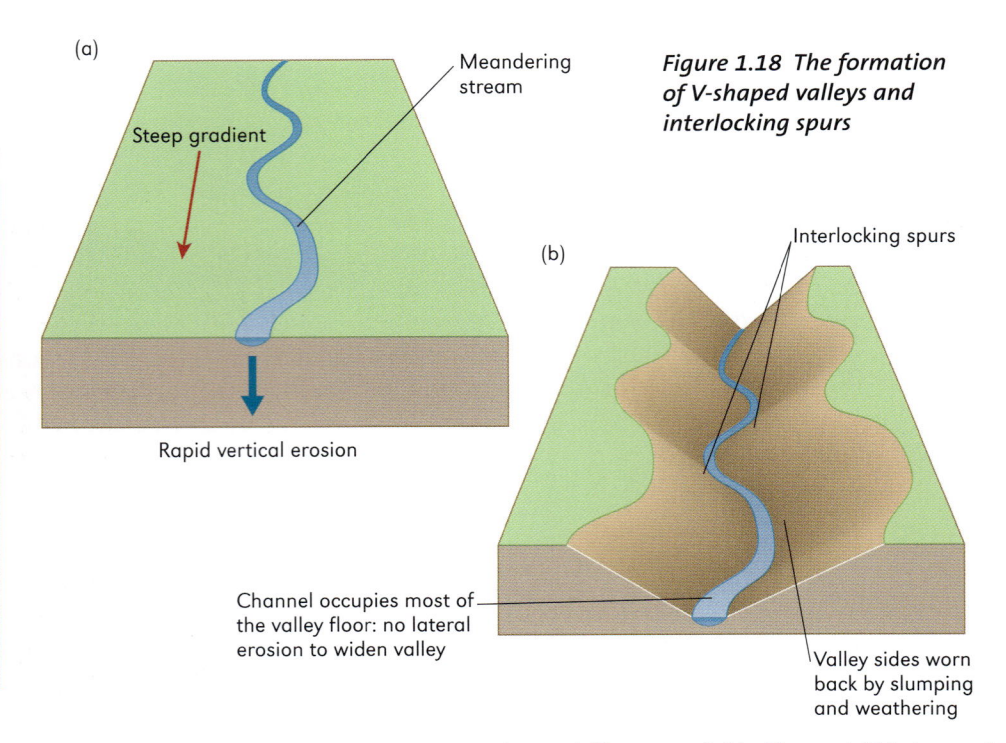

### V-shaped valleys

Upland river valleys like Buckden Beck (see Figure 1.17) have steep sides and narrow floors and are typically V-shaped in cross-section. Buckden Beck's valley was formed by the stream cutting downwards. This **vertical erosion** is due to the stream's steep gradient and coarse bedload, which scours the channel bed. Meanwhile, as the stream cuts down, the valley is opened out by weathering and other processes (e.g. landslides, slumping) which lower the valley slopes and create a characteristic V-shaped cross-section.

### Interlocking spurs

Even on the steepest slopes, most streams follow a winding (or sinuous) path. Thus as a stream deepens its valley by vertical erosion, it also creates a sinuous rather than straight valley. Standing in such a valley, and looking upstream, your view is blocked by a succession of interlocking spurs (see Figure 1.18).

### Waterfalls

Waterfalls are steep, rock steps in a stream or river's course. In upland areas, most waterfalls develop where more resistant bands of rock crop out in the stream channel. The waterfall in Figure 1.17 is located on Buckden Beck. It has formed where a layer of harder limestone, rests above a weaker rock layer (see Figure 1.19).

Waterfalls gradually retreat upstream as erosion of the weaker rock at the base undermines the more resistant rock above. As they retreat they often create a **gorge** with solid rock walls.

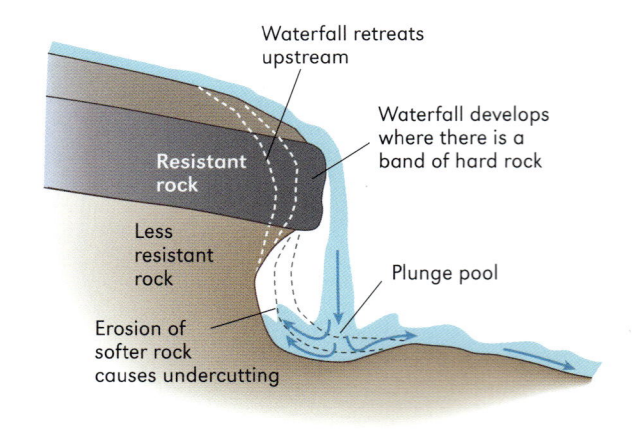

Figure 1.19 The formation of waterfalls

# Theme 1

## Fluvial landforms in the lowlands

Compared with upland rivers, rivers in the lowlands have gentler gradients and higher flow (or discharge). Gentle gradients mean that vertical erosion is no longer very important. However, the high discharge still gives lowland rivers more than enough energy for erosion. In contrast to upland rivers, most erosion is lateral, and takes place in curving sections of river channels known as **meanders**. At the same time, deposition of sediment becomes more important. The outcome of these processes is the development of new fluvial landforms in the lowlands. Among these landforms are meanders, floodplains and river cliffs.

### Meanders

Meanders are sinuous lengths of river channel, which are best developed in lowland areas where gradients are shallow (see Photograph 1.7). They are formed by sideways or **lateral erosion**. In a meander, the fastest current clings to the outside of the bend (see Figure 1.20). The concentration of energy there undercuts the outer bank (by abrasion and hydraulic action) and causes the bank to collapse. In this way the meander gradually migrates across the valley floor (see Photograph 1.9). Meanwhile, at high flow, deposition occurs on the inner bank, forming a bar of sand or gravel called a point bar.

*Figure 1.20 Lowlands and river landforms: the Lower Wharf valley*

In the lowlands, rivers have gentler gradients but higher discharge than in the uplands. They transport larger volumes of fine sediment (silt and clay) in suspension. Deposition is more obvious than in the uplands, and depositional features such as point bars and floodplains form. However, rivers still have surplus energy for erosion. Most erosion is sideways or **lateral** and is focused on the outer banks of river bends or **meanders**. Erosion not only creates meanders — it causes meanders to migrate gradually downstream and form wide, shallow valley floors or floodplains.

The fastest current clings to the outside of a river bend or meander. The concentration of energy here erodes the bank by abrasion and hydraulic action. In the lowlands, the silt and gravels (alluvium) that form the banks (and floodplain) collapse easily, leaving a vertical outer or cut bank. At high flow the inner bank is an area of lower energy. Deposition occurs here, forming a feature called a point bar.

As the river erodes the outer cut bank, and deposits sediment on the inner bank, its channel gradually migrates across the valley floor. Over thousands of years it criss-crosses every part of the valley. It removes any spurs and creates a wide, shallow valley. Meanwhile, floods deposit fine silt (the river's suspended load) across the valley floor and bars of sand and gravel that formed in the channel are abandoned. These river deposits (known as alluvium) fill in the valley floor and create the floodplain.

Rivers and coasts

# Chapter 1 Rivers

◀ **Photograph 1.7** A meander on the River Skirfare

▲ **Photograph 1.8** Sediment at point C in Photograph 1.7

Lateral erosion causes some meanders to become so sinuous that only a narrow neck of land separates the channel at the start and end of the meander. Eventually this neck is breached and the river straightens its course. The abandoned meander is known as an **oxbow** or **cut-off**. Initially it forms a shallow lake but this soon fills with sediment and disappears (see Figure 1.21).

## Floodplains

The River Skirfare, which is a major tributary of the River Wharfe (see Figure 1.16), can be seen meandering across its broad valley in Photograph 1.9. It erodes the outer bank on meanders and deposits sediment on the opposite inner bank. In this way, its channel gradually migrates across the valley floor, removing any spurs and widening the valley (see

**Figure 1.21** The development of an oxbow lake

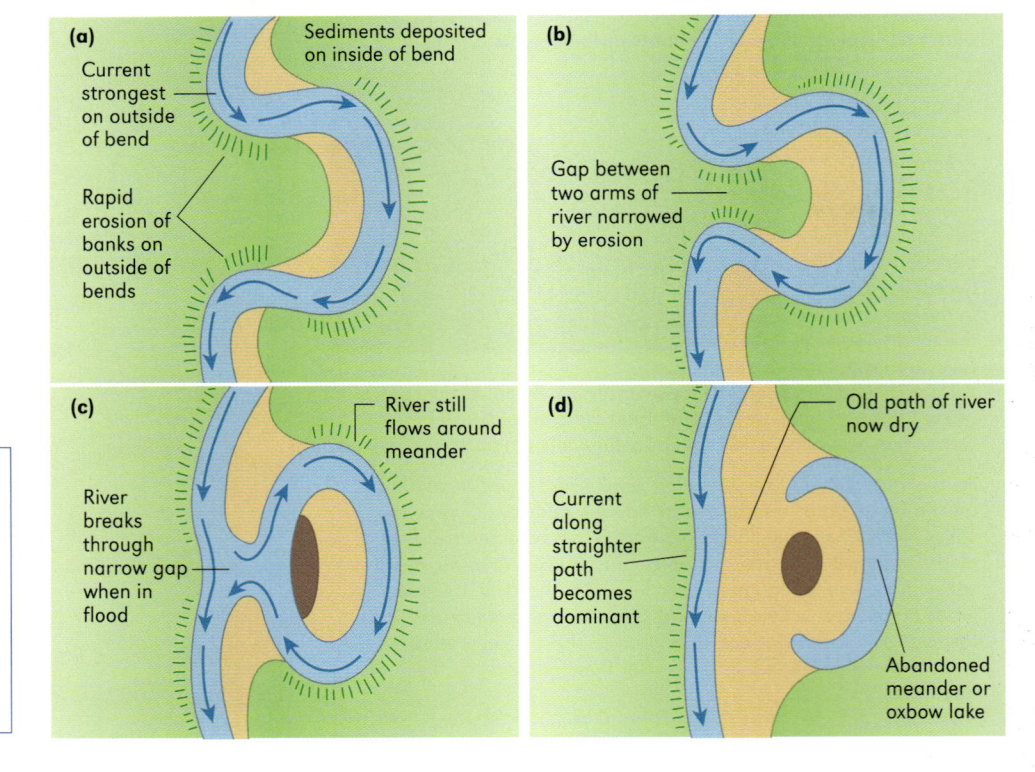

(a) Current strongest on outside of bend; Sediments deposited on inside of bend; Rapid erosion of banks on outside of bends

(b) Gap between two arms of river narrowed by erosion

(c) River still flows around meander; River breaks through narrow gap when in flood

(d) Old path of river now dry; Current along straighter path becomes dominant; Abandoned meander or oxbow lake

Key:
- Banks liable to erosion
- Newer deposits of sediment
- Older deposits of sediment
- Strongest current

OCR (B) GCSE Geography

## Theme 1

**◀ Figure 1.22 The formation of flood plains**

Valley side is undercut by river; slope collapse occurs, feeding new sediments into the river, widening the valley and creating a steep river cliff

Future position of meanders as they migrate across the floodplain (due to lateral erosion) and downstream

River cliff
Cut bank
Point bar
Point bar
Floodplain
Current of fastest flow
Bluff

50 metres

Alluvial fill — fine overbank deposits from valley floods overlie coarser channel deposits (old point bars and channel bars)

**▼ Photograph 1.9 The floodplain of the River Skirfare (a major tributary of the River Wharfe) with a well-developed meander**

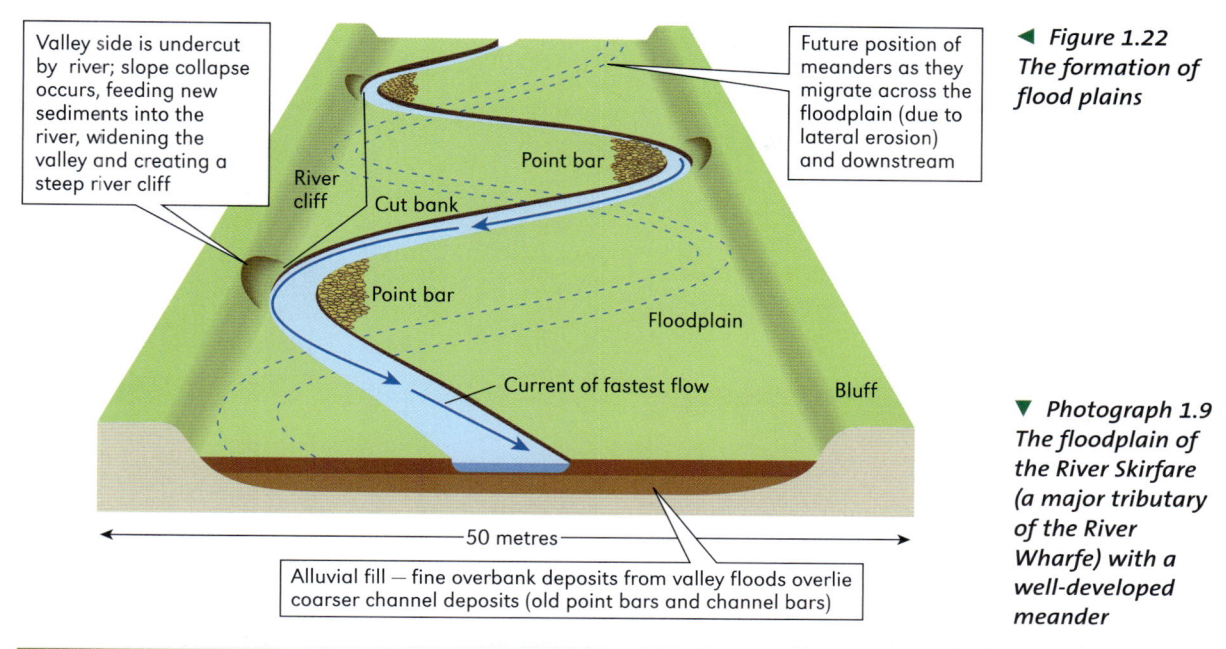

Figure 1.22). At the same time the valley is filled with river sediment known as **alluvium**. This alluvium comes from two sources. First from sand and gravel deposited in old channels that have been abandoned. And second, from floods which leave behind deposits of clay and silt on the valley floor. The result — a wide, flat valley, filled with alluvium — is known a **floodplain**.

Rivers and coasts

25

# Chapter 1 Rivers

## River cliffs

We have seen that rivers widen their valleys as meanders migrate across the valley floor. Widening occurs when a meander contacts the slope that marks the edge of the valley. In these areas of contact, the river undercuts the valley side making it unstable. Eventually the slope collapses, widening the valley and forming a steep **river cliff**. Photograph 1.10 shows the process of valley widening and the formation of a river cliff on Cow Beck in Upper Wharfedale.

### Activity 1.10

Study Photograph 1.7, which shows a meander on the River Skirfare, a tributary of the River Wharfe, and Photograph 1.8, which shows sediment at point C.

1. Using Figure 1.20 to help you, draw a sketch of a section across the meander between points A and B. Add the following labels to your section: cut bank, point bar, floodplain, areas of erosion, areas of deposition, faster flow, slower flow. Show the direction in which the meander is migrating with an arrow.

2. What evidence is there for erosion at point B?

3. (a) Name the type of load shown in Photograph 1.8.
   (b) What is attrition?
   (c) What evidence is there that the rock particles in Photograph 1.8 have been eroded by attrition?

Photograph 1.10 River cliff and valley widening on Cow Beck (a tributary of the River Skirfare)

OCR (B) GCSE Geography

# Theme 1 Rivers and coasts

# Chapter 2 Coasts

## Part 1 Coastal processes and landforms

The coastline is the place where land meets sea. Weathering helps to break up the rocks exposed along the coast while **waves**, generated far out at sea, erode the rocks to create familiar landforms such as cliffs and caves. Eroded rock particles, reduced to sand and mud, are transported along the coast by waves and currents. Eventually these particles are deposited elsewhere to form new features such as beaches, sand **dunes** and **salt marshes**.

### *Weathering*

Rocks exposed on the coast are broken down and weakened by moisture and temperature. This is the process of weathering. Frost weathering and chemical weathering operate on the coast as well in river environments (see Chapter 1). However, there are two other weathering processes which are unique to coastal environments: **salt weathering** and **biological weathering**.

> **Key ideas**
> 
> - The geomorphic processes responsible for distinctive coastal landforms are weathering, erosion, transport and deposition.
> - Some coastlines are dominated by erosional (destructive) processes; others by depositional (constructive) processes.
> - Geology influences the formation of coastal landforms.
> - Coastal landforms include cliffs, headlands, caves, arches, stacks, **beaches** and **spits**.

Unlike fresh water, sea water is salty. When rocks wetted by waves and sea spray dry out, salt crystals form in cracks and tiny air spaces in the rocks. As these crystals grow the surface layers of rocks weaken and crumble. This is salt weathering.

Rocks on the shoreline are also destroyed by the action of organisms such as algae, shellfish and sea urchins. Some marine organisms secret organic acids which cause chemical weathering. Meanwhile, softer rocks are attacked by rock-boring shellfish. Both processes are examples of biological weathering.

# Chapter 2 Coasts

*Table 2.1 Processes of coastal erosion*

| Process | Description |
|---|---|
| Abrasion | Waves erode the coastline by hurling pebbles against cliff faces. This happens most during storms, when high and powerful waves batter the coast. Abrasion is concentrated at the high-tide mark, where it forms a notch, causing overlying rocks to collapse. |
| Attrition | This is the wearing down and rounding of rock particles by wave transport as they collide with each other and abrade the coastal rocks. |
| Hydraulic action | Water and air at high pressure are forced into cracks and joints in rocks. This process weakens rocks and is a major cause of cliff collapse. The pounding of storm waves has a similar effect. |

*Table 2.2 Describing upland coastlines from OS maps*

| | |
|---|---|
| (1) | In which direction does the coastline run? |
| (2) | What is the average height of the coastline? |
| (3) | Is the coastline straight, or indented with bays, coves and headlands? |
| (4) | Are there any erosional landforms, such as cliffs, arches, stacks and shore (wave-cut) platforms? |
| (5) | Are there any coastal protection structures against erosion, such as **groynes**? |
| (6) | What are the main human activities along the stretch of coastline? |

### Factfile 2.1 Waves, coastal processes and landforms

- Waves erode the coast. They also transport eroded and weathered rock particles and deposit them elsewhere.
- The coastal processes of erosion are abrasion, attrition and hydraulic action.
- Wave erosion and the deposition of sand and **shingle** create distinctive coastal landforms.
- Erosion dominates upland coasts (destructive coastlines); deposition dominates lowland coasts (constructive coastlines).
- Erosion produces a sequence of distinctive landforms which includes cliffs, caves, arches and stacks (see Figure 2.1)

## Erosion

Erosion is the wearing away of the coastline by wave action. There are three main processes of coastal erosion. They are described in Table 2.1.

### Sediment transport and deposition

Waves and currents transport shingle, sand and mud, which are then deposited to form features such as **beaches**, sand dunes and **mudflats**. These landforms often dominate lowland coastlines.

### Waves and currents

**Waves** are movements of energy through water. Imagine a wave approaching parallel to the shore. As it gets close to the shore it enters shallow water and starts to change. First, it begins to 'feel' the sea bed and slows down. Then, as it

*Figure 2.1 Erosion of a headland*

Upland areas terminate at the coast in cliffs. Cliffs are steep-sided and plunge directly into the sea. Waves cut a notch at the base of the cliffs, which are slowly undermined.

Rain and frost (weathering) attack the top and face of the cliff

Cracks show weakness in the rock

Headland of hard rock

Arch

Shore or wave-cut platform

Notch — Cave — Notch — Stack — Stump

| Sea attacks line of weakness, opening up the crack or joint | As the joint erodes further, a **cave** forms | If the cave erodes right through the headland, an **arch** forms | The arch eventually collapses as it is widened by the sea and worn by the weather, leaving a **stack** | The weather and sea attack the stack until a **stump** is left, often covered by water at high tide | Shore or wave-cut platforms are the final stage in the destruction of cliffs. They are the base of the old cliffs and are only exposed at low tide. |

slows its height increases. Finally, the wave becomes unstable, breaks, and water surges up the beach as **swash**. Some of this water then returns down the beach as **backwash**. Swash and backwash can move sand and shingle in three directions: up and down beaches; along beaches; and between beaches and the sea bed immediately offshore.

## Onshore and offshore transport

The amount and direction of sand and shingle transported by waves depends on their energy. Low-energy waves are usually less than 50 cm high and have long distances between each **wave crest**. When they break, these waves collapse at a shallow angle, and their swash pushes sand and shingle up the beach (see Figure 2.2). The weaker backwash carries a smaller amount of sand and shingle back to the sea. As a result, low-energy waves tend to form beaches with steep gradients.

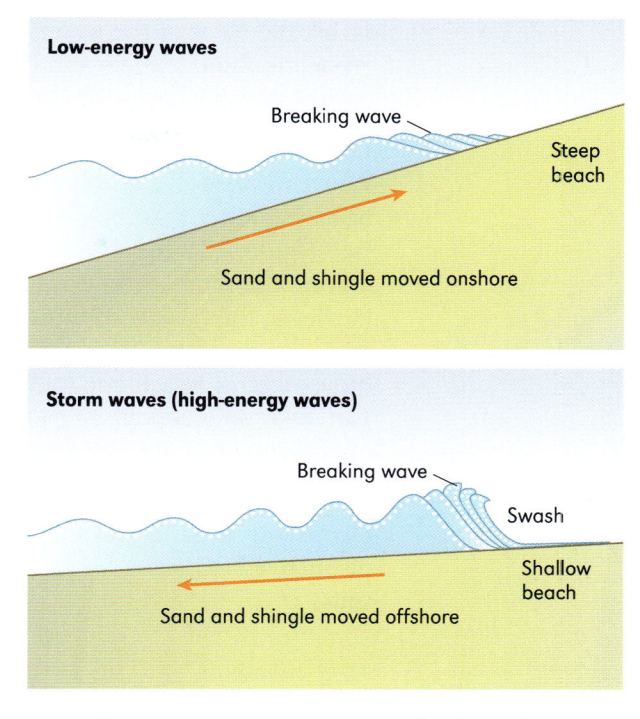

Storm waves (or high-energy waves) have the opposite effect (see Photograph 2.1 and Figure 2.2) These waves have lots of energy. When they

▲ Figure 2.2 Low-energy waves and storm waves (high energy waves)

◀ Photograph 2.1 Powerful storm waves on the coast of Maine, New England

Rivers and coasts

break, the force of the water is directed down onto the beach. In this way they erode sand and shingle and flatten beaches. The eroded sediments are then transported offshore and are stored in bars.

**Longshore transport**

When waves arrive at the coast obliquely, they move sand and shingle along beaches, rather than up and down them. This process is called **longshore drift** (see Figure 2.3). Because waves strike the coast at an oblique angle, the swash follows the same angle up the beach, carrying sand and shingle with it. However, the backwash returns down the beach on a straight path, at right angles to the shore. This means that each wave produces a saw-tooth movement of swash and backwash. As a result, sediments are shifted in a particular direction along the beach. While this beach drift is going on, the oblique angle of the waves produces a **longshore current**. This flows parallel to the shore, and transports large amounts of sand along the coast.

Deposition of sand and shingle by waves and currents is responsible for distinctive landforms on constructive, lowland coasts, especially beaches and spits.

*Figure 2.3 Longshore drift*

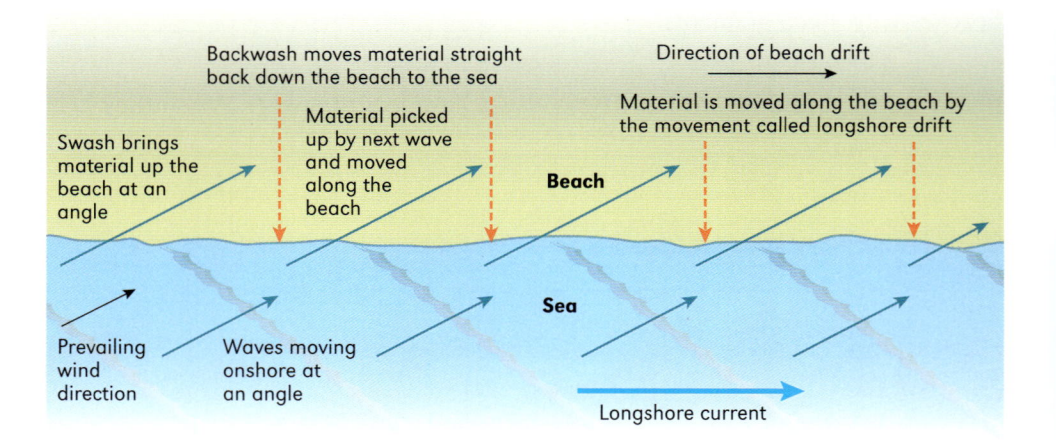

Table 2.3 Describing lowland coastlines from OS maps

| | |
|---|---|
| (1) | In which direction does the coastline run? |
| (2) | What is the average height of the coastline? |
| (3) | Is the coastline straight, or interrupted by river mouths and estuaries? |
| (4) | Are there any depositional landforms, such as beaches, bars, spits, tombolos, sand dunes, salt marshes and mudflats? |
| (5) | Are there any coastal protection structures against erosion (e.g. groynes) and/or flooding (e.g. flood embankments)? |
| (6) | What are the main human activities along the stretch of coastline? |

### Activity 2.1

Study the coastline on the 1:50,000 OS map extract of the Lleyn Peninsula in north-west Wales (Figure 2.4).

1 Using the questions in Table 2.3 as a guide, describe the main features of this stretch of coastline.

# Theme 1

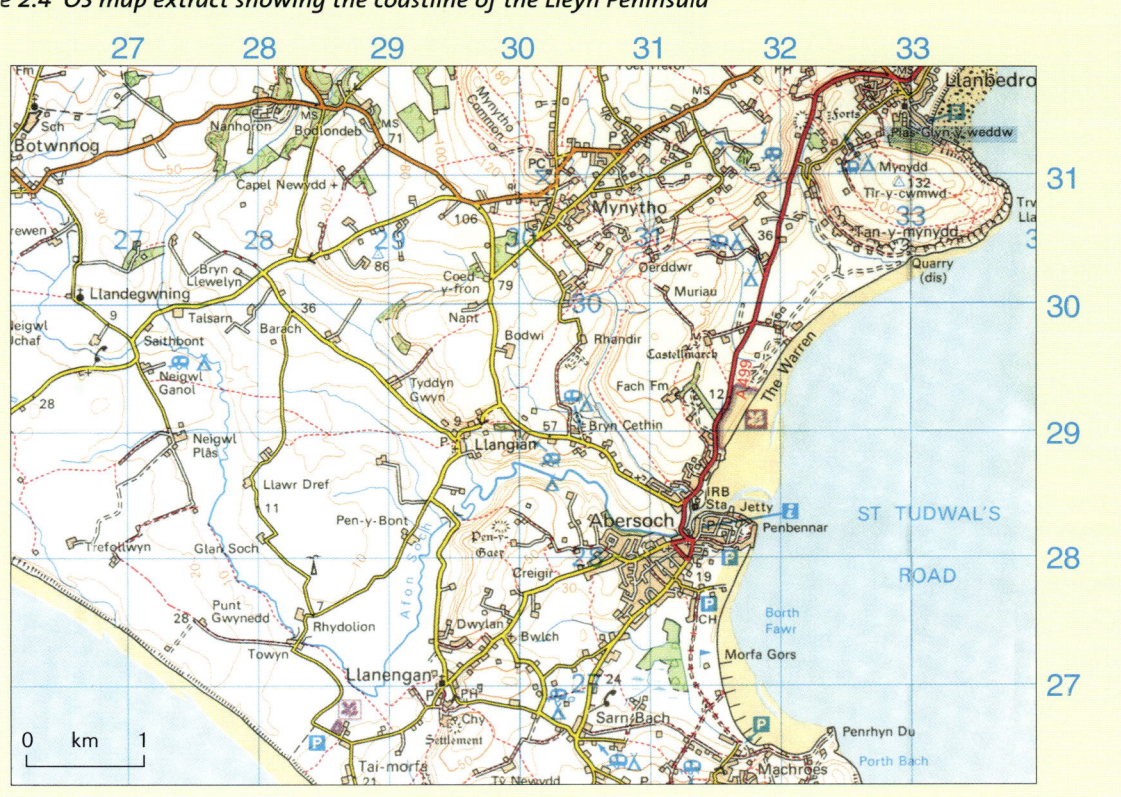

*Figure 2.4 OS map extract showing the coastline of the Lleyn Peninsula*

## Case study: The Yorkshire Coast — Flamborough Head to the Humber Estuary

### Flamborough Head

Flamborough Head in east Yorkshire, is a 15 km stretch of coastline formed where the Yorkshire Wolds meet the North Sea. It is an upland coast (50 to 60 m above sea level) dominated by erosional landforms (see Photograph 2.2).

*Photograph 2.2 Headlands and bays at Flamborough Head*

Rivers and coasts

# Chapter 2 Coasts

Flamborough owes much of its character to geology, relief and wave energy (see Figures 2.5 and 2.9). The main rock type is chalk, which crops out in horizontal layers. It is fairly resistant to wave erosion and produces impressive vertical cliffs. Resting above the chalk is a thick layer of soft boulder clay. Powerful waves from the north-easterly direction crash against the cliffs and have carved a classic sequence of erosional landforms including caves, arches and stacks.

## Erosional landforms

The principal erosional landforms at Flamborough are headlands, cliffs, caves, arches, stacks and shore (wave-cut) platforms.

### Headlands

Headlands are small peninsulas on upland coasts that project seawards. They are flanked on either side by

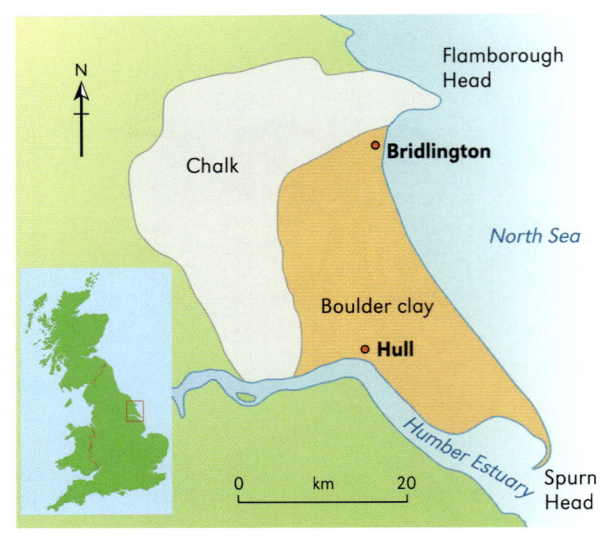

*Figure 2.5 Geology of the Yorkshire coast between Flamborough and the Humber*

### Activity 2.2

1 (a) Photograph 2.2 is the view from 257707 (see Figure 2.6 — OS map). In which direction was the camera pointing when this photograph was taken?
(b) Name the bay shown in Photograph 2.3a.

2 Describe the main features of the coastline between Flamborough Head (2570) and Thornwick Bay (2372) by answering the questions in Table 2.2.

*Figure 2.6 OS map extract: Flamborough*

32   OCR (B) GCSE Geography

bays or coves. Often headlands consist of resistant rocks that erode more slowly than the softer rocks in adjacent bays. Although Flamborough Head is carved from a single rock — chalk — in several places the cliffs jut out from the coast to form headlands (see Figure 2.6). This is probably due to differences in the density of jointing and faulting in the chalk. Bays such as Selwicks and Thornwick have developed where major joints and **faults** have been exploited by wave erosion. In contrast, the headlands, with fewer lines of weakness, have been eroded more slowly.

## Cliffs

The cliffs at Flamborough are made of chalk and boulder clay. Standing 50–60 m high, they are the tallest cliffs on the east coast of England, between Kent and Yorkshire. The cross-section or profile of the cliffs is clearly seen in the photographs in Figure 2.7. The lower part of the cliffs is almost vertical, and consists of horizontally bedded chalk. The upper part, formed from weak boulder clay, has a much lower angle, between 40 and 45 degrees. Because chalk is a hard rock, rates of erosion are fairly low, averaging just 0.3 mm a year. However, sudden rockfalls are not unusual (see Photograph 2.3a). These occur where wave erosion undermines the cliff base and forms a deep notch. Eventually the cliff becomes unstable and collapses.

### Activity 2.3

1 Study the photographs in Figure 2.7 and draw a labelled sketch diagram to show the profile of the cliffs at Flamborough. Add a scale to your diagram.

2 Draw sketch diagrams to show how (a) the cave and (b) the arch in Photograph 2.3c have formed.

*Figure 2.7 Cliffs, caves and arches: Flamborough and Selwick's Bay*

▲ *Photograph 2.3(a) Caves, cliffs and recent rockfall at Flamborough*

▶ *Photograph 2.3(c) Arch and cave at Selwick's Bay*

▲ *Photograph 2.3(b) Cliffs and shore platform at Selwick's Bay*

▼ *Photograph 2.3(d) Cliff profile and stack at Flamborough*

Rivers and coasts

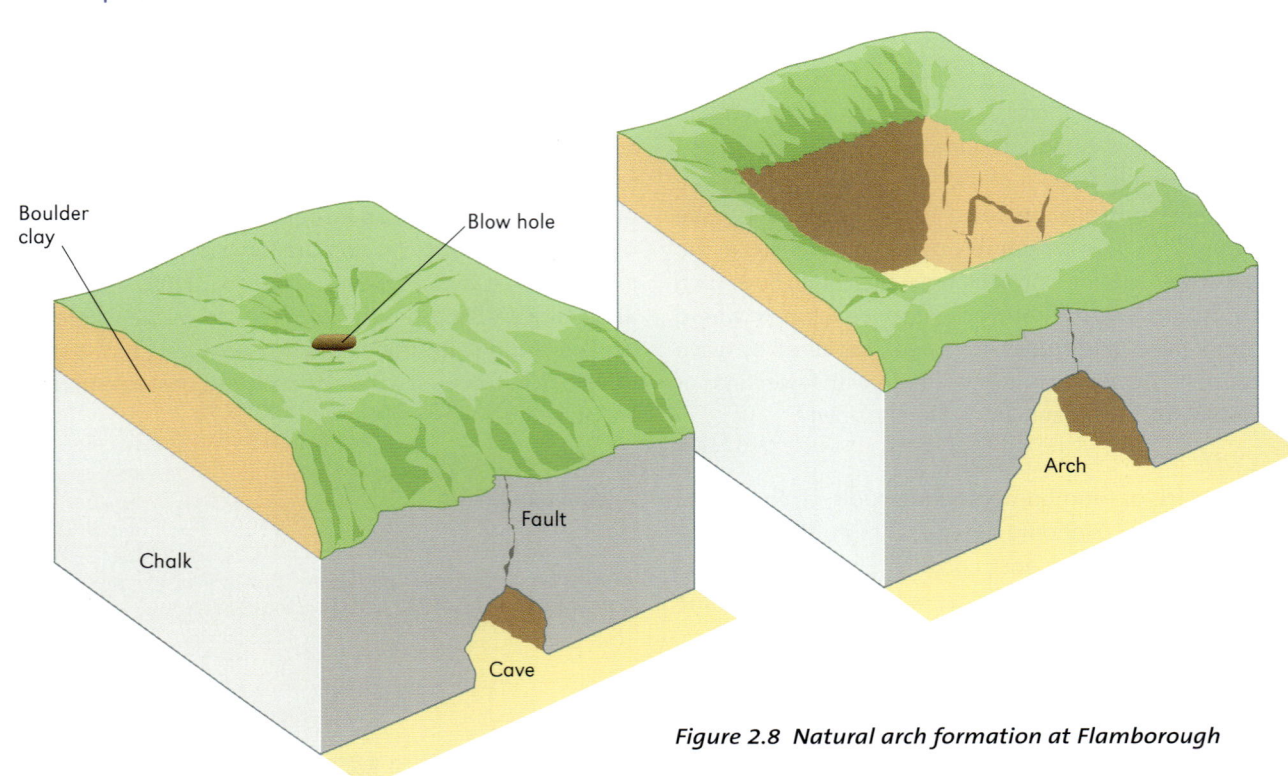

*Figure 2.8 Natural arch formation at Flamborough*

## Caves

Caves form in the chalk at the base of the cliffs (see Photograph 2.3a). The processes of wave erosion, especially hydraulic action and abrasion, are concentrated on lines of weakness such as faults, vertical cracks (or joints) and horizontal cracks or **bedding planes**. Gradually the cracks and joints are widened leading to rock collapse and the formation of caves. At high tide the caves are completely flooded. In Photograph 2.3c you can see how a cave has formed between the high and low water mark along a vertical fault line.

## Arches

If a cave roof partly collapses, the surviving roof section may form an arch. Some arches develop where a narrow fin of rock on an exposed headland is attacked on both sides by wave erosion. In this situation caves on opposite sides of the headland eventually meet, forming a tunnel. Further erosion and rockfalls increase the roof height to leave an arch.

At Flamborough, most arches lie parallel to the coastline (see Figure 2.8 and Photograph 2.3c). They seem to have formed by the partial collapse of caves that developed along major fault lines running at right angles to the cliffs. The collapse of the cave roof begins some distance from the shoreline where a master joint or fault reaches the surface as a **blow hole**.

## Stacks, stumps and shore platforms

Further wave erosion leads to the collapse of arches leaving an isolated rock pillar known as a stack (see Photograph 2.3d). In time, stacks, undercut by wave erosion, also collapse to form stumps that are submerged at high tide. The final landform in the sequence of erosion (see Figure 2.1) is the shore or wave-cut platform (see Photograph 2.3b), This is a flat expanse of solid rock than slopes gently seawards and is exposed at low tide. Shore patforms owe their formation not only to abrasion, but also to weathering processes such as wetting and drying, and the biological action of marine organisms like algae and molluscs.

# Theme 1

## Holderness and Spurn Head

### Depositional landforms

South of Flamborough, the Yorkshire coast has a very different character. This is a straight coastline of low boulder clay cliffs, and long, narrow beaches. Unlike Flamborough, beaches are prominent landforms, and deposition is an important process. Holderness is best known as one of Europe's most rapidly eroding coastlines.

### Beaches

Along the Holderness coastline the beaches consist of sand and shingle eroded from the local boulder clay cliffs (see Photograph 2.4). Holderness's beaches are narrow for two reasons. First the clay cliffs contain only small amounts of sand and gravel; and second there are no major rivers along this stretch of coast to bring new sediments into the coastal zone. The beaches extend for over 50 km and run parallel to

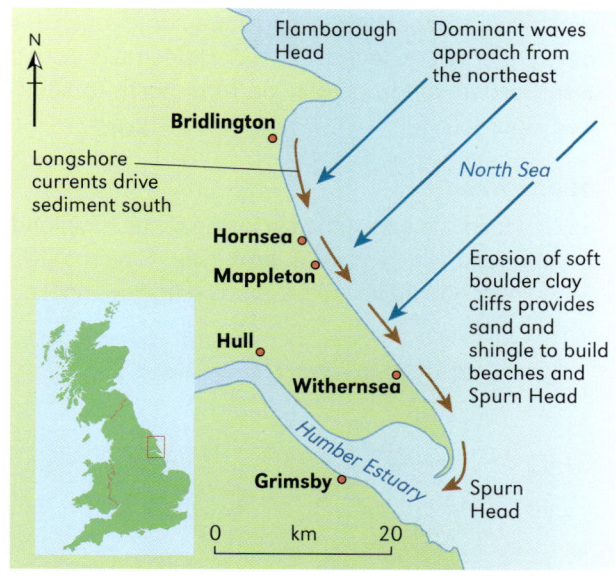

▲ Figure 2.9 Sediment movement along the east Yorkshire coast

Photograph 2.4 Holderness coastline: crumbling boulder clay cliffs and narrow beaches

Rivers and coasts

# Chapter 2 Coasts

the straight coastline. Longshore drift operates along the entire length of the Holderness coast, transporting sand and shingle from north to south (see Figure 2.9).

## Spurn Head

Spurn Head is a type of beach joined to the mainland at one end, known as a **spit** (see Figure 2.10). Made of sand and shingle, it forms a narrow, hooked peninsula, 6 km long, at the mouth of the River Humber (see Photograph 2.5). Several factors have contributed to the formation of Spurn Head:

- A supply of sand and shingle from the rapidly eroding cliffs of Holderness to the north.
- Longshore drift — the north to south movement of sand and shingle along the coast due to the dominant north-easterly waves striking the Holderness coast obliquely.
- The abrupt change in the direction of the coastline caused by the Humber Estuary.

As sediments are transported by longshore drift along the Holderness coast, Spurn Head spit has grown south across the inlet formed by the Humber Estuary. The hooked shape of Spurn Head is due to the movement of waves around the end of the spit.

**Figure 2.10** OS map extract: Spurn Head

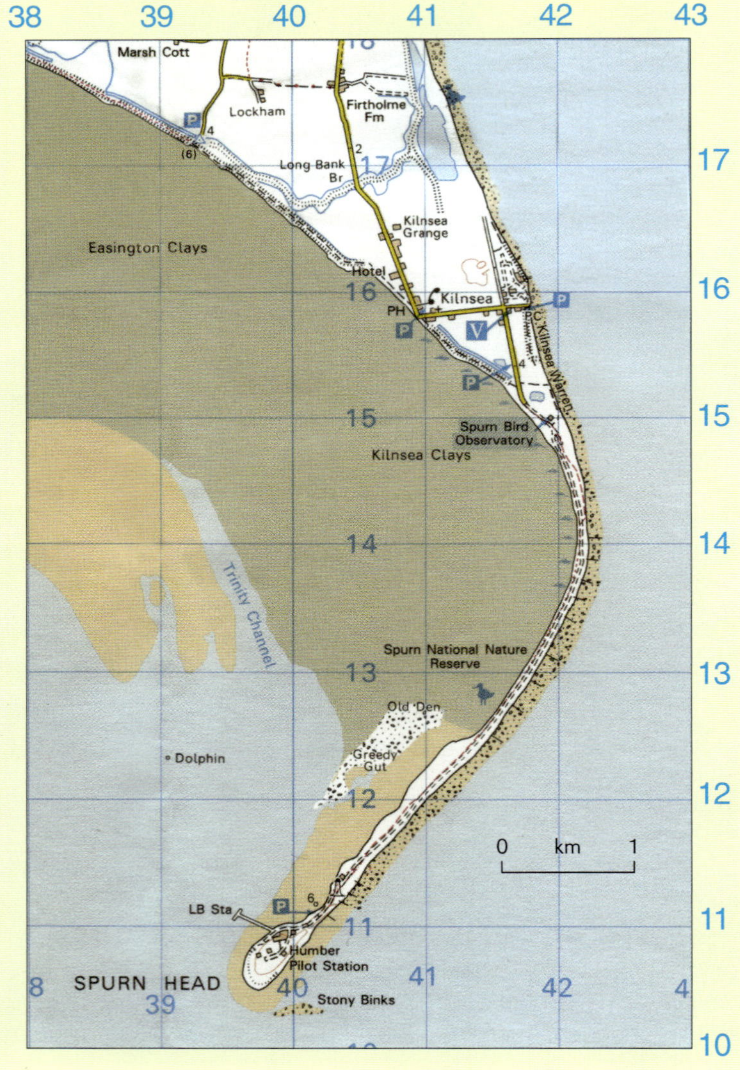

### Activity 2.4

Study the the 1:50,000 OS map extract of Spurn Head (see Figure 2.10).

1. What is the approximate length and width of Spurn Head between 420150 and its southernmost tip?

2. What evidence is there on the OS map of: (a) the direction of longshore drift (b) the value of Spurn to people (c) protection measures to reduce the risk of erosion?

3. With reference to the OS map and Photograph 2.5 draw a sketch map of Spurn Head. Add notes to your map to describe and explain its main features.

# Theme 1

◀ Photograph 2.5 Spurn Head looking north

# Part 2 Coastal management

There is a need to protect some stretches of coastline from erosion and flooding. For example, towns and cities, with massive investments in housing, businesses, public buildings and infrastructure, will be protected by 'hard' defences such as seawalls and flood barriers — regardless of cost. In this situation, whatever the costs of protection they are dwarfed by the value of the property and investments they defend. Coastlines with vital economic installations like nuclear power stations, gas terminals and oil refineries will also be given priority for defence.

Coastal protection may also be jusitified for environmental reasons. Sand dunes, which often support habitats for rare plants and animals, may be protected from erosion with **rock armour** blocks and brushwood fences. Similar protection may be given to sand spits such as Spurn Head, and Blakeney Point in Norfolk, which are important refuges for birds and marine mammals like common seals.

> **Key ideas**
> - There is a need to protect some stretches of coastline from erosion and flooding.
> - Coastlines can be protected from erosion and flooding in different ways.
> - Some strategies for coastal management are more sustainable than others.

## Case study: Coastal erosion at Happisburgh

### Background

Happisburgh is a small village (population 850) on the northeast coast of Norfolk. Following the disastrous floods of 1953, hard sea defences were built to protect the villages. These comprised **revetments** and groynes (see Figure 2.11). Then in 1990 a violent storm destroyed a 300 m length of the revetments southeast of the village. These were not repaired. This decision was in line with the government's policy of 'do nothing' and **managed realignment** for this stretch of coastline (see Table 2.4). As a result, erosion since 1990 has been spectacular. In 15 years, 26 seafront homes were lost, and today several others are under immediate threat.

Rivers and coasts

*Figure 2.11 Coastal defences: hard engineering structures*

**Groynes**

Wooden or concrete fences built at right angles to the shore. They trap the sand and shingle moved by longshore drift, which forms beaches and protects against erosion. If a wide and deep beach can be retained, there is less chance of waves reaching and eroding the cliffs behind.

Groynes interfere with the movement of coastal sediments. By trapping sand and shingle, groynes may starve beaches further down the coast of sediment and accelerate erosion there. They are intrusive and look unsightly.

**Sea walls**

Concrete walls or rock structures built along a stretch of coastline and designed to stop erosion and floods. Sea walls reflect waves, and give complete protection against erosion.

Sea walls are expensive to build (£1 million per km). Reflecting waves leads to scouring at the foot of the wall; without constant maintenance, sea walls can be undermined and collapse. By stopping erosion, sea walls reduce inputs of beach-building sediments (sand and shingle) to the coast.

**Gabions**

Wire cages filled with cobbles and stones placed where there is coastal erosion. The gaps between the cobbles and stones make them effective in absorbing wave energy and reducing erosion.

Gabions are cheaper than armour blocks but look unsightly.

**Revetments**

Latticed wooden fences built parallel to the shore. These allow shingle to build up behind them, creating beaches that give additional coastal protection. Unlike sea walls, they absorb wave energy.

Revetments reduce access to beaches and are unsightly.

**Armour blocks**

Boulders or concrete blocks placed at the foot of cliffs or at the base of sea walls. These absorb wave energy and have less impact on the environment than most other hard engineering structures.

Blocks (especially concrete ones) are ugly and reduce access to beaches.

# Theme 1

**Figure 2.12 Erosion cycle of the cliffs at Happisburgh, Norfolk**

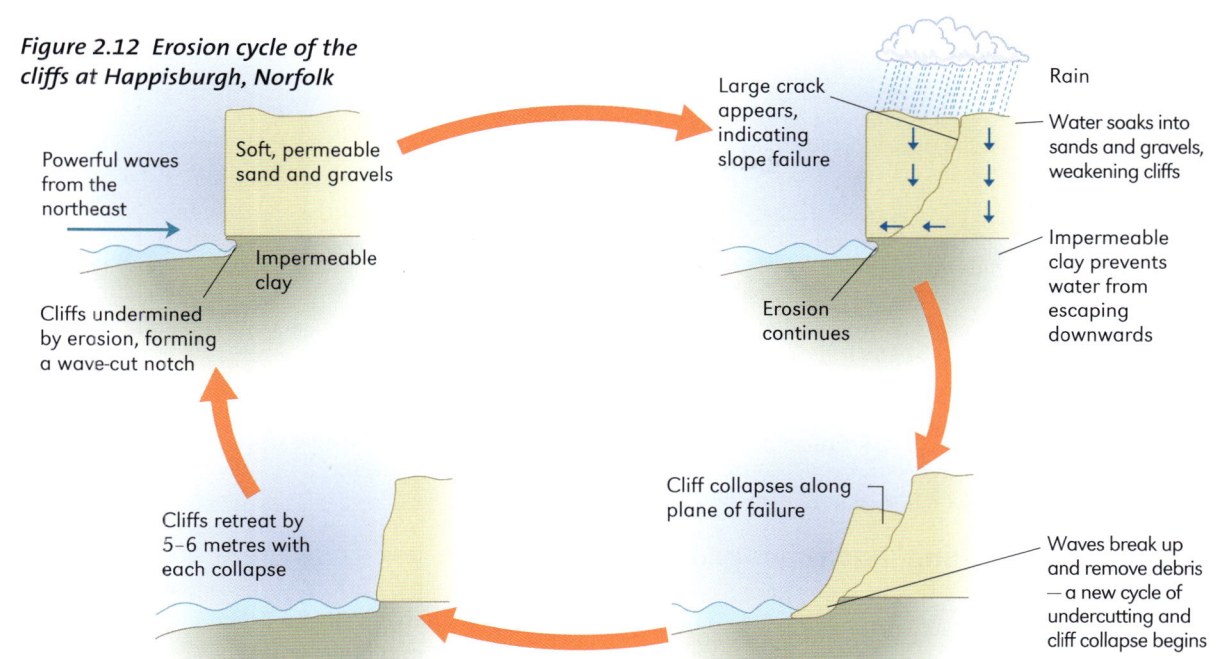

- Powerful waves from the northeast
- Soft, permeable sand and gravels
- Impermeable clay
- Cliffs undermined by erosion, forming a wave-cut notch
- Cliffs retreat by 5–6 metres with each collapse
- Cliff collapses along plane of failure
- Waves break up and remove debris — a new cycle of undercutting and cliff collapse begins
- Erosion continues
- Impermeable clay prevents water from escaping downwards
- Rain
- Water soaks into sands and gravels, weakening cliffs
- Large crack appears, indicating slope failure

Since the destruction of the revetments, rates of erosion at Happisburgh have averaged 5–8 metres a year. Already erosion has carved a shallow bay to the south of the village (see Photograph 2.6). Rapid erosion is explained by three factors:

▼ **Photograph 2.6** Happisburgh looking south, showing the shallow bay eroded since 1990

- Cliffs formed from soft glacial sands, gravels and clay (see Figure 2.12).
- The long fetch (i.e. expanse of open sea) to the northeast (see Figure 2.13) that generates powerful storm waves.
- Narrow beaches that give little protection from storms.

**Figure 2.13 Sediment movement in eastern England**

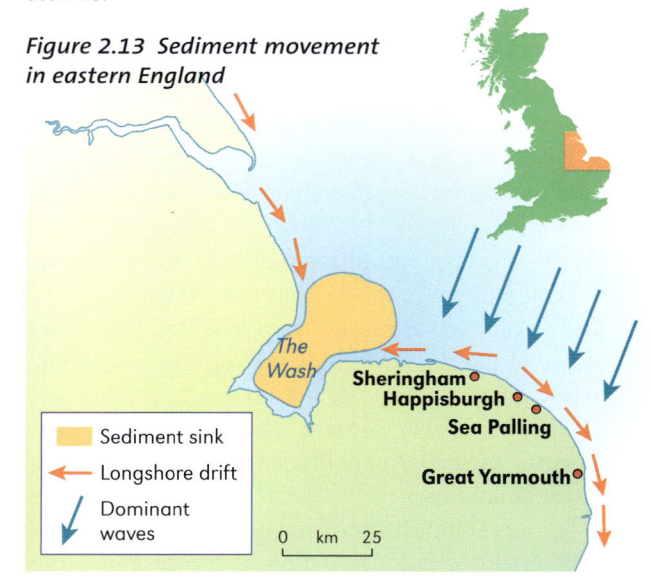

- Sediment sink
- Longshore drift
- Dominant waves

The Wash, Sheringham, Happisburgh, Sea Palling, Great Yarmouth

Rivers and coasts

## Chapter 2 Coasts

*Table 2.4 Coastal defences: soft engineering approaches*

| Beach replenishment/ renewal | Beaches absorb wave energy (energy is spent moving sand and shingle up, down and along beaches). A wide beach is the best defence against coastal erosion. Sand and shingle can be added artificially to beaches to protect the coastline against erosion and/or flooding. Beach replenishment also maintains beaches for tourism. |
|---|---|
| 'Do nothing' and managed realignment | It is too costly to build and maintain hard structures to defend the UK's entire coastline. Moreover, the costs of coastal defence will increase in future due to climate change and rising sea levels. This means that maintaining the UK's hard coastal defences is unsustainable. Where the value of threatened property is relatively low, erosion may be allowed to continue.<br><br>'Do nothing' is a controversial policy. It allows natural processes, such as the movement of sand and shingle, to operate, and it is sustainable. But people may lose their property without compensation.<br><br>Managed realignment allows some stretches of coastline to be flooded, either by letting the sea breach flood embankments or by dismantling sea defences. This has already happened in parts of Essex and Lincolnshire. A new, sustainable coastline is established further inland. Managed realignment may result in loss of farmland, but flooded land becomes new salt marsh and mudflat — important habitats for wildlife. |

## Impact of 'do nothing' and managed realignment

We have seen that the lack of hard defences at Happisburgh has led to dramatic increases in erosion since 1990 (see Photograph 2.7). In response to this situation a local pressure group — Coastal Concern Action Group (CCAG) — was formed to lobby North Norfolk District Council and the government to repair the sea defences. However, there is no legal obligation on the government to compensate people who lose their land, businesses and homes through coastal erosion.

## Protection against the sea

Grants for protection against coastal erosion are available from the government. They cover 40–50% of costs; the rest comes from the local authority. Applications for grants are considered against three criteria:
**(1)** Whether the cost of sea defences is greater than the value of the property being protected.
**(2)** The number of properties at risk and the vulnerability of the population (as measured by economic deprivation).
**(3)** Environmental benefits (e.g. creation of salt marshes, protection of heritage sites or Sites of Special Scientific Interest).

So far Happisburgh has not been awarded a government grant. The value of the property and land at risk is less than the cost of sea defences (revetments cost £1,500 per metre, and **sea walls** £5,000 per metre). At the moment only a few outlying houses and other properties at Happisburgh are threatened. The main part of the village is not in immediate danger.

## The current situation

CCAG's case for repairing the sea defences at Happisburgh is based on several arguments:
- Many local people bought their homes before 1990, when secure defences were in place and rates of erosion were only a fraction of those that have occurred since then.
- Erosion of the coast is not only due to natural processes. It has been accelerated by the following:
  – **Sea walls** to the north, which stop erosion and reduce the amount of sediment available to build beaches at Happisburgh.
  – Dredging sand and shingle from the sea bed off Great Yarmouth (from 1989 to 2002, 163 million tonnes were dredged), which starves beaches at Happisburgh of sediment.
  – Granite reefs built offshore near Sea Palling, which restrict the movement of sand and shingle from the sea bed to the coast.

However, in 2006, Happisburgh won a temporary reprieve when Norfolk County Council provided £200,000 to place nearly 5,000 tonnes of boulders

Photograph 2.7 Cliff-top houses at Happisburgh

### Activity 2.5

Study the information in Table 2.5 and in the case study of coastal erosion at Happisburgh.

1 State and explain your view on the issue.
2 As a resident of Happisburgh whose home is threatened by erosion, write a letter to your local newspaper expressing your views on:
(a) the policy that designates Happisburgh as a coastline of 'do nothing'/managed realignment
(b) the government's rejection of Happisburgh's application for a grant to put towards the cost of repairing the coastal defences
3 As a representative of North Norfolk District Council's planning department, give a presentation to the residents of Happisburgh, explaining the council's 'do nothing'/managed realignment policy.
4 Write a short scene (with dialogue) dramatising the meeting between Happisburgh's residents and representatives of the council and government in the village hall. The principal actors are: village residents, the chief planning officer for North Norfolk District Council, a junior minister from the government, and the MP for North Norfolk.

Rivers and coasts

at the foot of the most vulnerable cliffs. Remarkably, the villagers also managed to raise a further £50,000 for an additional 950 tonnes of rock. While the erosion problem has not gone away, these new defences will 'buy' Happisburgh and its residents another 10 years. It is hoped that by then the government will have found ways to help communities adapt to coastal change.

*Table 2.5 Arguments for and against defending Happisburgh from coastal erosion and/or compensating residents*

| Arguments for defending Happisburgh and/or compensating residents | Arguments against defending Happisburgh |
|---|---|
| There is a huge debate about the effects of coastal erosion on tourism. The negative side is that cliff-top properties like B&Bs and hotels will be lost.<br>*Gary Watson, coastal manager, North Norfolk District Council* | Spending money on coastal defences is a waste of resources; the money would be better spent on hospitals and schools.<br>*Professor Keith Clayton, environmentalist* |
| My mother and father's bungalow is now the second to go in the sea. I grew up in Happisburgh and am extremely upset, not only because I wanted to bring up my children there, but because it has caused so many people like my parents so much pain.<br>*Former Happisburgh resident* | It would be wholly unrealistic to defend every part of Britain's coastline.<br>*Gillian Shepherd, Minister for Agriculture, 1993* |
| | Controlled retreat is the only affordable and sustainable way to manage the coastline.<br>*Spokesperson for DEFRA* |
| Having worked all our lives to buy this property, it will mean we have nothing to leave our children. It seems to us that if the government can't get our assets the sea will.<br>*George Dixon, Happisburgh resident* | Sea defences interrupt natural coastal processes, such as longshore drift and sediment movement, leading to a shortage of sand to feed beaches.<br>*Gary Watson, coastal manager, North Norfolk District Council* |
| I would like to say how monstrous it is that people should lose their homes and businesses, for which they have worked and saved hard for so many years.<br>*C. E. Lilley, Happisburgh resident* | |
| It makes you question whether those who make decisions actually care about people. No one seems to mention the people who could lose their homes.<br>*Thomas and Gillian Beeby, Happisburgh residents* | The trouble with management of coasts is that changing one bit of coast means changing someone else's. Defending north east Norfolk would remove material that is being washed down the coast and protects the Broads.<br>*Professor Philip Stott, geographer* |
| The rate of erosion at Happisburgh is ten times the historic rate. No coastal authority would consider putting in a sea defence scheme in isolation without considering the effects on adjacent coastlines. So why do we tolerate this exact situation at Happisburgh?<br>*CCAG member* | Hard coastal defences are a waste of time and money. Defences save only cliff-top properties, and they destroy coastlines. We must make a mobile and unstable coast.<br>*Professor Tim O'Riordan, environmental scientist* |
| We are not starting with a natural coastline and this means that the abandonment of sea defences is highly irresponsible.<br>*Dr Clive Stockton, deputy leader, Norfolk District Council* | Managed realignment is the best answer for a sustainable coast.<br>*Tim Collins, English Nature* |
| Money should be spent by the government on sea defences...our coastline should be protected...we don't want to lose it.<br>*Andy Smith, Beach Holiday Village* | We want the coastline to do its own thing, not to be defended by man-made means. It needs to be dynamic and able to move around.<br>*Lisa Bray, Wildlife Trust* |
| The 'do nothing' policy has wiped thousands off the value of properties. The north Norfolk villages are now like prison camps — no one can buy in or out of them.<br>*Malcolm Kerby, coordinator of CCAG* | We should try to work with nature where we can. The coastline isn't fixed and as sea levels rise it will cost us more to defend.<br>*Peter Midgeley, Environment Agency* |
| People who bought properties on the understanding that it was a defended coastline have now had the goal posts shifted. Compensation is completely lacking and the issue has to be considered.<br>*Norman Lamb, MP for North Norfolk* | |

# Theme 2 Population and settlement

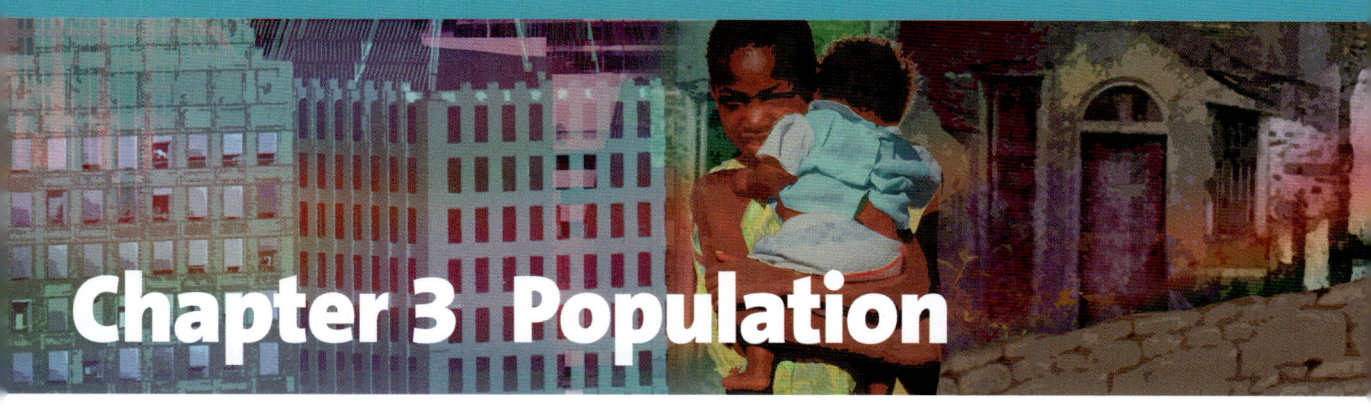

# Chapter 3 Population

## Part 1 Population structure

The population structure of a country describes two aspects: first, the percentage of the population in different age groups, such as children, adults and aged; second, the proportion of females to males.

The age and gender of a country's population are summarised in a special type of chart called a population pyramid (see Figures 3.1 and 3.2). Age is represented as horizontal bars, often in 5-year age groups, with males on the left side of the chart, and females on the right. Despite their name, population pyramids vary enormously in shape. Although some are triangular, others are straight-sided or rectangular; and few are perfectly symmetrical.

### Key ideas

- Countries at different stages of economic development (i.e. LEDCs and MEDCs) have contrasting population structures, including age and gender profiles.
- The population structure of individual countries changes over time.
- There are relationships between population structure and **birth rates** and **death rates**.

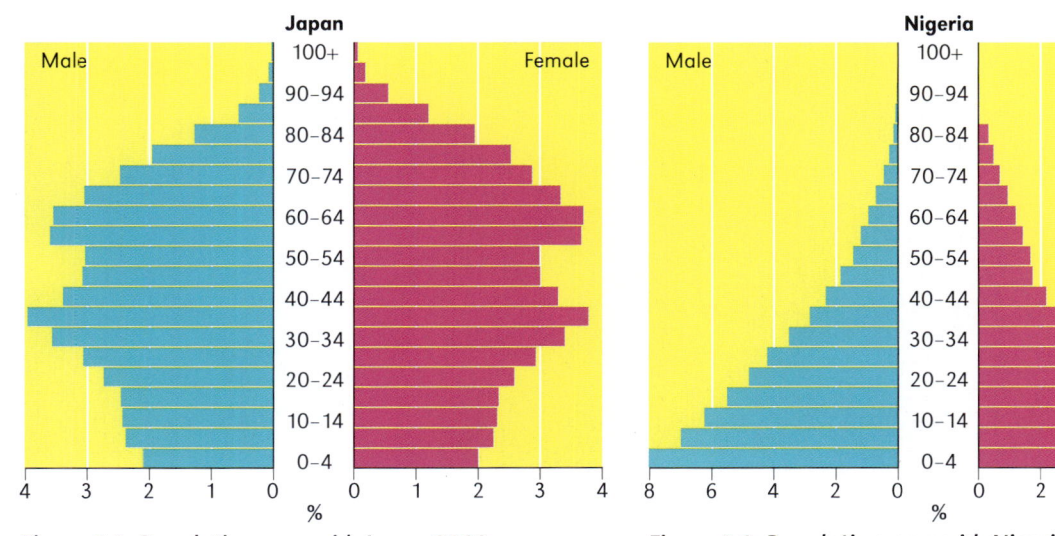

Figure 3.1 Population pyramid: Japan 2009

Figure 3.2 Population pyramid: Nigeria 2009

Population and settlement

## Contrasts in population structure: Japan and Nigeria

Nigeria and Japan are two countries at opposite ends of the development spectrum. Nigeria is a poor African LEDC with a **GDP** per capita of just US$2,100 in 2007 (see Photograph 3.1). Japan is a complete contrast: an MEDC, with a GDP per capita US$33,500 in 2007 (see Photograph 3.2).

These differences in economic development are associated with equally strong contrasts in population structure (see Figures 3.1 and 3.2).

### Nigeria

Like most LEDCs, Nigeria has a youthful population. Two-fifths of the country's 149 million people are aged between 0 and 14 years. This gives Nigeria's population pyramid a broad base. Meanwhile, only 3.1% of the population are aged over 65 years. The result is a classic triangular-shaped pyramid whose sides taper rapidly as each age group becomes smaller than the previous one. We describe this type of pyramid as 'progressive'. The narrow top or 'apex' of the pyramid indicates a population with very few elderly people.

The ratio of females to males in Nigeria is 961 per 1,000. Although women outnumber men in the older age groups, there are more men than women in every age group below 50 years.

*Table 3.1 Percentage of children, adults and aged in Nigeria and Japan in 2009*

| Age group | Nigeria | Japan |
|---|---|---|
| Children (0–14) | 41.5 | 13.5 |
| Adults (15–64) | 55.4 | 64.3 |
| Aged (65+) | 3.1 | 22.2 |

▶ *Photograph 3.1 Slums in Lagos: Nigeria is a poor African LEDC*

# Theme 2

## Japan

Compared with Nigeria, Japan has a much older population. More than a fifth of the population are aged 65 years and over, while the proportion of children is barely one third of that in Nigeria. These two features of Japan's population structure are typical of MEDCs. Japan's population pyramid is relatively straight-sided. It is only in extreme old age that age groups start to decline sharply.

The ratio of females to males in Japan is 1051 per 1,000. However, men outnumber women in all age groups up to 50 years (though the differences are smaller than in Nigeria). In the older age groups women outnumber men by 2 to 1.

## Births, deaths and population structure

Three factors control the shape of population pyramids: births, deaths and **migrations**. At the scale of individual countries, births and deaths have a far greater influence on population structure than migration.

▲ Photograph 3.2 The interior of the new Omotesando Hills luxury shopping mall in Tokyo reflects Japan's affluence

We normally standardise the number of births and deaths in a country per 1,000 of its population in a given year. Thus:
- the number of births per 1,000 people is the **crude birth rate** (CBR)
- the number of deaths per 1,000 people is the **crude death rate** (CDR)
- the difference between the CBR and the CDR is the **natural population change**, which is usually stated as a percentage per year. Where the CBR exceeds the CDR, **natural increase** occurs. If the CBR is less than the CDR the result is **natural decrease**.

Population and settlement

# Chapter 3 Population

*Table 3.2 Calculation of crude birth and death rates and natural population change*

| a | b | c | d | e | f | g |
|---|---|---|---|---|---|---|
| | Births | Deaths | Total population | CBR (b/d) × 1000 | CDR (c/d) × 1000 | Nat. pop change percentage per year (e−f)/10 |
| USA | 4,308,233 | 2,512,630 | 303,824,000 | 14.2 | 8.3 | 0.59 |
| UK | 649,053 | 612,486 | 60,943,912 | | | |
| Philippines | 2,537,950 | 494,718 | 96,061,683 | | | |
| Namibia | 48,436 | 29,388 | 2,088,669 | | | |

### Activity 3.1

1 Complete the calculations of the CBR, CDR and natural population change for the countries in Table 3.2.

2 Which country in Table 3.2 has the fastest growth rate?

3 The approximate time taken for a population to double is obtained by dividing its growth rate as a percentage, into 70. Using the percentage population growth rates you calculated in (1), estimate the doubling times for the USA, UK, Philippines and Namibian populations.

### Activity 3.2

1 Go to www.census.gov/ipc/www/idb/ and select two countries — an LEDC and an MEDC. For each of your chosen countries record the latest information on the following: CBR, CDR, natural population change, current population, forecast population in 2025, population density and age structure (i.e. percentage population aged 0–14, 15–39, 40–64, 65 and over).

2 Present the information as a table.

3 Describe and explain the differences in population growth and population structure between your chosen countries.

## Explaining population structure: Nigeria and Japan

The population pyramids of Nigeria and Japan are determined by trends in the CBR and CDR over a period of 80 or 90 years. Nigeria's population pyramid has a broad base, and a triangular shape. High CBRs (37/1,000 in 2009 and over 40 for most of the twentieth century) explain the pyramid's broad base. Its triangular shape and rapid tapering with age tell us that CDRs are also high, with significant losses in the number of people in each age group every 5 years. With high CDRs, few people survive to old age.

In contrast, Japan's pyramid has a narrow base and is fairly straight-sided. The narrow base indicates a low CBR and relatively few children in the population. In 2009, the CBR was just 7.6 per 1,000; a low rate that has been maintained over the past three or four decades. Because the CDR is also low (9.5 per 1,000 in 2009), unlike Nigeria, the vast majority of people in each 5-year age group survive to the next group. This explains the pyramid's straight-sided shape. Low CDRs also mean that many people survive to old age, giving the pyramid a distinctive top-heavy appearance.

### Population structure and economic development

The level of economic development in a country has a direct influence on its population structure. In terms of development levels, the United Nations divides countries into three broad groups: high, medium, and low. Highly developed countries or MEDCs have a relatively small proportion of children (usually between 15% and 20%), and a relatively large proportion of elderly people. By comparison, the poorest LEDCs

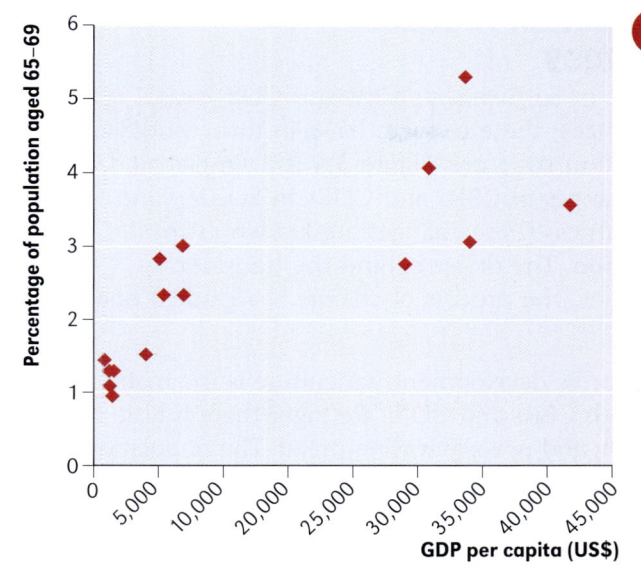

*Figure 3.3 The relationship between GDP per capita and age structure*

## Activity 3.3

Figure 3.3 shows a scatter plot for percentage of population aged 65–69 years and GDP per capita for the countries in Table 3.3. The countries in each of the three development groups were chosen at random.

1. Describe the relationship between development and the proportion of elderly people in a population.
2. Give a possible explanation for the relationship you described in (1).
3. Using the data in Table 3.3, construct a scatter chart to show the relationship between development and the percentage of children in a population.

Comment on the relationship shown on your scatter chart.

typically have large proportions of children (often over 40% of the population) and small proportions of elderly people. Medium developed countries like Thailand and Tunisia have population structures somewhere between these two extremes.

|  | GDP per capita US$ | % 0–14 |  |
|---|---|---|---|
| Iceland | 32,338 | 21.7 | High human development |
| Ireland | 40,987 | 20.9 | |
| France | 28,756 | 18.3 | |
| Austria | 31,990 | 15.4 | |
| Singapore | 26,712 | 15.6 | |
| Dominica | 5,809 | 26.1 | Medium human development |
| Thailand | 7,479 | 22.0 | |
| China | 5,453 | 20.8 | |
| Jordan | 4,317 | 33.8 | |
| Tunisia | 7,593 | 24.6 | |
| Senegal | 1,558 | 40.8 | Low human development |
| Rwanda | 1,321 | 41.9 | |
| Ivory Coast | 1,456 | 40.8 | |
| Burkina Faso | 1,117 | 46.8 | |
| Sierra Leone | 755 | 44.8 | |

◀ Table 3.3 Level of development (GDP per capita) and the proportion of children in a population.

Population and settlement

# Chapter 3 Population

### Factfile 3.1 Sweden

- In the first half of the nineteenth century Sweden was a poor country.
- During this period most people lived in rural areas and worked in farming; most were illiterate and standards of living were low.
- CDRs, particularly among children, were high, and relatively few people lived to old age.
- High CDRs were the result of poverty, diseases like typhoid and smallpox, and food shortages caused by poor harvests.
- CBRs were high, ensuring that enough children survived to adulthood.

## Changes in population structure: Sweden, 1800–2009

In the past 200 years or so, Sweden's CBR and CDR have undergone huge changes; these changes have, in turn, modified the country's population structure. Figure 3.4 is a simple model that describes the changes in CBRs and CDRs in Sweden and other European countries. These changes are known as the **demographic transition**. The driver behind the transition is economic development. The process of change is a gradual one, with four stages.

**Stage 1.** Before economic development, agriculture is the main economic activity. Both CBRs and CDRs are high; there is little or no population growth, and poverty is widespread. The population pyramid is triangular, with a broad base that tapers to a narrow apex (see Figure 3.5a). It is similar to the population pyramids of the poorest LEDCs today (see Figure 3.2).

**Stage 2.** As economic development and **industrialisation** gather pace, improvements in diet and environment (e.g. clean drinking water, sanitation) together with medical advances, cause a steep fall in the CDR. Diseases such as cholera, smallpox and measles disappear. As the CBR remains high, population grows rapidly. A comparison of the population pyramids for 1850 and 1920 (see Figures 3.5a and 3.5b) shows how Sweden's population expanded during this stage.

**Stage 3.** Economic growth brings rising prosperity and the majority of the population now lives in towns and cities. Contraception becomes widely available, and this, together with a decline in infant

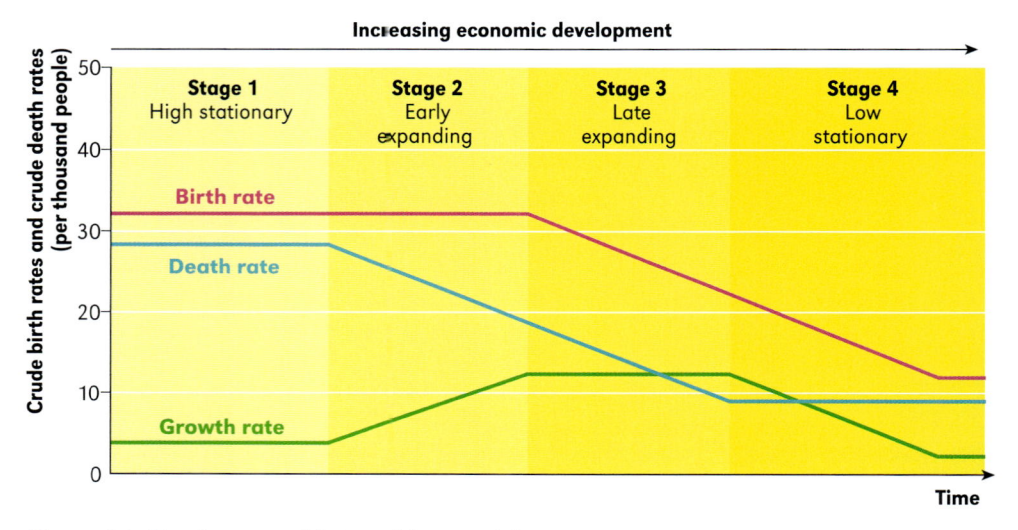

*Figure 3.4 The demographic transition model*

*Figure 3.5 Population pyramids for Sweden*

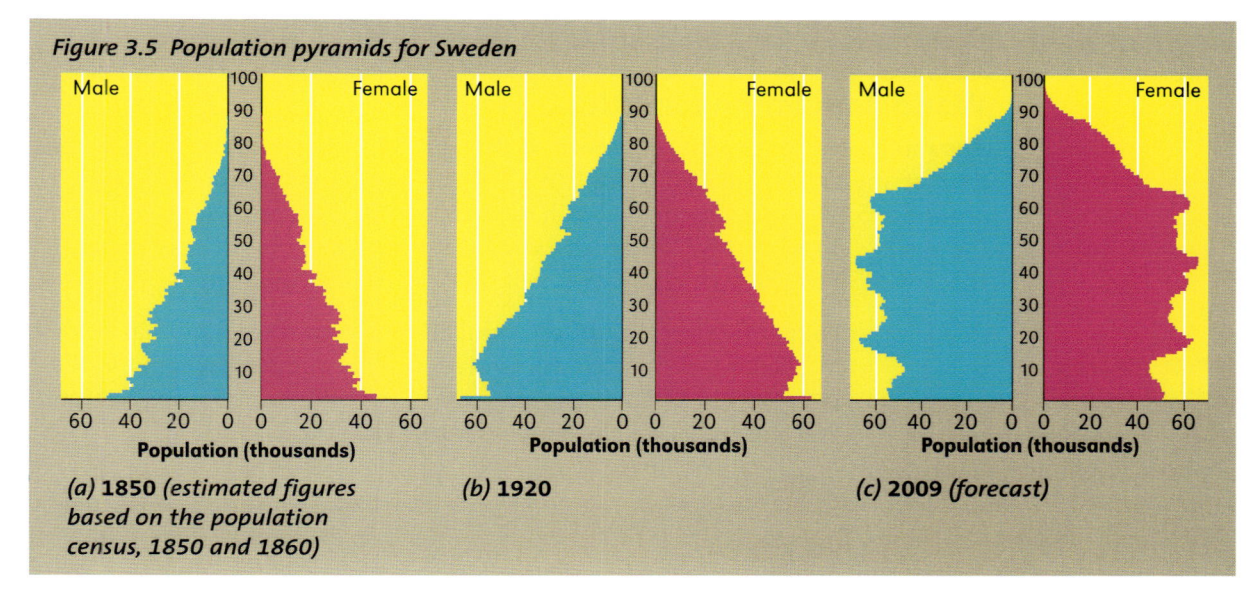

(a) 1850 (estimated figures based on the population census, 1850 and 1860)

(b) 1920

(c) 2009 (forecast)

death, leads, for the first time, to a lower CBR. Meanwhile the CDR continues to decline and high natural growth continues. The population pyramid for 1920 (see Figure 3.5b) has begun to narrow at the base, reflecting the falling CBR.

**Stage 4.** CBRs fall to the same low level as the CDR. Standards of living are high and employment is concentrated mainly in service activities in towns and cities. Few children die in infancy; contraception is universal; men and women have equal status; and there are few economic advantages to large families. Thanks to high standards of living and advanced medical technology, average life expectancy is close to 80 years. Sweden's population pyramid (see Figure 3.5c) is straight-sided, with a relatively narrow base, and tapers only after 70 years. Variations in the size of age groups between 0 and 70 years are largely due to short-term changes in economic conditions.

*Table 3.4 CBRs and CDRs in selected countries: 2009*

|  | CBR | CDR |
|---|---|---|
| Bangladesh | 28.4 | 7.9 |
| Mexico | 19.7 | 4.8 |
| Sierra Leone | 44.9 | 21.9 |
| Morocco | 21.1 | 5.5 |
| Cameroon | 34.1 | 12.2 |
| Norway | 11.0 | 9.3 |
| Niger | 49.1 | 19.9 |
| Spain | 9.7 | 10.0 |

### Activity 3.4

1. Make a copy of the demographic transition diagram in Figure 3.4.

2. Identify the four stages of the demographic transition from the descriptions below. Add the descriptions as labels to your demographic transition diagram.

   **Stage ?** Falling CBRs and low CDRs; population growth

   **Stage ?** High CBRs and high CDRs; little population growth

   **Stage ?** Low CBRs and low CDRs; little population growth

   **Stage ?** High CBRs and low CDRs; rapid population growth

3. Add the countries in Table 3.4 to the appropriate stage of the demographic transition in your diagram.

Population and settlement

## Chapter 3 Population

# Part 2 Population change

## World population growth

The rate of world population growth in the past 50 to 60 years has been faster than at any time in human history. In 1950 the world's total population was around 2.5 billion. Today the world has 6.8 billion inhabitants, and each year the world's population grows by an extra 80 million. Some estimates suggest that by 2050 the human population will number nearly 10 billion.

Ninety-five per cent of all population growth since 1950 has been in LEDCs (see Figure 3.6). Growth has been especially rapid in the poorest 50 LEDCs. However, rates of growth are beginning to slow and this trend will continue in future (see Figure 3.7).

### Key ideas

- The growth of population on a global scale is due to changes in CBRs and CDRs.
- Rates of population change vary over time.
- Population growth can result in overpopulation.
- Natural population change can be influenced by government strategies.
- The age structure of populations has economic and social implications.

### Factfile 3.2 Growth of the human population

- In 1800 the human population reached nearly one billion for the first time.
- It took 127 years to add the second billion, 33 years to add the third billion and 24 years to reach 4 billion.
- The global population doubled in 37 years, from 2.5 billion to 5 billion between 1950 and 1987.
- In 2009 there were expected to be 135 million births and 55 million deaths: 370,000 children born every day — four every second!

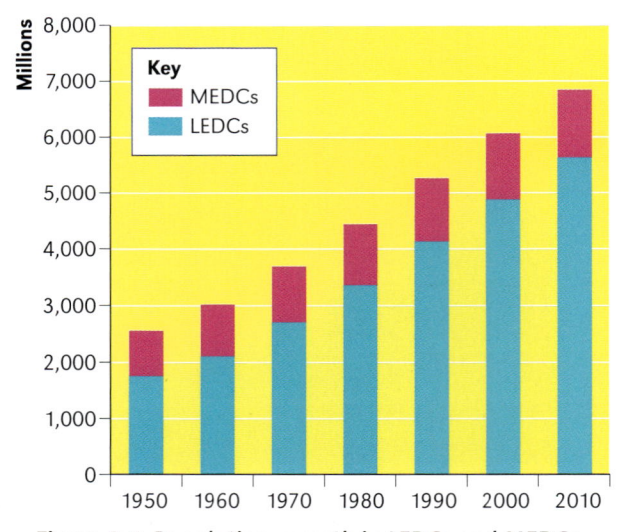

Figure 3.6 Population growth in LEDCs and MEDCs, 1950–2010

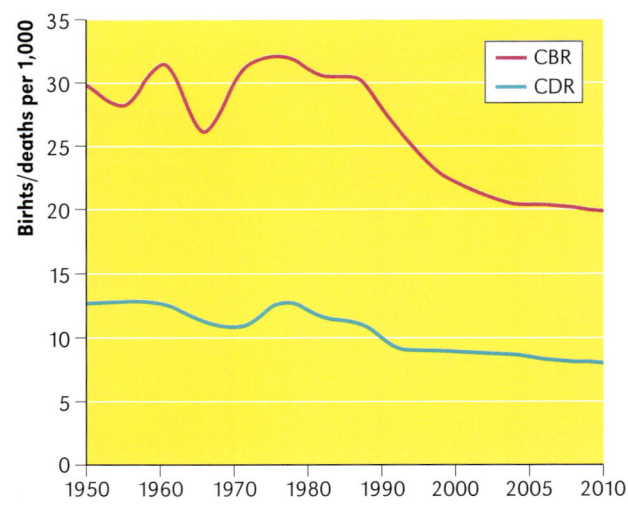

Figure 3.7 Changes in global crude birth rates and global crude death rates, 1950–2010

OCR (B) GCSE Geography

## Explaining world population growth

If we look at the global trends in birth and death rates since 1950 (shown in Figure 3.7), the cause of the world's rapid population growth becomes clear. The CBR was much higher than the CDR for the whole of the period 1950–2009. With many more births than deaths, the world's population grew rapidly.

Why have birth rates been so much higher than death rates? The answer is surprisingly simple. Improvements in housing, diet and medical care lower death rates and prolong life. However, it has not been so easy to convince people to have fewer children. Many people continue to have large families for religious, economic and social reasons (see Table 3.5), while others, who might want fewer children, often have no access to contraception and family planning advice.

Table 3.5 Factors that influence CBRs and CDRs

| | |
|---|---|
| **Age structure** | A high proportion of women of reproductive age (15–49) in a population increases the CBR. Equally, a high proportion of elderly people increases the CDR. |
| **Diet, housing, environmental conditions** | A balanced diet and sufficient food intake lower CDRs, especially among children. Good quality housing, proper sanitation and clean drinking water also lower CDRs. |
| **Medicine and healthcare** | The availability of medicines, hospitals and doctors reduces CDRs and increase life expectancy. |
| **Family planning and contraception** | CBRs in many LEDCs are high because women do not have access to family planning services and contraceptives. Where family planning and contraceptives are easily available, CBRs often fall dramatically. |
| **Economic conditions** | In rural areas in many LEDCs, children are an economic asset. They often work in farming and craft industries at an early age and contribute to family incomes. Opportunities for child employment are lower in urban areas. As a result CBRs in LEDCs are often higher in rural than in urban areas. In many LEDCs children are viewed as insurance in old age. In MEDCs children are engaged in full-time education for at least 11 to 13 years. During this time they are supported by their parents and are non-productive. The average cost to parents of a child from 0 to 21 years is £200,000 in the UK. Thus for most parents, large families do not make economic sense. |
| **Social and religious factors** | The status and education of women is an important influence on CBRs in LEDCs. Where women have equality with men, and are well educated, they choose to have fewer children. Some religions (or customs) forbid contraception and in some societies girls marry in their mid-teens. Both increase CBRs. |
| **Political factors** | Governments adopt policies that may either encourage or discourage births. For example, governments can promote births by banning abortion or the sale of contraceptives, or by giving families with children financial benefits. Currently, most population policies (particularly in LEDCs) aim to reduce population growth by encouraging family planning. |

Chapter 3 Population

## Population growth and overpopulation

The rapid growth of population in some Asian and African countries in the past 50 years raises the question: are these countries overpopulated?

### Case study: Bangladesh — the effects of overpopulation

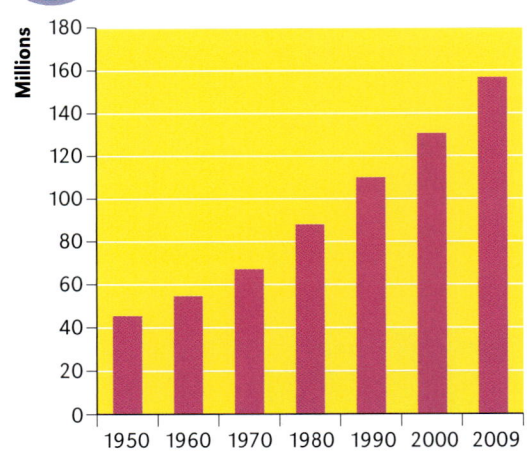

*Figure 3.8 Bangladesh population growth, 1950–2009*

There is a widely held view that Bangladesh is overpopulated. Its population has indeed grown rapidly in the past 60 years (see Figure 3.8): from 46 million in 1950 to 157 million in 2009. Although the rate of growth is falling, the population is still likely to double by 2050.

Bangladesh is a small country with few natural resources. Its land area is about the same size as England, yet its population is two and a half times greater. This makes Bangladesh one of the most densely populated countries in the world. And unlike densely populated countries in the economically developed world, which are highly urbanised, three-quarters of Bangladesh's

### Factfile 3.3 Overpopulation

- Overpopulation occurs when the resources available to a society are insufficient to provide the people with a decent **standard of living**.
- Overpopulation implies that a reduction in population would increase resources per person, and raise standards of living.
- High **population density** and overcrowding are not the same as overpopulation. Many countries with very high population densities such as Singapore, the Netherlands and the UK are prosperous and their citizens have high standards of living.
- Symptoms of overpopulation include: widespread poverty; food shortages; unemployment; and environmental degradation.

*Figure 3.9 Bangladesh*

OCR (B) GCSE Geography

# Theme 2

◀ Photograph 3.3 Planting rice in Bangladesh

▼ Photograph 3.4 A char in Bangladesh, which will eventually erode and force settlers to move on

population still live in rural areas and depend on farming.

Most of Bangladesh occupies the Ganges-Brahmaputra-Meghna delta (see Figure 3.9). Conditions there are ideal for intensive farming. Soils are fertile; water for irrigation is plentiful; and the climate is warm and subtropical. These favourable conditions allow farmers to get two or even three crops a year from the same piece of land (see Photograph 3.3).

Despite this, Bangladesh's huge rural population places its farming resources under extreme pressure. Moreover, the delta is a hazardous environment. Powerful rivers, annual floods and the constant risk of **storm surges** put millions at risk. So why live there? Well, land shortages and overpopulation mean that farmers have little choice. So, they either live in the delta and accept the risks or starve.

So desperate are people for land that they occupy temporary islands of silt that emerge in the delta after the annual floods. These islands, known as 'chars', are settled on and cultivated for a few years (see Photograph 3.4). Eventually they erode and disappear forcing the char-dwellers to move on and find another place to live.

Apart from fertile soils, water and climate, Bangladesh has few other natural resources. There are no significant deposits of oil, coal, gas or mineral ores. And with adult literacy levels of just 48%, the country's human resources are limited too.

Overpopulation is partly to blame for widespread poverty. According to the **World Bank**, more than one person in three in Bangladesh lives in extreme poverty (i.e. on less than US$1/day). Pressure of

Population and settlement

## Chapter 3 Population

### Activity 3.5

Study Figure 3.10.

1. Describe the trends in population growth and crop production in Bangladesh between 1971 and 2006.
2. What evidence in Figure 3.10 suggests that Bangladesh might solve the problem of overpopulation?

population and the custom of dividing up farms equally between heirs, means that 80% of farms are too small — less than one hectare — to support a family. In addition, nearly half of all households in rural areas are landless. These people and smallholders work as farm labourers for wages that barely average US$1/day.

### Strategies to limit population growth in Bangladesh

#### Policies and their effect

Faced with acute poverty and overpopulation, successive Bangladeshi governments have tried to reduce natural population growth. The main focus has been to limit the number of births through family planning. Two approaches have been tried:
- Home delivery of contraceptives and family planning advice by fieldworkers.
- Family planning clinics (including mobile ones) which also offer a range of other health services to mothers and their children.

Legislation has also raised the age of marriage to 18 years for women, and 21 years for men. Later marriage reduces the total number of children a woman will have, and improves the health of young mothers and the survival chances of children. The government's target is to reduce the average number of children born to each woman (the fertility rate) to 2.1 by 2010. This figure, known as the replacement level, should, in the long term, bring population growth to an end.

Generally, Bangladesh's population policies have been successful. The fertility rate fell from 6.4 in 1970 to 2.9 in 2006 (see Figure 3.11). Meanwhile, over the

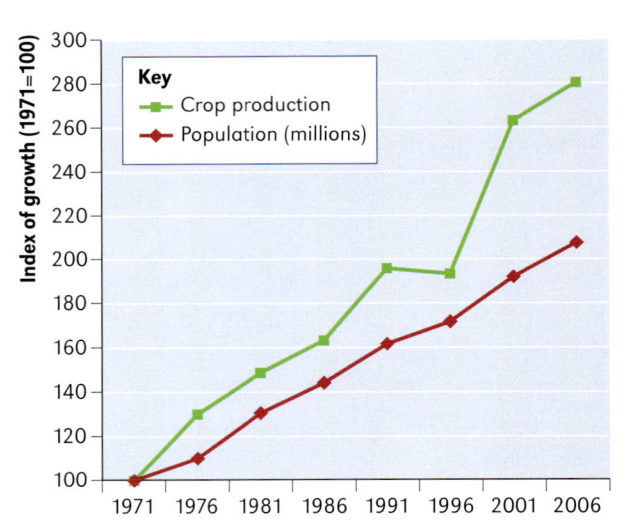

Figure 3.10 Trends in crop production and population growth in Bangladesh, 1971–2006

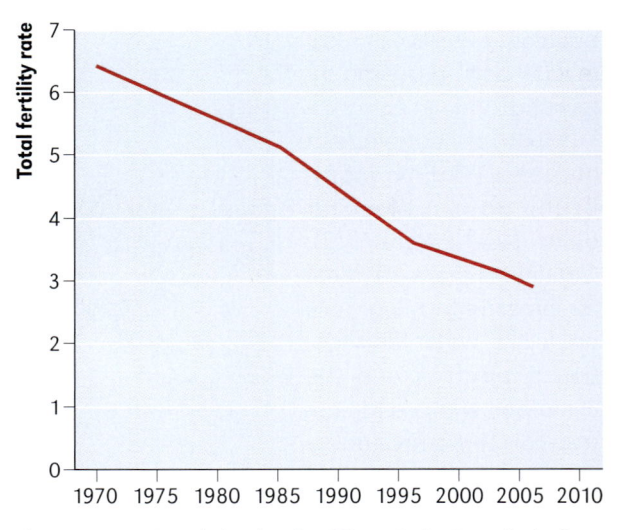

Figure 3.11 Trends in the fertility rate in Bangladesh, 1970–2006

past three decades, the proportion of young women using contraceptives has risen from 8% to 54%.

#### Problems

The fact that nearly half of all young women do not use artificial contraception is cause for concern. It shows the deeply traditional nature of the society, and the isolation and unequal status of women. This is especially true in rural areas. These difficulties ended the policy of handing out contraceptives door-to-door.

Now contraceptives and family planning advice are only available in health clinics. This has a number of advantages. First, the health of mothers as well as children can be checked. Second, mothers speak to each other about the benefits of smaller families. And third, advice can be given to women in private, without pressure from their husbands.

Thanks to legislation, the average age of marriage for women has risen from 14 years to 17 years. However, traditions and customs are difficult to overcome, and a large proportion of young women continue to marry well below the legal age of 18 years. Indeed, over half of young women have had their first child by the age of 19 years.

### Future

Despite the success of family planning in Bangladesh, the country's population will continue to grow. UN forecasts suggest that replacement level may not be reached until 2030, making the government's current target look hopelessly unrealistic. Even if replacement level were reached in the next 5 or 10 years, there are just so many young adults and children in the population that growth will continue until mid-century.

## The problems of age dependency

Age structure causes economic problems in both rich and poor countries. These problems usually relate to issues of age dependency. Increasingly, rich countries face the problem of ageing populations, while poor countries have the opposite problem — too many children. In economic terms, the ideal age structure for a country is one with a large proportion of the population in the adult age group. These people are most likely to be in work, and being productive they create wealth, which drives the economy.

### Factfile 3.4 Measuring age dependency

- A country's simplified age structure comprises three groups: children (0–14), adults (15–64) and elderly people (65+).
- Dependency (the dependency ratio) is calculated by dividing the combined percentage of children and elderly people by the percentage of adults.
- Dependency ratio = (% children + % elderly people)/% adults
- Youthfulness (the juvenility index) is calculated by dividing the percentage of children by the combined percentage of adults and elderly people.
- Juvenility index = % children/(% adults + % elderly people)
- Old age (the old age index) is calculated by dividing the percentage of elderly people by the percentage of adults.
- Old age index = % elderly people/% adults.

### Activity 3.6

A family planning worker visits a young Bangladeshi farmer and his wife who are not using any artificial contraception. They already have three children.

1 As the family planning worker, set out the arguments you would use to persuade the couple to use contraceptives and limit their family to just three children.

2 Give reasons why the farmer and his wife might reject the idea of family planning.

### Activity 3.7

Table 3.6 Simplified age structure of Germany, Swaziland and Venezuela in 2009

|  | % 0–14 | % 15–64 | % 65+ |
|---|---|---|---|
| Germany | 13.7 | 66.1 | 20.3 |
| Swaziland | 39.4 | 56.9 | 3.7 |
| Venezuela | 30.5 | 64.3 | 5.2 |

1 Calculate the age dependency ratio, the juvenility index and the old age index for the countries in Table 3.6

2 Which country has the highest: (a) age dependency (b) juvenile dependency (c) old age dependency?

Chapter 3 Population

## The ageing crisis in MEDCs

Ageing populations and rising proportions of retired people are beginning to create real economic problems in many MEDCs. Average life expectancy in MEDCs reached 77 years in 2009 and is rising fast. By 2025 almost one in four people in the economically developed world will be aged 65 and over. In Japan the proportion will be nearly 30%.

Ageing causes problems because retired people are consumers rather than producers. In MEDCs this group also receives state pensions. Elderly people also make heavier demands on medical services than younger adults, while growing numbers of elderly people (aged 80 and over) often require expensive nursing care (see Photograph 3.5). The resources needed to support elderly people are provided by taxation, the bulk of which comes from employed adults. However, problems arise in MEDCs because the number of elderly people is increasing faster than the number of adults in work. The outcome is increased dependency.

▲ Photograph 3.5 Elderly people tend to make heavier demands on medical services than younger adults

Governments have yet to find a solution to this population 'time-bomb'. Some suggestions include:
- encouraging immigration of young adults with skills required by the economy
- giving couples financial incentives (e.g. tax credits, family allowances) to have children
- raising the age of retirement — this means that older people work longer, draw their state pension later, and pay more tax
- raising taxes on the working population

### Youthful populations in LEDCs

Many of the world's poorest countries, including the vast majority of states in sub-Saharan Africa, have very young populations (see Photograph 3.6). Although many children are economically active in these countries, they make

# Theme 2

◀ *Photograph 3.6 Although education makes a heavy demand on the economy, young people equipped with skills become a huge asset for the future*

heavy demands on the economy through education and healthcare. However, suitably equipped with skills, young populations become a huge asset for the future. As they join the workforce they provide the labour to drive the economy, accumulate savings, and attract investment. India, China and other emerging economies are currently in this position. This so-called 'demographic dividend' is particularly strong where a declining CBR is at the same time reducing the proportion of children and therefore dependency.

### Activity 3.8
What is your solution to the problem of ageing populations in MEDCs? Explain your reasoning in full, and be prepared to state and justify your solution in a class discussion.

# Part 3 Migration

Migration is the permanent relocation of an individual or group. It usually refers to population movements over some distance, at least from one region to another. International migration describes population movements between countries. Those migrants entering a country are known as immigrants, while those leaving are emigrants.

Migrations vary not only in their length, but also in their direction. Today, in the economically developing world, rural to urban migration is common. This contrasts with migration movements in MEDCs, which are mainly in the opposite direction, from urban to rural areas.

## The causes of migration
People migrate for many different reasons. Economic migrants are probably the most common group. Their decision to migrate is strongly influenced by job prospects and the desire to achieve a higher standard

### Key ideas
- **Push and pull** factors influence migration.
- Local areas are affected by the movement of people between urban and rural areas.
- The consequences of **international migration**, urbanisation and counter-urbanisation require careful management.

Population and settlement

## Chapter 3 Population

▲ Figure 3.12 Push and pull factors

### Activity 3.9

For each of the following population movements say whether or not it is migration. Give reasons for your answer.

- nomadic herders moving with their livestock
- people moving from the countryside to live in towns
- students attending university and living there during term time
- people spending time in their second home in the country
- old people moving from a city to retire by the coast
- journey to work
- the evacuation of people from a flood disaster area

of living for themselves and their families. Political migrants may be forced to leave their homes because of war or fear of persecution because of political, religious and ethnic intolerance. Migrants may also move for social reasons such as greater educational opportunities for children and better medical facilities and healthcare. Environmental migrants are an increasingly important group. They move because of environmental disasters such as droughts, floods and land degradation.

### Push and pull factors

The reasons for migration fall into two groups: push factors and pull factors (see Figure 3.12). Push factors are the disadvantages of a migrant's place of origin. They might include a shortage of jobs, low wages, poor services or religious persecution.

▶ Photograph 3.7 A family in the doorway of their one-room wooden shack in Mexico

OCR (B) GCSE Geography

◀ Photograph 3.8 The business centre buildings in Tucson, Arizona

Pull factors are the opposite: they describe the attractions of a migrant's intended destination such as good wages and religious tolerance.

However, a combination of powerful push and pull factors does not always result in migration. Figure 3.12 shows that potential migrants face a number of obstacles. In order to enter a country legally, international migrants may require a visa or work permit. Language is also an obstacle to international migration; so too is distance and the cost of transport.

### Activity 3.10

Study Photographs 3.7 and 3.8. State and explain possible push and pull factors that might encourage the people in Photograph 3.7 to migrate to the city shown in Photograph 3.8.

### Factfile 3.5 Migration

- Migration may take place internationally or within a country.
- Migration is often selective in terms of age, skills and gender.
- Groups such as young adults, skilled workers and the better educated are most likely to migrate. In some parts of the world, such as southern Africa, men migrate more often than women. The reverse is true in many South American countries.
- Migration brings benefits to receiving areas such as a young workforce but can create problems of housing shortages and place excessive pressure on services in these areas.
- Migration often has disadvantages for sending areas: they may lose their most skilled young people and out-migration may lead to an unbalanced age and gender structure.
- Migrants often send money home, which supports many poor communities, especially in LEDCs.

Population and settlement

## Chapter 3 Population

# Case study: International migration from Mexico to the USA

The land border between the USA and Mexico is one of the few places where the rich, economically developed world meets the poor, economically less developed world. The economic contrasts between both sides of the border have resulted in one of the biggest population movements in US history. In 2008 there were nearly 12 million Mexican-born people living permanently in the USA. Every year around one million Mexicans enter the USA, most of them illegally. On average, 70% are caught by the immigration authorities and returned to Mexico.

Three-quarters of Mexican (and other Hispanic) immigrants to the USA have settled in just four states: California, Texas, Arizona and Illinois. With the exception of Illinois, these states share a common border with Mexico. Most Mexican and other Hispanic immigrants are unskilled: they account for 85% of farm workers, and over half of all jobs in construction.

## Causes of migration

The causes of migration from Mexico and other central American countries are mostly economic. The contrasts on either side of the USA-Mexico border are stark. In Mexico in 2006, average GDP per capita was less than one fifth of that in the USA, infant mortality was twelve times higher, and the rate of poverty was more than double. Meanwhile, wages in the USA are far higher than in Mexico and other countries in the region. These differences create a series of push and pull factors that make the USA a very attractive destination for millions of Mexicans (as well as other nationalities in central America and the Caribbean) (see Figure 3.13). Also adding to the attractiveness of the USA is its geographical proximity to Mexico and central America, allowing migrants to move to the USA relatively quickly and cheaply

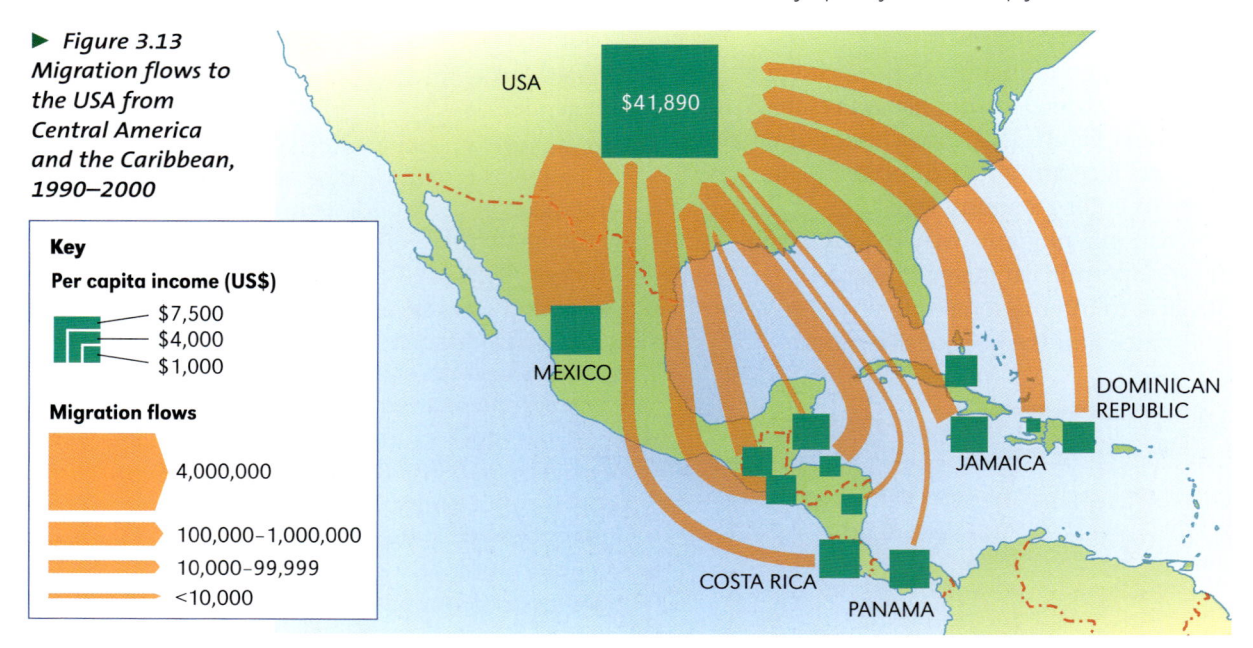

*Table 3.7 Percentage of population of Hispanic origin in selected US cities: 2000*

| Los Angeles (California) | 46.5 |
|---|---|
| San Diego (California) | 25.4 |
| Phoenix (Arizona) | 29.2 |
| El Paso (Texas) | 76.6 |
| San Antonio (Texas) | 58.7 |
| Houston (Texas) | 37.4 |

▶ Figure 3.13 Migration flows to the USA from Central America and the Caribbean, 1990–2000

## Theme 2

◄ Table 3.8 The consequences of Mexican migration to the USA

| Consequences for the USA | |
|---|---|
| **Positive** | **Negative** |
| The majority of immigrants are young adults who join the workforce, pay taxes and help support America's 'greying' population. | Immigrants have larger families than native-born Americans and make relatively greater demands on education and healthcare. Older immigrants on retirement may draw benefits that they have not paid for. |
| Immigrants are consumers of goods and services. They increase demand and help to create jobs and wealth. | Many immigrants are poorly educated and unskilled. There is a limited demand for this type of labour in a modern economy. |
| Immigrants take low-paid jobs (e.g. farm work, construction) that native-born Americans find unattractive. | Immigrants may depress wages and take jobs otherwise filled by native-born Americans. |
| **Consequences for Mexico** | |
| **Positive** | **Negative** |
| Mexico receives money sent by migrants (remittances) worth US$24bn per year (2007). Eight per cent of Mexico's poorest families depend on these remittances; 2.2% of Mexico's GDP comes from remittances. They generate more foreign exchange than the country's tourism industry. | Emigration is selective by age and sex. Communities experiencing heavy out-migration lose young adults who are the most productive members of society. Sex ratios become unbalanced with single males more likely to migrate than females, undermining the fabric of rural societies. |

## Consequences of migration

The migration of Mexicans and other Hispanic people to the USA has economic and social consequences. Given the large scale of this population movement, the consequences are felt in the USA, and in Mexico and other sending countries. The consequences are summarised in Table 3.8.

## Managing migration

The USA controls international immigration through a system of quotas and entry visas. But for many years the government has been concerned about the

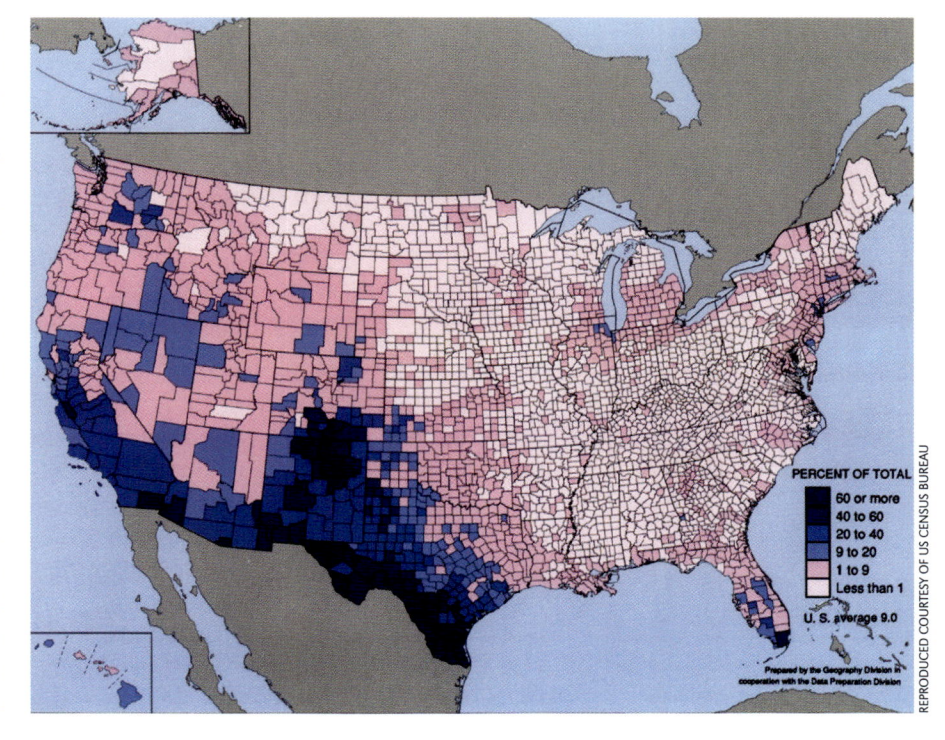

▼ Figure 3.14 Distribution of the Hispanic population in the USA

Population and settlement

## Chapter 3 Population

▶ Photograph 3.9 US border patrol with illegal Mexican migrants in the Arizona desert

### Activity 3.11

Study Figure 3.14.

1. Describe the distribution of the Hispanic population in the USA.
2. Using an atlas, place the following states in rank (1 to 6) in order of their concentration of Hispanic people: Iowa, Texas, Washington, New Mexico, California, Nebraska.
3. Suggest reasons for the distribution you described in (1).

Study Table 3.8, which outlines the consequences of Mexican immigration to the USA.

4. Describe the advantages and disadvantages of Mexican immigration to the USA.
5. State your view on the issue of illegal immigration to the USA. In your opinion, what should the US government do to resolve this issue?

scale of illegal immigration into the country, particularly from Mexico. Its long-term aim is to control the flow of immigrants and reduce the volume. However, cooperation between the US and Mexican governments on border enforcement has proved difficult and immigration reform has stalled.

In 2008, 350,000 illegal immigrants, most of them Mexican, were deported from the USA. A majority of the deportees will return to the USA. Currently the immigration debate in the USA centres on whether there should be an amnesty for illegal immigrants, allowing them to become US citizens.

Meanwhile policy emphasis has been on greater security along the 3,000 km US-Mexican border and at ports. The most popular illegal crossing points on the border, in Texas, California and cities such as San Diego and El Paso, have been reinforced by a fence patrolled by security guards. Tragically, the border fence has diverted many migrants to sections of the border that are less secure. This often means an 80 km crossing of the Sonoron Desert in Arizona (see Photograph 3.9). Inadequately equipped, over 200 illegal immigrants died attempting the desert crossing in 2005.

# Theme 2 Population and settlement

# Chapter 4 Settlement

## Part 1 Urban and rural populations

Since 1950, the number of people living in towns and cities has increased much faster than the number of people living in rural areas (see Table 4.1). In 1950 fewer than one person in every three lived in an urban area; today more than half of the world's population are urban dwellers.

Three factors explain the rapid growth of urban populations since 1950:

(1) Rural–urban migration.
(2) Many rural settlements have grown into towns.
(3) There is a higher natural population growth in towns and cities than in rural areas.

### Urbanisation

Urbanisation is an increase in the proportion of people living in towns and cities. At present, urbanisation is mainly occurring in LEDCs (see Table 4.2). What the figures in Table 4.2 don't show is that more than two in every three urban dwellers live in LEDCs.

#### Mega cities

One effect of rapid urbanisation has been to create **mega cities** — huge cities with 10 million or more inhabitants. In 2009 there were 25 mega cities. This compares with just two — New York and Tokyo — in 1950.

> **Key ideas**
> 
> - Urbanisation is caused mainly by the migration of people from rural to urban areas.
> - The consequences of urbanisation are economic, social and environmental and give rise to a range of management responses.
> - Counterurbanisation is caused mainly by the migration of people from urban to rural areas.
> - The consequences of counterurbanisation are economic, social and environmental and give rise to a range of management responses.

*Table 4.1 Changes in the proportion of the world's population living in urban areas, 1950–2030*

|  | 1950 | 1975 | 2010 | 2030 |
|---|---|---|---|---|
| World's population living in urban areas (%) | 29 | 37 | 51 | 60 |

*Table 4.2 Percentage of population living in urban areas in MEDCs and LEDCs, 1950–2030*

|  | 1950 | 1975 | 2010 | 2030 |
|---|---|---|---|---|
| MEDCs | 52.5 | 67.2 | 75.0 | 80.6 |
| LEDCs | 17.9 | 26.9 | 45.3 | 56.0 |

# Chapter 4 Settlement

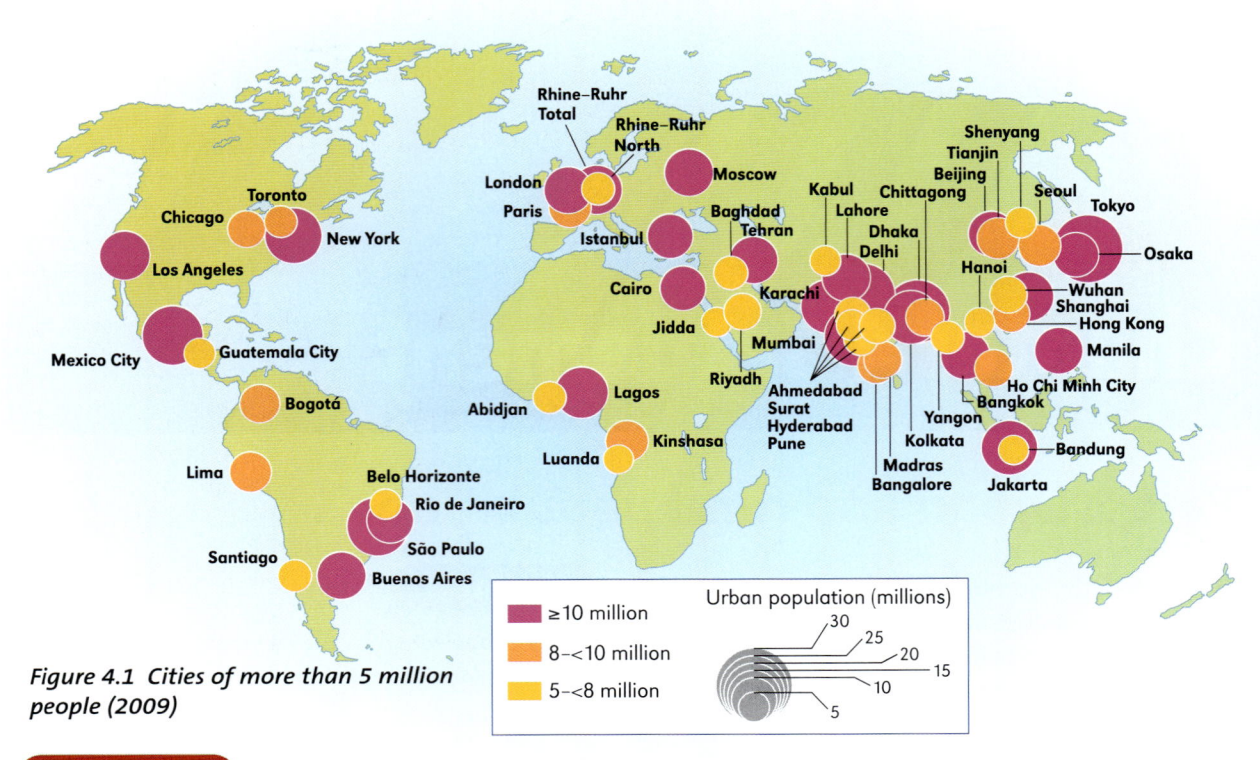

Figure 4.1 Cities of more than 5 million people (2009)

## Activity 4.1

Study Table 4.1 and Table 4.2.

1. Describe the trends in urban and rural populations from 1950 to 2030.
2. When did the world's urban population start to outnumber the rural population?

Study Figure 4.1, the map of the world's largest cities in 2009.

3. Draw a bar chart to show the number of cities by continent with populations of 5–8 million, 8–10 million and over 10 million.
4. Which continent has the greatest concentration of cities with 5 million or more people?

Despite the rapid growth of **mega cities**, they account for less than 5% of the world's total urban population. In fact, most urban dwellers live in smaller cities with populations of less than 500,000. But it is these smaller cities that are currently growing most rapidly.

## Case Study Urbanisation in Bolivia

In 1950 one third of Bolivia's population lived in towns and cities. By 2009 this proportion had risen to two thirds (see Figure 4.2). Urbanisation will continue. Three quarters of Bolivia's population are likely to inhabit urban areas by 2020.

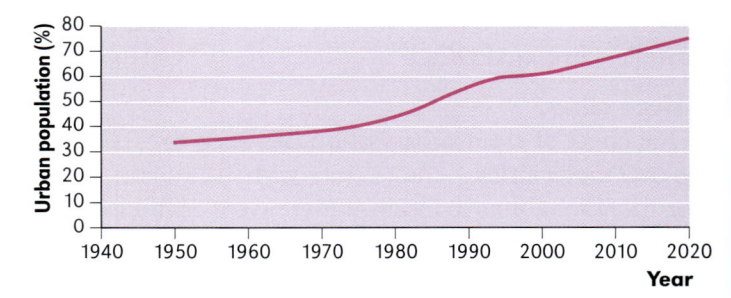

Figure 4.2 Urbanisation in Bolivia ▶

OCR (B) GCSE Geography

# Theme 2

*Figure 4.3 Bolivia*

### Factfile 4.1 Bolivia

- Bolivia is landlocked (i.e. it has no coastline) and is one of the poorest countries in South America.
- Bolivia's land area is equal to that of France and Spain combined.
- In 2009 Bolivia's total population was 10 million — this is three times larger than it was in 1950.
- Bolivia's CBR is 22 and its CDR is 7. Its rate of natural increase is 1.5% per year.
- Bolivia is divided into three natural regions: the eastern lowlands, or Llano; the steep-sided valleys of the Central Region; and the high plains of the Altiplano in the west. These three regions contain 29%, 30% and 41% respectively of the country's total population.
- La Paz is Bolivia's capital and the largest city: the agglomeration contains 1.69 million inhabitants.

The main cause of urbanisation in Bolivia is rural–urban migration. This migration is driven by push factors, especially low standards of living and poverty in the countryside.

## Rural–urban migration

Two thirds of Bolivia's urban growth is due to rural–urban migration. The main destination for migrants is La Paz, Bolivia's capital and largest city (see Figure 4.3).

The most important reason for rural–urban migration is poverty in rural areas, especially the Andes and Altiplano (see Photograph 4.1). These regions, which are between 3,700 and 4,500 m above sea level, are among the highest inhabited places in the world. They are harsh environments in which to make a living, and this

*Photograph 4.1 The southern Altiplano, Bolivia*

Population and settlement

harshness contributes to rural poverty. People move away to the cities to improve their **quality of life**. The main **push factors** that drive out-migration are listed in Table 4.3.

Unfortunately most people moving to the city simply exchange rural poverty for urban poverty. Despite this, a majority of migrants believe life is better in the cities. Señora Valdez de Sajama moved from the countryside to the **slums** of El Alto, a suburb of La Paz, a decade ago. She says:

> In the countryside, when you run out of food you starve. Here, whether you are rich or poor, there is always something. I don't know how to read or write, but my children have learned. I've suffered so much, but my children will suffer less.
>
> *Wall Street Journal*, 30 August 1994

## Urbanisation: good or bad?

Urbanisation in Bolivia has advantages and disadvantages for both rural and urban areas. The advantages are as follows:
- It provides a pool of cheap workers for jobs in industry and services in towns and cities.
- It concentrates the population geographically. This makes it easier and cheaper to provide people with basic services, such as piped water, electricity and education. For example, in Bolivia's ten largest cities

*Table 4.3 Push factors causing rural–urban migration in Bolivia*

| | |
|---|---|
| **Extreme poverty** | This results in a low standard of living and causes high rates of infant mortality. More than 80% of rural dwellers live in poverty, compared with 50% of people in urban areas. |
| **Lack of basic services** | Lack of healthcare, education, electricity, piped water and roads results in a low quality of life. |
| **Low productivity farming** | Many farms are too small to support families. The land has been **over-cultivated** and deforestation is widespread. Much farmland is degraded and soil eroded. |
| **Employment** | There are few jobs available in rural areas apart from farming and mining. The jobs that are available are poorly paid. Wages in urban areas are on average four times higher than those in rural areas. |

### Activity 4.2

1. What is meant by the term urbanisation?
2. Urbanisation is taking place rapidly in LEDCs. Do you think that, on balance, urbanisation is good or bad for an LEDC such as Bolivia? Give reasons for your view.

84% of people have piped water and 95% have electricity. In the poorer rural areas the comparable figures are 31% and 18%.
- It reduces the pressure on rural areas that has led to **deforestation**, **soil erosion** and **land degradation**, making agriculture **unsustainable**.
- Most people who move to urban areas get jobs and send money back to their families in the countryside. Many rural people depend on this source of income.

The disadvantages are as follows:
- The loss of the most educated and most able people from rural areas.
- The weakening of rural communities. Young adults are most likely to migrate, leaving behind an **ageing population**.
- Increases in traffic congestion in urban areas. For example, the steep mountain slopes where La Paz is sited make road widening and building car parks difficult.
- Increases in pollution, especially contamination of streams and rivers where local communities have no proper sanitation.
- The growth of **squatter settlements** (known as *barrios* in Bolivia) and a lack of jobs in the **formal sector** to provide employment for migrants.

## El Alto

In 1950 El Alto was little more than a suburb a few kilometres west of La Paz. It had a population of 11,000. Today it has 677,000 inhabitants. Almost as big as the capital itself, El Alto is one of the world's most rapidly growing cities (see Photograph 4.2).

Essentially El Alto is a huge **shanty town** suburb, the consequence of rapid and unplanned urbanisation.

# Theme 2

**Photograph 4.2** El Alto is one of the world's most rapidly growing cities

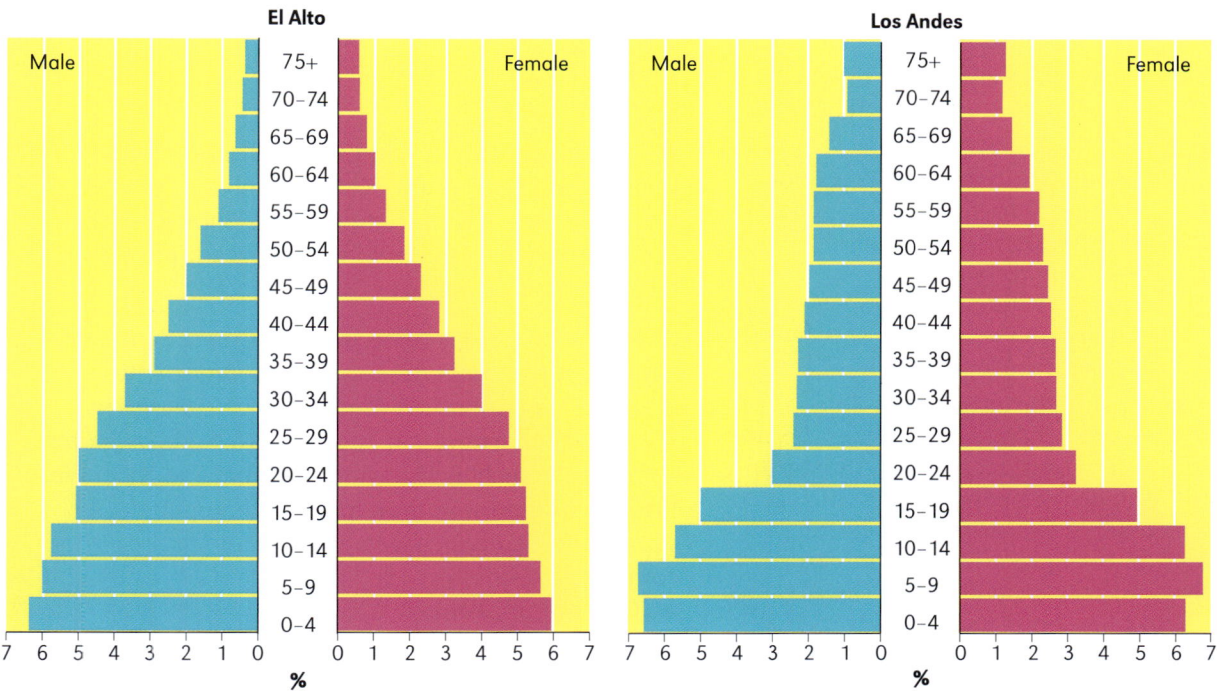

*Figure 4.4 Population pyramids for El Alto and Los Andes*

Population and settlement

# Chapter 4  Settlement

Houses are crammed into the built area at high density. They are self-built, with mud walls and corrugated iron roofs. Most residents work in La Paz. At 3,500 m above sea level, the weather in El Alto is often bitterly cold and the slum housing is inadequate. Over 70% of residents in El Alto live in poverty. Basic services are poor with few schools, churches and parks. There is just one hospital with 33 beds to serve the entire population, and on average there is one telephone for every 100 people.

### Activity 4.3

Figure 4.4 shows population pyramids for El Alto and Los Andes in Bolivia. As a suburb of La Paz, El Alto forms one of the largest urban areas in Bolivia. Los Andes, in contrast, is a remote rural area in the mountains.

1. What are the main differences between the population pyramids for El Alto and Los Andes?
2. El Alto is experiencing urbanisation and receiving large numbers of migrants from the countryside. What evidence is there for this in the shape of El Alto's population pyramid?
3. Many people are leaving Los Andes for urban areas like El Alto. What evidence is there for this out-migration in Los Andes's population pyramid?

### Factfile 4.2 Improving squatter settlements

With the help of organisations such as the World Bank and the United Nations, many cities have improved squatter settlements:

- Squatters are given legal title to land. This gives residents the security to invest in their homes.
- Services that the squatters cannot provide themselves are upgraded. For example, roads are paved, overcrowding is reduced, piped water is provided, electricity is installed and people can get loans to improve their homes.
- Site-and-service schemes are established. Local authorities prepare a site, construct a simple street plan, and provide basic services, such as roads, water, sewers and electricity, for each plot. The plots are rented and may include house 'shells' (a roof and two walls). Residents may also get cheap loans to buy building materials.

## Impact of urbanisation in LEDCs

Ninety per cent of the world's urban population growth is taking place in cities in LEDCs. Such is the speed and scale of growth that it stretches the resources of city authorities to the limit. It is estimated that 1 billion people worldwide are poor and lack basic services; three out of every four poor people live in urban areas, and one third of all urban dwellers in LEDCs live in informal (or squatter) settlements and **slums**.

### Squatter settlements

Because city authorities in LEDCs cannot provide housing and services for everyone, millions of poor urban dwellers rely on self help. The poor solve their housing problems by squatting on vacant plots and building their own shacks.

Clusters of shacks develop into squatter settlements. Squatter settlements have many different names — for example, they are called *favelas* in Brazil, *barrios* in Mexico and *townships* in South Africa. Some squatter settlements, such as Daravi in Mumbai and Kibera in Nairobi, house more than half a million people. All squatter settlements have a number of features in common:

- They are unplanned.
- The squatters do not own the land they occupy.
- At least initially, they have few services such as piped water, proper sanitation, electricity and paved roads.

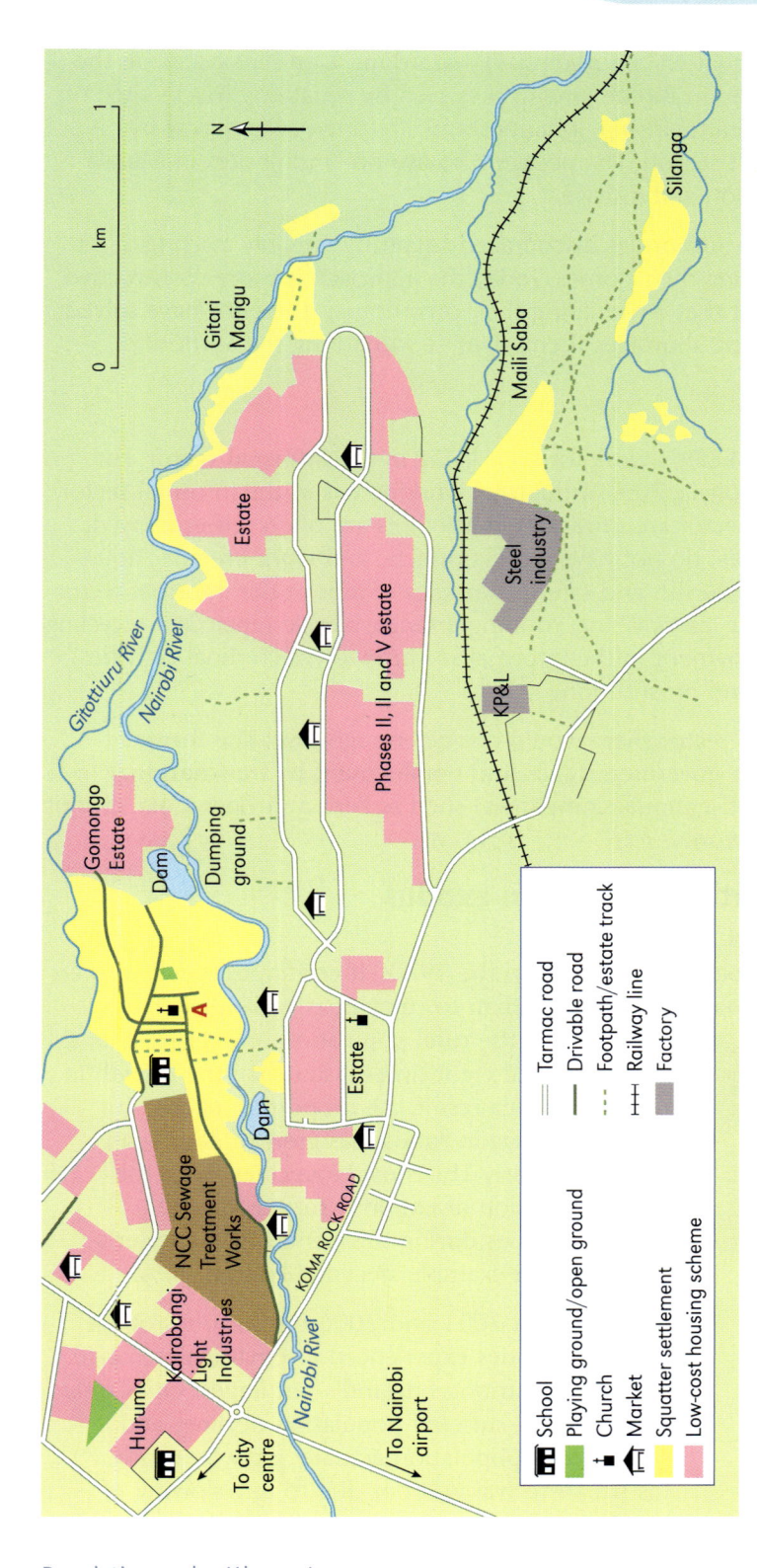

Figure 4.5 Squatter settlements, the Dandora and other low-cost housing schemes in Kariobangi District, Nairobi

## Activity 4.4

Study the map in Figure 4.5 of Kariobangi District squatter settlements in Nairobi, Kenya.

1. Give another name for areas of low-quality housing in cities in LEDCs.
2. State and explain two possible advantages and two disadvantages for people living in squatter settlement A in Kariobangi.
3. What evidence in Figure 4.5 tells you that attempts are being made to improve housing in Kariobangi?

Population and settlement

Many sites used by squatters are potentially hazardous. Landslips occur on the steep, deforested slopes in Rio de Janeiro occupied by squatters. Shacks sited on riverbanks in Alexandra township, Johannesburg, are often swept away by floodwaters in the wet season. The people who live on landfill sites in Manila are exposed to pollution and disease.

In the past, many city authorities discouraged squatting, forcibly evicting residents and destroying their homes. Today the approach is more constructive. The authorities accept that, by building their own homes, the poor have solved the problem of housing shortages themselves — something the authorities cannot do.

### Employment

Most city dwellers in LEDCs work for their living in the **informal sector**. For example, in El Alto, Bolivia, 70% of the total workforce is in the informal sector. Jobs in the informal sector are unregulated. Workers are often self-employed; they avoid paying taxes; do not have legal contracts; and work irregular hours with little concern for health and safety. Examples of jobs in the informal sector include street hawking, car washing, running errands, bicycle repair and recycling activities. Some employment in the informal sector involves criminal activities, such as drug selling and prostitution.

Without the informal sector there would not be enough jobs. The **formal sector**, which includes government jobs and employment by **transnational corporations** (or multi-national companies) such as Ford and Coca-Cola, cannot provide work for everyone.

## Counterurbanisation: the urban exodus

### Counterurbanisation in the UK

In the UK, counterurbanisation started in the 1970s. It continues today, with an average of 1,700 people moving from urban to rural areas each week. From 1991 to 2001 the rural population of England and Wales increased eight times faster than the growth in urban areas. As a result, the proportion of the population living in rural areas grew to 28.5%, an increase of nearly 1%. Most large cities (with the notable exception of London) suffered heavy population losses during this period. Manchester's population, for example, declined by over 10%.

Then, between 2001 and 2006 the fortunes of the UK's largest cities experienced a remarkable change. For example, among England's ten largest cities only one, Liverpool, suffered population decline; and Manchester's population actually grew by nearly 7%! This urban revival was not due to any slowing of

> **Factfile 4.3 Urbanisation and counterurbanisation**
>
> Urbanisation is creating a new population geography in LEDCs. The driving force behind this change is rural–urban migration. Change is also taking place in MEDCs but in the opposite direction. In MEDCs people are moving out of large towns and cities to live in smaller towns and rural areas. This process is called **counter-urbanisation**. It results in a relative increase in the rural population.

Theme 2

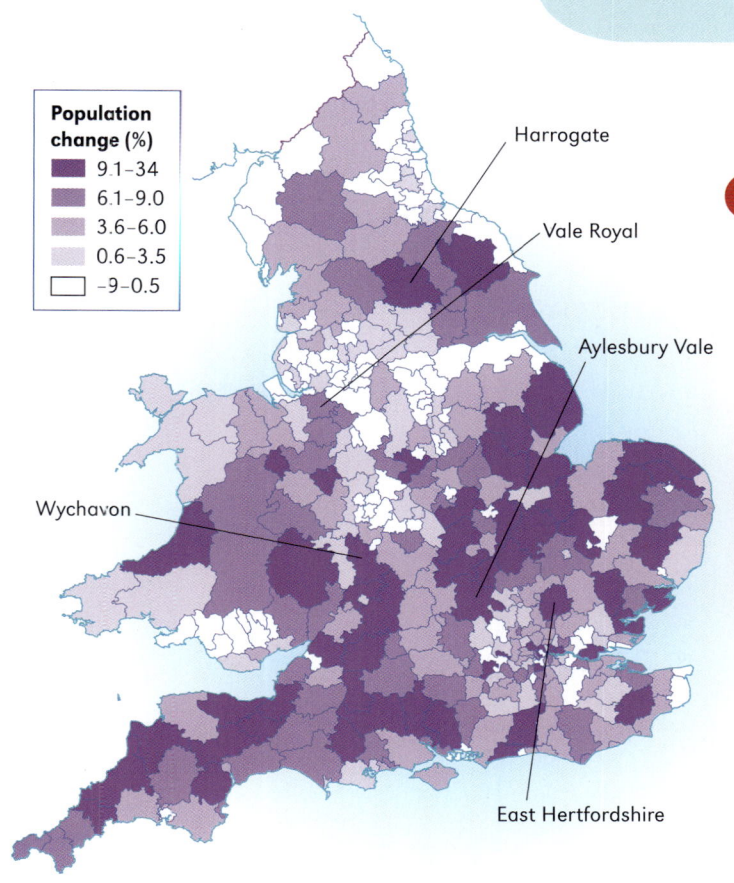

◀ Figure 4.6 Population change in England and Wales, 1991–2001

Population change (%)
- 9.1–34
- 6.1–9.0
- 3.6–6.0
- 0.6–3.5
- −9–0.5

Labelled districts: Harrogate, Vale Royal, Aylesbury Vale, Wychavon, East Hertfordshire

### Activity 4.5

1. Describe the distribution of local authority areas in Figure 4.6 that have rates of population change between 1991 and 2001 of:
   (a) more than 6.0%
   (b) less than 0.5%
2. What is meant by the term counter-urbanisation?
3. Referring to Figure 4.6, explain how the population changes between 1991 and 2001 in England and Wales show evidence of counterurbanisation.

Table 4.4 Rural population change in England and Wales, 1991–2000

| Total population | Natural change | Net migration change | Total change |
|---|---|---|---|
| 13,302,000 | −18,600 | +839,400 | +821,000 |

counterurbanisation; between 2001 and 2006 the rate of population growth in rural areas was still double that of urban areas. Nor was it due to rural–urban migration within the UK. Its cause was massive international immigration, especially from eastern Europe, which was concentrated mainly in large cities.

### Activity 4.6

Give two reasons why people in MEDCs may wish to leave cities to live in the countryside.

### Causes of counterurbanisation

Urban–rural migration is the main cause of counterurbanisation (see Table 4.4). From 1991 to 2000, migration added nearly 840,000 people to the population of rural areas in England and Wales. This trend continued between 2001 and 2006, although at a lower rate of around 35,000 a year.

Table 4.5 Population growth in some accessible rural districts, 1991–2001

| Rural district | Population growth (%) | Nearby conurbation/city (Activity 4.7) |
|---|---|---|
| Aylesbury Vale | 12.61 | |
| East Hertfordshire | 9.87 | |
| Harrogate | 7.92 | |
| Vale Royal (Cheshire) | 6.99 | |
| Wychavon (Worcs) | 10.84 | |

Population and settlement

# Chapter 4  Settlement

▶ **Figure 4.7** Population change in northern England, 1991–2007

*Bar chart showing percentage population change by Authority:*
- York: ~11
- West Yorkshire: ~4.5
- Tyne and Wear: ~-3.5
- Stockton: ~8
- South Yorkshire: ~0
- Redcar and Cleveland: ~-5
- Northumberland: ~1
- North Yorkshire: ~9
- Northeast Lincolnshire: ~-2
- Middlesbrough: ~-5
- Merseyside: ~-4
- Lancashire: ~4
- Hull: ~-3.5
- Hartlepool: ~0
- Greater Manchester: ~1
- East Riding: ~12.5
- Durham: ~0
- Darlington: ~0
- Cumbria: ~1.5

**Percentage population change**

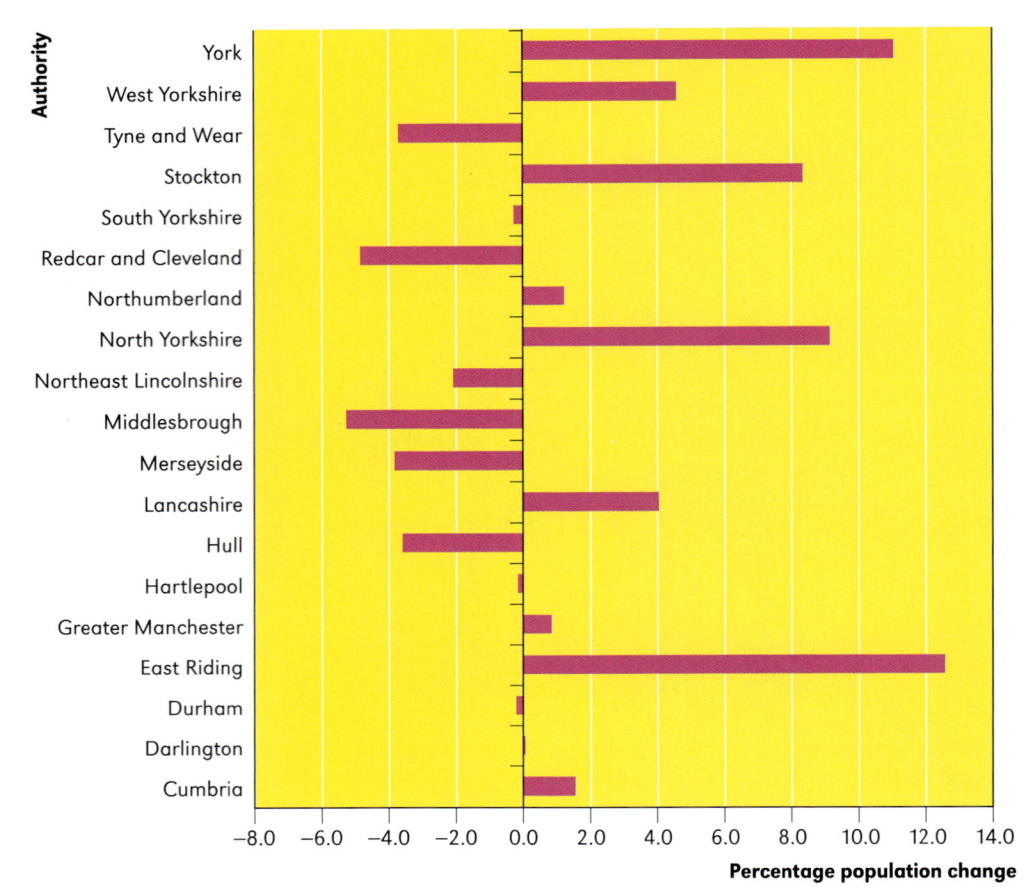

▼ **Table 4.6** Local authorities in Figure 4.6 arranged by type

| Mainly rural | Mainly urban | Urban and rural |
|---|---|---|
| East Riding | Darlington | Cumbria |
| North Yorkshire | Durham | Lancashire |
| Northumberland | Greater Manchester | |
| | Hartlepool | |
| | Hull | |
| | Merseyside | |
| | Middlesbrough | |
| | Northeast Lincolnshire | |
| | Redcar and Cleveland | |
| | South Yorkshire | |
| | Stockton | |
| | Tyne and Wear | |
| | West Yorkshire | |
| | York | |

Both **push** and **pull factors** explain why so many people moved from urban to rural areas. High crime rates, antisocial behaviour, pollution, traffic congestion, lack of community, a rundown physical environment and poor services are just some of the unattractive features of life in large towns and cities. Most British people seem to prefer rural life and believe that quality of life is better in small towns and rural areas.

Most urban–rural migrants continue to work in the cities they have left. As a result they need to live within commuting distance of their workplace. This explains the rapid

OCR (B) GCSE Geography

*Table 4.7 Impact of counterurbanisation on rural communities*

| | |
|---|---|
| **Economic effect** | People migrating to rural areas are relatively well-off commuters or retired people. They push up house prices, which leads to a lack of **affordable housing**, so young people cannot afford to buy property and have to leave.<br><br>Commuters often prefer to use services in nearby urban centres — where they work — rather than local services. Without local support village shops and post offices close, and bus services are withdrawn. This causes hardship for some groups, particularly women, the elderly and young people.<br><br>Incomers are mainly older professionals or retired people who have little demand for services such as local schools. Falling pupil numbers may lead to the closure of primary schools, which are often a focal point for village life.<br><br>In Ryedale in North Yorkshire around three quarters of villages have no shop or primary school; around half have no post office or pub; and almost one third have no public transport service. Counterurbanisation adds to the problems of service decline in rural areas. |
| **Social effect** | Incomers want to 'take over' the village; commuters don't integrate into village life. Longstanding local residents don't welcome incomers. The sense of community is undermined and village traditions decline. |
| **Environmental effect** | The demand for housing in more accessible rural areas may lead to new housing projects on greenfield sites. Amenities are lost, and population growth means more traffic and noise. |
| **Demographic effect** | The older age profile of incomers increases the ageing of the population and creates unbalanced age structures. Ageing also results from the out-migration of young adults who cannot afford to stay in villages. |

### Activity 4.7

1. Use an atlas to find the names of the conurbations or cities adjacent to the five rural districts marked in Figure 4.6. They experienced population growth between 1991 and 2001 due to counter-urbanisation.

2. Complete Table 4.5 with the information you find.

3. Study Figure 4.7. Which local authority had:
   (a) the largest population increase between 1991 and 2007?
   (b) the largest population loss between 1991 and 2007?

4. Table 4.6 shows the authorities in Figure 4.7 arranged by type.
   (a) (i) How many mainly urban authorities lost population between 1991 and 2007?
   (ii) How many mainly rural authorities gained population between 1991 and 2007?
   (b) Look up the locations of Hull and the East Riding in an atlas. Explain one possible reason for the East Riding's population growth between 1991 and 2007.
   (c) What evidence is there in Figure 4.7 to show that counterurbanisation occurred in northern England between 1991 and 2007?
   (d) What evidence is there in Figure 4.7 to show the revival of population in the UK's largest urban centres that occurred between 2001 and 2006?

population growth in many rural counties and rural districts close to major cities and conurbations (see Figure 4.6 and Table 4.5). It also explains why most migrants are relatively high earners. Only the better-off can afford the extra housing and commuting costs.

But counterurbanisation is not just about commuters. Many people move to more scenic areas when they retire, such as the south coast of England, north Norfolk and the Lake District. In addition an increasing number of people work from home (using ICT and other electronic systems) and therefore have the freedom to move away from cities and live in rural areas.

Population and settlement

Chapter 4 Settlement

# Part 2 Land use patterns in cities

### Key ideas

- The different areas of land use within cities reflect economic, social and cultural factors.
- Land use patterns change within cities: some changes are more sustainable that others.
- The need for sustainable development affects urban planning and the management of change.

Every town and city has its own land use patterns made up of commercial, industrial, housing and recreational areas (see Table 4.8). These patterns are the result of a range of physical, economic, social and technological factors operating over several decades or centuries.

At first sight the distribution of land use in cities appears to be rather haphazard. However, on closer inspection it is clear that urban land use has structure and order. At the heart of all cities there is a commercial core, dominated by shops and offices. This area is known as the **central business district** or CBD. As we move away from the CBD, land use often changes in a predictable pattern. In British cities a zone of warehousing and small manufacturing industries surrounds the CBD. This is succeeded by the late nineteenth and early twentieth century **suburbs** or **inner city**. Further out are the suburbs added in the mid- and late-twentieth century, until finally we come to the edge of the built-up area and the rural fringe.

Two simple models have been devised to describe urban land use (see Figure 4.8). One describes land use as a series of concentric rings or zones organised around the CBD. The other shows land use arranged in sectors or wedges radiating from the city centre.

*Table 4.8 Urban functions and land use in UK cities*

| Functions | Land use |
|---|---|
| Residential | Housing types: detached, semi-detached, terraced, apartments, maisonettes |
| Commercial | Retailing (shops), warehousing, offices, hotels |
| Administrative | Offices: government (e.g. town hall); public utilities |
| Other public services | Schools, hospitals, swimming pools, sewerage works, cemeteries, crematoria, electricity sub-stations, landfill sites |
| Transport | Roads, railways, canals, airports |
| Industrial | Manufacturing, energy supply (power stations), mining, quarrying |
| Recreational | Parks, playing fields, allotments, woodland |
| Non-functional | Derelict land/waste land; land awaiting development |

▶ Figure 4.8 Urban land use

1. Central business district
2. Manufacturing industry
3. Low-class residential
4. Medium-class residential
5. High-class residential

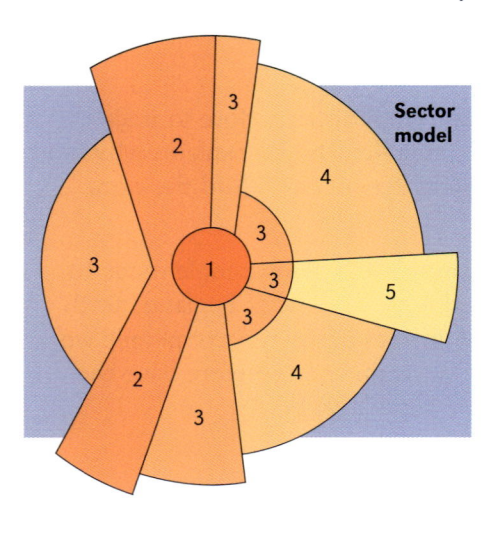

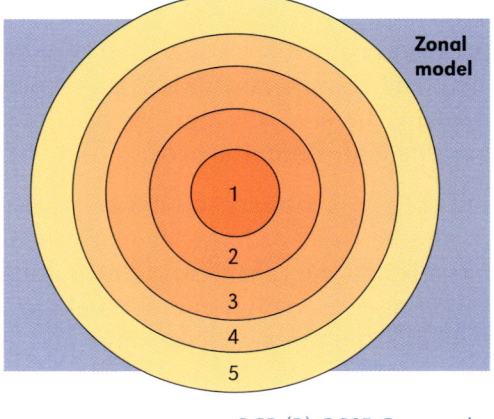

Sector model

Zonal model

OCR (B) GCSE Geography

# Theme 2

## Case study: Land use areas in Bradford

Industrial development in the nineteenth century caused the rapid growth of Bradford's population (see Figure 4.9). This led to the massive expansion of the city's built area, with the addition of new houses, factories, roads and railways.

Like most cities, Bradford expanded outwards from its historic core. Each period of growth added a new ring of development around the edge of the city. The result was a series of concentric rings or zones around the city centre or CBD (see Figure 4.10).

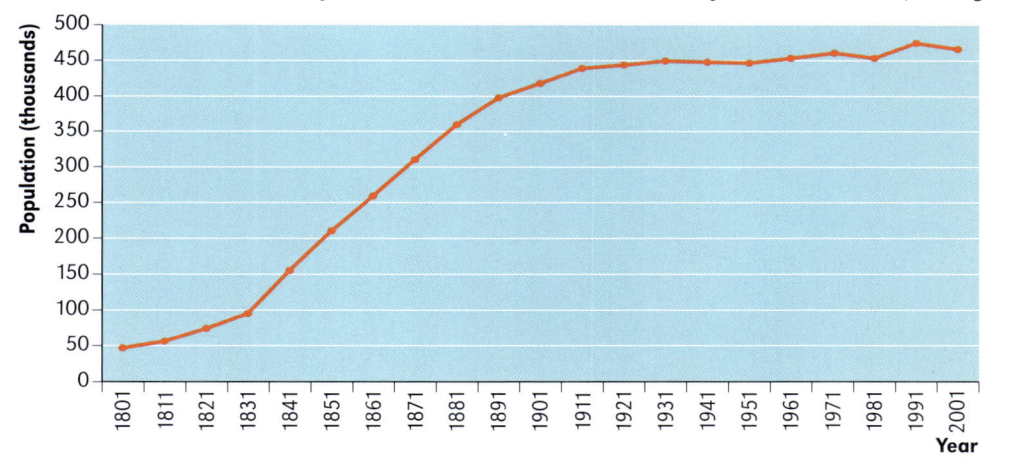

◀ *Figure 4.9 Population growth in Bradford, 1801–2001*

### The central business district

The CBD is the city's historic centre. It is a zone of high density development and intensive land use, with concentrations of shops, offices and leisure activities. The CBD also includes important public buildings such as the cathedral and city hall. Because land is scarce and demand is high, multi-storey buildings dominate the centre.

### Activity 4.8

Study Figure 4.10 which shows the main housing areas in Bradford.

1. What is the furthest distance from the city centre to the outer edge of the inner city?
2. Estimate the average width of the inner city.
3. Which housing zone covers the largest area?
4. Suggest one reason why the inner city occupies a smaller area than the suburbs.
5. Explain why land use in cities often forms a series of concentric zones.

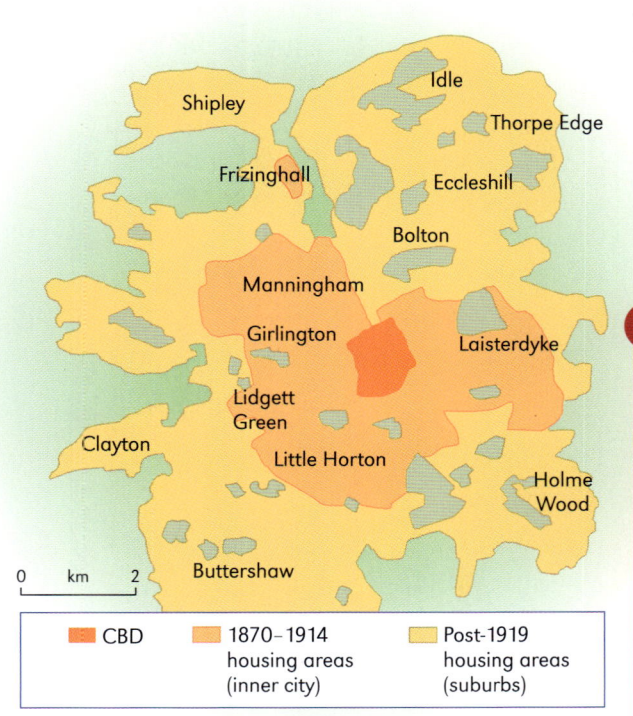

*Figure 4.10  Housing areas in Bradford*

Population and settlement

# Chapter 4  Settlement

*Figure 4.11  OS map of Bradford*

76

OCR (B) GCSE Geography

# Theme 2

## Activity 4.9

Study the grid squares 1632 and 1633 in Figure 4.11 that cover Bradford's CBD. From the evidence in Figure 4.11, describe the following features of the CBD: pattern of major roads; density of development; typical CBD functions.

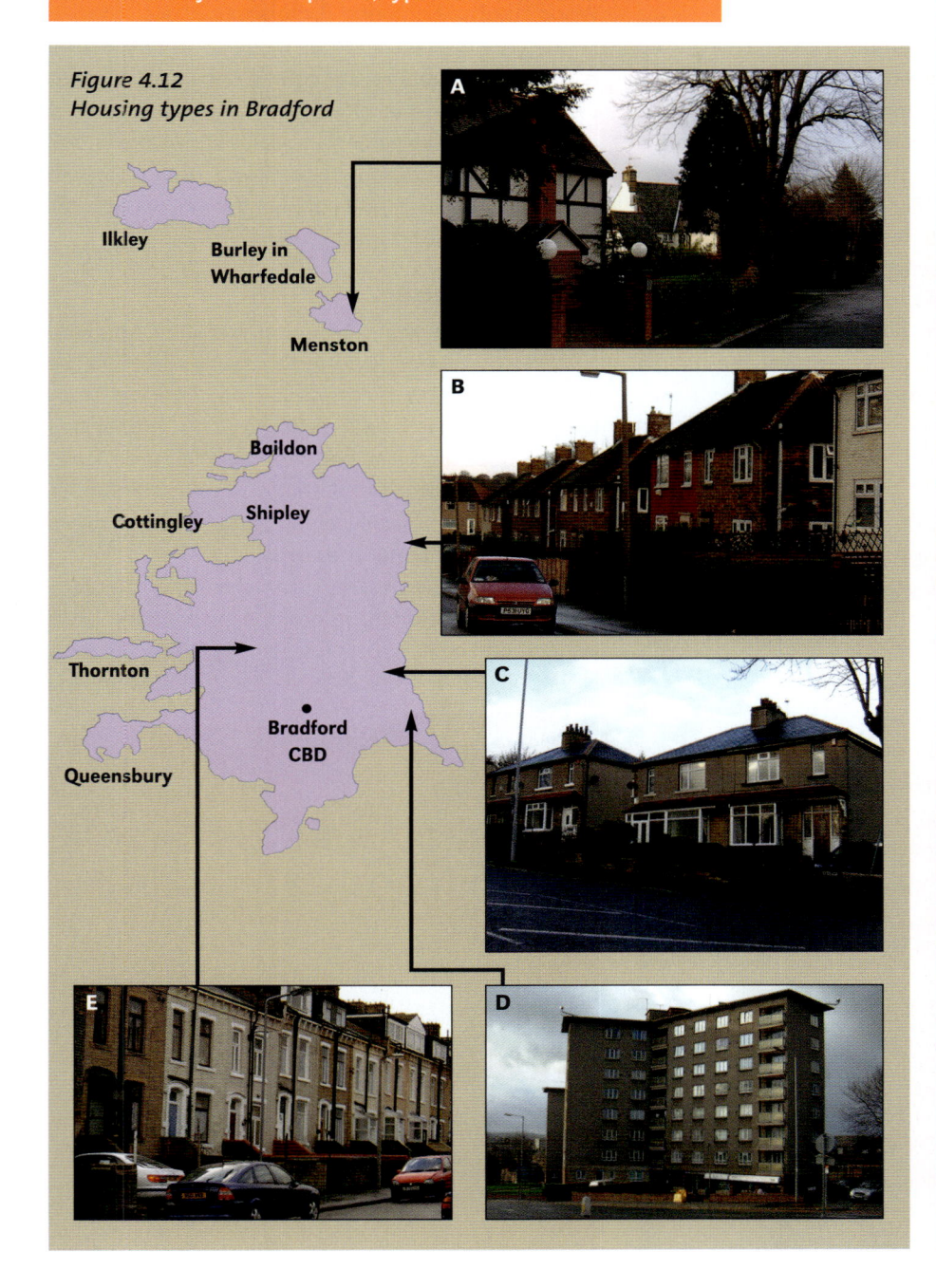

## Activity 4.10

Study Photographs A–E in Figure 4.12.

1. Construct a table with the following headings to summarise the main features of each of the houses/flats shown:
   (a) Type of housing (detached, semi-detached, terraced, flat/apartment)
   (b) Age
   (c) Location (inner city, inner suburbs, outer suburbs, commuter zone)
   (d) Density (high, medium, low)
   (e) House quality (high, medium, low)
   (f) Size (small, medium, large)
   (g) Number of storeys (single, two, multiple)
   (h) Quality of neighbourhood (high, medium, low)

2. Housing types D and E are found in the inner city of Bradford, but one is much older than the other. How can you explain this?

3. State and explain the likely income levels of the people who occupy housing types A–E.

Figure 4.12 Housing types in Bradford

Population and settlement

Well-known high street retailers such as Boots, Marks and Spencer and WH Smith locate in the centre, attracted by the heavy pedestrian flows (footfall).

## The inner city

Between 1870 and 1914, urban growth in Bradford added a zone of terraced houses and industry between 1 km and 3 km from the city centre. Today this area is known as the inner city. It includes neighbourhoods such as Manningham, Girlington and Little Horton. In some parts of the inner city the old terraced houses and factories have been replaced by modern housing developments.

Most inner-city terraced houses occupy small plots without gardens, built at high density. Their street layout follows a simple gridiron pattern. The people who originally lived in the inner city were mill workers who needed to be within walking distance of the mills.

## Suburbs

The suburbs sprawl beyond the inner city to the edge of the built area. Constructed in the interwar (1919–39) and postwar (after 1945) years, the suburbs mainly consist of detached and semi-detached housing. Most of the housing is privately owned. However, Bradford's suburbs also include several large local authority estates, such as Holme Wood, Thorpe Edge and Buttershaw.

The growth of the suburbs is known as **suburbanisation**. The suburbs are newer and have a lower density than the inner city. Most houses have gardens and there are more open spaces, such as parks and playing fields. Instead of the rigid gridiron street layouts, suburban streets are less formal with cul-de-sacs, crescents and radial roads.

## Commuter zone

In the past 50 years urban growth has extended northwards beyond Bradford's suburbs and into the more rural districts of Wharfedale and Airedale. Small towns and villages, such as Ilkley, Otley, Bingley and Silsden, have grown as better-off people have moved there from Bradford and Leeds. These settlements, which are not physically joined on to Bradford, are in the **commuter zone** or **exurbs**.

Although places in the commuter zone are physically separated from Bradford and Leeds, commuters living there continue to rely on the cities for jobs. Essentially, the small towns and villages in the

*Table 4.9 How to describe housing areas from OS maps*

| |
|---|
| (1) How far is the housing area from the city centre? |
| (2) Is the housing area in the inner city, suburbs or commuter zone/exurbs? |
| (3) Does the street layout have a formal, grid-like pattern? |
| (4) Does the street layout have a less formal pattern, with crescents, cul-de-sacs and radial roads? |
| (5) Approximately how old is the housing? |
| (6) How do the street patterns and the distance of the housing area from the city centre support your estimate of age? |
| (7) Is the housing area low, medium or high density? |
| (8) Is the housing likely to be terraced, detached or semi-detached? |
| (9) Are there any factories or mills in the immediate neighbourhood of the housing area? |
| (10) Are there many open spaces in the immediate neighbourhood, such as parks, schools, reservoirs or woodland? |

### Activity 4.11

Study Figure 4.11 again, the 1:25,000 OS map extract of Bradford.

1. Give the four-figure grid reference for Bolton Wood quarries.
2. Give the six-figure grid reference for the mosque in grid square 1534.
3. Using the questions in Table 4.9 as a guide, describe the housing areas in grid squares 1534 and 1235.
4. Explain how the location of the housing in grid square 1534 suggests that it is older than the housing in grid square 1235.
5. Describe the possible advantages and disadvantages of living in these two areas.

commuter zone are **dormitory settlements** for people working in Bradford and Leeds. The movement of people out of large urban centres to smaller towns and rural areas has occurred on a large scale in the UK and other MEDCs in the past 40 years. This process is called **counterurbanisation** (see pages 70–73).

## Activity 4.12

Look at Table 4.10, which shows population changes in the Bradford district between 1991 and 2001.

*Table 4.10 Population change in the Bradford district, 1991–2001*

|  | Population in 1991 | Population in 2001 | % change |
|---|---|---|---|
| Inner city | 108,721 | 113,271 | +4.19 |
| Suburbs | 207,614 | 207,240 | −0.18 |
| Commuter zone | 99,712 | 105,385 | +6.14 |

1. Which zone had:
   (a) The largest percentage increase in population between 1991 and 2001?
   (b) The largest total increase in population between 1991 and 2001?
2. Draw a bar chart to show population changes in the inner city, suburbs and commuter zone in the Bradford district between 1991 and 2001.
3. What is meant by the term counterurbanisation?
4. Did counterurbanisation occur in the Bradford district between 1991 and 2001? Explain your answer.

## Changing patterns of land use within cities

Rapid urbanisation in the past 50 years, especially in LEDCs, means that more than half of the world's population now lives in towns and cities. Urbanisation has had huge environmental effects. Cities have expanded at the expense of farmland, forests, wetlands and open spaces. Meanwhile, millions of urban dwellers have been forced to live in appalling conditions in overcrowded slums.

**Geographical Information Systems** (GIS) allow geographers to map and understand rapid urban growth and its environmental impact. Data are gathered from satellites, air photography, ground surveys and other sources, are stored in computers and then identified by their location. By mapping data for the same locations at different times we can measure the changes, assess their impact, and develop strategies for managing and planning change.

▼ *Figure 4.13 The location of New Delhi*

### New Delhi

New Delhi in northern India is one of the world's largest cities (see Figure 4.13). Its population has soared in the past three or

## Chapter 4 Settlement

▶ Photograph 4.3 Slums on the outskirts of New Delhi

▼ Figure 4.14 Urban growth in New Delhi, 1974–1999

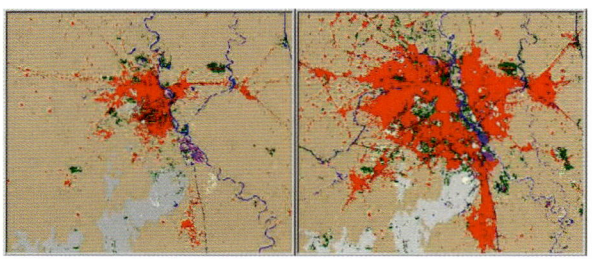

(a) 1974   (b) 1999

four decades. In 1977 New Delhi had 4.4 million inhabitants. This figure rose to 12.9 million in 2001 and to 16.6 million in 2007. The forecast for 2015 is 21 million. This growth is due largely to in-migration. Average population densities exceed 9,000 persons per km², and there is acute poverty, overcrowding and slum housing problems (see Photograph 4.3).

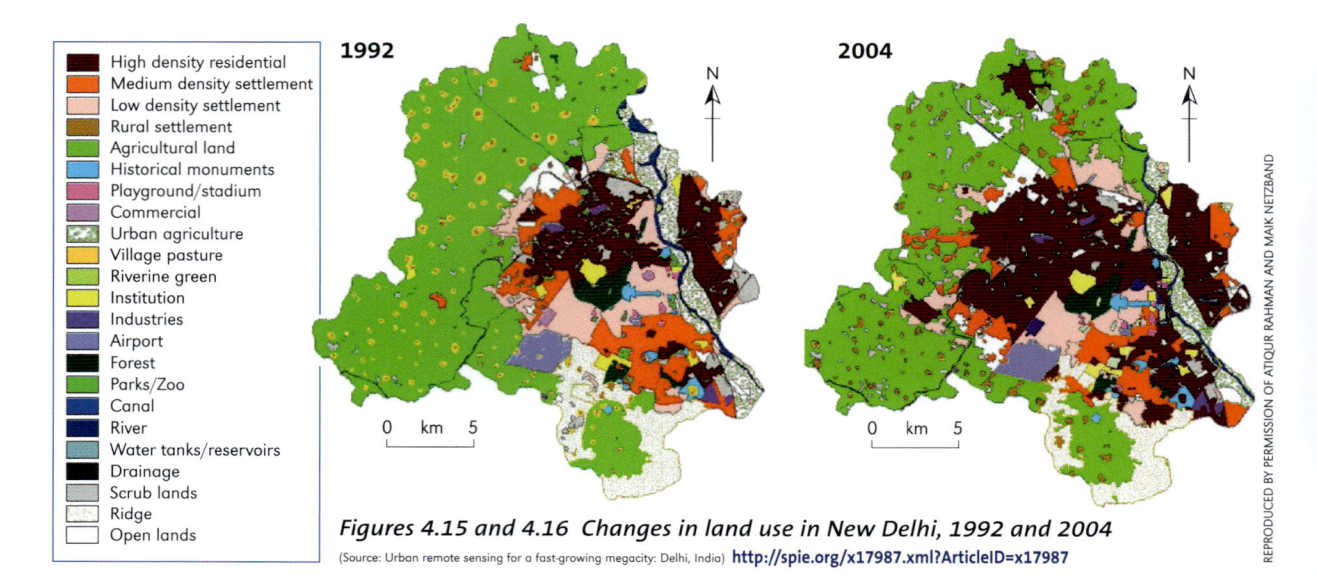

Key:
- High density residential
- Medium density settlement
- Low density settlement
- Rural settlement
- Agricultural land
- Historical monuments
- Playground/stadium
- Commercial
- Urban agriculture
- Village pasture
- Riverine green
- Institution
- Industries
- Airport
- Forest
- Parks/Zoo
- Canal
- River
- Water tanks/reservoirs
- Drainage
- Scrub lands
- Ridge
- Open lands

1992        2004

Figures 4.15 and 4.16 Changes in land use in New Delhi, 1992 and 2004

(Source: Urban remote sensing for a fast-growing megacity: Delhi, India) http://spie.org/x17987.xml?ArticleID=x17987

OCR (B) GCSE Geography

## Activity 4.13

1. Estimate the increase in the extent of New Delhi's built-up area between 1974 and 1999 (see Figure 4.14).
2. Study the land use maps of New Delhi (see Figures 4.15 and 4.16) and summarise the main changes in land use in New Delhi by completing a table like the one opposite (Table 4.11).
3. Using the evidence of land use change in New Delhi (see Figures 4.15 and 4.16) describe how population density has changed in the city between 1992 and 2004. Explain how you came to your conclusion.

Table 4.11 Principal land use changes in New Delhi 1992–2004

|  | Land use changes | Location of changes |
|---|---|---|
| High density settlement |  |  |
| Medium density settlement |  |  |
| Low density settlement |  |  |
| Agricultural land |  |  |
| Open space/ridge |  |  |

The impact of urban growth on New Delhi and the surrounding region can be measured using GIS. Figure 4.14 is based on remote sensing from the Landsat satellites and show how the city's built area expanded between 1974 and 1999. Data from satellites has also helped geographers to identify and map detailed land uses in the city. Figures 4.15 and 4.16 were compiled from GIS data and show changes in land use in New Delhi from 1992 to 2004.

### Austin, Texas

Recent land use change in cities in MEDCs is often due to societal changes, such as increases in the number of households, rather than population growth. However, many cities in rich countries have also experienced rapid population growth since the 1970s. In the USA, rapid population growth has occurred in the southern and western states in cities such as Houston, Dallas and Austin in Texas, Phoenix in Arizona, Miami in Florida and Las Vegas in Nevada.

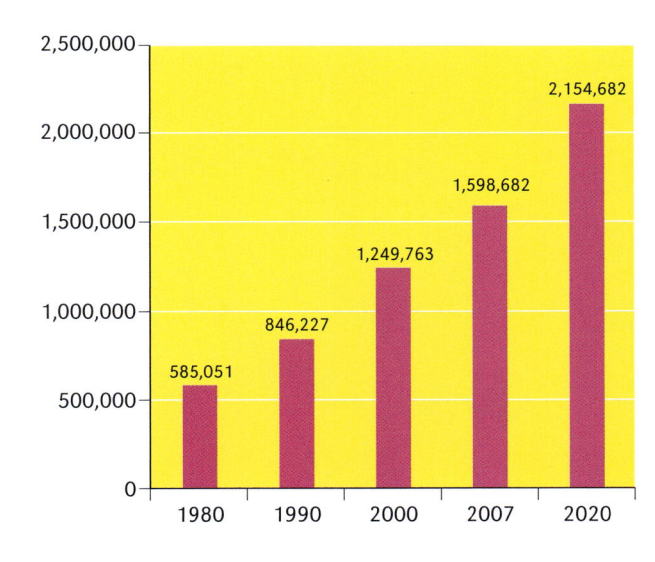

Between 1990 and 2007, Austin was one of the fastest growing cities in the US (see Figure 4.17). Its population increased by 48% in the 1990s, and by 28% between 2000 and 2007. These rates of increase were four times faster than the national average. Population growth on this scale is largely due to a single factor: migration. Thousands of people flooded into Austin from all over the USA, attracted by the warm climate, high quality of life and the low costs for businesses (see Photograph 4.4).

▲ Figure 4.17 Population change in Austin, 1980–2020

Bar chart values: 1980: 585,051; 1990: 846,227; 2000: 1,249,763; 2007: 1,598,682; 2020: 2,154,682

Population and settlement

## Chapter 4 Settlement

**Photograph 4.4** Austin, Texas

As in New Delhi, massive population growth has resulted in urban expansion and land use change. These changes have been monitored by GIS, which has enabled the city to produce detailed land use maps, and plan for future growth (see Figures 4.18 and 4.19). Most of these changes have occurred in the suburbs and on the edge of the city and have involved the growth of housing, commercial activities (e.g. offices, shopping malls, storage and distribution) and industry (business and science parks).

▼ *Figure 4.18 Plan for land use change in a district of Austin, Texas: 1990–2000*

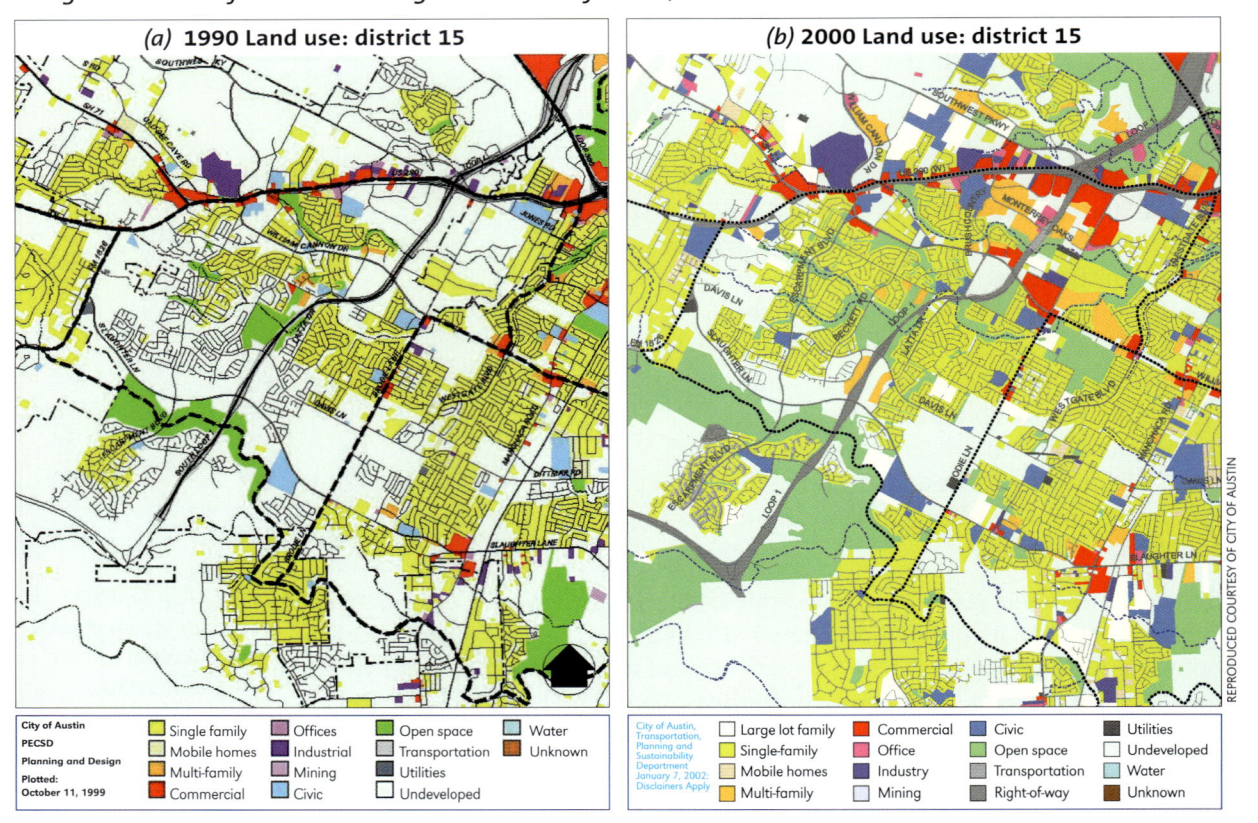

(a) 1990 Land use: district 15

(b) 2000 Land use: district 15

City of Austin PECSD Planning and Design Plotted: October 11, 1999

- Single family
- Mobile homes
- Multi-family
- Commercial
- Offices
- Industrial
- Mining
- Civic
- Open space
- Transportation
- Utilities
- Undeveloped
- Water
- Unknown

City of Austin, Transportation, Planning and Sustainability Department January 7, 2002: Disclaimers Apply

- Large lot family
- Single-family
- Mobile homes
- Multi-family
- Commercial
- Office
- Industry
- Mining
- Civic
- Open space
- Transportation
- Right-of-way
- Utilities
- Undeveloped
- Water
- Unknown

OCR (B) GCSE Geography

# Theme 2

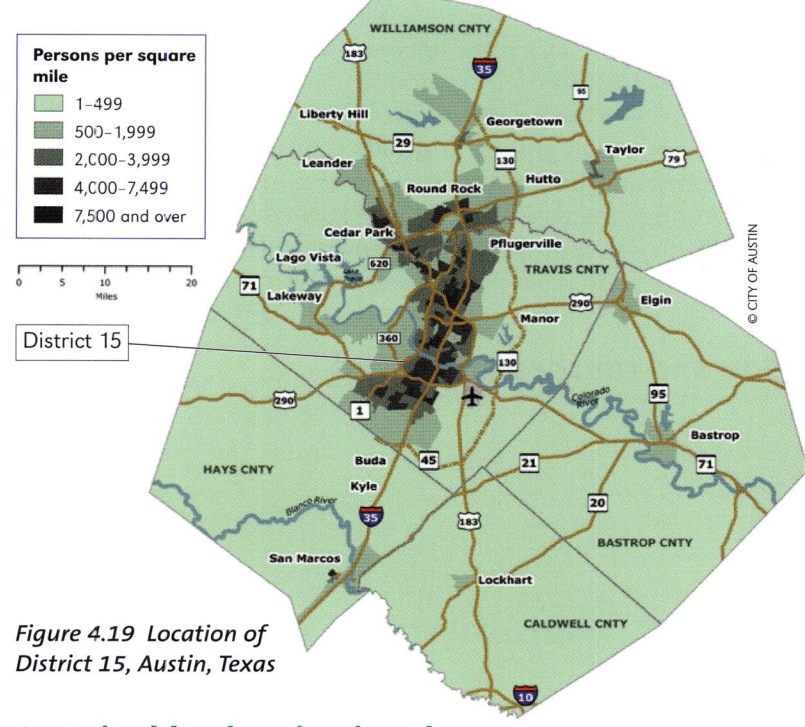

**Persons per square mile**
- 1–499
- 500–1,999
- 2,000–3,999
- 4,000–7,499
- 7,500 and over

District 15

Figure 4.19 Location of District 15, Austin, Texas

### Activity 4.14

Study Figures 4.18a and 4.18b, which show the pattern of land use in district 15 in Austin in 1990 and 2000. District 15 covers part of the southwest suburbs and is close to the edge of the city (see Figure 4.19). The land use maps in Figures 4.18a and 4.18b have been compiled from GIS satellite information and ground surveys.

1. Estimate percentage increase in areas of
   (a) new housing
   (b) commercial areas
   (c) open space
2. Describe the main changes that have occurred in the type, extent and location of urban land use in district 15 between 1990 and 2000.

## Sustainable planning in urban areas

Cities make huge demands on the environment. They consume **raw materials**, energy and water. In the process they produce waste gases such as carbon dioxide; and harmful solids and liquids that pollute the environment. Sustainable cities enable their citizens to meet their own needs and improve their well-being without damaging the environment, or degrading the living conditions of others. Their impact on the environment — their ecological footprint — should be minimal.

▼ Table 4.12 Some features of sustainable urban living

| | |
|---|---|
| **Food, water and other materials sourced locally** | Reduces the costs of transport, including emissions of carbon dioxide and nitrogen oxide, and conserves non-renewable fossil fuels like oil. |
| **Citizens live close to their place of work** | Citizens can walk or cycle to work, reducing emissions of carbon dioxide and nitrogen oxide, and conserving oil. |
| **Urban land is recycled** | Urban land used previously for housing or industry or commerce is re-used. Developing **brownfield** sites protects the countryside and wildlife habitats from development. |
| **Domestic solid waste is recycled** | Paper, glass, plastic and metal waste are sorted and recycled. This reduces the demand for landfill sites in semi-rural areas on the edge of the city. |
| **Electricity is generated from renewable resources** | Electricity generated from renewable sources such as wind power and hydro power. Coal-fired power stations that emit sulphur dioxide and create spoil heaps of ash are gradually phased out. |
| **Waste water treatment** | Waste water from domestic and industrial users is treated before being discharged into rivers. With treatment, water may be recycled in the public water supply or for irrigation. |
| **Controls on the release of toxic waste, noise pollution etc.** | Laws aimed at restricting emissions of polluting gases as well as solid and liquid waste. Similar restrictions on urban noise, e.g. around airports. |

Population and settlement

# Chapter 4 Settlement

Today, urban management in MEDCs plans for more sustainable urban living. It aims to reduce a city's ecological footprint by implementing the sort of ideas described in Table 4.12. While cities in rich countries have the resources to give priority to the environment, urban growth in LEDCs remains largely unplanned. Such is the scale and speed of urban development in these countries, that the authorities cannot even meet the demand for basics such as affordable housing and essential services. In these circumstances, the environment has low priority and is often badly degraded.

## Case study: Urban change in London and southeast England

In the past 20 years not enough houses have been built to meet demand in southeast England. As a result the region has a serious housing shortage. Two factors explain this increased demand for housing:
- Population growth. The population of the southeast grew by just over 500,000 between 1991 and 2006. In the same period, London's population increased by nearly 700,000.
- Changes in society. There are more households due to higher divorce rates, more young adults living alone, and older people living longer.

Housing shortages are also blamed on the difficulties developers face in getting planning permission to build on green-belt land.

### Planning for growth

The government wants to tackle housing shortages in London and southeast England with a massive house building programme. By 2021, 325,000 new houses will have been completed. But housing shortages are only part of the problem. House prices have soared in the region, putting homes beyond the reach of many first-time buyers. **Affordable houses** are also needed to attract key workers such as nurses and teachers.

Sixty per cent of new homes in London and the south-east will be built on **brownfield** (previously used) land. The recycling of existing urban land is one aspect of the government's commitment to sustainable development. Even so, large tracts of countryside may have to be built on if the government is to achieve its housing targets. Planning controls that currently protect the green belt will have to be relaxed.

As Figure 4.20 shows, most new housing will be concentrated in four growth areas: the Thames gateway, Ashford, Milton Keynes and the south Midlands, and the Stansted–Cambridge corridor. In each growth area public transport links to London will be improved. This will encourage commuters to abandon their cars, reducing traffic congestion and pollution. Meanwhile, planning will ensure that **Areas of Outstanding Natural Beauty** such as the Chilterns and the North Downs are protected against development.

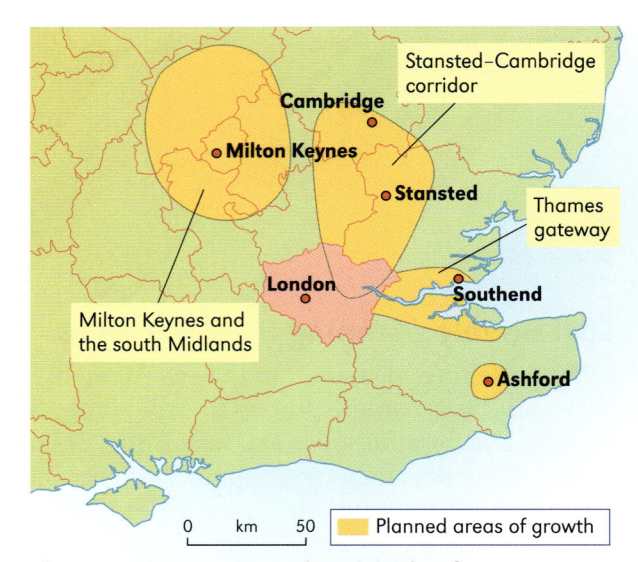

*Figure 4.20 Government housing plan for southeast England*

# Theme 2

## Case study: Conflict over the West Stevenage green belt

There has been a long-running battle over the issue of building 10,000 new homes in the green belt west of Stevenage, Hertfordshire (see Figure 4.21). The West Stevenage Development Project will provide high density, affordable homes for thousands of people. Those groups supporting development include Stevenage Borough Council and two development companies, Persimmon and Taylor Woodrow. Ranged against them are a local pressure group called the Campaign Against Stevenage Expansion (CASE), Hertfordshire County Council and many local residents.

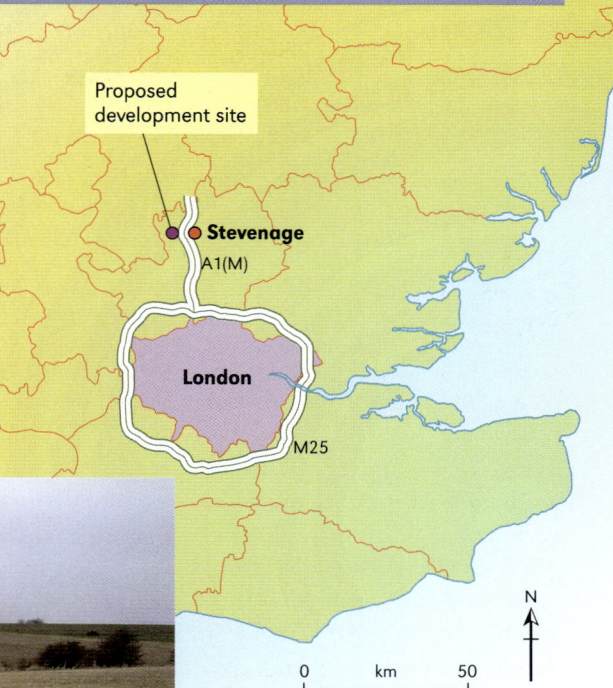

▲ Figure 4.21 Map showing the location of Stevenage

◄ Photograph 4.5 Stevenage green belt

## Factfile 4.4 West Stevenage development proposals

- Build 10,000 houses.
- Of these new houses, 27.5% will be affordable dwellings.
- Housing density will average 37 dwellings per hectare, exceeding the government target of 30 per hectare. High densities will reduce the loss of **greenfield** land and are inconsistent with the idea of sustainable development.
- Building will take place on green-belt land, which is currently used for agriculture (see Photograph 4.5).
- Developers aim to achieve sustainability objectives by:
  (a) avoiding any loss of biodiversity
  (b) reducing peak journeys by 30% and doubling the number of journeys on foot, bicycle and bus
  (c) reducing water consumption by 30% for each dwelling
  (d) recycling 40% of household waste

Population and settlement

## Chapter 4 Settlement

*Figure 4.22 People's views on the West Stevenage Development Project*

Every day my postbag is filled with letters from constituents desperate for homes...obviously new land needs to be found and released.

There is no more sustainable greenfield site in the county than that west of Stevenage. The proposal would provide much needed housing for Hertfordshire.

*Barbara Follett, MP for Stevenage*

In Harlow the vast majority of new homes went to people from London. They helped push up prices, leaving young local people unable to afford the houses. I suspect the same thing is happening in Stevenage.

*Tony, Harlow resident*

Developers want to destroy much of Stevenage's green belt, but do they really want such a bad public image? Persimmon's shareholders should ask why the company is taking on this hugely unpopular development.

*Spokesperson for Friends of the Earth*

The new residents will breathe new life into the town, supporting the economic case for the regeneration of the town centre.

If we don't build homes somewhere, how will our children have affordable homes to live in? A well-planned development of 10,000 homes in West Stevenage is better than a scattering of small developments on the fringes of villages across the county.

*Paul Griffiths, Milton Keynes resident*

They should build these houses because there are too many people without homes. Perhaps the protesters would think differently if they were unable to buy a house in this area. More affordable houses should be built for young people.

*David, Stevenage resident*

It's a difficult situation, people saying they don't want development, because if it wasn't for development in the first place then I wouldn't have my home. So in a way it's a bit naughty of us who have homes to say we don't want others coming in. It's hypocritical then, isn't it?

*Roger Millard, Stevenage resident*

There is a Tory agenda on the county council aimed at not having the West Stevenage development. It's causing immense problems. If they had allowed it to go ahead we would not have had pressure about filling in and cramming every little space. It means the rest of us have to suffer.

*Malcolm MacMillan, Labour leader, Stevenage Borough Council*

The assumption that we can build 10,000 new homes on brownfield land is laughable. The number of brownfield sites in the area are nowhere near big enough. Brownfield is also more expensive to build on, therefore pushing up the price of houses.

*Christopher, Knebworth resident*

The green belt's going to be swallowed up...I think about the fields where I live and I think where are the rivers going to run? The wildlife is part of our country and if you do away with that out here you have nothing left. It's all about people making money, that's all it is.

*J. P. Cleverly, resident living on the outskirts of Stevenage*

I really don't know how the green-belt area of the town is going to cope...I think there are a lot more brownfield sites which they could have used and I'm really sorry that the green belt is going to suffer because of this.

*Douglas Moulding, Stevenage resident*

The bypass here can't cope with the traffic at the moment and that will obviously get worse and worse as more people arrive.

*Roger Millard, 68 years old, Stevenage resident since 1958*

Most of these new homes will be used to accommodate people moving from London. These people then clog up the surrounding roads trying to get back into London. It's telling that these homes are built so close to the A1(M).

*Jess, Hitchin resident*

Having lived in Stevenage for over 40 years we have witnessed during this time field after field being lost to bricks and mortar, concrete and tar. Our flora and fauna have suffered and lost too much already and we simply cannot allow our remaining countryside to be destroyed any further.

*Pauline, Stevenage resident*

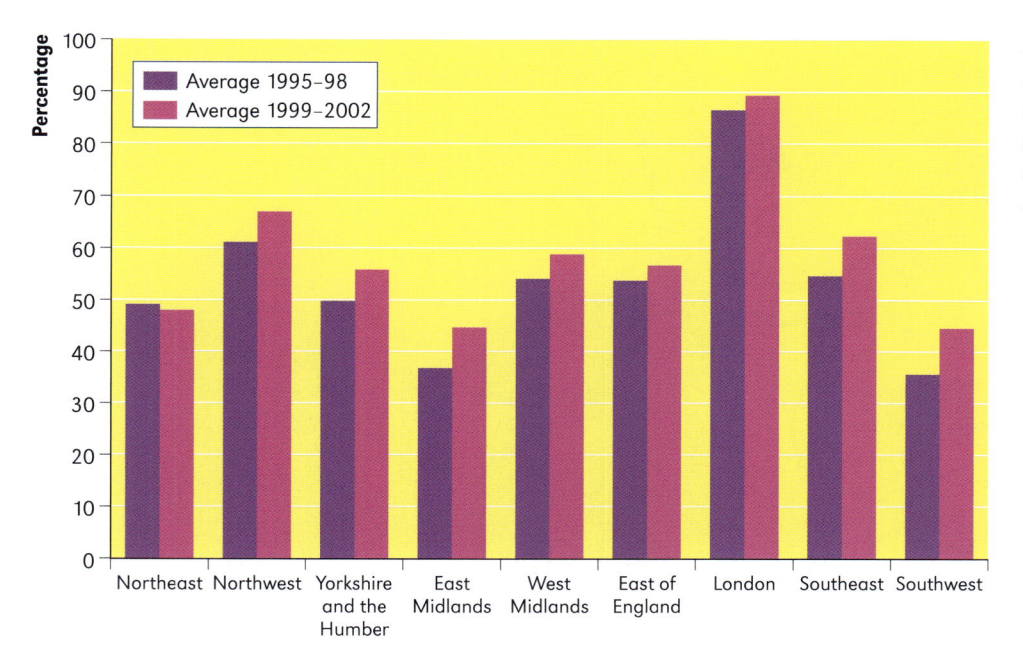

◄ *Figure 4.23 New dwellings built on brownfield land by region, 1995–98 and 1999–2002*

Hertfordshire is one of the most densely populated counties in England and is already highly urbanised. House prices in north Hertfordshire are 25% above the national average, and 50% above the average in south Hertfordshire.

### Activity 4.15

1 Write an article for the *Stevenage Mercury* about the issue of housing development in West Stevenage. Remember to:
(a) provide some background to the proposal, including the housing shortages in the region
(b) give some details of the development proposals
(c) consider the positive and negative viewpoints of people who have an interest in the proposals (see Figure 4.22)
(d) state whether, in your own view, the proposal is likely to be accepted based on the strength of evidence

### Activity 4.16

Study Figure 4.23.

1 Which UK region made (a) the most use and (b) the least use of brownfield land from 1999 to 2002?

2 Suggest one reason why some regions make more use of brownfield land than others.

3 How did the use of brownfield land change between 1995–98 and 1999–2002?

Study the 1:50,000 OS map extract of Stevenage (Figure 4.24).

4 Estimate the size of the proposed site for development, west of the A1(M). Is it:
(a) 7 km$^2$? (b) 9 km$^2$? (c) 11 km$^2$? (d) 13 km$^2$?

5 Name two features of historic interest on the development site, and give their six-figure grid references.

6 Describe the relief of the development site.

7 Using the evidence of the map, suggest how the site chosen for housing could support the aim of substainable development.

8 Explain how the development of West Stevenage might benefit the people who live in Stevenage.

9 Suggest two reasons why people living in Rush Green and Langley might oppose the development.

Population and settlement

# Chapter 4 Settlement

*Figure 4.24 OS map extract of Stevenage, showing the proposed development site*

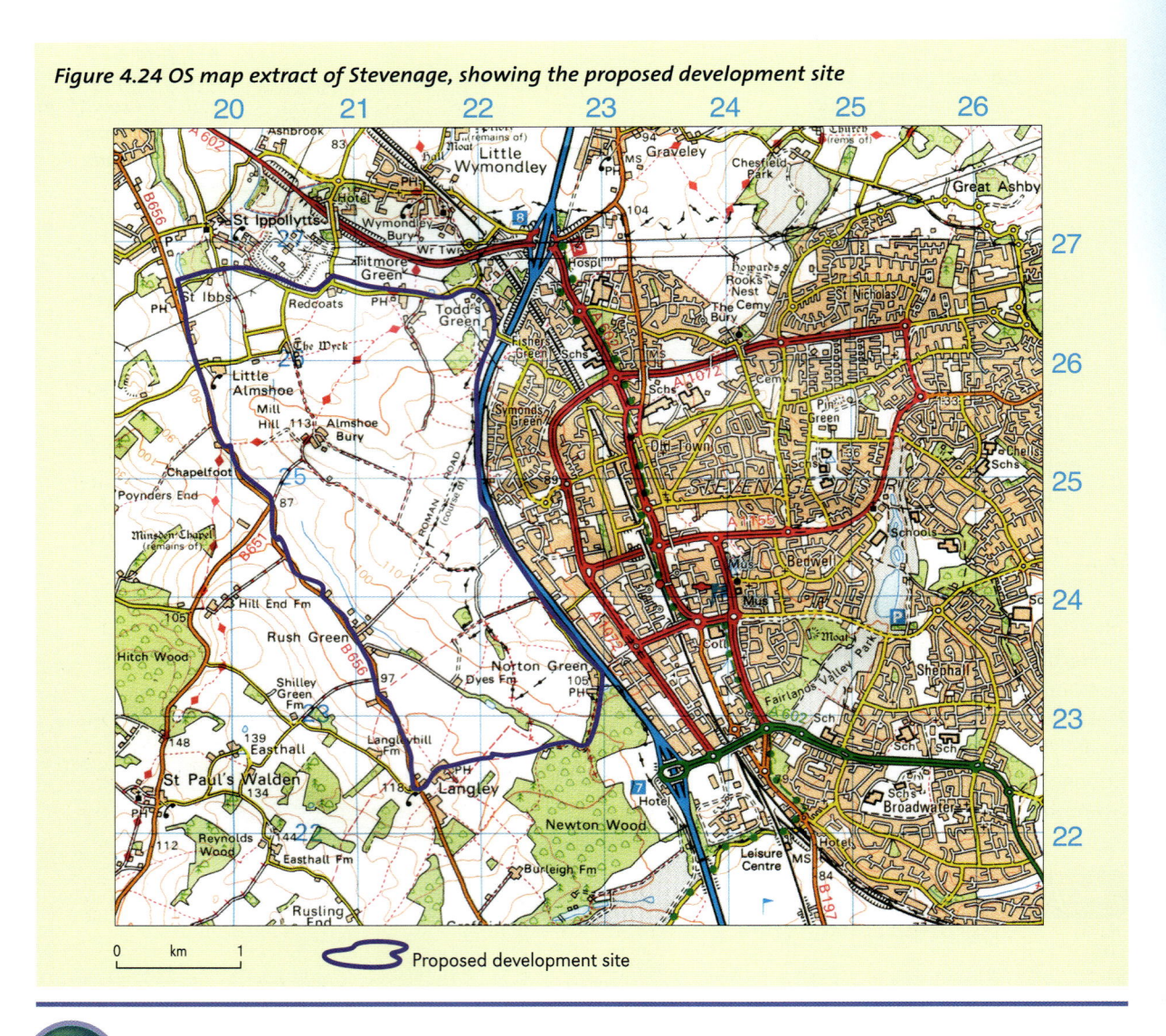

## Case study: Unsustainable urban growth in Johannesburg

Johannesburg is the largest city in southern Africa (see Figure 4.25). Its population is 3.3 million and growing rapidly. Johannesburg exists for one reason: gold. The discovery of gold in 1886 led to rapid urban growth and inequality between racial groups.

### Alexandra township

Alexandra is one of around 20 black townships dotted around Johannesburg (see Figure 4.26). It is home to an estimated 350,000 people, 86% of whom are black. First established in 1912, Alexandra grew rapidly in the apartheid years as a **dormitory settlement** for black Africans. They provided a cheap workforce for Johannesburg's **central business district** (CBD) and the white northern suburbs.

The contrasts between quality of life and standard of living in Alexandra and the predominantly white suburb of Sandton, just a few kilometres to

# Theme 2

▲ Figure 4.25 Location of Johannesburg

### Factfile 4.5 Apartheid

- Apartheid was the South African government's policy of separate development from 1948 to 1990.
- Its laws forced white and non-white people to live apart. The white minority controlled the government; non-whites made up the workforce for South Africa's industries and mines.
- Apartheid created huge inequalities in South African society.
- Apartheid ended in 1994, but inequalities remain. For example, although black people make up 70% of South Africa's population, they account for only 29% of the country's wealth.
- Apartheid created its own geography. White people lived in prosperous suburbs; non-white people occupied poverty-stricken slums known as townships.
- Pass laws restricted the movement of non-white South Africans. They prevented blacks settling legally in the cities, confining the majority to rural areas.

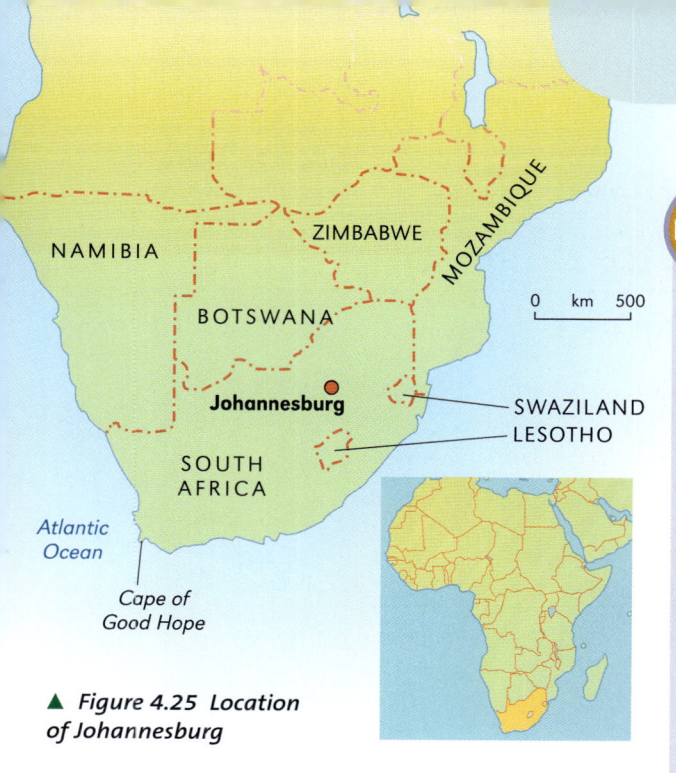

the west, underline inequality in Johannesburg (see Table 4.13).

## Standard of living and quality of life in Alexandra

Following the collapse of apartheid and the ending of the pass laws, Alexandra's population grew rapidly. This growth has been unsustainable and has placed enormous strain on the township's housing and **infrastructure**. As a result the people of Alexandra face major social, economic and environmental problems.

▼ Table 4.13 Comparison of the black township of Alexandra and the predominantly white suburb of Sandton

|  | Alexandra | Sandton |
|---|---|---|
| **Population** | 350,000–700,000 | 180,000 |
| **Average household income** | £5,075 | £20,962 |
| **Unemployment rate (%)** | 60 | 6 |
| **Percentage white population** | 14 | 63 |
| **Age** | 70% under 35 years | Large percentage aged 35–64 years |
| **Gender** | Male dominated | Male/female balance |
| **Percentage adults with higher education** | 12 | 42 |
| **Percentage formal dwellings** | Less than 50 | 96 |
| **Number of informal dwellings** | 20,658 | 1,806 |
| **Occupations** | Mainly unskilled | High skill levels; large percentage of professionals |

Population and settlement

# Chapter 4 Settlement

**Figure 4.26** Map of Alexandra township

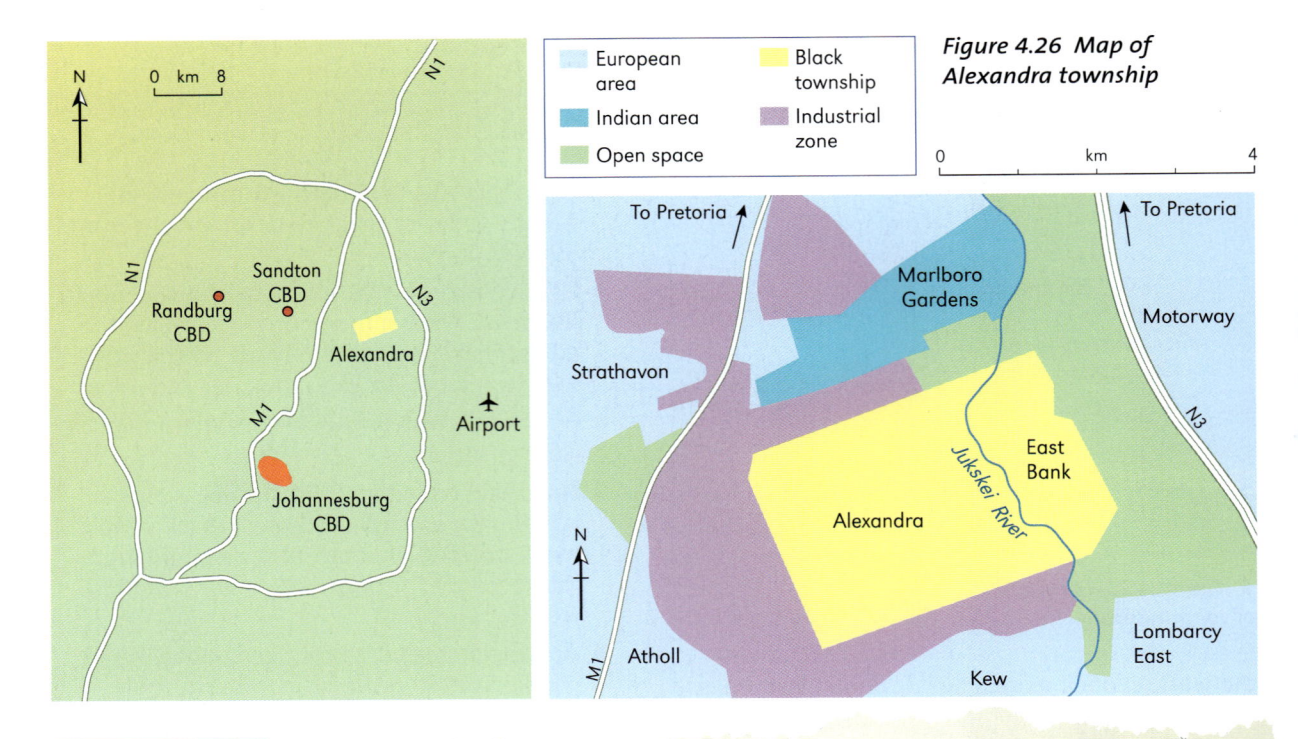

Legend:
- European area
- Indian area
- Open space
- Black township
- Industrial zone

## Activity 4.17

1. Describe the location of Alexandra township in Figure 4.26.
2. State two advantages of Alexandra's location.
3. Study the information on Alexandra and Sandton in Table 4.13. Summarise the main differences in standard of living and quality of life between the two areas.

# Life in Alexandra

*By Eric J. Lyman*

In Alexandra, most people are without jobs. Statistics show that life expectancy in South African shanty towns like this is 37 years, and infant mortality rates are six times higher than in the developed world. Crime is rampant, electricity and clean water are rare, and, locals say, hope is even rarer.

Michael Hattingh, 33, is a lifelong resident of the area. With one arm withered from birth, he carries his sleeping 4-year-old son Moses in the other. Like more than a third of the people in the township, both father and son are infected with HIV — the virus that causes AIDS. Both are covered with dirt and grime and they walk through the filthy dirt streets in bare feet. And they are alone: the boy's mother died of AIDS-related tuberculosis several months ago, and a younger daughter died as a baby.

Other residents told similarly hopeless tales: a mother of two who died last week because she bled to death after cutting her arm on broken glass; the boy who was beaten by a resident for trying to steal a sickly chicken.

Walking through Alexandra and seeing young children play in the same muddy fields used to dispose of the human and animal waste from the neighbourhood, one wonders how things became so desperate.

Source: United Press International

**Figure 4.27** ▶

▶ Photograph 4.6
Alexandra township

Hubert Ngomana, a resident of Alexandra, sums up the feelings of despair in the township:

> We have been forgotten. We cannot buy new cars and clothes and eat in expensive restaurants and so we are not important. Maybe places like this and the people's lives here are too depressing for the world to pay attention to.

## Overcrowding and housing

In the past 20 years thousands of shacks have mushroomed on every available space in Alexandra. For example, 7,500 households have sprung up on the banks of the polluted Jukskei River and its tributaries. These unplanned areas are overcrowded and are exposed to flooding in the rainy season.

Population densities rise to 80,000 km$^2$ in the oldest parts of Alexandra. Although houses in these areas were originally well built and had gardens, over the years the gardens have been sublet and occupied by backyard shacks. The estimated 7,000 shacks located in backyards are some of Alexandra's worst slums.

## Services

As most shacks in Alexandra are not connected to the electricity grid, many inhabitants resort to the dangerous practice of tapping power

### Activity 4.18

Read Figure 4.27, an account of life in Alexandra.

1 Name a problem referred to in the article. Suggest a reason for the problem.
2 Give three reasons why the quality of life in Alexandra is low.
3 Study Photograph 4.6 — shacks alongside the Jukskei River in Alexandra township. Describe the possible disadvantages of living close to the Jukskei River.

Population and settlement

lines. Only two thirds of households have access to piped water. Some people draw water from the heavily polluted Jukskei River. In 2001 contaminated river water caused an outbreak of cholera, which killed over 100 people. Roads are unpaved and are often obstructed by the uncontrolled growth of shacks. Fewer than 20% of Alexandra's inhabitants have their own private toilet facilities, and only 65% have regular refuse collections.

### Environmental and social problems

Air pollution is responsible for high levels of respiratory diseases such as asthma. In dry weather, dust blown from mining spoil heaps fills the air. Township residents rely heavily on coal for fuel, and the resulting smoky conditions lower air quality even further.

Crime is a major concern for Alexandra's residents. South Africa has the highest murder rate in the world, and serious crime rates in Alexandra — violence, kidnapping and rape, as well as murder — far exceed the national average. Educational standards are low (15% of Alexandra's population is illiterate), and **malnutrition** and AIDS are widespread.

## Upgrading Alexandra township

The Alexandra Renewal Project, an ambitious scheme to upgrade Alexandra township, began in 2001. Over a period of 7 years and at a cost of $130 million, the project aimed to improve the quality of life of one of South Africa's poorest suburbs by:
- reducing overcrowding
- reducing unemployment
- creating a healthier living environment (e.g. supplying piped water, improving air quality, increasing sanitation)
- providing affordable basic services
- reducing crime and violence
- upgrading existing housing and building affordable housing
- creating parks and recreational areas

At the start of the project families living in unsafe locations in Alexandra were forcibly removed. These removals included 5,500 families who were living in shacks on flood-prone land by the Jukskei River, and 3,800 families who were living on a landfill site.

New housing has been built for both private ownership and to be rented. In the first year of the project almost 1,000 new housing units were completed and occupied. Hostels for single adults were redeveloped and backyard shacks upgraded. Housing has been provided for people suffering from AIDS, AIDS orphans, the elderly and the disabled.

Unemployment is being tackled by creating jobs, helping local people to set up small businesses, and organising training programmes to improve skills.

# Part 3 The provision of goods and retail services

### Key ideas

- A number of factors influence the provision of goods and retail services in rural and urban settlements.
- The provision of goods and retail services changes over time due to changes in transport and market forces.

With the exception of isolated farms and small hamlets, all rural and urban settlements support a range of retail functions. These retail functions provide goods such as food and clothing, and services like hairdressers and restaurants to local inhabitants who live in the settlement and the surrounding area. Factfile 4.6 gives a summary of the main characteristics of retail provision in rural and urban settlements.

# Theme 2

## Factfile 4.6 Retail provision in rural and urban settlements

The shops found in a settlement are generally those that can be supported profitably by the local population. Each shop (or retail function) needs a minimum number of customers or spending to survive. This is known as the **threshold** population (or threshold spending).

- Shops sell two types of goods and services: **convenience** and **comparison**.
- **Convenience goods and services** are bought regularly and therefore need only a few hundred customers to be profitable. In other words they have low thresholds.
- In cities there are hundreds of shops selling convenience goods and services. Many convenience goods and services are needed on a daily basis so they are usually available locally. Typical convenience shops/services include newsagents, chemists, grocers, fast food outlets, banks and hairdressers.
- **Comparison goods and services** are more expensive and are bought less often. Large numbers of customers — several thousand — are needed to make these shops profitable.
- Comparison shops therefore have higher **thresholds** than convenience shops. Because comparison goods are bought infrequently and are relatively expensive, shoppers are prepared to travel longer distances to buy them.
- Compared to convenience shops, comparison shops are fewer in number. Examples of comparison shops/services are shoes, clothing, electrical goods, estate agents and solicitors.
- The **settlement hierarchy** reduces the distance people travel to shop. Convenience goods and services are bought frequently and have to be available locally. In cities this means in a small neighbourhood shopping centres; and in rural areas in villages and market centres. Comparison goods and services which are bought only occasionally are available further away. In urban areas they are concentrated in district centres, **regional centres** and the CBD. In rural areas they are found in market centres and other small towns.
- As shopping centres increase in size, shops owned by multiple retailers become more numerous. Multiples are large high street retailers, such as Marks and Spencer, Boots, PC World and WH Smith, which have branches throughout the country.

## Case study: Retail provision in an urban settlement: Leeds

### Urban shopping hierarchies

Leeds is a large city and centre of the Yorkshire and the Humber region. It provides retail goods and services for over two million people in West Yorkshire, and serves up to five million in the wider region.

Like other big cities, there is a **hierarchy** of shopping centres in Leeds (see Table 4.14 and Figure 4.28). This hierarchy is the best way to provide people with the goods and services they need. It consists of an ordering of shopping centres defined by their size and importance. At the base of the hierarchy there are large number of small local centres. Above them are neighbourhood, district and regional centres. Finally, at the top of the hierarchy, is the city centre or central business district (CBD). A feature of the shopping hierarchy is that there are progressively fewer centres at each higher level in the hierarchy.

### Changing patterns of shopping in Leeds

In the past 30 years many shops have moved out of city centres and have relocated to the suburbs.

Population and settlement

## Chapter 4 Settlement

*Table 4.14 Hierarchy of urban shopping centres*

| Shopping centre type | Characteristics |
|---|---|
| Local centre  | Local centres usually have five or six shops and serve a **catchment area** of 5,000–10,000 people.<br><br>Most shops in local centres are independently owned and sell low-order **convenience goods** and services (see Factfile 4.6). Because shoppers buy these goods and services often, local centres are within walking distance of their homes.<br><br>◀ *The Alwoodley centre, a local shopping centre* |
| Neighbourhood centre  | Neighbourhood centres comprise 20–30 shops and serve a catchment of 10,000–20,000 people. This allows them to support a few **comparison shops**, such as opticians, estate agents and travel agents.<br><br>Neighbourhood centres are easier to get to than local centres and are often located on major roads and at busy junctions. Most are within walking distance of shoppers' homes.<br><br>◀ *Moortown Corner, a neighbourhood centre* |
| District centre  | District centres serve 25,000–50,000 people. A typical district centre has a large supermarket, several smaller stores and lots of parking for shoppers.<br><br>◀ *Moor Allerton, a district shopping centre* |
| Regional centre | **Regional centres** serve catchments of up to 80,000 people and offer a wide range of convenience and comparison shops. Most of the shops in **regional centres** are **multiples** (see Factfile 4.6). Some regional centres, such as Cross Gates in east Leeds, also have a shopping mall. |
| Central business district | The city centre tops the **urban shopping hierarchy**. There are over 1,000 shops in Leeds's CBD, mostly selling high-order comparison goods and services. Central Leeds is dominated by multiples, including department stores such as Harvey Nichols, Debenhams and House of Fraser. People come from all over the Yorkshire and Humber region to shop in large stores in central Leeds. |

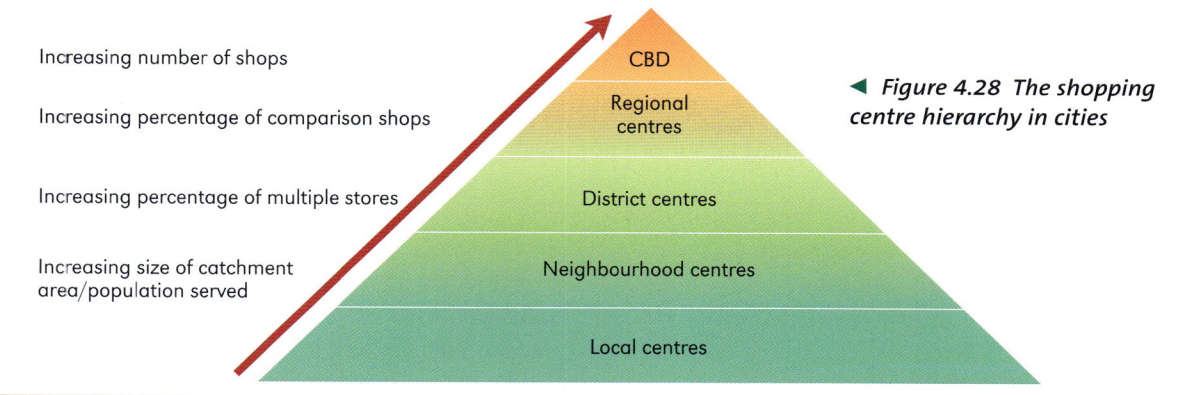

# Theme 2

Increasing number of shops

Increasing percentage of comparison shops

Increasing percentage of multiple stores

Increasing size of catchment area/population served

CBD
Regional centres
District centres
Neighbourhood centres
Local centres

◀ Figure 4.28 The shopping centre hierarchy in cities

## Activity 4.19

Study Figure 4.29, which shows a local shopping centre in Alwoodley, Leeds, and Figure 4.30, which shows part of the Street Lane neighbourhood shopping centre in Roundhay, Leeds.

1. Name one group of people that has benefited from the growth of large supermarkets in the suburbs and one group that has suffered. Explain your choices.

2. Compare the following features of the Alwoodley and Street Lane shopping centres:
   (a) number of shops
   (b) type of shops (i.e. convenience and comparison)
   (c) number of multiples

3. Using the evidence of Figures 4.29 and 4.30, suggest why the Street Lane shopping centre is likely to serve a larger population than the Alwoodley shopping centre.

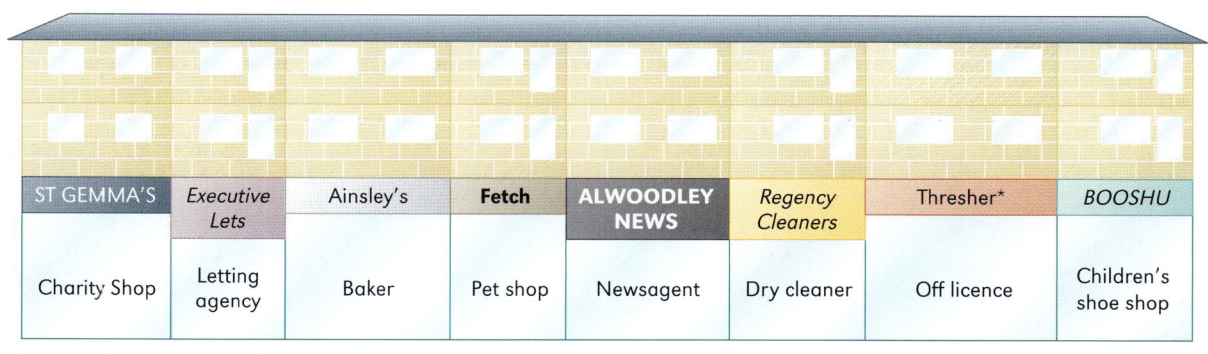

| ST GEMMA'S | Executive Lets | Ainsley's | Fetch | ALWOODLEY NEWS | Regency Cleaners | Thresher* | BOOSHU |
|---|---|---|---|---|---|---|---|
| Charity Shop | Letting agency | Baker | Pet shop | Newsagent | Dry cleaner | Off licence | Children's shoe shop |

Figure 4.29 Alwoodley local shopping centre

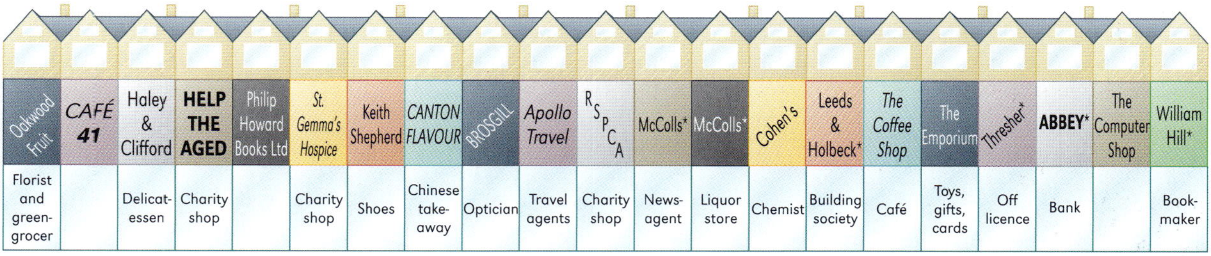

| Oakwood Fruit | CAFÉ 41 | Haley & Clifford | HELP THE AGED | Philip Howard Books Ltd | St. Gemma's Hospice | Keith Shepherd | CANTON FLAVOUR | BROSGILL | Apollo Travel | RSPCA | McColls* | McColls* | Cohen's | Leeds & Holbeck | The Coffee Shop | The Emporium | Thresher* | ABBEY* | The Computer Shop | William Hill* |
|---|---|---|---|---|---|---|---|---|---|---|---|---|---|---|---|---|---|---|---|---|
| Florist and green-grocer | Delicat-essen | Charity shop | Charity shop | | Charity shop | Shoes | Chinese take-away | Optician | Travel agents | Charity shop | News-agent | Liquor store | Chemist | Building society | Café | Toys, gifts, cards | Off licence | Bank | | Book-maker |

* Multiples

Figure 4.30 Street Lane neighbourhood shopping centre

Population and settlement

95

This process is known as decentralisation. Today, the suburbs are where retailers such as supermarket chains, DIY, furniture, carpet and electrical goods stores want to be.

There are three advantages to moving out of the city centre:
- The suburbs have more space for large supermarkets, retail warehouses and car parks.
- Land is cheaper in the suburbs.
- Stores in the suburbs are closer to the bulk of their customers.

Most retail warehouses are located in planned retail parks, such as Crown Flatts in south Leeds and Guiseley in the northwest suburbs. Many large supermarkets also favour planned shopping centres, such as Owlcotes in Pudsey and Moor Allerton in north Leeds. Decentralisation has even affected shops selling clothing and shoes. The Owlcotes centre on the Leeds ring road includes a large M&S store, and the White Rose shopping mall close to the M62 has over 80 shops, including a Debenhams department store.

## Economic and social impact of retail change

Changes in retailing in the 1980s and early 1990s raised a number of issues: the decline of city centres; disadvantages for low-income groups; and the closure of many small **independent stores**.

### The decline of shopping in the CBD

The loss of food, furniture, carpet, electrical goods and clothing shops from the CBD to the suburbs in the 1980s and 1990s threatened to undermine shopping in city centres. The government responded by tightening planning controls, making it more difficult for retailers to move to the suburbs. At the same time, city centres were made more attractive. For example, in Leeds the main shopping street, Briggate, was pedestrianised (see Photograph 4.7); city centre malls such as the Merrion Centre were refurbished; and new malls such as The Light were built.

▼ Photograph 4.7 Briggate, the main shopping street in Leeds

Large cities like Leeds also adapted by developing new entertainment and leisure facilities, such as clubs, cafés, cinemas, bars and restaurants. These services attracted young people from the wider region, as well as tourists and other visitors. As the number of visitors grew, new hotels were built in the centre, creating more jobs.

Booming entertainment and leisure facilities have made city centres attractive places for young, professional people to live. Over 9,000 people now live in the centre of Leeds. They occupy newly built apartments and converted offices and warehouses, many with riverside locations. Living in Leeds city centre also gives easy access to jobs in the CBD, particularly in retailing, finance and legal services.

### The decline of small shops and the growth of supermarket chains

In the past 40 years there has been a huge decline in the number of small, independent shops in the suburbs. In the late 1950s, in the northern inner city of Leeds, there were almost 1,000 small shops, of which 300 were grocers and greengrocers. By 1983 this number had been reduced to fewer than 150, and only 28 sold fresh food. This decline is due to competition from the four major supermarket chains — Tesco, Asda, Sainsbury's and Morrisons.

Eighty per cent of all food shopping in the UK is done in the four major supermarket chains. This concentration of food shopping in large supermarkets disadvantages those people without a car, including low-income groups, the elderly and the disabled. Furthermore, food prices in the main supermarket chains are relatively high, and most supermarkets prefer to locate close to higher-income residential areas. Thus, poverty and lack of mobility combine to create inequality of access to healthy food for many people.

### Regional shopping centres

**Regional shopping centres** are large, purpose-built shopping malls that occupy out-of-town sites. In the UK around a dozen regional shopping centres were built between the early 1980s and the mid-1990s. Most have between 150 and 300 shops and sell high-order comparison goods, such as clothing and footwear. However, regional centres are more than simply shopping centres. They have a variety of leisure and entertainment services and are attractive places for family days out. MetroCentre at Gateshead, for example, has a bowling alley, a multi-screen cinema, an indoor funfair and over 50 cafés and restaurants.

### Activity 4.20

1. Explain what is meant by these terms:
   (a) shopping catchment area
   (b) high-order goods

2. State and explain two reasons for the location of the regional shopping centres in Figure 4.31.

3. Give one reason why there are relatively few regional shopping centres in the UK.

Figure 4.31 Regional shopping centres in England

1. Lakeside, Thurrock
2. Bluewater, Dartford
3. Cribbs Causeway, Bristol
4. Merry Hill, Dudley
5. Meadowhall, Sheffield
6. Trafford Centre, Manchester
7. MetroCentre, Gateshead

Population and settlement

## Chapter 4 Settlement

▶ Table 4.15
The UK's largest regional shopping centres

| Centre | Turnover (£m) | Number of shops | Number of parking places |
|---|---|---|---|
| Bluewater | £1,224 | 330 | 13,000 |
| Trafford Centre | £1,016 | 280 | 10,000 |
| Meadowhall | £977 | 270 | 12,000 |
| Lakeside | £723 | 300 | 13,000 |
| MetroCentre | £627 | 350 | 13,000 |
| Merry Hill | £583 | 200 | 10,000 |
| Cribbs Causeway | £554 | 150 | 7,000 |
| Westfield (London) | (open Oct 08) | 265 | 4,500 |

Most visitors travel to regional centres by car, but public transport links are also important. MetroCentre and Meadowhall in Sheffield have their own mainline train stations as well as frequent bus services.

Table 4.15 lists the eight largest regional shopping centres in the UK. Bluewater at Dartford in Kent ranks overall as the seventh largest shopping centre in the UK — even larger than Liverpool, Newcastle and Leicester city centres.

Regional shopping centres compete directly with city centre shops. Studies show that Sheffield's city centre has suffered as a result of competition from nearby Meadowhall. Shoppers now spend more money in Meadowhall than in Sheffield's city centre. But Sheffield is an exception. The impact of MetroCentre on Newcastle or the Trafford Centre on Manchester has been relatively small. However, many smaller shopping centres close to regional centres have experienced decline. This is the case at Dudley, which is close to Merry Hill, and at Gateshead, which is near MetroCentre.

### The White Rose Shopping Centre, Leeds

The White Rose Shopping Centre was completed in 1997 (see Photograph 4.8). It is situated on the south-east outskirts of Leeds and is one of the smaller regional shopping centres. It comprises a shopping mall on two floors. At either end of the mall are the two largest stores: Debenhams and Sainsbury's. The centre has 102 shops. Most of these are well-known high street retailers, such as Next, Principles, Etam and River Island. Over one third are fashion and footwear stores.

The centre is located close to the M62, M621 and M1, and 2.1 million people live within a 75-minute drive time. There are nearly 5,000 parking spaces and most visitors arrive by car. Around 170,000 shoppers visit the White Rose Centre each week. On average they travel 13 km and spend £54 per trip.

The White Rose Centre has had little effect on shopping in the centre of Leeds. It has, however, hit smaller centres such as Morley and Pudsey quite hard.

### Activity 4.21

Study Figure 4.32.
1. How long does it take to drive to the White Rose Centre from:
   (a) Barnsley?
   (b) Wakefield?
   (c) Keighley?
2. Describe the effect of the motorway network on drive times to the White Rose Centre.

# Theme 2

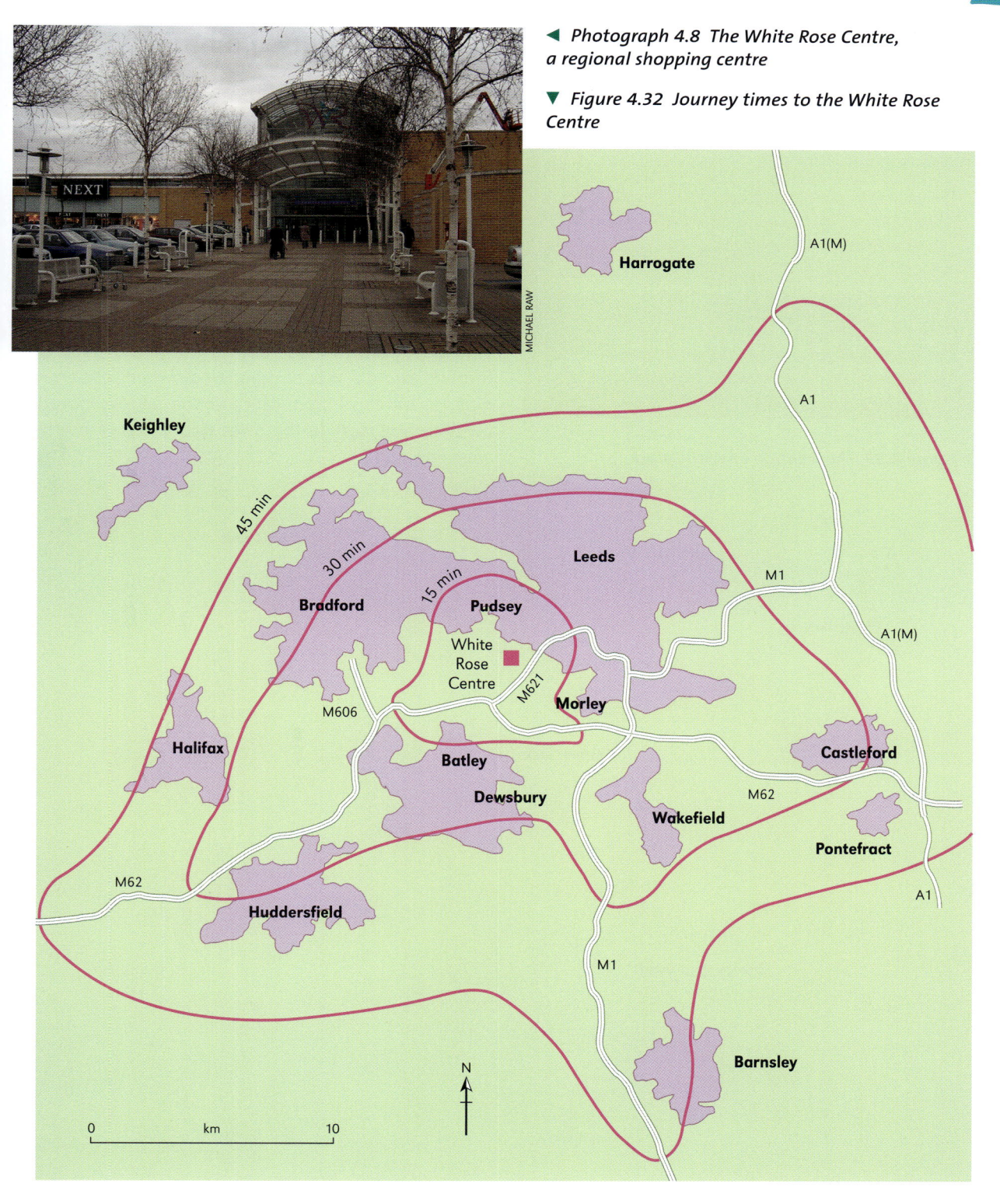

◄ Photograph 4.8 The White Rose Centre, a regional shopping centre

▼ Figure 4.32 Journey times to the White Rose Centre

Population and settlement

Chapter 4 Settlement

## Case study: Changes in rural service provision — Witherslack, Cumbria

Witherslack is a small village in south Lakeland (see Photograph 4.9). Located a few kilometres inside the Lake District **National Park** and close to Morecambe Bay, its nearest large service centres are Kendal and Grange-over-Sands (see Figure 4.33).

### Population change

Witherslack's population peaked in the late nineteenth century and then declined steadily until 1971. This **depopulation** was due to the loss of jobs in farming and the lack of other employment opportunities in the local area. Many young people moved away to find work in the cities and towns of north-west England.

### Activity 4.22

1. Using the evidence of Figure 4.33 and Photograph 4.9, suggest reasons why Witherslack is an attractive place for retired people and commuters.
2. Plot the population figures in Table 4.16 as a bar chart.
3. Explain why the growth of population in Witherslack has not stopped the decline in the village's services since 1971.

▼ *Figure 4.33 The location of Witherslack*

*Photograph 4.9 The countryside around Witherslack, south Lakeland*

Then, after 1971 the population trend reversed. Between 1971 and 1991 Witherslack's population grew by nearly one third, with a further 10% increase between 1991 and 2003. This remarkable turnaround was due to in-migration by retired people, and commuters working in nearby towns like Kendal and Lancaster.

## Service decline

In the past 50 years and in common with villages throughout rural Britain, the number of services in Witherslack has declined. Until the 1970s, this decline was associated with falling demand caused by depopulation. In the past three decades, other factors explain the loss of village services:

- Commuters living in Witherslack often use the shops and other services in the towns where they work.
- Retired people live in smaller households and therefore have less demand for village retail services.
- The increase in the number of **second homes** (19 out of 169 households were second homes in 2001) also reduces the demand for local services.
- The growth of large supermarkets in nearby towns (e.g. Asda and Morrisons in Kendal) offering lower prices and wider range of products.
- Increased levels of car ownership, making it easier than ever for local residents to travel to larger service centres.

The closure of the pub, general store and sub-post office in 2006 was a considerable blow to Witherslack.

*Table 4.16 Population change in Witherslack: 1971–2003*

| 1971 | 1981 | 1991 | 2001 | 2003 |
|------|------|------|------|------|
| 330  | 411  | 428  | 452  | 485  |

Population and settlement

It meant that the nearest food shop and post office were 6 km away in Grange-over-Sands. With no public transport in the village, local residents without cars could not easily access even the most basic retail services. A resident summed up the problems:

> 'Our village has many older people who find it difficult to drive to neighbouring villages and miss Witherslack's services terribly. Young people with children are in a similar position. There is a loss of independence for those who don't drive…while the closure of the village shop and post office prevents the coming together of a whole range of age groups who don't naturally meet anywhere else.'

The local community and MP for Kendal responded to the closure of the village shop by creating a new shop facility on a temporary site next to the pub. The shop, which opened in September 2008, is owned by the community through shares and fund raising, including a £20,000 grant from the Lake District National Park, and is staffed by volunteers. However, its survival will depend on the level of usage by local people.

*Table 4.17 Changing service provision in Witherslack*

| Services in 2009 | Changes in the past 25 years |
|---|---|
| Community grocery store | Closure of sweet shop and tobacconist; closure of village pub (2006); closure of post office and general store (2006) |
| St Paul's parish church | None |
| Village Hall | None |
| Primary school | None (28 pupils on roll in 2007) |
| Mobile services: library | Butcher and fishmonger withdrawn |
| GP surgery — open 2 days/week | None |

# Theme 3 Natural hazards

# Chapter 5 Tectonic hazards

## Part 1 The distribution and causes of earthquakes and volcanoes

### The distribution of earthquakes and volcanoes

At the global scale earthquakes and volcanoes often occur close together (see Figures 5.1 and 5.2). They also cluster along the edges or margins of the tectonic plates (see Figure 5.3). The areas of greatest earthquake activity are around the Pacific Basin, especially in Japan, Indonesia, Chile, Peru, Mexico, California and Alaska. Earthquakes also occur in mountainous regions where volcanoes are largely absent. Thus the Himalayas, Iran, central China and north Africa are highly active earthquake zones. Earthquakes are not confined to the continents. They occur frequently in mid-ocean along the **mid-ocean ridges**.

> **Key ideas**
> - Tectonic **hazards** (earthquakes and volcanoes) have specific global distributions.
> - Most earthquakes and volcanoes are caused by movements of **tectonic plates**.
> - The processes involved at tectonic plate margins affect the global distribution of tectonic hazards

### Factfile  5.1 Tectonic plates

- The outermost rocky layers of the Earth are the **lithosphere** and the **crust**.
- The lithosphere and crust are not a uniform shell; instead they are broken into a number of large tectonic plates (see Figure 5.3).
- There are seven major tectonic plates — Pacific, North American, Eurasian, South American, Indo-Australian, African and Antarctic — and many more smaller ones, e.g. Nazca, Caribbean, Juan de Fuca.
- Tectonic plates can be grouped according to the proportion of oceanic and continental crust they contain. The Pacific plate is entirely oceanic; the Eurasian plate is largely continental; and the Indo-Australian plate includes significant slabs of both oceanic and continental crust.

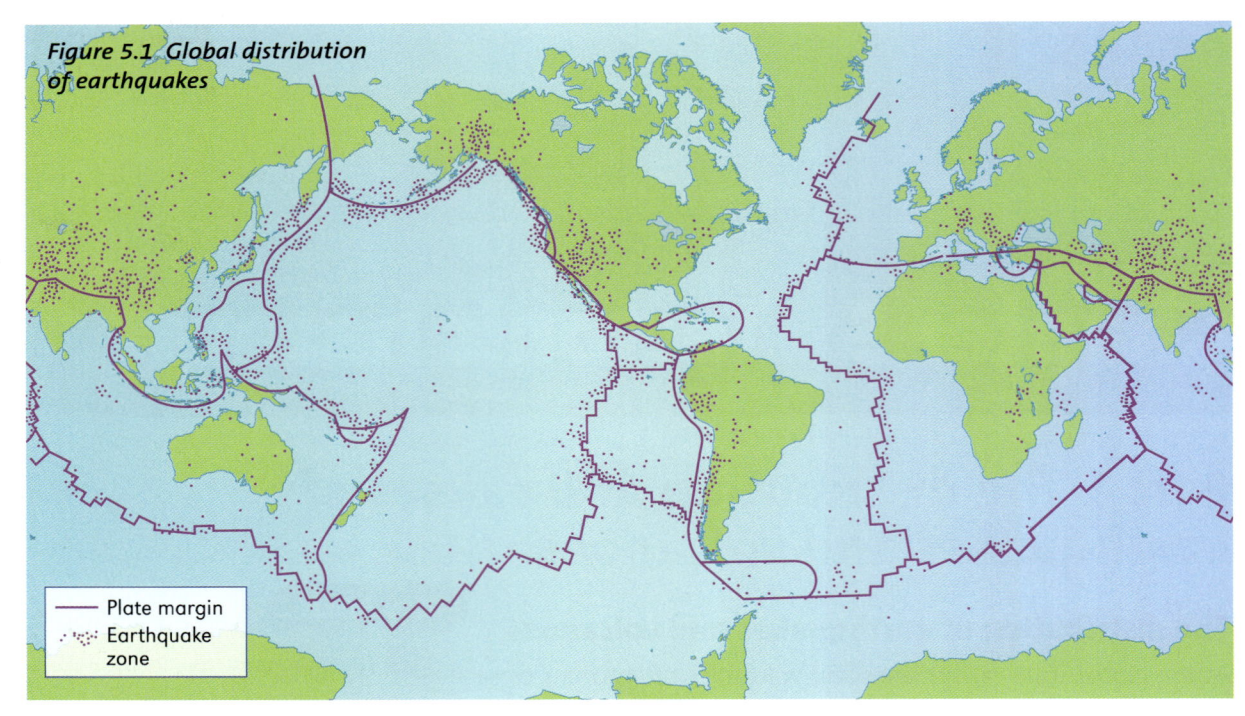

# Chapter 5 Tectonic hazards

**Figure 5.1** Global distribution of earthquakes

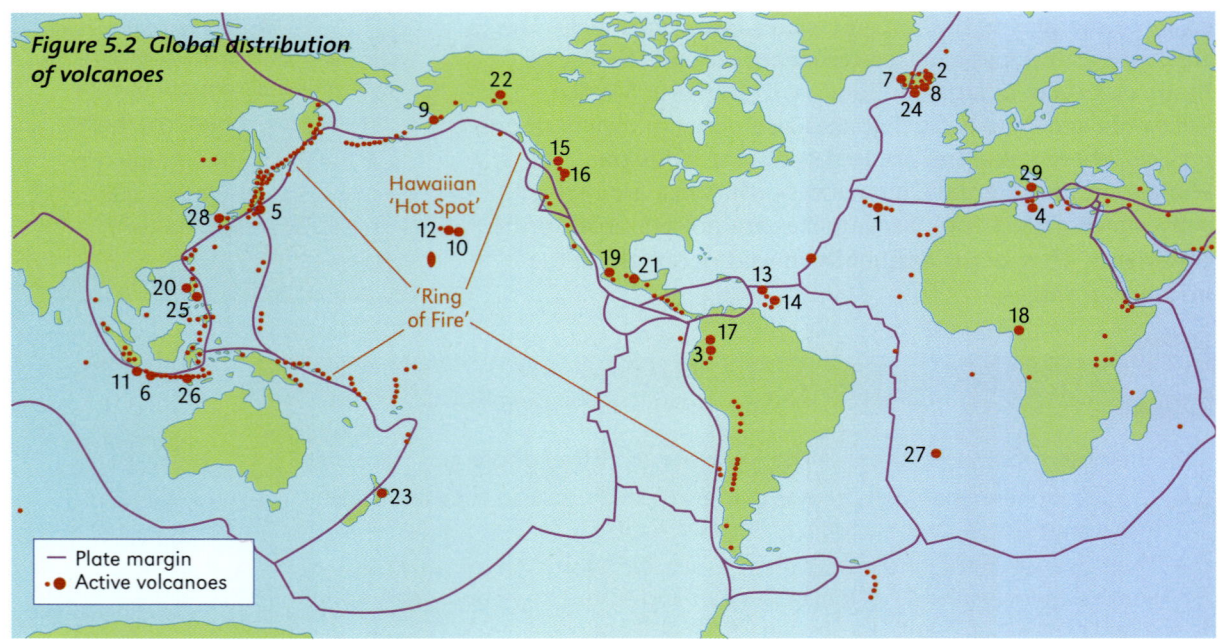

- Plate margin
- Earthquake zone

**Figure 5.2** Global distribution of volcanoes

- Plate margin
- Active volcanoes

| | | | | | |
|---|---|---|---|---|---|
| 1 Azores | 6 Galunggung | 11 Krakatoa | 16 Mt St Helens | 21 Popocatépetl | 26 Tambora |
| 2 Bardarbunga | 7 Grímsvötn | 12 Mauna Loa | 17 Nevado del Ruiz | 22 Redoubt | 27 Tristan da Cunha |
| 3 Cotopaxi | 8 Heimaey | 13 Soufrière Hills | 18 Nyos | 23 Ruapehu | 28 Unzen |
| 4 Etna | 9 Katmai | 14 Mt Pelée | 19 Parícutin | 24 Surtsey | 29 Vesuvius |
| 5 Fujiyama | 10 Kilauea | 15 Mt Rainier | 20 Pinatubo | 25 Taal | |

OCR (B) GCSE Geography

# Theme 3

▲ *Figure 5.3 Tectonic plates*

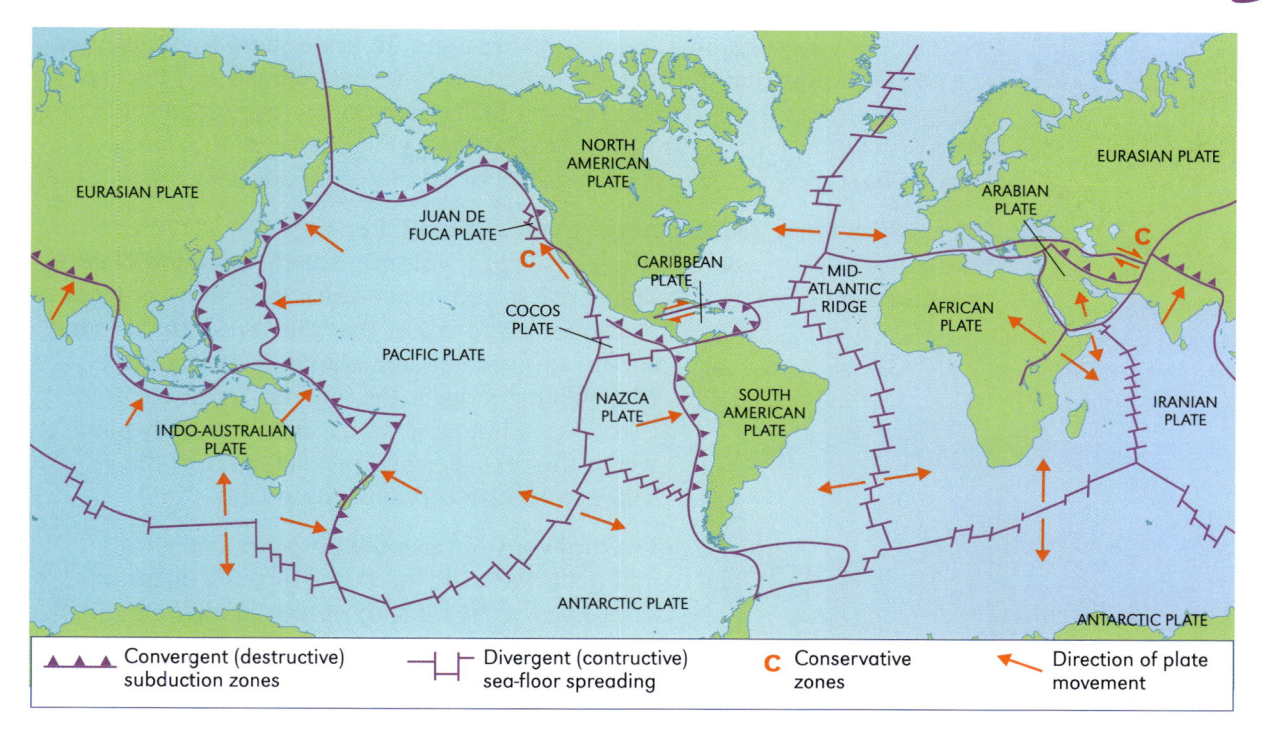

Volcanoes have a similar global distribution to earthquakes, being strongly concentrated along plate margins, and especially around the Pacific Ocean in the Ring of Fire (see Figure 5.2). There are currently around 500 active volcanoes in the world, over half of them in the Ring of Fire. Some of the world's best known volcanoes such as Mount Fuji, Mount St Helens, Krakatoa, Cotopaxi and Aconcagua are in this zone.

## Tectonic plate boundaries

Tectonic plates are moving all the time. This movement is slow — just a few centimetres a year — but over geological time, even the slowest movements add up to thousands of kilometres. It is at the tectonic plate boundaries, where great slabs of crust and lithosphere either converge, diverge, or slide past each other, that most earthquakes and volcanoes are found.

We will now look in more detail at what is going on at these plate boundaries. To do this we recognise three types of plate boundary: constructive, destructive, and conservative.

### Constructive boundaries
New crust forms continually at **constructive plate boundaries** in mid-ocean (see Figure 5.4). These areas, known as mid-ocean ridges, consist of a deep, undersea valley, bounded on

### Activity 5.1

Study Figure 5.3 and an atlas map showing the countries of the world. Link the following countries with their correct tectonic plates.

*Table 5.1 Tectonic plates*

| USA | Caribbean plate |
|---|---|
| Nigeria | Arabian plate |
| Iraq | Pacific plate |
| Barbados | Indo-Australian plate |
| Russia | Eurasian plate |
| New Guinea | South American plate |
| Fiji | African plate |
| Argentina | Juan de Fuca plate |

Natural hazards

# Chapter 5 Tectonic hazards

both sides by steep, submarine mountain ranges. To understand these features we need to know that the crust in mid-ocean is being stretched and torn apart by tension. As a result, parallel cracks or faults develop, causing sections of crust to sink down to form a **rift valley**. This faulting, which often results in the sudden fracturing of rocks, is responsible for earthquakes in mid-ocean.

▼ Figure 5.4 Constructive plate boundary

Meanwhile, rifting relieves pressure and allows molten rock (basalt) to well up to the ocean floor where it forms new crust. Volcanic activity is common along constructive boundaries and gives rise to submarine volcanoes. Some of these volcanoes are so active, that they break the ocean surface to form volcanic islands. Iceland, on the Mid-Atlantic Ridge is the world's largest volcanic island (see Photograph 5.1), and is the only place where the rift valley and parallel faults of the mid-ocean ridge can be seen on land.

Over millions of years the pressure of new rock adding to the crust forces the tectonic plates on both sides of the ridge to move sideways. So the two plates, like a slow-moving conveyor, move in opposite directions away from each other (i.e. they diverge). We call this process **sea floor spreading**.

Photograph 5.1 Thingvellir rift valley, Iceland

## Destructive boundaries

Although new crust is continually forming at constructive plate boundaries, there is no evidence that the Earth is getting bigger. This suggests that old crust must be destroyed at roughly the same rate as new crust forms; and this is exactly what happens at **destructive plate boundaries** or **subduction zones** (see Figures 5.5 and 5.6).

At subduction zones, one tectonic plate plunges steeply into the Earth's interior. However, this movement is often jerky and intermittent rather than smooth and continuous. Where friction halts subduction, huge pressure can build up. Eventually something has to give. Rocks bend, fracture and snap, releasing massive amounts of energy as earthquakes.

As the subducted plate is pushed further into the Earth's interior it begins to melt. Some of this molten rock or **magma** rises slowly to the surface to form volcanoes. The volcanoes in the Pacific Ring of Fire have formed in this way. These, like most other active volcanoes at subduction zones, often erupt explosively and are extremely hazardous.

# Theme 3

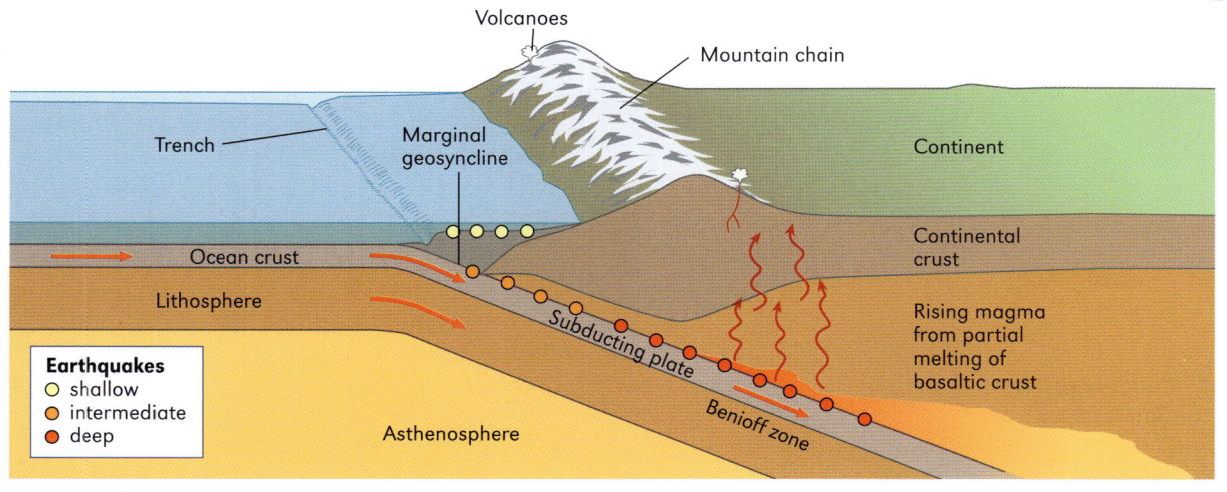

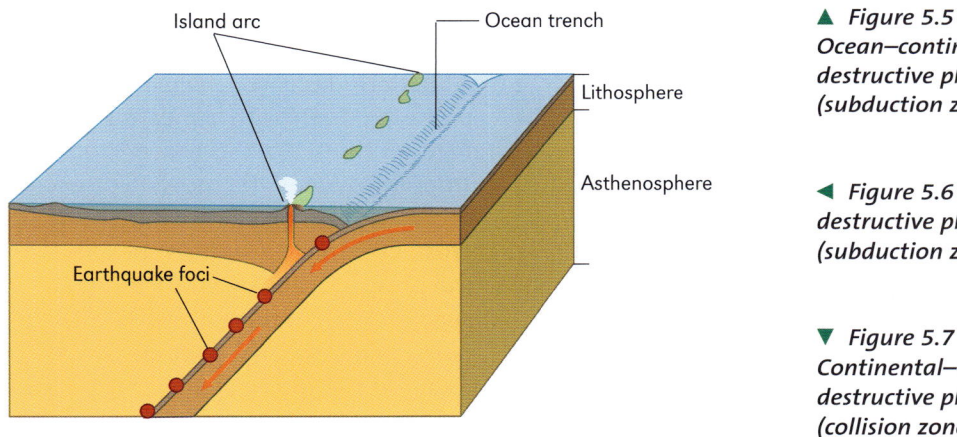

▲ **Figure 5.5** Ocean–continental destructive plate boundary (subduction zone)

◀ **Figure 5.6** Ocean–ocean destructive plate boundary (subduction zone)

▼ **Figure 5.7** Continental–continental destructive plate boundary (collision zone)

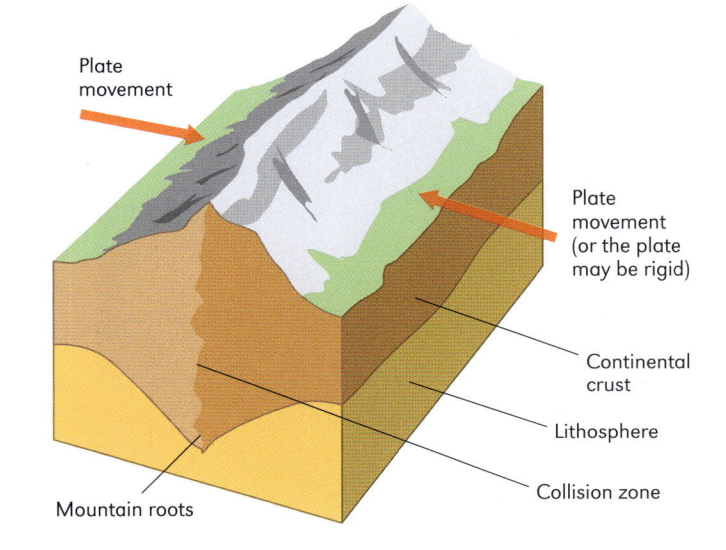

### Factfile 5.2 Types of destructive boundary

- Only oceanic plates are subducted.
- The subducted plate is denser than the non-subducted plate.
- There are three types of destructive plate boundaries: ocean-continental, ocean-ocean and continental-continental (Figures 5.5–5.7).
- Major earthquakes occur at all three destructive boundaries.
- Volcanic activity occurs only at ocean-continental and ocean-ocean boundaries (subduction zones).

Natural hazards

# Chapter 5 Tectonic hazards

▶ Table 5.2 Types of destructive boundary

| | | | |
|---|---|---|---|
| | Ocean-continental | Figure 5.5 | Examples of this type of subduction zone include the Pacific coasts of South America and North America. Subduction is responsible for forming deep **ocean trenches** offshore, and fold mountain ranges like the Andes in South America and the Cascades in the USA. Most volcanoes are explosive and erupt andesitic rock. |
| | Ocean-ocean | Figure 5.6 | When two oceanic plates converge, the denser plate is subducted. This type of subduction zone is found in the Caribbean, where the North American plate is subducted beneath the Caribbean plate. Ocean-ocean plate margins create **volcanic island arcs**, such as the Lesser Antilles. Several islands in this group, including Montserrat and Martinique, have active, explosive volcanoes. |
| | Continental-continental | Figure 5.7 | When two continents collide the result is massive fold mountains, unusually thick crust, and an absence of volcanic activity. Large earthquakes are common. The collision between the Indo-Australian and Eurasian plates has created the Himalayas, the world's highest mountain chain. |

▼ Photograph 5.2 The San Andreas fault, southern California

## Conservative boundaries

At conservative boundaries crust is neither added nor destroyed. Instead the plates slide past each other with a shearing motion (see Figure 5.8). Again, this movement is rarely smooth. Where little movement occurs over several decades, great pressure build ups in the crust. Eventually a sudden movement releases the pressure, causing an earthquake. In 1906 such a quake occurred along the San Andreas fault, a **conservative plate boundary**, in California (see Photograph 5.2). It destroyed the city of San Francisco, killed an estimated 3,000 people and left 225,000 homeless.

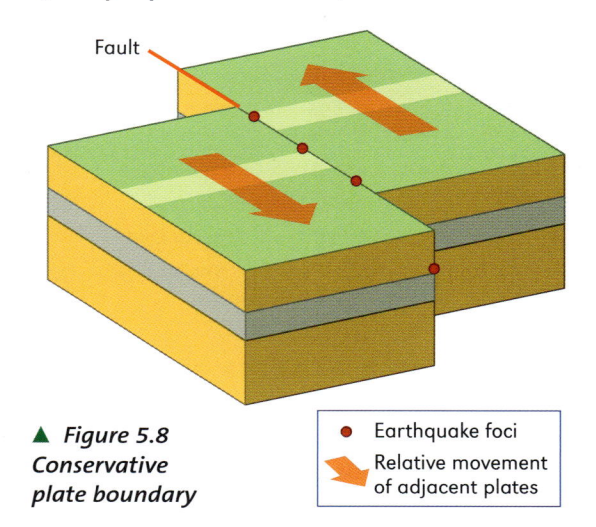

▲ Figure 5.8 Conservative plate boundary

- Earthquake foci
- Relative movement of adjacent plates

OCR (B) GCSE Geography

## Activity 5.2

Use the Global Volcanism website **www.volcano.si.edu/** and the map of plate boundaries (see Figure 5.3) to find the following features of the volcanoes listed in Table 5.3: (a) the country in which they are found; (b) the type of plate margin they are situated on.

Table 5.3 Twelve active volcanoes

| Fuji | Krakatoa | Galeras |
|---|---|---|
| Galeras | Surtsey | Kefla |
| Mount Rainier | Etna | Nyiragongo |
| Vesuvius | Soufrière Hills | Unzen |

## Activity 5.3

1. Investigate the distribution of earthquakes in the past 7 days by logging on to the USGS website: **www.earthquake.usgs.gov/eqcenter/recenteqsww/**
2. Make a copy of the world map showing the distribution of earthquakes during the past 7 days and describe the distribution and magnitude of the quakes (see Factfile 5.2).
3. Explain the distribution of earthquakes by comparing your map with the global map of tectonic plates (see Figure 5.3).

# Part 2 Earthquake and volcanic hazards

## Natural hazards

Natural hazards are naturally occurring events such as earthquakes and volcanic eruptions that have a damaging impact on people and society. They often cause death and injury, and destroy property and infrastructure such as roads, bridges and pipelines. It is important to emphasise that a natural event like a volcanic eruption only *becomes* a hazard when it affects people. For example, if a volcano erupts on an uninhabited island it will not be hazardous. Natural hazards that result in major loss of life, injury and economic damage, are called **natural disasters**.

### Earthquake hazards

Earthquakes are sudden movements of the crust caused by pressure, tension and shearing and are impossible to predict. Earthquake waves travel outwards from the origin or **focus** of the quake deep within the crust (see Figure 5.9). Places on the

▶ Figure 5.9 Earthquake epicentre and focus

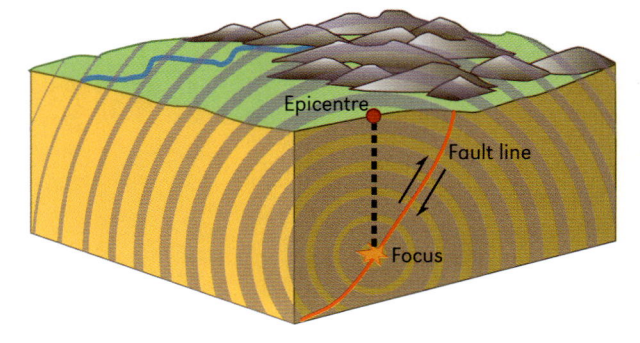

## Key ideas

- **Natural hazards** occur when naturally occurring events such as earthquakes and volcanic eruptions adversely affect people and society.
- Earthquakes are responsible for a number of natural hazards such as ground shaking, liquefaction and landslides.
- Volcanoes are responsible for natural hazards such as lava flows, pyroclastic flows and lahars.
- **Primary hazards** are the direct hazardous effects of earthquakes and volcanoes, such as ground shaking and lava flows.
- **Secondary hazards** are indirect hazardous effects, triggered by primary hazards. Landslides are secondary hazards produced both by earthquakes and volcanic eruptions.

# Chapter 5 Tectonic hazards

*Table 5.4 Earthquake hazards*

| Primary hazards | |
|---|---|
| Ground shaking | Ground shaking from earthquake waves causes widespread damage and loss of life through building collapse and subsequent fires. Buildings may collapse or suffer damage hundreds of kilometres from the epicentre. |
| **Secondary hazards** | |
| Liquefaction | Ground shaking may result in saturated soils and sands taking on a liquid state, allowing them to flow laterally. Liquefaction undermines the foundations of buildings and is one of the most destructive earthquake hazards. |
| Landslides | Landslides occur because of ground shaking in areas of steep slopes. |
| Tsunamis | Tsunamis are generated by undersea earthquakes. They can cause widespread coastal flooding and may impact areas thousands of kilometres from the earthquake centre. |

surface directly above the focus are at the **epicentre** of the quake and experience the most powerful shocks and greatest damage.

The main hazards associated with earthquakes are violent shaking of the ground, liquefaction, landslides and tsunamis (see Table 5.4). Shock waves and tremors are primary hazards. Secondary hazards such as liquefaction, landslides and tsunamis are triggered by the shock waves (see Photograph 5.3). Other secondary hazards that may develop in the aftermath of an earthquake are diseases and food shortages.

Around 130 million people worldwide are exposed to earthquake hazards. Between 1980 and 2005, earthquakes and related hazards killed over 600,000 people. The highest death tolls were in Indonesia, Pakistan and Iran.

▼ *Photograph 5.3 The impact of the 2004 tsunami on a Sumatran village*

## Volcanoes and volcanic hazards

Volcanoes are openings in the Earth's crust, surrounded by a cone of ash and lava, where molten rock and gases reach the surface. Most volcanoes are found at constructive and destructive plate margins. The exceptions are those near the centre of tectonic plates, at hot spots like Hawaii.

Volcanoes fall into two types: steep-sided and cone-shaped **strato-volcanoes**, comprising alternate layers of ash and lava (see Figure 5.10 and Photograph 5.4); and broad-based, **shield volcanoes** with gentle slopes

**Crater**
This is created after an eruption when the top is blown off the volcano

**Secondary vent**
Smaller outlets through which magma escapes

**Main vent**
The main outlet for the magma to escape

**Magma chamber**

Earth's crust

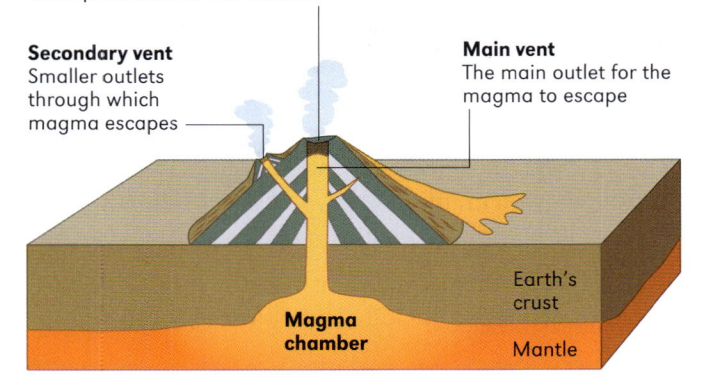

Mantle

▲ Figure 5.10 Strato-volcano

### Factfile 5.3 Measuring the power of earthquakes

- The Richter scale measures earthquake magnitude.
- The scale is logarithmic, with each whole number representing a 10-fold increase in magnitude.
- The scale has no upper limit, though the most powerful earthquake ever recorded measured 9.5.
- A moderate earthquake measures around 5 on the Richter scale; a strong earthquake is 6 and above.
- The Indian Ocean earthquake of 2004, which caused a devastating tsunami, measured 9.3; the San Francisco quake (1906) and Sichuan quake (2008) were magnitude 8 events.
- The Richter scale does not express the amount of damage caused by an earthquake. Apart from magnitude, several other factors, such as population density and hazard mitigation, influence damage levels.

◀ Photograph 5.4 Mount Teide, Tenerife — a strato-volcano

# Chapter 5 Tectonic hazards

▲ Photograph 5.5 Mauna Loa, Hawaii — a shield volcano

▲ Photograph 5.6 Lava flow

(see Photograph 5.5). Because of their thick **andesite** magma, eruptions from strato-volcanoes are often extremely violent. In contrast, shield volcanoes produce quiet eruptions of runny lava known as basalt.

Like earthquakes, volcanoes create a number of different hazards (see Table 5.5). Primary hazards, directly related to eruptions, include lava flows, pyroclastic

▼ Table 5.5 Volcanic hazards

| **Primary hazards** | |
|---|---|
| Lava flows | Masses of molten rock can pour from volcanoes during an eruption (see Photograph 5.6). Lava flows bulldoze everything in their path, burying farmland and entire settlements. However, lava flows rarely threaten human life. |
| Volcanic blasts | Lateral blasts from explosive eruptions carry rock debris at high speeds, causing complete devastation in the blast zone (see Photograph 5.7). They destroy buildings and kill plants and animals by abrasion, impact, burial, and heat. |
| Pyroclastic flows | These ground-hugging avalanches of hot ash, rock fragments and superheated gas can reach speeds of 100 km/h and destroy everything in their path. The pyroclastic flow from the Mount Pelée eruption on Martinique in 1902 killed 28,000 people. |
| Ashfalls | Fall-out from the eruption of ash disrupts economic activity over a wide area. Ashfalls cause buildings to collapse, blanket the landscape and smother farmland. |
| **Secondary hazards** | |
| Lahars | These mudflows, with the density of wet concrete, are formed by rain washing ash and other debris from a volcano's slopes. Lahars can transport rocks up to 10 m in diameter at speeds of 50 km/h. They cause serious economic and environmental damage. |
| Sulphur dioxide and acid rain | Sulphur dioxide is emitted during volcanic eruptions. The gas can cause respiratory problems. Mixed with rainwater, sulphur dioxide forms acid rain, which damages crops and forests. |
| Landslides | Violent eruptions trigger landslides on the slopes of volcanoes. The Mount St Helens eruption in 1980 created the largest landslide ever recorded. |

flows, and ashfalls. Among the secondary hazards are lahars, acid rain, landslides and earthquakes.

Although nothing can be done to prevent a volcanic eruption, a range of methods is available to give early warning and reduce the impact of volcanic hazards. They include monitoring volcanoes, hazard mapping and the diversion of lava flows (see Table 5.6).

Photograph 5.7 Blast zone around Mount St Helens

▶ Figure 5.11 Volcano hazards around Mount Ranier

Table 5.6 Measures to reduce the impact of volcanic eruptions

| Monitoring volcanoes | Volcanic eruptions are often preceded by earthquakes and tremors. Their frequency gives early warning of an eruption. |
| --- | --- |
| | Gravity measurements at the surface tell scientists how magma is moving deep inside the volcano. |
| | Rising emissions of gases such as sulphur dioxide and hydrogen chloride are evidence of impending eruptions. |
| | The build up of magma inside the volcano causes the ground surface temperature to rise — again evidence that an eruption is likely. |
| | When an eruption is imminent in MEDCs, automatic alerts and evacuation of the population at risk are triggered. |
| Hazard mapping | The paths followed by old lahars or mudflows (see Figure 5.11) can be mapped to show areas of greatest risk. |
| Diversion of lava flows | Small lava flows on the flanks of Mount Etna in Sicily have been successfully diverted away from settlements. At Heimaey in Iceland in 1973, the fishing harbour was saved by spraying a lava flow with sea water. |

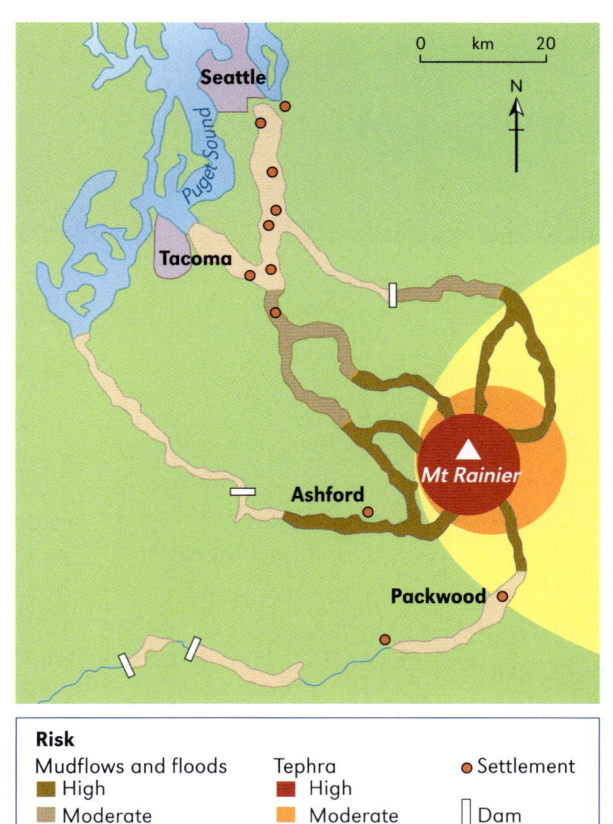

**Risk**

Mudflows and floods
■ High
■ Moderate
□ Low

Tephra
■ High
■ Moderate
□ Low

● Settlement
▯ Dam

Natural hazards

Chapter 5 Tectonic hazards

◀ **Photograph 5.8** Mount Ranier: an active volcano in the Cascade Range, Washington state

### Activity 5.4

Log on to **www.vulcan.wr.usgs.gov/Volcanoes/ framework.html**. Select a volcano and write a report about it, with photos, charts and maps. Your report should cover: location, type of volcano, recent eruptions, volcanic hazards caused by eruptions, and the impact of a recent eruption on people.

### Activity 5.5

Mount Rainier (see Photograph 5.8) is an active volcano in Washington state, USA, with 22 small glaciers clustered around its summit. Study the volcanic hazards map of Mount Rainier (see Figure 5.11).

1. Name two natural hazards caused by an eruption of Mount Rainier.
2. Describe and explain the distribution of these hazards.
3. Describe the specific hazard risks faced by the residents of Packwood and Ashford

## Part 3 The impact of earthquakes

### Key ideas

- Human activities can affect the impact of natural hazards.
- A range of methods are used to reduce the impact of natural hazards.
- A range of methods can be used to predict the location, frequency and severity of natural hazards.

The human impact of natural hazards depends on several factors (see Figure 5.12). Among these factors are the scale or magnitude of the hazard event, the number of people exposed to the hazard, and society's preparedness (i.e. level of planning and preparation available to reduce the hazard impact). In this section we shall look at the variable impact of two earthquakes. The first case study describes the impact of the Sichuan earthquake in central China in 2008; the second deals with the Northridge earthquake in California in 1994.

▶ **Figure 5.12**

Earthquake impact = Magnitude + Population risk ÷ Preparedness

# Theme 3

## Case study: Earthquake in an LEDC: Sichuan, China

On 12 May 2008 the province of Sichuan in central China was struck by a 7.9 magnitude earthquake. The quake, which lasted for four minutes, devastated a large area around the epicentre (see Figure 5.13). In places the land rose by up to 6 m. Estimates of the number of deaths varied from 80,000 to 87,000. A further 375,000 people were injured and 4.8 million were made homeless.

### Cause

Sichuan is located in the collision zone between the Indo-Australian plate and the Eurasian plate. Over millions of years the collision has uplifted the Himalayas and the Tibet Plateau. Meanwhile, the resulting compression has created thousands of fault lines. Slippage along one of these faults was responsible for the Sichuan quake.

## Earthquake hazards

### Ground shaking — the primary effect

Loss of life, injury and the economic cost of the Sichuan quake were huge. Ground shaking resulted in the collapse of 6.5 million houses, and damaged a further 23 million. Schools were badly affected. In total, 7,000 classrooms were destroyed, killing 19,000 school children. Chengdu, the capital of Sichuan province, was badly shaken but compared with Dujiangyan City, close to the epicentre, (see Figure 5.13 and Photograph 5.9) it escaped lightly. In Dujiangyan there was total devastation; buildings were reduced to rubble and bodies lay in the streets. Fewer than 60 out of 900 children survived when a three-storey school building collapsed.

Damage to infrastructure was also extensive. Ground shaking destroyed roads, power lines, water pipelines, dams, embankments and hydroelectric power stations.

### Landslides and quake lakes — secondary effects

In the mountains the quake caused widespread slope failure. The town of Beichuan (see Figure 5.13) was partly buried by landslides, which bulldozed

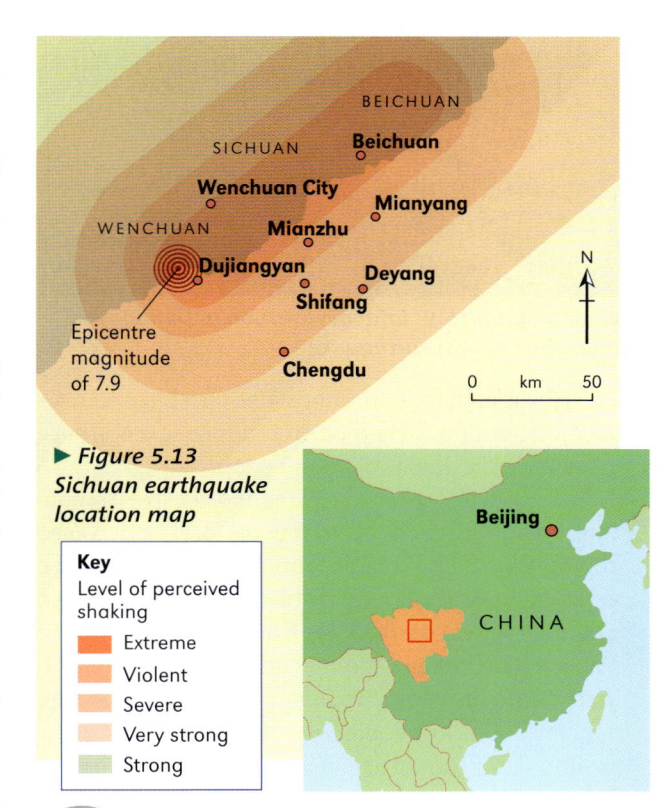

▶ **Figure 5.13** Sichuan earthquake location map

**Key**
Level of perceived shaking
- Extreme
- Violent
- Severe
- Very strong
- Strong

### Factfile 5.4 China

- China is a relatively poor country with an **emerging economy** that is growing rapidly.
- In 2006, China's GDP per capita was US$2,034 while its position in the UN's **human development** league table was 94th out of 179 countries.
- Nearly 60% of China's population live in rural areas.
- 56% of the population have inadequate sanitation.
- Urbanisation due to rural-urban migration is occurring rapidly — rates of urban population growth are around 3.5% per year.

Natural hazards

# Chapter 5 Tectonic hazards

▲ Photograph 5.9 Total devastation in Dujiangyan after the Sichuan earthquake

### Activity 5.6

Read the report on the impact of the Sichuan earthquake in Figure 5.14.

1. Name three natural hazards caused by the earthquake.
2. Describe the impact of the earthquake in Hanwang and in the mountains.

everything in their path. Landslides also blocked river valleys, creating 34 temporary 'quake lakes'. These lakes posed a potential flood hazard.

The quake lakes were monitored by remote sensing information from the air and space (see Photograph 5.10). Tanigiashan Lake, formed by the landslide at Beichuan, which blocked the White River, was the biggest quake lake. Rising water levels and rising water pressure threatened to breach the earth dam and cause catastrophic flooding downstream. Initially 250,000 people were evacuated to higher ground, until an artificial channel, completed on 7 June, drained the lake.

## Impact of the earthquake

The impact of an earthquake depends on a number of factors. The magnitude of the quake is important: the Sichuan quake was large, measuring nearly 8.0 on the Richter scale. Just as important is the number of people living close to the epicentre. Sichuan province is relatively densely populated, with 15 million people living in the earthquake zone.

These two factors help to explain the huge loss of life, but they are not the whole story. Take a look at Table 5.7. You will see that most of the countries that have suffered major loss of life due to earthquakes since 1990 are LEDCs. Of course, major earthquakes are not just confined to LEDCs. Japan and California, two of the richest parts of the economically developed world, are exposed to high earthquake risks. However, two big quakes in California in 1989 and 1994 caused only 120 deaths. Although the death toll

▲ Photograph 5.10 Satellite images of quake lake formation in Sichuan

OCR (B) GCSE Geography

# Theme 3

## 'The mountains are sliding down'

*Tania Branigan reports from Hanwang, a temporary haven for thousands of survivors of China's devastating earthquake*

Perhaps half the buildings here (in Hanwang) have collapsed; those still standing hang at crazy, alarming angles. Hundreds, probably thousands, of residents are buried, almost certainly dead.

Tang Xinfen threw herself in the dust, weeping as she pleaded with someone, anyone, to airlift medicine to survivors still trapped in Qingping by the mountains, which surround it. She had tramped for six hours to find aid.

"Please, use helicopters to bring medicine in. The roads are blocked [by landslides] and nobody can get there," she said. "People are dying every hour."

Almost every house on her street had crashed down within 10 or 20 seconds of the shock, she explained. People were thrown out of their homes and onto the road by the force of the quake. But Tang insisted thousands could be saved if only aid reached them in time.

"Some people are still alive, but they are badly injured and they need medical care," she said. "Because the weather is warm, their wounds are becoming infected."

A helicopter drop of water and food had proved fruitless: the bottles and packages broke and spilled open as they hit the ground.

"People couldn't get out with us because they were kids or too old," Shi Yunfang said. Her husband, Tang's brother, was missing.

"Others who are young and strong stayed to take care of them. But there is no completely safe place inside Qingping — the mountains are sliding down."

Their neighbour Zhou Yuan said earth and debris had dammed the river in the town, increasing the risk of flooding and further slippage. As many as 2,000 workers were unable to escape from a phosphorus mine there, she added.

In the late afternoon, a faint shudder and muffled rumble sent panic coursing through the crowds in the main square.

"We can't do anything, but don't want to leave," Zhang Shunyu said as she stood by the single-storey remains of what had been a five-storey block. Her 20-year-old daughter was buried under four floors of rubble. Further on, a man waited patiently as rescuers combed what was left of Hanwang County Central primary school. The whimpers rescue workers had heard from the rubble had fallen silent overnight. Behind him, bodies lay sheathed in plastic on the concrete pingpong tables in the playground.

"I came here minutes after the quake, but my daughter was already dead," he said. "I could see her body, but they still haven't got it out.

"My wife's parents died when the hospital collapsed, and mine have gone to Deyang. But my wife and I are staying until we have our little girl. I have a coffin ready for her. I want to bury my daughter."

Source: the *Guardian*, 14 May 2008

▲ Figure 5.14 Newspaper article about the Sichuan earthquake

### Activity 5.7

Photograph 5.10 shows the formation of Yansai quake lake, following the Sichuan earthquake on 12 May 2008. The lake formed when a landslide, triggered by the quake, blocked a mountain valley upstream of Beichuan city.

1. Draw an annotated sketch map to show how the rising waters of Yansai lake affected the two villages, roads, bridge (on right hand side) and farmland by (a) 14 May and (b) 19 May.
2. Outline the potential hazards from Yansai lake (a) upstream and (b) downstream from the lake.

*Table 5.7 Major earthquakes since 1990*

| Date | Location | Magnitude | Estimated deaths |
|------|----------|-----------|------------------|
| 2008 | Chengdu, Sichuan | 7.9 | 80,000 |
| 2005 | Kashmir | 7.6 | 80,000 |
| 2004 | Sumatra, Indonesia | 9.0 | 176,000 |
| 2003 | Bam, Iran | 6.5 | 26,000 |
| 2002 | Northern Algeria | 6.8 | 2,300 |
| 2002 | Northern Afghanistan | 5.8 | 1,000 |
| 2001 | Gujurat, India | 7.9 | 13,000 |
| 1999 | Taiwan | 7.6 | 2,400 |
| 1999 | Western Turkey | 7.4 | 17,000 |
| 1999 | Western Colombia | 6.0 | 1,171 |
| 1998 | Northern Afghanistan & Tajikistan | 6.9 | 5,000 |
| 1995 | Kobe, Japan | 7.2 | 6,000 |
| 1994 | Northridge, California | 6.7 | 57 |
| 1993 | Latur, India | 6.0 | 10,000 |
| 1990 | Northwest Iran | 7.5 | 50,000 |

Natural hazards

## Chapter 5 Tectonic hazards

in the Kobe quake in Japan in 1995 was much higher, a similar quake in a LEDCs would almost certainly have led to a much greater loss of life.

This tells us that the impact of earthquakes depends not just on the size of the quake and the number of people at risk, but also on how well prepared a society is to resist earthquakes. Earthquake resistance includes: strict building codes designed to prevent the collapse of houses, bridges, office blocks and other buildings; planning to prevent building on known fault lines; and disaster planning for evacuation and emergency relief.

Despite the power of the Sichuan quake, and the large population, the number of deaths was still exceptionally high. This points to one conclusion: Sichuan was ill-prepared for a major earthquake. In the months after the quake, it became clear that poor design and shoddy construction of buildings had contributed to the loss of life. China does have a strict earthquake building code aimed at preventing building collapse. However, most construction only gave protection up to a magnitude 7 quake. Many buildings (especially schools), collapsed due to a combination of poor workmanship, inferior design and failure to implement the building code. Building on known fault lines also contributed to the disaster.

Other aspects of earthquake preparedness, including short-term emergency planning to help survivors, were effective. Although China is a relatively poor country, it has the world's second largest economy and huge resources. A massive humanitarian relief effort was mounted by the Chinese authorities and **non-government organisations (NGOs)** such as the Red Cross and Red Crescent, providing food parcels, safe water supplies, warm quilts, hygiene items and tents. The long-term focus is on rebuilding. Reconstruction will cost around US$150bn and will provide millions of new homes, as well as new schools, health clinics and water and sanitation infrastructure. The World Bank is providing loans of nearly US$1bn to assist reconstruction.

## Case study: Earthquake in an MEDC: Northridge, California

On 17 January 1994 a large earthquake (magnitude 6.7) struck southern California. Its focus was the small town of Northridge close to Los Angeles (see Figure 5.15). The quake killed 57 people, injured 9,000 and left 20,000 homeless. While the human costs of the Northridge quake were relatively light, the economic costs — US$20 billion — were huge. At the time, the quake was the costliest natural disaster in US history.

### Cause

Southern California is one of the most active earthquake regions in the world. Between 1978 and 2004, five large earthquakes were recorded in the Los Angeles basin. Earthquakes are generated by the San Andreas fault, a conservative plate boundary, which runs parallel to the Pacific Ocean in southern California (see Figure 5.15). The North American and Pacific tectonic plates slide past each other along this fault

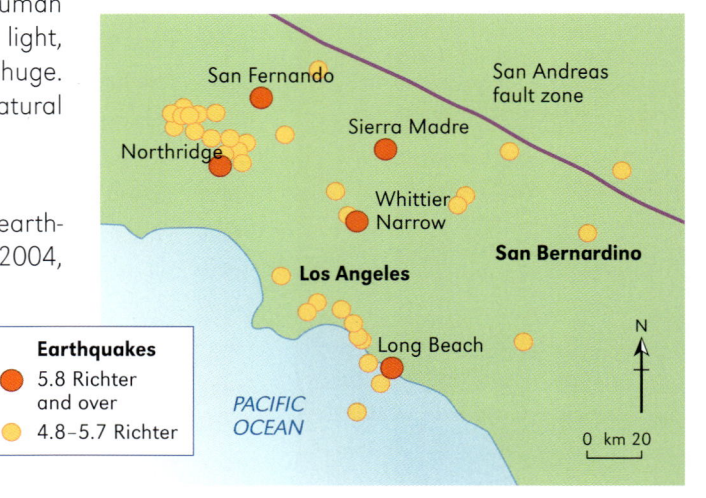

▶ Figure 5.15 The San Andreas fault: earthquakes in the Los Angeles basin since 1933, and the location of Northridge

*Photograph 5.11 Freeway damage caused by the Northridge earthquake*

boundary. In southern California this movement has compressed the crust and formed hundreds of hidden faults deep below the surface. It was a sudden movement along one of these faults that caused the Northridge quake.

## Earthquake hazards

### Ground shaking — the primary effect

Loss of life, injury and damage were mainly due to the primary effect of ground shaking. Ten to 20 seconds of strong shaking collapsed buildings, brought down freeway interchanges and damaged bridges and pipelines. Seven freeway interchanges suffered varying degrees of collapse (see Photograph 5.11) and 170 bridges were damaged. A number of low-rise apartments built above open parking spaces also collapsed, killing 16 people in one building. Many steel-framed buildings, including schools and hospitals, were also damaged. A 2,500 multi-storey car park, 3 km from the epicentre, collapsed.

### Landslides and fires — secondary effects

The Northridge quake triggered landslides in the surrounding mountains. These slides blocked roads and damaged water pipelines. The landslides also damaged some housing. Fortunately, because the Northridge area has a dry soil, liquefaction and ground failure effects were few.

Up to 50 fires broke out in the San Fernando Valley following the earthquake. Their main hazard was natural gas leaks. In addition a few wildfires resulted from arcing of overhead power lines. There was no loss of life from fire.

### Factfile 5.5 California

- California is the most populous US state: in 2006 its total population was 36.5 million.
- Nearly 95% of California's population lives in towns and cities.
- California is a wealthy state: in 2006 its GDP per capita was US$41,663 — comparable to Sweden's.
- California has the eighth largest economy in the world.
- 13% of California's population live below the poverty line.

# Chapter 5 Tectonic hazards

▶ **Photograph 5.12** Skyscraper in San Francisco showing earthquake-proof construction

▼ **Figure 5.16** Design for an earthquake-resistant multi-storey building

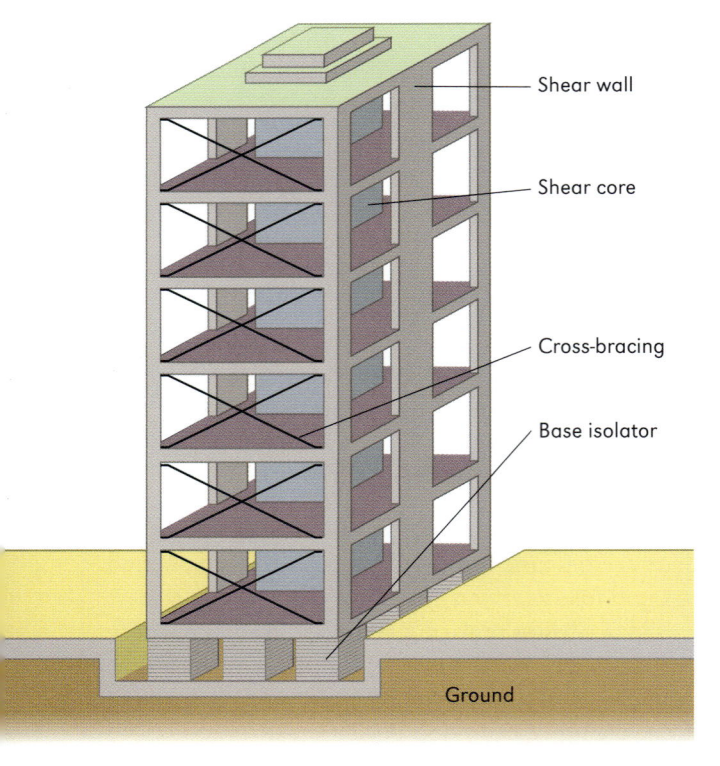

## The impact of the earthquake

Although the economic costs of the Northridge quake were large, compared with Sichuan, the death toll, number of injuries and disruption to society were relatively small. However, the Northridge quake was powerful and with nearly three million people living within 20 km of the epicentre, potentially it could have been disastrous.

*Table 5.8 Building methods to resist earthquakes*

| Design | Description |
|---|---|
| Bolting | Buildings bolted to their foundations |
| Shear walls | Made of reinforced concrete (i.e. concrete with steel rods embedded); help strengthen the building and resist rocking forces; often located in the centre of a high-rise building around the elevator shaft (shear core) |
| Cross bracing | Walls reinforced with diagonal steel beams |
| Shock absorbers | Inserted in foundations; made of layers of steel and elastic material such as synthetic rubber; absorb some of the sideways motion that damages buildings |

OCR (B) GCSE Geography

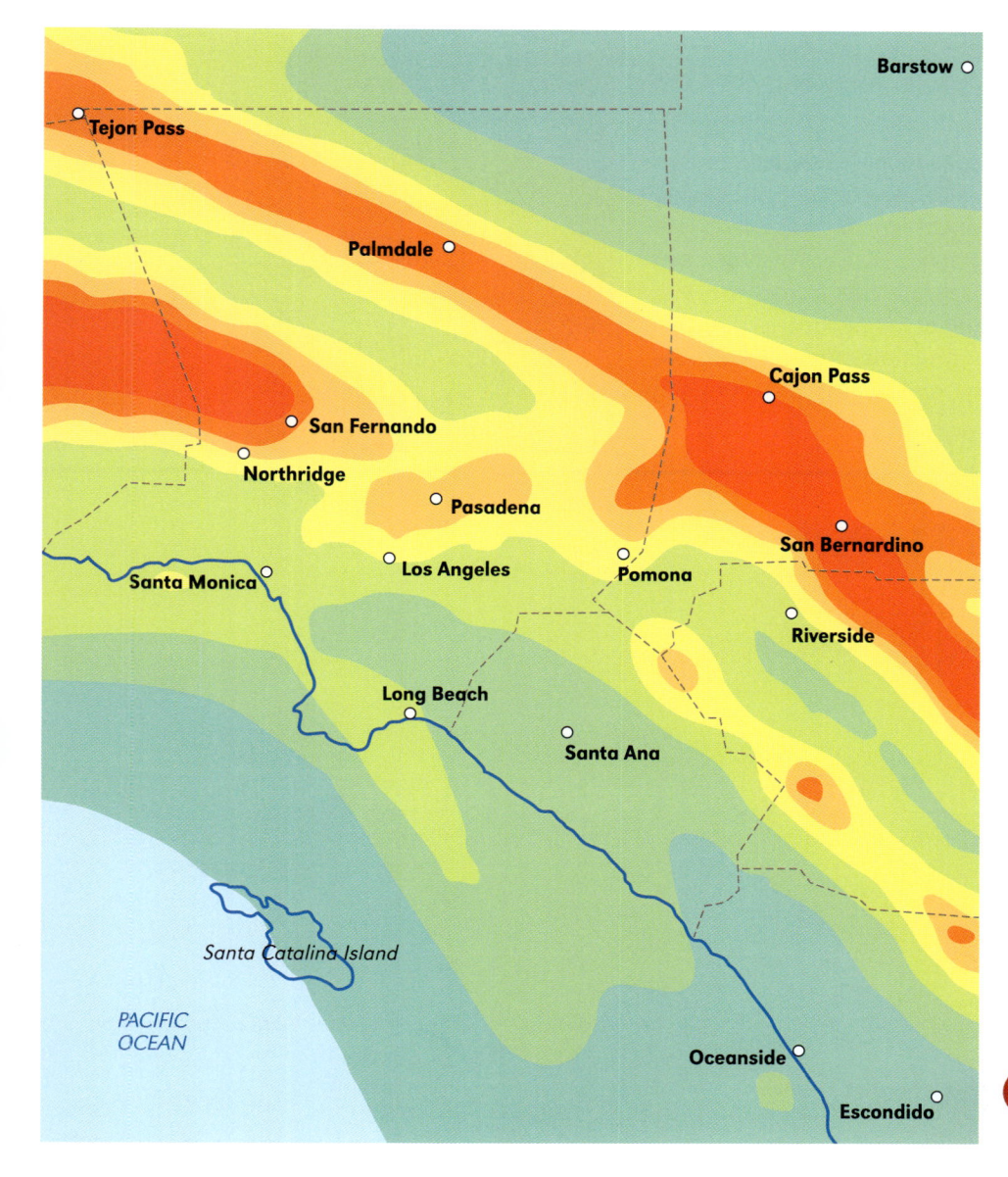

*Figure 5.17 Earthquake hazard map (ground shaking) for Los Angeles basin*

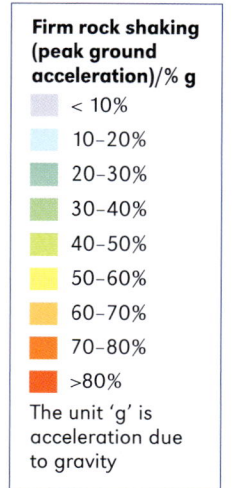

**Firm rock shaking (peak ground acceleration)/% g**
- < 10%
- 10–20%
- 20–30%
- 30–40%
- 40–50%
- 50–60%
- 60–70%
- 70–80%
- >80%

The unit 'g' is acceleration due to gravity

So why did California get off relatively lightly? Figure 5.16 suggests an answer: the USA and other MEDCs have the resources to prepare and plan for major earthquakes and so to reduce their impact. Earthquake preparedness includes:
- constructing buildings that will not collapse (see Table 5.8 and Figure 5.16) and making them fireproof
- preparing hazard maps that show fault lines, sites of past earthquakes, and areas at risk from liquefaction and landslides (see Figure 5.17). These maps help planners to control the building of unsafe structures in areas of high risk. They are used in the design of buildings, bridges, highways, power lines and pipelines, etc. so structures can withstand earthquake shaking.

### Activity 5.8

Describe and explain the main features of the multi-storey building in Figure 5.16 that are designed to make it earthquake resistant.

Natural hazards

- educating the people in earthquakes zones in basic procedures to reduce the risk of injury and loss of life

Skyscrapers in earthquake-prone cities such as San Francisco and Los Angeles require special building techniques to make them earthquake-proof (see Figure 5.16 and Photograph 5.12). They include deep foundations and a reinforced steel framework with stronger joints than ordinary skyscrapers. The steel framework makes the structure strong yet flexible enough to resist shaking and collapse.

> **Activity 5.9**
>
> Study Figure 5.17, which maps the ground shaking hazard caused by earthquakes in the Los Angeles basin.
>
> 1 Rank the following places in order of their vulnerability to ground shaking: Santa Monica, San Bernardino, Oceanside, Santa Ana, San Fernando.
>
> 2 Suggest how the hazard map might influence (a) the location of a new power station and (b) the construction of a multi-storey building in San Fernando or San Bernardino.

# Theme 3 Natural hazards

# Chapter 6 Climatic hazards

## Part 1 Tropical storms

The most violent storms on the planet occur in the tropics. In the North Atlantic and Caribbean they are known as **hurricanes**. Similar storms in south Asia are called **tropical cyclones**, and in east Asia, **typhoons**. The intensity of tropical storms, is measured by their average wind speed. Storms become hurricanes (or tropical cyclones or typhoons) when their average wind speed reaches 119 km/h. The most powerful storms are ranked as category 5 events on the Saffir–Simpson hurricane scale (see Table 6.1).

### The distribution of tropical storms

Globally, tropical storms have a very specific geographical distribution. They develop over the ocean between latitudes 8° and 20° (see Figure 6.1). However, once formed, they often move outside the tropical belt. For example: in the USA, where hurricanes sometimes track north from the Gulf of Mexico and hit Georgia and the Carolinas (30°–35°N); and in Japan (30°–40°N) where typhoons occur regularly in late summer and autumn.

Table 6.1 *The Saffir–Simpson hurricane scale*

| Scale | Wind speed (km/h) | Storm surge height (m) |
|---|---|---|
| 1 | 119–153 | 1.2–1.5 |
| 2 | 154–177 | 1.8–2.4 |
| 3 | 178–209 | 2.7–3.7 |
| 4 | 210–249 | 4.0–5.5 |
| 5 | >249 | >5.5 |

### Key ideas

- Tropical storms have specific global distributions.
- Specific climatic conditions lead to the formation of tropical storms, which affects their global distribution.

### Factfile 6.1 Tropical storms

- **Hurricanes, cyclones and typhoons** are powerful tropical storms with sustained wind speeds of at least 119 km/h.
- Tropical storms are areas of low pressure; they have a roughly circular shape, tightly packed **isobars** and winds that rotate anticlockwise in the northern hemisphere.
- Tropical storms are extreme weather events which can bring total devastation to parts of the tropics and sub-tropics through a combination of high winds, storm surges and heavy rainfall.

# Chapter 6 Climatic hazards

*Figure 6.1 Areas of oceans where tropical storms form*

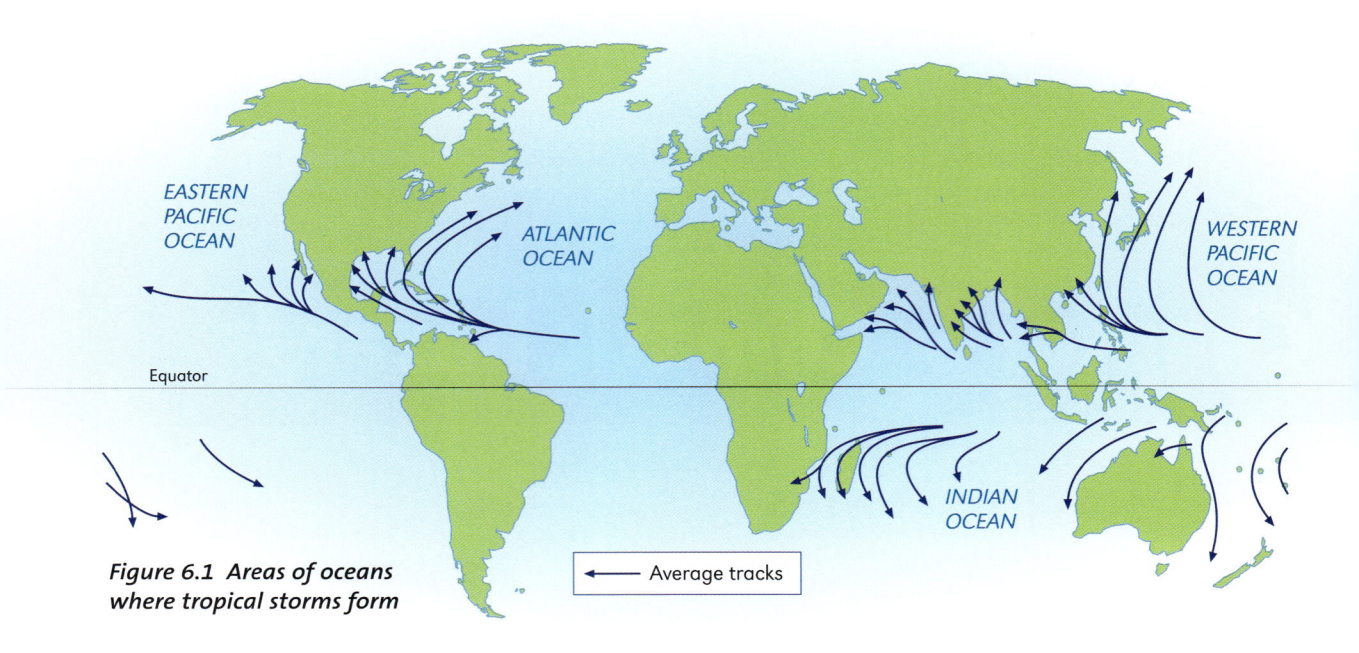

▲ *Photograph 6.1 Satellite image of Hurricane Katrina*

## The causes of tropical storms

Hurricanes, cyclones and typhoons form over tropical oceans where surface water temperatures are 26.5°C or higher (see Figure 6.1). Favourable temperature conditions occur in summer and early autumn in the North Atlantic and Indian and Pacific Oceans. Seen from space (see Photograph 6.1) hurricanes resemble giant catherine wheels of cloud, typically 500 to 600 km in diameter. As they move across the ocean, their thick bands of cloud rotate anticlockwise around the central eye.

Hurricanes and other tropical storms get their energy from the evaporation of water from the warm ocean. As the vapour rises it cools and forms clouds. This process releases energy as latent heat, which provides further energy for more evaporation. In this way the storm increases in intensity and power.

At the same time, hurricanes and other tropical storms act like massive chimneys (see Figure 6.2). They draw air in at the

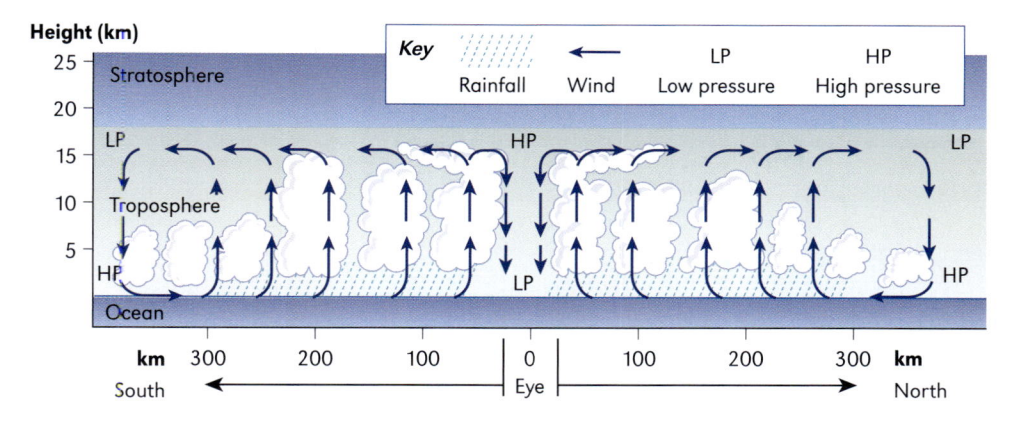

◀ **Figure 6.2** Cross-section through a hurricane

▼ **Figure 6.3** The distribution of surface ocean currents

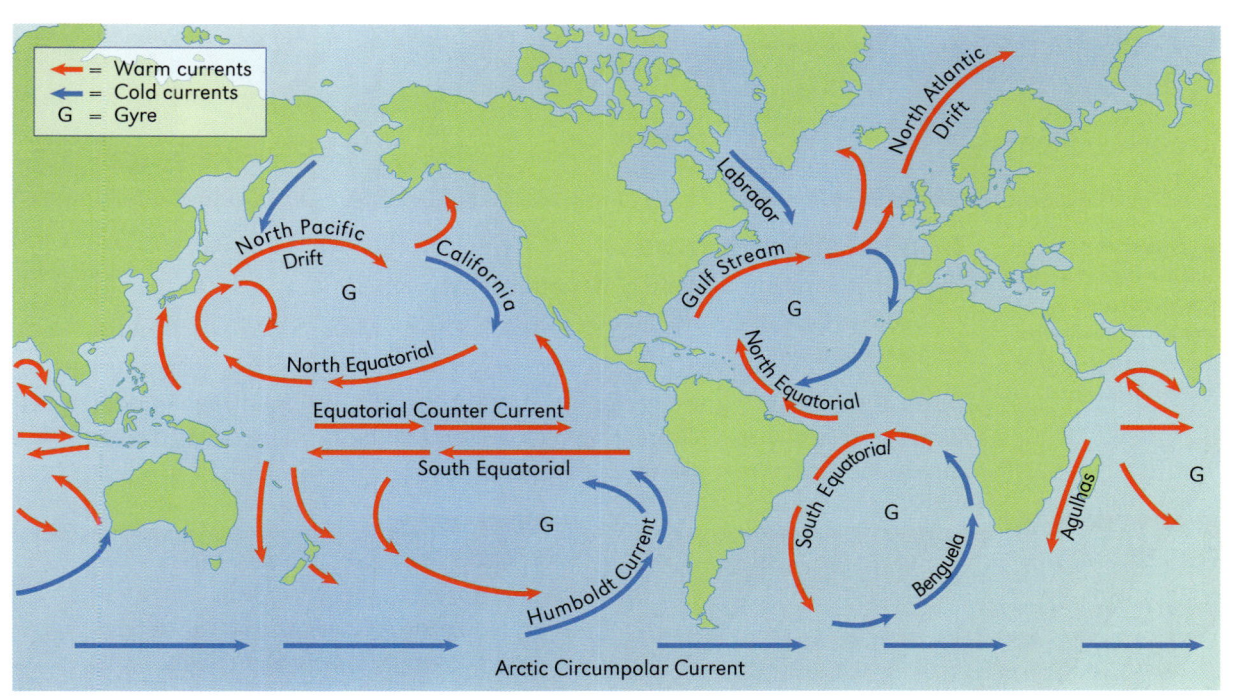

surface, which rises steeply, and flows outwards at high level. However, the surface winds never reach the exact centre of the storm. Instead, the centre is a cylinder of calm, sinking air. This is the 'eye'.

Although hurricanes take weeks to form, once they reach land and lose their supply of water vapour, they quickly decay.

### Activity 6.1

Compare the distribution of tropical storms (see Figure 6.1) and the distribution of ocean currents (see Figure 6.3).

1. Name the ocean currents found along the coasts of northwest Africa, south-west Africa, California, and Pacific South America.
2. What do these ocean currents have in common?
3. Although these coastal areas are in the tropics or sub-tropics, they are not associated with tropical storms. Explain why.

Natural hazards

# Chapter 6 Climatic hazards

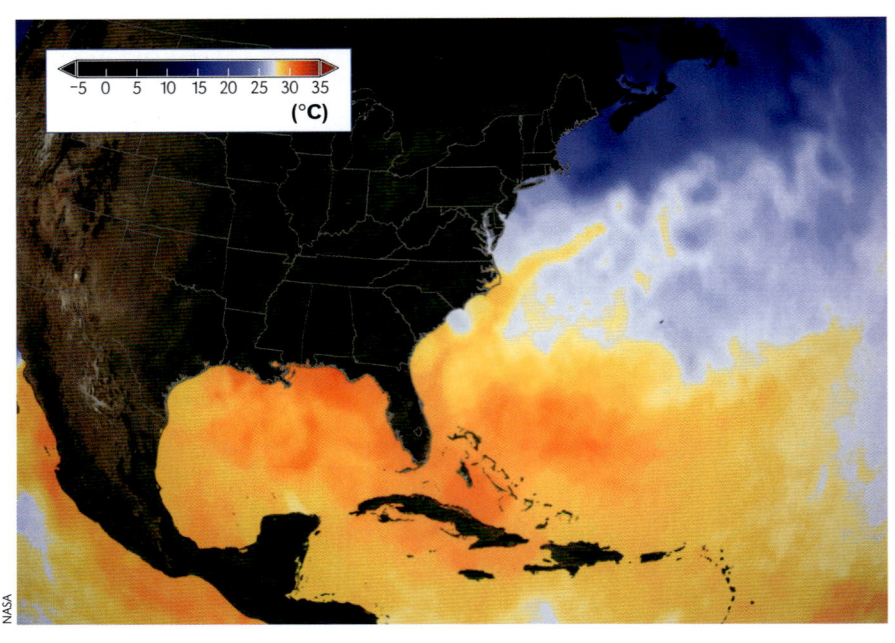

## Activity 6.2

Study the satellite image showing sea surface temperatures (SSTs) in the Gulf of Mexico, Caribbean and north Atlantic on 1 August 2008 (Figure 6.4).

1. Describe the distribution of SSTs in the Gulf of Mexico, Caribbean and north Atlantic.

2. Suggest where tropical storms (hurricanes) are likely to form. Explain your reasoning.

▲ Figure 6.4 Sea surface temperatures in the Gulf of Mexico, Caribbean and the North Atlantic

## Tropical storm hazards

Tropical storms are extremely hazardous. Between 1980 and 2000 they killed 250,000 people and cost billions of dollars in damage to property and infrastructure.

Tropical storms bring three types of natural hazard: sustained high winds, storm surges and heavy rain. Damaging high winds are the primary hazard: storm surges and heavy rain are secondary hazards.

## Activity 6.3

Study Figure 6.5, which shows the number of people exposed to hurricanes (and tropical cyclones and typhoons) by country, and the average number of deaths caused by hurricanes each year.

1. Which country has:
   (a) the highest number of average deaths from hurricanes?
   (b) the largest population exposed to hurricanes?

2. Describe the relationship between the population exposed to hurricanes and the average number of deaths per year.

3. Suggest possible reasons why Japan, which has similar numbers of people exposed to hurricanes as Bangladesh and the Philippines, has far fewer deaths than those countries.

## Key ideas

- Natural hazards occur when naturally occurring events such as tropical storms adversely affect people and society.
- Tropical storms are responsible for a number of natural hazards such as hurricane force winds, storm surges, floods and landslides.
- Primary hazards are the direct hazardous effects of tropical storms, such as structural damage caused by violent winds.
- Secondary hazards are indirect and are triggered by primary hazards. Tropical storms produce secondary hazards such as storm surges, river floods and landslides.

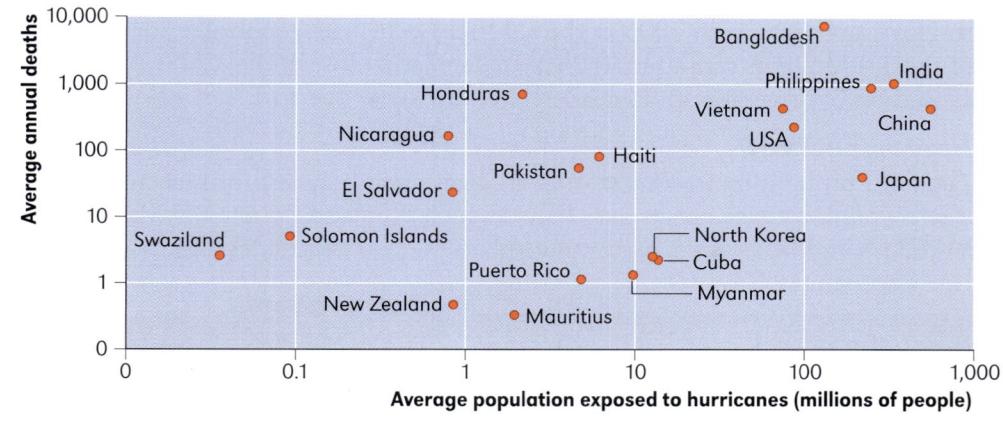

◀ *Figure 6.5 Vulnerability to hurricanes, 1980–2000*

▼ *Photographs 6.2 and 6.3 Storm damage and floods caused by Hurricane Katrina in 2005*

## Winds

Wind speeds can average 250 km/h in tropical storms, with gusts sometimes reaching 360 km/h. Destruction is caused by direct impact and flying debris (see Photograph 6.2). Violent winds damage trees, crops and can flatten entire forests. Tall buildings, buffeted by winds, can collapse; sudden pressure changes can cause buildings to explode; while suction can lift roofs and wooden buildings. However, most wind damage results from flying debris such as roof sheets and tiles.

## Storm surges

Storm surges occur when the force of the wind piles up water at sea and drives it towards the land. At the same time low atmospheric pressure at the centre of the storm raises the sea surface. A surge, combined with a high tide can increase water levels 5 m or more. The result is severe flooding in low-lying coastal areas (see Photograph 6.3). In fact, storm surges (and river floods) are usually far more hazardous than high winds. The storm surge generated

Natural hazards

# Chapter 6 Climatic hazards

by Hurricane Katrina in 2005 in the southern USA was responsible for most of the 1,400 deaths caused by the storm. Similarly most of the 4,000 deaths caused by Cyclone Sidr in Bangladesh in 2007 were due to a 5 m storm surge.

## Heavy rainfall

The rains brought by tropical storms are heavy and may last for several days. Intense rainfall creates secondary hazards such as inland flooding by rivers, landslides and other mass earth movements such as mudslides and mudflows (see Photograph 6.4).

▼ *Photograph 6.4 Mudflow in the Philippines*

### Activity 6.4

Investigate a hurricane from the past 10 years. Use the internet as your data source and present your results in either hard copy or CD format. Your investigation should cover some of the following:

1. The development of the hurricane and its movement.

2. The path or track of the hurricane. You can download a tracking map from **www.nhc.noaa.gov/AT_Track _chart.pdf** and positional data for the Atlantic, Pacific and Indian Oceans from websites such as: **http://weather.Unisys. com/hurricane/atlantic/2004/ index.html**

3. The intensity of the hurricane (i.e. central pressure) and its status on a scale of 1–5 (classification based on wind speed, where a force 5 hurricane has sustained winds of more than 250 km/h — see Table 6.1).

4. A satellite image of your chosen hurricane.

5. A description of the hazards associated with the hurricane (e.g. winds, floods, landslides) and the scale of their impact (e.g. loss of life, damage to property).

# Protecting people and places from tropical storm hazards

## The USA

Tropical storms are more closely monitored than any other natural hazard. Satellites, aircraft, ships and buoys moored in the oceans, are used to track the movement of existing storms, monitor the development of new ones and provide essential data on temperature, humidity and wind speed (see Table 6.2). In the USA this technology makes accurate forecasting possible, giving people and businesses time to prepare for storm hazards. The National Hurricane Center has responsibility for measuring and monitoring storms in the Atlantic and eastern Pacific.

## Cuba

The impact of extreme weather events like tropical storms depends partly on a country's level of preparedness. As a rule, poor countries are less well prepared than rich countries. However, there are exceptions. Cuba, an island state in the Caribbean (see Figure 6.15, page 137), is an example of a **less economically developed country** (**LEDC**) that has

> **Key ideas**
> - A range of methods are used to reduce the impact of tropical storms.
> - A range of methods can be used to predict the location, frequency and severity of tropical storms.

*Table 6.2 Measuring and monitoring tropical storms*

| | |
|---|---|
| Monitoring begins during the early stages of storm development out in the ocean using satellites, ships and buoys. Closer to land, aircraft and radiosondes provide data. All the data are fed into computer models that forecast storm intensities and storm tracks. ||
| **Satellites** | Provide data on the size, intensity and movement of storms |
| **Ships and buoys** | Provide air and sea surface temperatures, wind speed, wave height, wind direction etc. |
| **Aircraft** | Fly into storms to measure wind speed, pressure, temperature and humidity |
| **Radiosondes** | Balloons, carrying weather instruments and transmitters, are released into storms; they also provide data on wind speed, pressure, temperature and humidity |
| **Radar** | Radar images provide information on rainfall intensity |
| In the USA, the National Weather Center issues two categories of warning on approaching storms: ||
| **Hurricane watch:** hurricane conditions are possible within the next 36 hours. ||
| **Hurricane warning:** sustained winds of 119 km/h and above are expected in the next 24 hours. ||

### Factfile 6.2 Economic development and the impact of natural hazards

- Extreme weather events such as tropical storms usually hit less economically developed countries (LEDCs) harder than **more economically developed countries** (**MEDCs**).
- Poor people often have little choice but to live in areas at risk from tropical storms and other natural hazards, e.g. on steep slopes exposed to landslides, or in river valleys vulnerable to flooding.
- Poor people may live in houses that provide little protection against events such as hurricane-force high winds.
- Many people in poor countries live in isolated rural areas, which are difficult for emergency services to reach following a disaster.
- Governments in LEDCs may have few resources to devote to early warning of disasters, disaster planning and emergency relief.

Natural hazards

## Chapter 6 Climatic hazards

successfully protected its population against hurricanes. When Hurricane Georges swept through the Caribbean in 1998 it killed over 1,000 people. Yet the death toll in Cuba was just four. Perhaps even more remarkable was the impact of Hurricane Charley in 2004. This hurricane was directly responsible for 30 deaths in Florida, USA, but caused only two deaths in Cuba.

Cuba's success is based on a low-cost approach aimed at reducing people's vulnerability. Disaster prevention and preparedness are compulsory parts of the Cuban school curriculum, and children and adults are trained to cope with extreme weather events. Television and radio give early warning of hurricanes; and emergency plans are put into operation 48 hours before a hurricane hits the island. These include evacuation and the use of schools and hospitals as temporary shelters.

In the poorest countries more lives could be saved by a few simple measures, such as improved warning systems, building better housing, locating housing away from known flood and landslide areas, tying down roofs and covering windows and glass panels.

# Part 2 Droughts

A drought is an unusual weather pattern that produces a prolonged shortage of rain. Droughts may last from a few weeks to several months or even years.

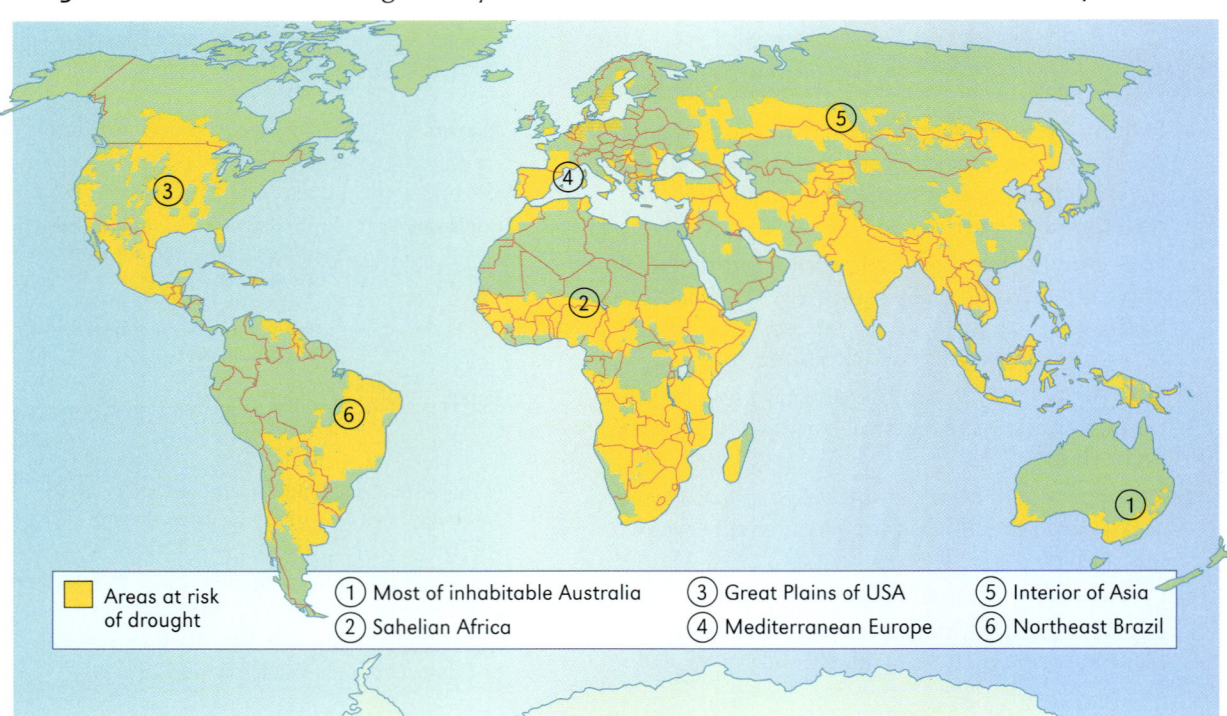

*Figure 6.6 Global distribution of drought risk areas*

Areas at risk of drought
1. Most of inhabitable Australia
2. Sahelian Africa
3. Great Plains of USA
4. Mediterranean Europe
5. Interior of Asia
6. Northeast Brazil

# Theme 3

## The distribution of droughts

Nearly two-fifths of the world's land area experiences drought (see Figure 6.6). Worst affected are tropical and sub-tropical regions with alternating wet and dry seasons, such as the Sahel in Africa, southern Africa, northeast Brazil and India. Other drought-prone regions include the Mediterranean, and continental interiors in the USA, Canada, China and Argentina.

## The causes of droughts

Periods of low rainfall leading to drought are linked to changes in pressure patterns in the atmosphere. Even in a country with a wet climate like the UK, droughts sometimes occur. Much of southern England experienced drought between 2004 and 2006, when water supplies declined to seriously low levels. How did this happen? Normally the UK's weather is controlled by storms from the Atlantic, which bring cloud and rain. However, sometimes high-pressure systems, known as **anticyclones**, develop and can dominate the weather for months. These 'blocking highs' divert Atlantic storms to the north and south of the British Isles, and bring long, dry spells and drought (see Figure 6.8 and Factfile 6.3).

### Key ideas

- Droughts have specific global distributions.
- Specific climatic conditions lead to the formation of droughts, which affect their global distribution.

### Activity 6.5

Study the global distribution of drought (see Figure 6.6) and rainfall (see Figure 6.7).

1. Name two types of rainfall region in Figure 6.7 that are least affected by drought. Explain why drought has little impact on these regions.

2. Describe how rainfall patterns influence the distribution of drought in Africa and South America.

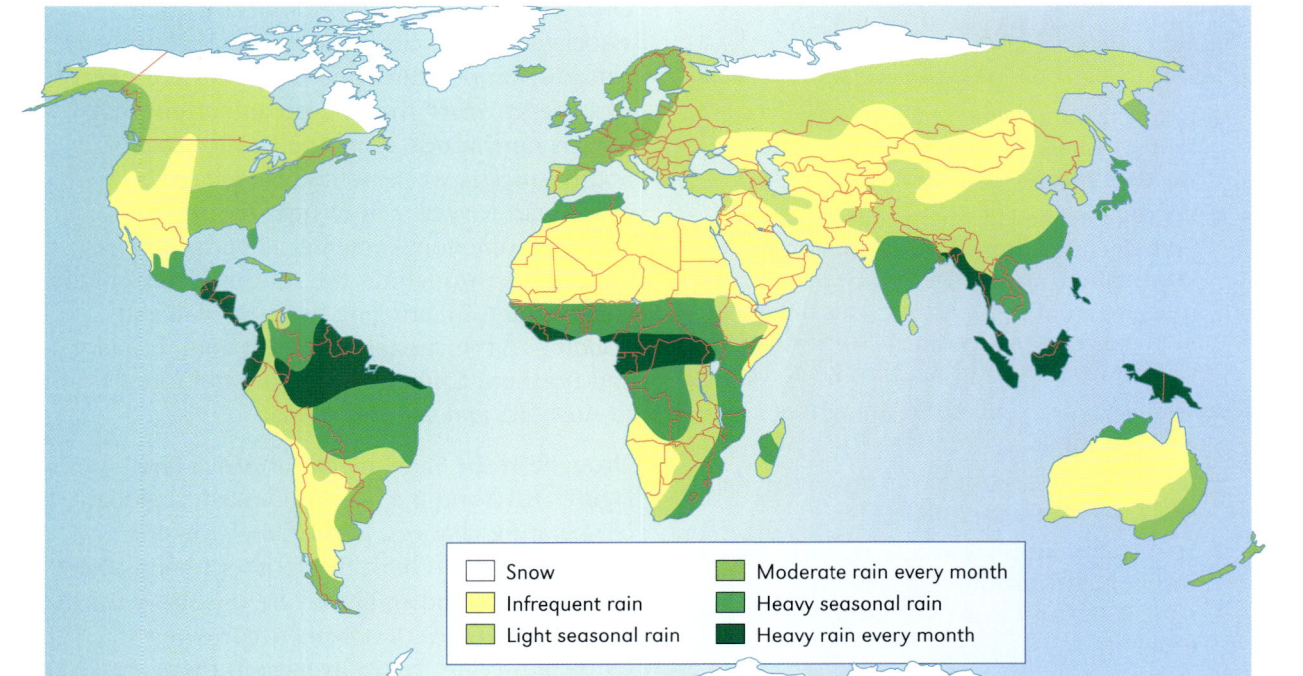

*Figure 6.7 Seasonal rainfall distribution*

Legend:
- Snow
- Infrequent rain
- Light seasonal rain
- Moderate rain every month
- Heavy seasonal rain
- Heavy rain every month

Natural hazards

# Chapter 6 Climatic hazards

*Figure 6.8 Weather chart showing a blocking situation over much of Europe*

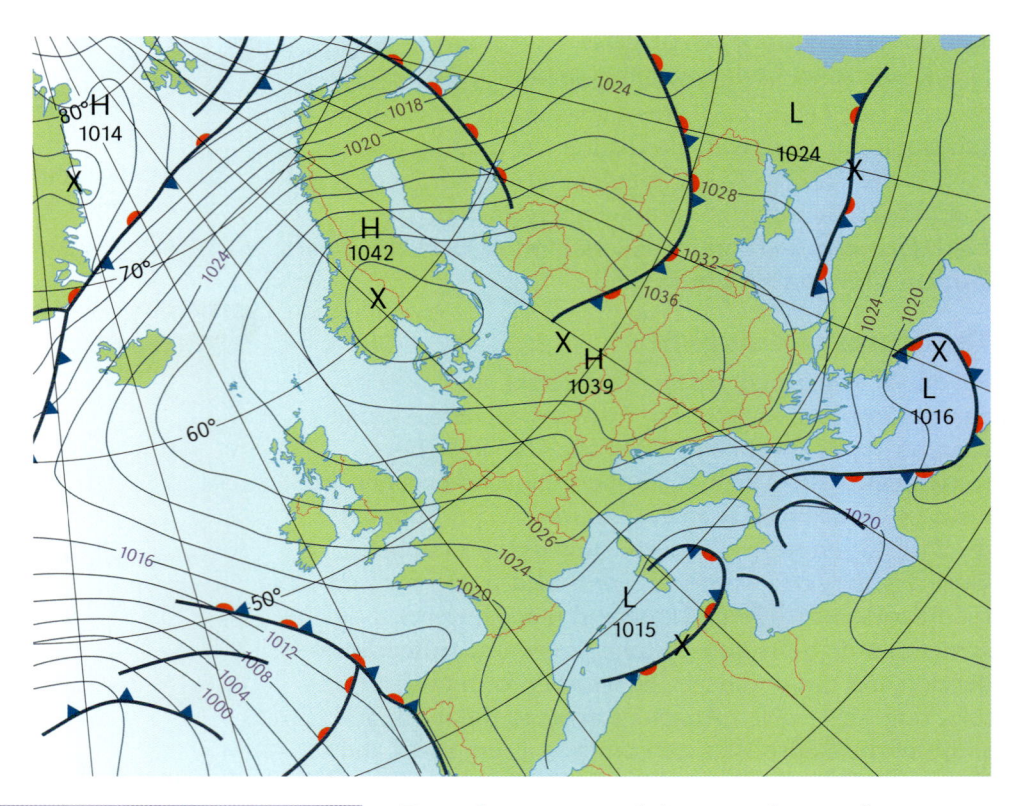

### Factfile 6.3 Causes of drought in the UK

- Drought occurs when high pressure (anticyclones) becomes established over western Europe for several weeks.
- Weather in the UK is controlled by two permanent pressure systems in the Atlantic: low-pressure around Iceland, and high pressure around the Azores. This difference in pressure — the so-called North Atlantic Oscillation (NAO) — tends to be cyclic.
- The NAO determines the strength of the westerly winds.
- Large differences result in strong westerlies and above average rainfall.
- Small differences lead to weaker westerly winds, higher pressures, below average rainfall and an increased likelihood of drought.

Droughts on a much larger scale are often associated with cyclic changes in global pressure patterns, temperatures and ocean currents. Every six or seven years, the cold ocean current that sweeps northwards along the Pacific coast of South America weakens, and is replaced by much warmer water from near the equator. This phenomenon, known as El Niño, disrupts the climate throughout the southern hemisphere (see Figure 6.9), bringing heavy rainfall and flooding to the coastal regions of Peru, Ecuador and northern Chile, and drought and forest fires to Australia and southeast Asia.

Drought in the Sahel region of Africa (see Figures 6.10 and 6.11) is also linked to global temperature changes. In the Sahel, the driest years occur when both the southern hemisphere and the north Indian Ocean are unusually warm. Meanwhile the wettest years occur when temperatures are below average in these areas.

# Theme 3

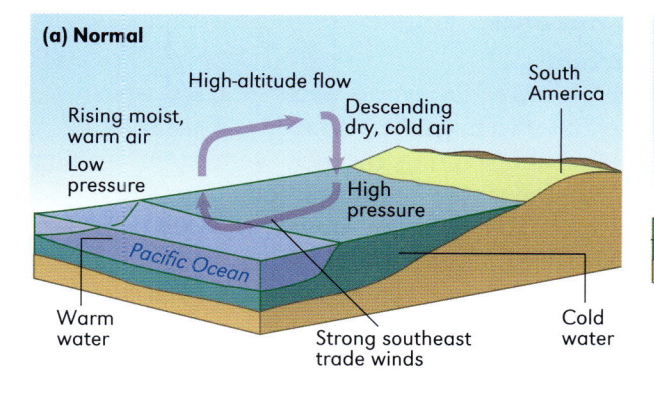

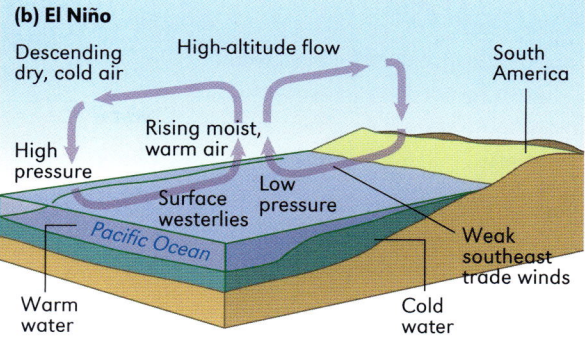

**(a) Normal**

Labels: High-altitude flow; Rising moist, warm air; Low pressure; Descending dry, cold air; High pressure; South America; Pacific Ocean; Warm water; Strong southeast trade winds; Cold water

**(b) El Niño**

Labels: Descending dry, cold air; High-altitude flow; High pressure; Rising moist, warm air; Low pressure; South America; Surface westerlies; Pacific Ocean; Warm water; Cold water; Weak southeast trade winds

▲ *Figure 6.9 The El Nino phenomenon*

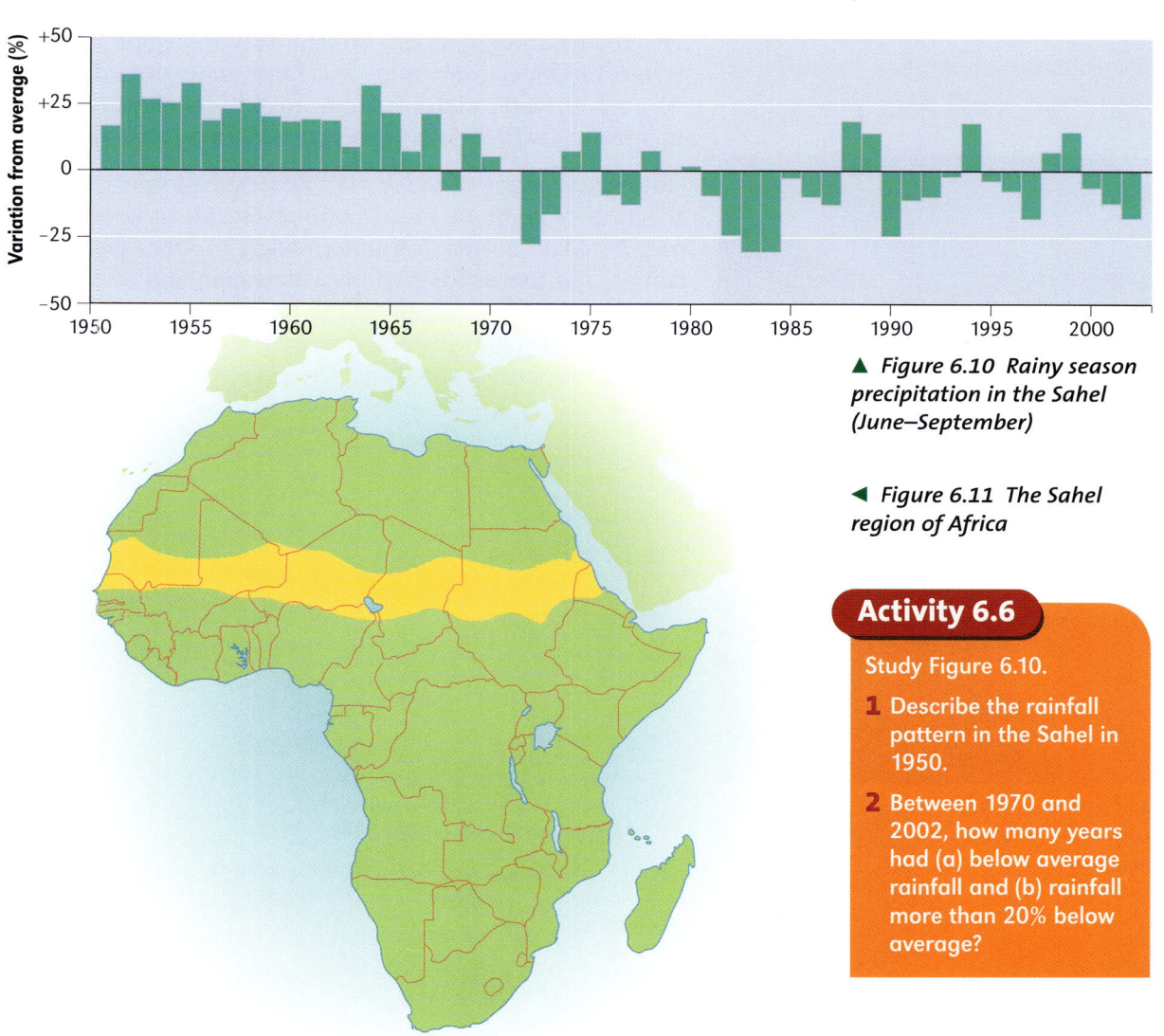

▲ *Figure 6.10 Rainy season precipitation in the Sahel (June–September)*

◀ *Figure 6.11 The Sahel region of Africa*

## Activity 6.6

Study Figure 6.10.

1. Describe the rainfall pattern in the Sahel in 1950.
2. Between 1970 and 2002, how many years had (a) below average rainfall and (b) rainfall more than 20% below average?

Natural hazards

133

## Chapter 6 Climatic hazards

### Key ideas

- Natural hazards occur when naturally occurring events such as droughts adversely affect people and society.
- Droughts are responsible for hazards such as water shortages, **wildfires**, crop failure and famine.
- Primary hazards are the direct effects of drought, such as water shortages.
- Secondary hazards are indirect and are triggered by primary hazards. Droughts cause secondary hazards like fires and damage to wildlife.

## Drought hazards

### Primary hazards

The primary hazard of drought is water shortage, which can have serious effects on the availability of water for domestic use, manufacturing, electricity generation, farming and the environment (see Photograph 6.5). Drought (and heat) across Europe in the summer of 2003 proved disastrous for farmers. In the UK the wheat harvest fell by 12%; in France it was down by 20%; and in eastern Europe by nearly three-quarters. The total cost to European farming was estimated to be US$7 billion.

### Secondary hazards

Southern England, the driest part of the UK, is often badly affected by drought. When drought hits the region extra water is pumped from rivers and from underground rocks. As a result, **water tables** fall and small rivers may dry up completely, with serious consequences for aquatic life.

However, in many of the world's poorest countries, the effects of drought are much more severe. In summer 2005, over 3 million people in southern Niger in Africa faced famine, and thousands died from starvation and disease (see Figure 6.12). A report by the Food and Agriculture Organisation (FAO) blamed the crisis on drought that lasted 13 months and reduced the grain harvest by a quarter.

▲ Photograph 6.5 Low reservoir level in Spain

▶ Figure 6.12 Map of Niger

Drought has also contributed to land degradation in Niger and the Sahel belt (see Figure 6.13). When the rains fail, farmers and their livestock put extra pressure on grazing land and woodland. Often the result is overgrazing, deforestation and soil erosion, and a permanent loss of resources (see Photograph 6.6).

Finally, drought, together with excessive heat, can lead to outbreaks of wildfire. The 2003 drought and heatwave in Europe sparked over 25,000 wildfires, mainly in Portugal, Spain, Italy and France. In total, 6,500 km² of forest was burned. More than half the destruction was in Portugal. On the Côte d'Azur in southern France, five people were killed by forest fires. The economic costs of drought in Europe in 2003 were considerable. Wildfires cost Portugal more than €1 billion. Water levels on many navigable rivers were so low that cargo transport came to a standstill. Meanwhile, there was reduced electricity output from power stations due to insufficient cooling water, and huge losses were suffered by farmers.

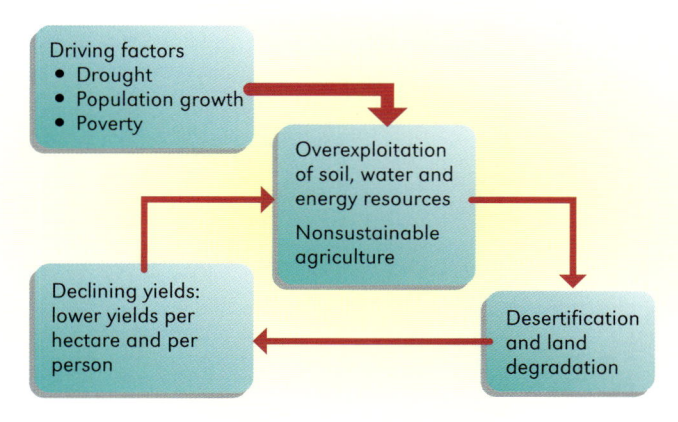

*Figure 6.13 Causes of desertification and land degradation*

## Protecting people and places from drought hazards

Water shortages often result from drought and inadequate rainfall. However, water shortages can also result from excessive water demand, rather than insufficient rainfall. As it is impossible to modify weather patterns, protecting people against drought often means managing the supply of water so that society can cope with extended periods of low rainfall.

*Photograph 6.6 Land degradation in the Sahel*

# Chapter 6 Climatic hazards

## Drought in the UK

Water shortages in southeast England are likely to increase in future for two reasons: demand will continue to rise; and climate change will increase evaporation and reduce rainfall, especially in summer. One possible response is to build more reservoirs and store surplus rain that falls in winter. A more costly solution is to develop a water grid. This would allow the transfer of water from water-rich areas in the north and west to southeast England (see Figure 6.14). Some inter-regional water transfers already take place: Birmingham and Liverpool get a large part of their public water supply from Wales, and Manchester relies on water transferred from the Lake District.

Society can also protect against drought by reducing water demand. During droughts water authorities can impose drought orders, which ban non-essential uses such as washing cars and watering gardens. Consumers can be encouraged to save water by taking showers rather than baths and by recycling 'used' water. Water meters also help to cut wasteful usage, while water authorities have targets to reduce leaks from the mains.

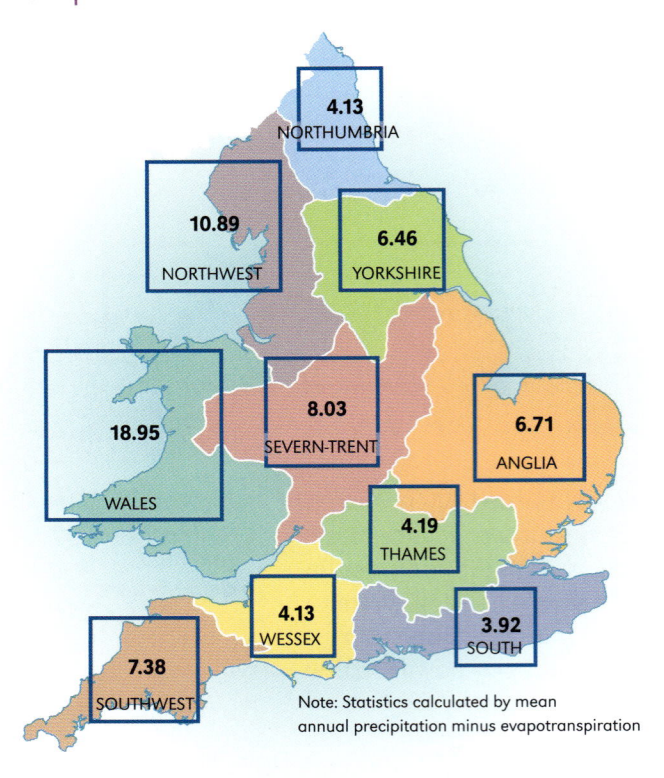

*Figure 6.14 Potential water available in the UK by region (km³/yr)*

Values by region:
- NORTHUMBRIA: 4.13
- NORTHWEST: 10.89
- YORKSHIRE: 6.46
- WALES: 18.95
- SEVERN-TRENT: 8.03
- ANGLIA: 6.71
- THAMES: 4.19
- WESSEX: 4.13
- SOUTH: 3.92
- SOUTHWEST: 7.38

Note: Statistics calculated by mean annual precipitation minus evapotranspiration

## Drought in sub-Saharan Africa

While drought in MEDCs may be inconvenient, in many of the world's poorest countries drought can be a matter of life or death. This is because most people rely on food produced locally and use local resources of water, soil and pasture. Any prolonged dry period spells disaster in terms of food production. Furthermore, drought encourages the overexploitation of natural resources, which ultimately leads to land degradation (see Figure 6.13).

Societies in this situation can be protected by increasing water supply and water security. NGOs like *Water Aid* specialise in providing water to the world's poorest people (see Chapter 7). Bore holes, wells and pumps can tap underground supplies of fresh water for people and livestock. This water can also be used to irrigate crops to ensure against secondary drought hazards such as food shortages and famine.

### Activity 6.7

Study Figure 6.14.

1. Which region has:
   (a) the largest water resources?
   (b) the smallest water resources?
2. Apart from rainfall and evaporation, state one other factor that might influence the total water resources in the regions in Figure 6.14.

OCR (B) GCSE Geography

# Theme 3

# Part 3 Case studies of tropical storms and drought

## Case study: Hurricane Mitch

Hurricane Mitch, a category 5 hurricane, struck central America and the Caribbean in late October 1998. Mitch was one of the most powerful storms ever to hit the region. At its peak, its central pressure dipped to 905 mb and wind speeds reached 280 km/h. The countries worst affected were Honduras and Nicaragua. In Honduras, 625 mm of rain fell in a single day.

Hurricane Mitch formed in early October in the eastern Atlantic. It moved through the Caribbean, making landfall on 29 October in Honduras. It then tracked slowly across Honduras and Nicaragua (see Figure 6.15). As it crossed the mountains it deposited huge amounts of rain (1,000–2,000 mm fell in just 3 or 4 days). The results were catastrophic. Violent flash floods and landslides killed thousands of people, and destroyed crops, homes, roads and bridges.

### Factfile 6.4 The impact of Hurricane Mitch on central America

- 11,000 people killed, the vast majority in Honduras and Nicaragua.
- 3 million people made homeless; and in the immediate aftermath there were serious shortages of food and medicines.
- 70% of crops destroyed; estimated crop losses were US$900 million.
- 92 bridges badly damaged; 70–80% of Honduras' transport infrastructure was destroyed.
- Damage estimated at US$6 billion.

### Activity 6.8

Study Figure 6.15 and Factfile 6.4.

1. Describe the path of Hurricane Mitch between 22 October and 4 November 1998.
2. Between 29 October and 4 November wind speeds dropped and Hurricane Mitch was downgraded to tropical storm status. Explain why this change occurred.

▼ Figure 6.15 Path of Hurricane Mitch

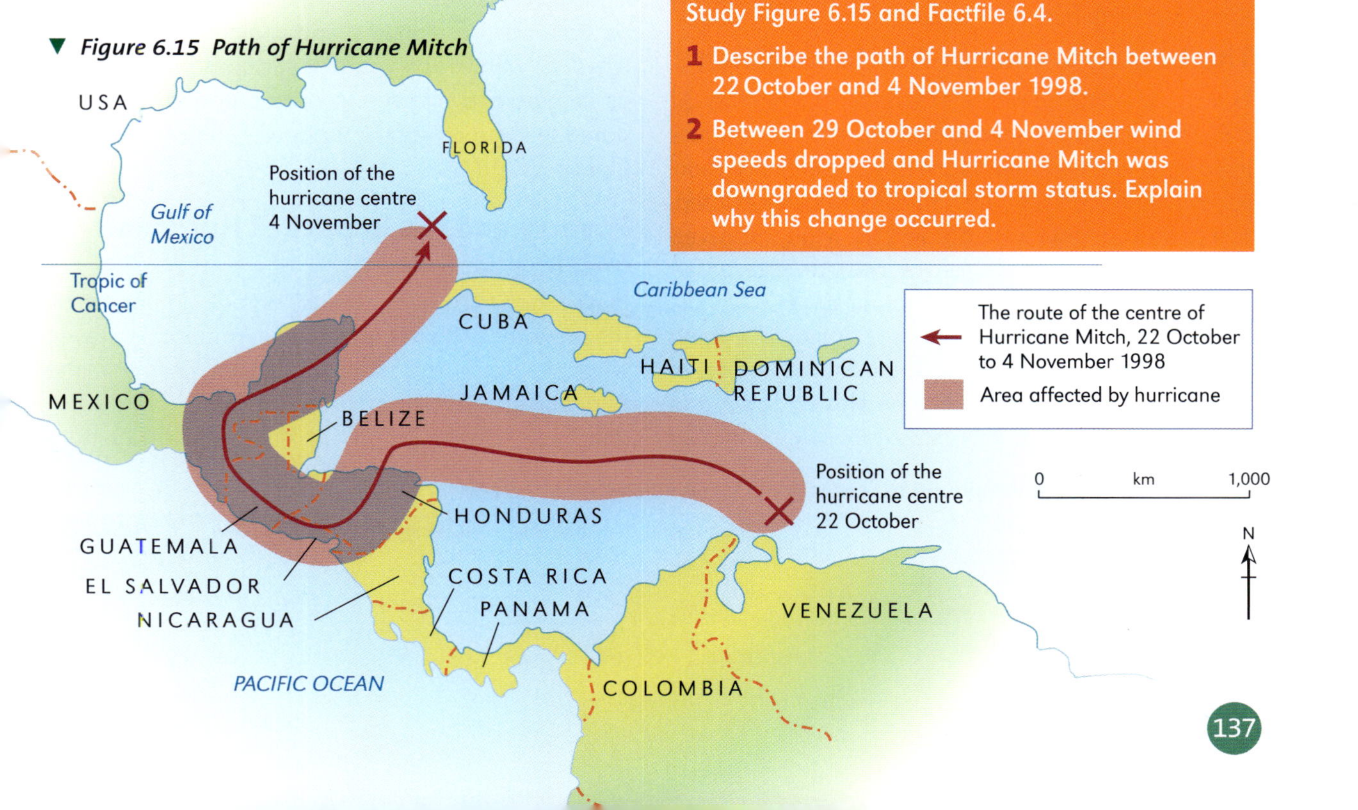

## Chapter 6 Climatic hazards

It has not stopped raining. There are no bridges and the streets are flooded. We are also without water and the electricity. Last night hurricane Mitch was directly over Tegucigalpa. The truth is that I had never seen anything like it. The streets are like rivers. Thousands of houses have collapsed. Even the prison building collapsed. Criminals threw themselves into the water to escape with the police shooting at them. There is no communication with other cities; all the bridges in the country are destroyed. This is a huge disaster. Really, I am very scared. We have no money. The banks and airports are closed; we have no more candles, and no bread. Bodies are floating in the river. I hope it stops raining. The coast is even worst hit by floods and hurricane-force winds. Here it is the rain and rising river levels that are the biggest threat.

▲ *Photograph 6.7 Children in Honduras among the devastation caused by Hurricane Mitch*

◀ *Figure 6.16 Eyewitness account of Hurricane Mitch, Tegucigalpa, Honduras, 1 November 1998*

### The human impact of Hurricane Mitch

Hurricane Mitch directly affected 10% of the 31 million people who live in central America. This figure includes the dead and injured and the many thousands who either lost their homes or were evacuated. The poorest people were hardest hit. Many occupied flimsy houses and were forced to live in areas exposed to floods and landslides (see Photograph 6.7). Whole villages were swept away by floods and mud rushing down mountainsides. In Tegucigalpa, the capital of Honduras, a landslide buried one **shanty town** and partly destroyed two others. Meanwhile, a lack of proper sanitation and poor levels of nutrition created secondary hazards such as disease.

The floods and landslides that accompanied Hurricane Mitch crippled the economy of central America. Damage was estimated at US$6 billion. Agricultural losses were enormous. Export crops, such as bananas, pineapples and melons, were devastated, as were crops for domestic consumption, such as cereals and oil seed. Nearly one quarter of the damage was to roads, bridges, power lines and pipelines.

### Poverty and the impact of Hurricane Mitch

Hurricane Mitch had a hugely damaging impact on the economy and society of central America. However, when we study the effect of similar storms in the Atlantic region, a clear pattern emerges. While the five deadliest Atlantic storms of the twentieth century

*Table 6.3 Levels of development in central America compared with the USA*

|  | Nicaragua | Honduras | Guatemala | El Salvador | USA |
|---|---|---|---|---|---|
| **GDP per capita US$** | 1,023 | 1,256 | 2,735 | 2,618 | 44,155 |
| **Human development index (rank 1–178)** | 120th | 117th | 121st | 101st | 15th |
| **Infant mortality rate per 1000** | 25 | 26 | 29 | 22 | 6 |

*Photograph 6.8 Landslide damage in Honduras caused by Hurricane Mitch*

caused thousands of deaths in central America and the Caribbean, they caused little loss of life in the USA.

It seems that tropical storms, like other natural hazards, hit poor countries (see Tables 6.3 and 6.4) much harder than rich countries. This difference is due almost entirely to poverty. In poor, debt-ridden countries like Honduras, Guatemala and Nicaragua, poverty increases risk for two reasons. First, thousands of people are forced to live in areas exposed to hazards such as storm surges, floods and landslides. Second, governments simply do not have the resources to plan and prepare for natural disasters and so reduce their effects.

Flood and landslide hazards triggered by Hurricane Mitch were made worse by poverty. Poverty, linked to rapid population growth, had already caused severe environmental damage in Nicaragua and Honduras. Steep mountain slopes had been deforested by peasant farmers desperate for land and fuel wood. Forest fires added to the destruction. Without tree cover, heavy rainfall made slopes unstable, generating landslides and mudflows (see Photograph 6.8). Meanwhile many wetlands, which would normally hold back floodwaters, had been drained by peasant farmers desperate for land.

The fact that governments in central America were ill-prepared for a category 5 hurricane added to the disaster. Although the US National Hurricane Center

### Activity 6.9

Read the section in this chapter on protecting people and places from tropical storms (pages 129–130). Suggest ways in which countries such as Honduras, Guatemala and Nicaragua could reduce the risk from tropical storms such as Hurricane Mitch.

*Table 6.4 The five deadliest Atlantic hurricanes*

| Rank | Name | Date | Deaths | Worst affected countries/regions |
|---|---|---|---|---|
| 1 | Mitch | 1998 | 11,000–18,000 | Central America |
| 2 | Fifi | 1974 | 8,000–10,000 | Central America |
| 3 | Unnamed | 1930 | 2,000–8,000 | Dominican Republic |
| 4 | Flora | 1963 | 7,000–8,000 | Cuba, Haiti |
| 5 | Jeanne | 2004 | 3,000–3,500 | Haiti (c. 3,000 deaths), Dominican Republic (18 deaths), Puerto Rico (8 deaths), Florida (5 deaths) |

Natural hazards

issued warnings, once Mitch struck there was no effective disaster planning. Governments simply reacted to emergencies as they arose. Fortunately, the international community responded quickly, providing emergency aid. Over 40 countries gave relief support including equipment, personnel, food and debt forgiveness. Even so, it will take 15 to 20 years for Honduras and Nicaragua to recover fully.

## Case study: Drought in southern Spain

In 2005 Spain experienced its worst drought for 60 years (Figure 6.17). In the first 4 months of the year the country received just one fifth of its normal rainfall. In some areas, there had been hardly any rain for nearly a year. Wildfires in the tinder-dry countryside killed 11 firefighters in July.

### Southern Spain

Southern Spain suffered more than any other region. However, drought and water shortages are common there (see Table 6.5 on page 142). In the past, people learned to live with drought and water shortages, particularly during the summer months.

Today the situation is different. The increase in tourism (see Photograph 6.9) and residential development on the coast, together with the growth of irrigated agriculture (see Photograph 6.10), has doubled the demand for water every 7 years. Water shortages are particularly acute in the Almería-Murcia-Alicante region. So, the problems of drought have been made much worse by major increases in the demand for water in the past 30 years.

By the autumn of 2005, 20% of reservoirs in Mediterranean Spain contained water that was little more than sludge. Overpumping of groundwater had caused a dramatic fall in the water table over wide areas, threatening wildlife in the Doñana National Park and land degradation elsewhere.

### Reducing the impact of drought

In an attempt to solve southern Spain's problems of drought and water shortage, water has been imported from central Spain. In 1979, a large-scale **water transfer scheme** was completed. It linked the

Photograph 6.9 Mass tourism in southern Spain

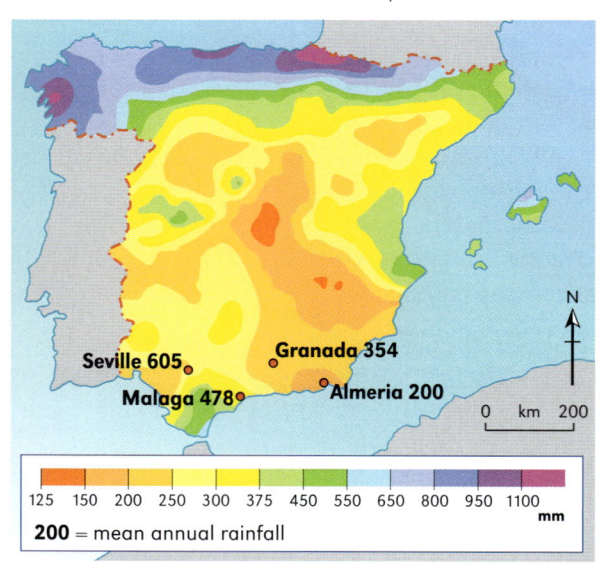

Figure 6.17 Rainfall in Spain, September 2004–August 2005

**Photograph 6.10** Giant plastic greenhouses used in irrigated agriculture in southern Spain

KEVIN BORMAN

### Factfile 6.5 Problems with the Tagus–Murcia water transfer scheme

- The disadvantages of this scheme are economic, social and environmental. It has created problems for both the receiving region (Almería-Murcia-Alicante) and the sending region (the Tagus River basin).
- Water shortages have doubled in the Almería-Murcia-Alicante region since the completion of the scheme in 1979. The availability of water has simply led to greater use.
- The scheme has promoted intensive irrigated agriculture, which is unsustainable.
- Irrigated agriculture has destroyed thousands of hectares of wildlife habitats, and nitrates from chemical fertilisers have contaminated water supplies.
- There has been a 60% reduction in the flow of the Tagus River.
- During periods of drought, flows in the Tagus River are too low to keep the river healthy.
- The reduced flows in the Tagus River are insufficient to dilute polluted tributary waters from Madrid.
- Water transfers have mainly benefited prosperous large farms (i.e. **agribusiness**), rather than small farmers.

### Activity 6.10

1. Using the temperature and precipitation figures in Table 6.5, plot a climate graph for Almería.
2. Calculate the mean annual precipitation for Almería (i.e. sum the monthly totals) and find out what proportion of precipitation normally falls between May and September?
3. Study the rainfall map for Spain from September 2004 to August 2005 (see Figure 6.17). Compare the actual rainfall at Almería, Granada, Malaga and Seville during this period with the expected rainfall.

Natural hazards

## Chapter 6 Climatic hazards

*Table 6.5 Mean monthly temperature and precipitation at Almería, southern Spain*

| Month | Jan | Feb | Mar | Apr | May | Jun | Jul | Aug | Sep | Oct | Nov | Dec |
|---|---|---|---|---|---|---|---|---|---|---|---|---|
| Mean temperature (°C) | 13 | 13 | 14 | 16 | 19 | 22 | 26 | 26 | 24 | 20 | 16 | 13 |
| Average precipitation (mm) | 28 | 18 | 20 | 25 | 13 | 8 | 0 | 0 | 10 | 28 | 30 | 20 |

area to the Tagus River basin, which lies to the north, by canal (see Figure 6.18).

The scheme provided water for **tourism** along the coast and for over 100,000 hectares of melons, tomatoes, broccoli, lettuce, celery and fruit grown in polythene greenhouses. Annual agricultural production tops 1 million tonnes a year, most of which is exported to supermarkets in Germany and the UK. However, the Tagus–Murcia water transfer scheme is controversial (see Factfile 6.5).

Currently, the fastest growing demand for water in the south is from residential development and the tourism industry on the coast. Spain built 700,000 new homes in 2004. Half of these were holiday homes on the south coast meant for foreign buyers. These developments, with swimming pools, showers and golf courses, suck up precious water (see Figure 6.19). A single golf course uses as much water as a town of 20,000 people. With 40 new courses planned for Murcia, and a similar number for Almería and Alicante, the sustainability of these developments, in a drought-prone region, is highly questionable.

Already there are signs that water resources are running out in southern Spain. In some places, the water table has fallen by 250 m in just 20 years, suggesting that the limits of sustainable supply have been reached. Despite this, the government wants to increase supplies by using more water transfer schemes, wells and even desalination plants on the coast.

▲ Figure 6.18 The Tagus River and the Almeria-Murcia-Alicante water transfer scheme

Figure 6.19 Golf courses in southern Spain

### Activity 6.11

Calculate the amount of water consumed in a year by an average 18-hole golf course in southern Spain. Assume that 360,000 m² need irrigating and 9 litres of water are used per m² for 300 days a year.

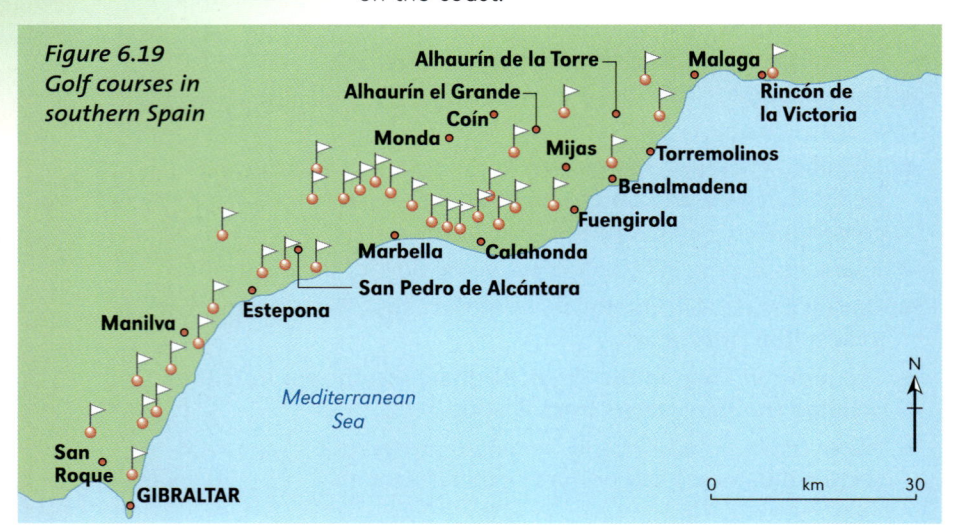

# Theme 4 Economic development

# Chapter 7 Development and employment

## Part 1 What is development?

### Measuring development

There are several ways of measuring development. One is to look at country's wealth. The most common measure of a country's wealth is GDP per capita (see Figure 7.1). Using GDP per capita enables us to define rich countries as 'more developed' and poor countries as 'less developed'. However, measures of income like this do not show how

> **Key ideas**
> - The concept of development includes economic well-being and quality of life.
> - Economic well-being and quality of life can be measured by a range of economic and social indicators.
> - Countries are at different stages of development.

### Factfile 7.1 Measures of development

**GDP per capita**
- GDP per capita is the total value of goods and services produced by a country or region, divided by its population.
- GDP per capita can often give a misleading idea of the average wealth of a country or region because:
  - a disproportionate share of a country's income may be in the hands of a small minority (e.g. Saudi Arabia, United Arab Emirates)
  - foreign companies may produce a large proportion of GDP (e.g. Namibia); much of the income that these companies generate could go to shareholders overseas
  - it does not always take account of prices and the cost of living, i.e. purchasing power parity
- GDP does not take quality of life into account, e.g. education, healthcare, freedom from crime, access to clean water and an unpolluted environment.

**Human development index (HDI)**
- The HDI was devised by the UN to describe human development (i.e. both economic and social well-being) within countries.
- The HDI is based on three factors: life expectancy, literacy and GDP per capita.
- The HDI varies from 0 (least developed) to 1 (most developed).

# Chapter 7 Development and employment

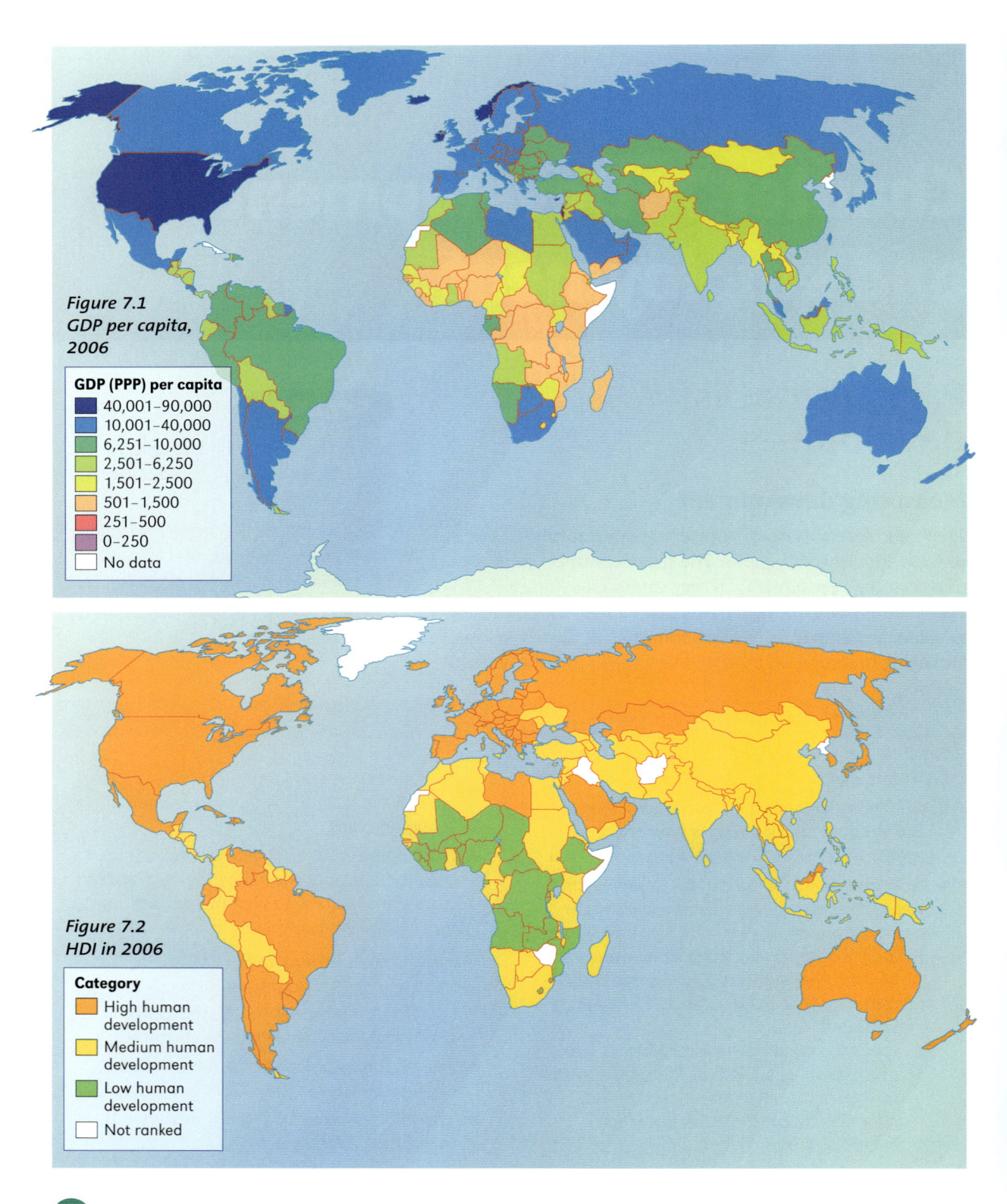

*Figure 7.1 GDP per capita, 2006*

**GDP (PPP) per capita**
- 40,001–90,000
- 10,001–40,000
- 6,251–10,000
- 2,501–6,250
- 1,501–2,500
- 501–1,500
- 251–500
- 0–250
- No data

*Figure 7.2 HDI in 2006*

**Category**
- High human development
- Medium human development
- Low human development
- Not ranked

wealth is shared out or what access people have to essential services such as education and healthcare.

The United Nations (UN) argues that development is about improving people's social well-being as well as their economic well-being. This is human development rather than economic development. For instance, people with low incomes may nonetheless have a decent **quality of life**, if they have free healthcare, free education and clean water.

The UN publishes a **human development index** (**HDI**) for 179 countries (see Factfile 7.1). In 2006 Iceland topped the HDI rankings; Sierra Leone in west Africa ranked lowest (see Figure 7.2).

## Global patterns of development

It is clear that, whether measuring it by GDP per capita or the HDI, there are large contrasts in global development. At the simplest level countries can be divided into two groups: more economically developed countries (MEDCs) and less economically developed countries (LEDCs). However, this division has weaknesses. It takes no account of **social development** or the large number of countries that are neither very rich nor very poor (e.g. Argentina and Thailand). On the basis of the HDI, the UN divides countries into three groups: high, medium and low human development. The 2006 ranking placed 75 countries in the 'high' category, 77 in the 'medium' category, and 25 in the 'low' category.

Geographically, the global pattern of development is very uneven. Most MEDCs are in the northern hemisphere, in Europe and North America. The main exceptions are Japan, South Korea and Singapore in Asia, and Australia and New Zealand in the southern hemisphere. Most LEDCs are either in the tropics or in the southern hemisphere, in Africa, South America and Asia. Because of the uneven geography of development, a distinction is often made between the 'rich North' and the 'poor South'. The boundary separating them is known as the **Brandt Line** (see Figures 7.1 and 7.2). The UN's HDI classification underlines the low development status of much of Africa: of the 25 countries in the low development category, 24 are in sub-Saharan Africa.

## Cuba: developed or less developed?

The example of Cuba shows just how difficult it is to label a country 'more developed' or 'less developed'. Cuba is the largest island in the Caribbean and in 2009 had a population of 11.5 million (see Figure 7.3). In economic terms it is

*Table 7.1 Comparison of GDP per capita and HDI rankings by country (2006), in which 1 is most developed and 179 is least developed*

|  | GDP per capita rank | HDI rank |
|---|---|---|
| Botswana | 61 | 126 |
| China | 111 | 94 |
| Costa Rica | 73 | 50 |
| Cuba | 97 | 48 |
| Iran | 87 | 84 |
| Poland | 51 | 39 |
| Saudi Arabia | 42 | 55 |
| South Africa | 70 | 125 |
| Sweden | 9 | 7 |
| UK | 13 | 21 |

### Activity 7.1

1 Put the countries in Table 7.1 in rank order, for GDP per capita and for HDI.

2 Which countries have a quality of life (measured by HDI) that is:
(a) Better than you would expect from their GDP per capita rank?
(b) Worse than you would expect from their GDP per capita rank?

3 Which three countries show the largest differences between GDP per capita and HDI?

Economic development

## Chapter 7 Development and employment

### Activity 7.2

1. Use the information on development to fill in the missing words in the following paragraph:

   The ........ Line divides countries into two groups: the more economically developed (MEDCs) and the ........ ........ ........ (LEDCs). Most MEDCs are found in the ........ hemisphere, north of the tropics. Australia and New Zealand are exceptions: they are MEDCs that are located in the ........ hemisphere. Most LEDCs are found in the tropics and in the ........ hemisphere, in Africa, South America and ........ . Canada, one of the world's richest countries, is an MEDC, and Niger, one of the poorest, is a LEDC. Niger is a country in the poorest continent — ......... .

2. Development can be measured using a number of indicators, such as GDP per capita, life expectancy and infant mortality rate. Explain what each of these measures means.

3. Select one other indicator you could use to measure development. Explain your choice.

a relatively poor country. Table 7.1 shows that Cuba's GDP per capita ranked it 97th in the world in 2006. However, its HDI ranking placed it 48th. In terms of the quality of healthcare and education, Cuba is not far behind the US and Canada.

The explanation for Cuba's impressive social development is its government. Following the communist revolution in 1959, the Cuban government pledged to reduce poverty and promote social development. The results have been remarkable.

In 1960, the average life expectancy at birth was less than 60 years; today it is 77.5 — comparable to the USA. Progress in reducing infant mortality has been even more impressive. Cuba's infant mortality rate fell from 43.9 per 1,000 in 1970 to 5.8 per 1,000 in 2009 (see Figure 7.4) — a level that is even lower than the USA. Everyone has access to free medical care. Progress in education has also been impressive: today, 96% of the adult population can read and write; primary school enrolment is 100%; and 14% of the population are graduates (see Photograph 7.1).

Clearly, economic measures of development fail to provide an accurate picture of well-being and the quality of life in Cuba. Cubans may be relatively poorly off in terms of income, but they are as healthy and well educated as most people in Europe and North America.

▶ Figure 7.3 Location of Cuba

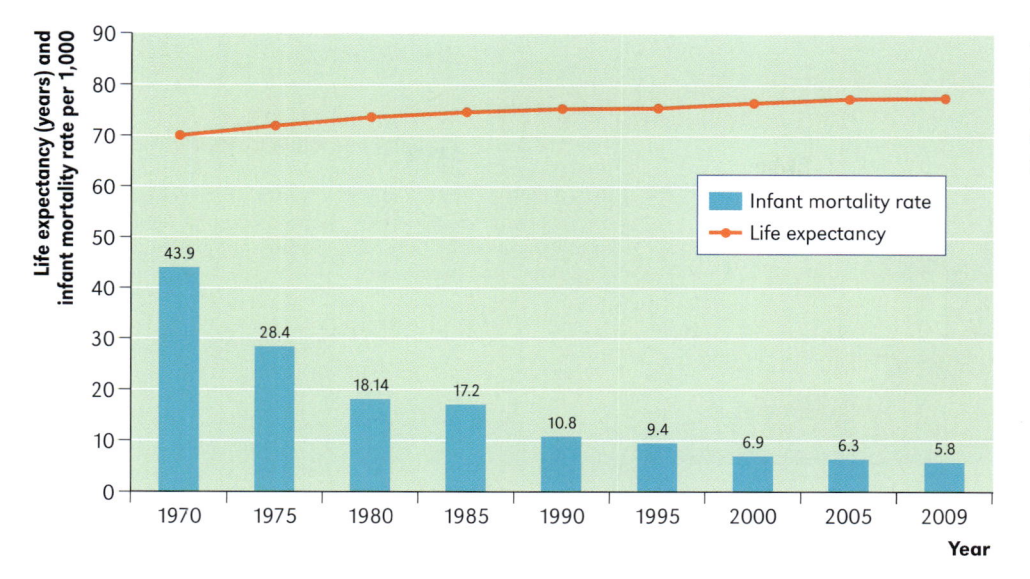

◀ *Figure 7.4 Infant mortality rate and life expectancy in Cuba, 1970–2009*

## Explaining differences between countries in levels of development

Many factors explain the differences in levels of development between countries. They include a country's natural and human resources; its population, geography, history; and its government (see Figure 7.5).

*Photograph 7.1 A school in Cuba; the standard of education is as high as in Europe and the USA*

# Chapter 7 Development and employment

*Figure 7.5*

### Resources ▲

Natural resources include fuels, metallic ores, timber, soils, climate, etc. that are valuable to people. Some MEDCs, such as Canada, Australia and Saudi Arabia, owe their development in part to their rich natural resource base. These resources have assisted manufacturing and industrial growth and wealth creation. However, many countries with few natural resources, such as Japan and the Netherlands, are among the most successful in the world. This is largely due to the quality of their workforces, which are highly educated and highly skilled. Unlike natural resources, these human resources are essential to development.

### Population ▶

Population growth and population structure (see Chapter 3) play a key role in development. Over the past 50 years most poor countries have doubled, and in some cases tripled, their populations. Growth on this scale often exceeds economic growth and holds back development. Overwhelmed by sheer numbers, many LEDCs have been unable to grow the economy fast enough to provide jobs, housing, education and other basic services. Rapid population growth also produces unbalanced age structures, with unusually large proportions of children and high rates of dependency. An ideal structure for successful economic growth is one where a large proportion of the population comprises economically productive adults (aged 18 to 65 years).

### Geography ▼

The location of a country can influence its development. Remote and landlocked countries without direct access to the coast are disadvantaged in terms of international trade and economic development. Isolation can be reinforced by mountainous relief (e.g. Tibet, Nepal) and dense forests (e.g. Brazil and Indonesia).

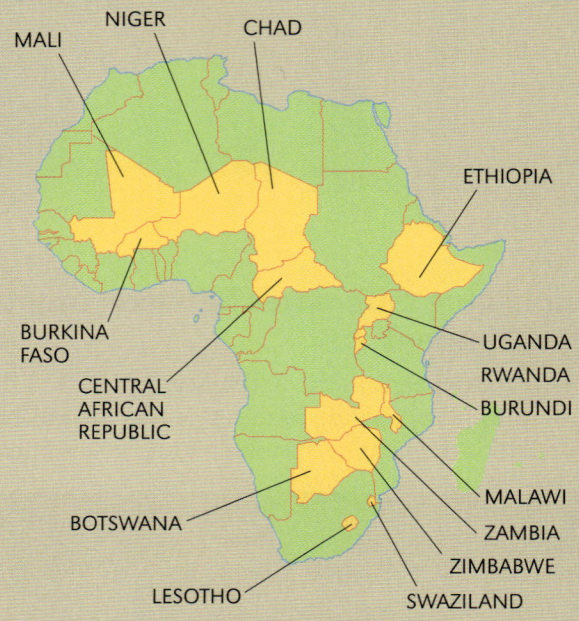

▲ *Land-locked countries of Africa*

OCR (B) GCSE Geography

## Theme 4

### History ▶

The colonial history of many LEDCs, particularly in Africa, has stifled their development. These countries, as colonies of imperial powers such as Britain and France, were used as sources of raw materials, and markets for exports of manufactured goods. This one-sided relationship was designed to benefit the imperial power. Although independent today, these countries continue to depend on exports of primary goods to MEDCs. Many are also burdened with huge debts that further limit their prospects for economic development.

### Politics ▼

Poor governance has handicapped dozens of LEDCs in their drive to development. Many governments are corrupt, channelling money that could be used for development to the military or to the governing elite. In the mid-twentieth century, political independence from former imperial powers created states that had little sense of national coherence. Tribal conflicts, and meddling by outside countries in their internal affairs, have triggered numerous civil wars in Africa.

▲ *Africa in colonial times*

Economic development

Chapter 7 Development and employment

# Part 2 Development and international aid

## Key ideas
- Development can be affected by international aid.
- Aid should be sustainable in terms of economic costs, impacts on the environment and effects on people.

## What is international aid?

International aid is money or resources transferred from rich to poor countries. Crucially the donor countries (or organisations like the UN and World Bank) do not expect full or direct repayment.

There are two types of international aid. Bilateral aid is assistance given by a donor government to a recipient country. In 2007, nearly 70% of all international aid was bilateral. Bilateral aid mainly consists of technical assistance, debt relief and humanitarian aid. Multilateral aid is provided by donor agencies such as the World Bank and IMF, and NGOs. These organisations are funded by the world's richest countries that belong to the Organisation for Economic Cooperation and Development (OECD).

## Why countries give international aid

The main purpose of international aid is economic. For recipient countries international aid increases investment, helps pay interest on foreign debt, provides foreign exchange (e.g. US$) to pay for imports and assists the development of infrastructure such as roads, ports and airports. Donor countries may also provide aid for humanitarian reasons, such as alleviating poverty.

▶ Figure 7.6 Percentage GNI given as international aid, 2007

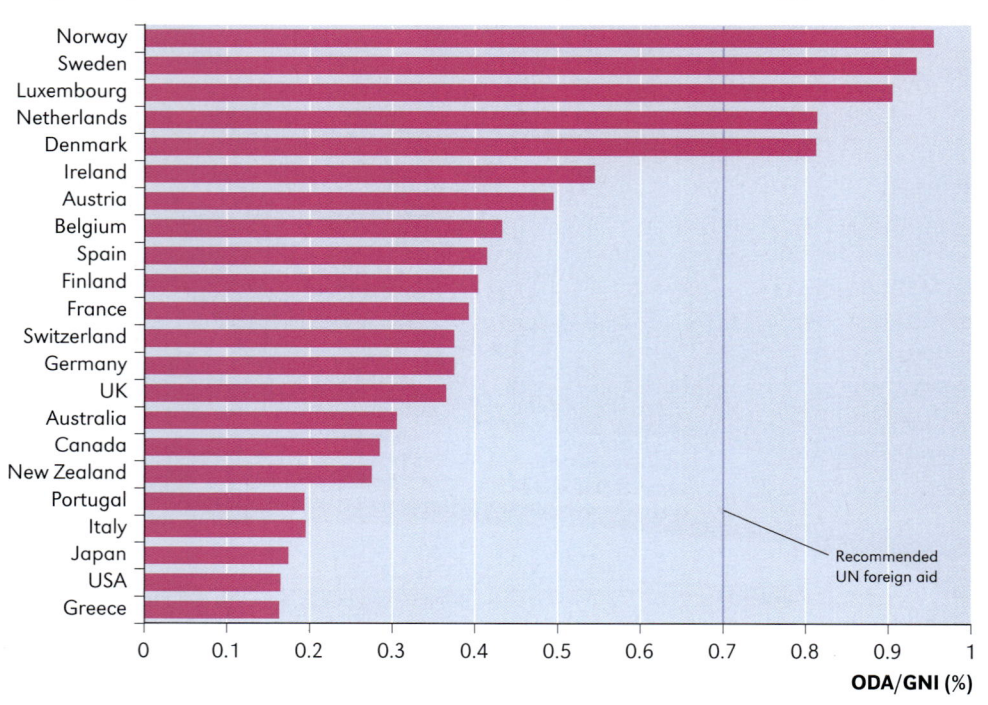

Theme 4

## Factfile 7.2 International aid

- **International aid** is the transfer of money, food, equipment and technical assistance from rich countries to poor countries.
- Long-term international aid should promote development, be sustainable and reduce poverty.
- Aid given by one country to another is called **bilateral aid**.
- Multilateral aid is assistance given to poor countries by international bodies such as the United Nations (UN), the International Monetary Fund (IMF), the World Bank, and non-governmental organisations (NGOs) like Oxfam, Christian Aid and Red Crescent.
- Since 1970, the UN has recommended that rich countries should give 0.7% of their gross national income as international aid.
- The average proportion of gross national income given in aid by rich countries is just 0.23% (see Figure 7.6). The most generous donors are Norway, Sweden, Luxembourg and the Netherlands. The least generous are Greece, the USA, Japan and Italy. In 2006 the UK gave aid worth 0.36% of its income.

However, the benefits of bilateral aid are not all one way. Recipient countries may offer a market for the exports of a donor country, or a source of essential raw materials and energy supplies. For example, in the last few years China has provided significant bilateral aid to the Democratic Republic of Congo (DRC), giving China privileged access to the DRC's vast mineral wealth. Multilateral aid often has conditions attached. To receive aid from the IMF or World Bank, recipient governments must implement strict economic policies.

## Sustainable development aid

Sustainable development aims to 'meet the needs of the present without compromising the ability of future generations to meet their own needs.' Ideally, all

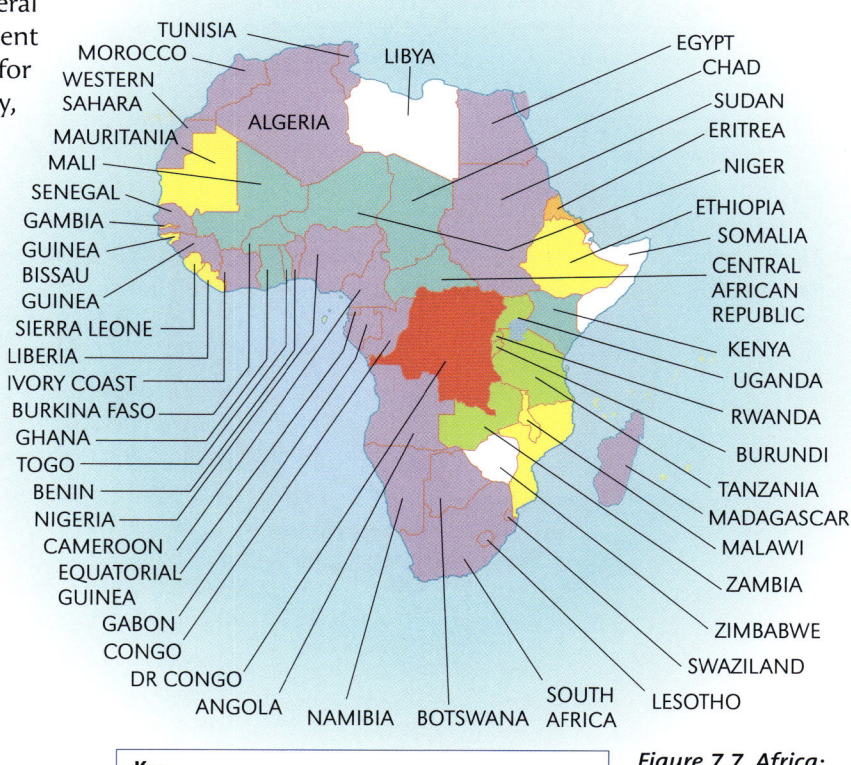

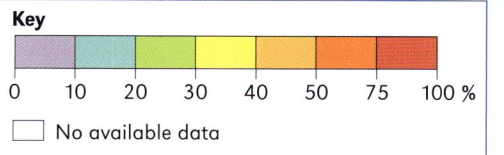

Figure 7.7 Africa: dependence on international aid

Key: 0 10 20 30 40 50 75 100 %
No available data

Economic development

# Chapter 7 Development and employment

## Activity 7.3

According to the Organisation for Economic Cooperation and Development (OECD) Africa receives about a third of the total aid given by governments around the world.

1. Compare and contrast the dependence of African countries on international aid (see Figure 7.7) with levels of poverty, defined by GDP per capita (see Figure 7.1) and the human development index (see Figure 7.2).
2. The Democratic Republic of Congo (DRC) is heavily dependent on international aid. Give an account of the international aid deal between the Congo and China by searching the internet. Start by watching the BBC video report at: **news.bbc.co.uk/1/hi/programmes/newsnight/7347686.stm**.

development aid, targeted at reducing global poverty, should achieve this aim. It should not, for example, cause environmental damage, diminish **renewable resources** such as water, fertile soils and forests, or increase inequalities within society. Development projects are only sustainable if:

- consumption of the new resources made available remains in balance with with supply
- the technologies and resources needed to maintain them are accessible to local people and will remain so in the future

## Case study: Large-scale development aid: the Nam Theun 2 dam project in Laos

The Nam Theun 2 (NT2) is a US$1.3 billion project to build a dam on the Nam Theun River, a tributary of the Mekong River, in Laos, southeast Asia (see Figure 7.8). Due for completion in 2009, the dam will be 50 m high and 320 m long, and it will flood a 450 km² area on the Nakai Plateau. Water stored in the reservoir will be diverted into 40 km long tunnels leading to a power station on the Xe Bang Fai River (see Photograph 7.2). The project is funded by loans from the **World Bank** (an organisation that provides finance to support development projects in LEDCs) and the Asian Development Bank. It will generate 1,000 MW of electricity, most of it for export to nearby Thailand.

Laos is one of the poorest countries in Asia. In 2006, its GDP per capita was just US$590; life expectancy at birth was 55 years; and nearly three quarters of its population survived on less than US$2 a day. By exporting electricity, the project should provide foreign currency and help tackle poverty in the country.

### Controversial issues

NT2 is one of several big dam projects in Laos and is controversial. Building the dam is a massive project that relies heavily on loans and foreign aid. There is also the question of its sustainability. The key issue is whether the economic benefits of the scheme outweigh its social, economic and environmental costs. Some views on the scheme are given in Table 7.2.

◀ **Figure 7.8** Location of the Nam Theun 2 dam project

# Theme 4

## Factfile 7.3 The economic, social and environmental impact of NT2

- The Laos government estimates that the project will earn US$150 million each year by exporting electricity to Thailand. This is a lot of money for a poor country like Laos. However, the scheme will saddle the country with a large foreign debt.
- The reservoir created by the dam will flood one third of the Nakai Plateau and displace 4,500 people.
- Flooding will destroy habitats and wildlife in one of the largest remaining areas of rainforest in southeast Asia.
- The livelihoods of over 100,000 villagers who live downstream and rely on the Xe Bang Fai and Nam Theun rivers for fish, drinking water and agriculture could be threatened (fish migration will be severely disrupted, and gardens currently irrigated for farming will disappear).
- Big dam projects like NT2 are often criticised as unsustainable. Many critics argue that they cause environmental degradation, destroy farming and fisheries, and increase inequality and poverty.

## Activity 7.4

1 Describe how the NT2 project will bring both advantages and disadvantages for the local population on the Nakai Plateau and in the valleys of the Nam Theun and Xe Bang Fei rivers.

2 Describe two ways in which the dam will affect the environment.

3 Complete the second column of Table 7.2. The first row has been completed for you.

4 Study all the information relating to NT2 (including Table 7.2) and then prepare a statement (for discussion in class) saying whether you support or oppose the project. You should consider the project's social, economic and environmental impacts and its sustainability.

Photograph 7.2 The Nam Theun dam under construction

Economic development

## Chapter 7 Development and employment

*Table 7.2 Arguments for and against the NT2 project*

| Views on the NT2 scheme | Does the speaker support or oppose the scheme? Why? |
|---|---|
| The NT2 project is an essential part of the country's long-term development plan. *Laos government minister* | Supports the scheme. Laos is a poor country. Development is a long-term process and NT2 will play a key part in the government's long-term strategy. |
| The NT2 power project is an ideal project, which will bring income and wealth to the Laos people in future. *Nakai district chief* | |
| The revenue this project generates will help the government improve the lives of some of the poorest people in Asia. *Asian Development Bank (ADB) spokesperson* | |
| We believe that selling electricity is the best way for Laos to increase the money it can invest in health, education and basic infrastructure for the benefit of the poor. *World Bank president* | |
| We fear for the lives of tens of thousands of poor Laotian farmers who will lose land, fisheries and other resources. *Aviva Imhof, IRG (US environmental group)* | |
| Villagers will be given small plots of land [as compensation] with soil that is heavily leached, infertile and poorly suited to crop production. *Aviva Imhof, IRG (US environmental group* | |
| The Nakai-Nam Theun protected area ranks among the most important in the world. Over 400 species of birds occur there, including 50 species threatened with extinction. *Spokesperson for World Wide Fund for Nature* | |
| NT2 is not needed because Laos already produces more power than it needs and Thailand currently has a surplus electricity capacity. *Spokesperson for IRG* | |

# Theme 4

## Case study: Small-scale development aid: improving water supplies in Ghana

Ghana is a poor country in west Africa (see Figure 7.9 and Factfile 7.4). Like many other African countries, it suffers serious water shortages. In the capital, Accra, only one quarter of the population has a 24-hour water supply. Thirty-five per cent have supplies for just 2 days a week, and on the outskirts of the city around 10% have no piped water at all. Water supplies in rural areas are even more limited — only 44% have piped water.

### Water and human health

Lack of clean water and poor sanitation blight the lives of millions of people in Ghana. Diarrhoea kills thousands of children every year. Intestinal parasites, such as hookworms, affect 80% of children in rural areas, causing anaemia and other serious illnesses. Many people die because they are not educated about the dangers of contaminated water and poor sanitation (see Photograph 7.3).

Figure 7.9 Map showing the location of Ghana

### Aid to improve water supplies in Asampombisi

Asampombisi is small village of 680 people in eastern Ghana. This is a remote region where extreme poverty is the norm. In Asampombisi the villagers grow millet and other crops, live in mud houses, and until recently

Photograph 7.3 People collecting drinking water in Ghana, west Africa

### Factfile 7.4 Ghana

- Population: 23.22 million
- Rate of population growth per year: 1.9%
- **Life expectancy** in years: 60
- **Infant mortality** rate per 1,000: 51
- Average **GDP per person** per year: US$573
- Population living in poverty: 44.8%
- Population with access to improved water supplies: urban — 93%; rural — 46%
- Improved water sources include piped water, public taps, boreholes with pumps, protected wells, protected springs and rainwater

Economic development

had no access to safe drinking water or proper sanitation. The only source of water, both for villagers and animals, was a muddy stream. Women and girls spent several hours a day collecting water; and because the water was contaminated, sickness and diarrhoea, especially among children, were common.

Water Aid is a British charity that provides safe domestic water, sanitation and hygiene education to the world's poorest people in Africa and Asia. Its solutions are low-cost, sustainable and based on simple technology. At Asampombisi, safe water was provided by digging a 10 m deep well and providing a hand pump. Clean water is now available all year round, even during the dry season. This single event has transformed the lives of local people. Apoyanga Nash, a mother with five children, explains:

> In the time I have lived here in Asampombisi, our lives have improved now that we have clean water. Now our health is changing and improving. We don't suffer from diarrhoea and stomach pains any more. Now I don't spend as much time collecting water, I have time to do other work around my home, like washing and cooking, and I have enough time to weave baskets. I am happy that my new baby will have good water and not suffer the way the other children did. I hope the clean water will help my children to develop, to go to school and finish their education.

### Activity 7.5

1. State three benefits Apoyanga and her family gain from the provision of clean water.
2. Explain how the Asampombisi project is an example of sustainable international aid.

With the help of Water Aid, sanitation in the village is also being improved. The first toilets have been built to provide safe sanitation, which will prevent any contamination of water supplies during the wet season. As a result everyone in the village should have a healthier and brighter future.

The help provided by Water Aid at Asampombisi is small scale, and low cost, but it has made a positive difference to the lives of some of Africa's poorest people. Moreover, because it improves the quality of life of local people without in any way compromising the quality of life of future generations, it is truly sustainable.

# Part 3 Employment structures and patterns

## Employment structures and patterns

Employment is divided into three main sectors: primary, secondary and tertiary/quaternary (see Factfile 7.5). Together these sectors are known as the employment structure. Employment structures are not fixed, but change in the course of a country's economic development. Normally, economic development triggers the following sequence of change in employment structure: first a rapid reduction in the primary sector, followed by moderate growth of the secondary sector, and finally a large expansion of the tertiary/quaternary sector.

### Key ideas

- Employment structures vary between countries.
- Employment structures change over time and may change in future.

### Global contrasts in employment structures

Large differences exist between countries in the size and importance of their primary, secondary and tertiary sectors (see Figure 7.10). For example, compare China with the UK. Forty-three per cent of China's workers are in the primary sector, compared with just 2% in the UK;

# Theme 4

## Activity 7.6

Arrange the following activities into primary, secondary and tertiary/quaternary (i.e. services) sectors:

- Water supply
- Fertiliser production
- Paper making
- Forestry
- Textile production
- Banks
- Publishing
- Iron and steel production
- Estate agents
- Taxi firms

## Factfile 7.5 Employment sectors

There are three main employment sectors: **primary**, **secondary** and **tertiary/quaternary**.

- The **primary sector** comprises activities that produce food and source energy, minerals and raw materials. Examples of primary industries are farming, fishing and mining.

- The **secondary sector** consists of manufacturing industries. Most manufacturing industries either process **raw materials** (e.g. oil refining), fabricate semi-finished products (e.g. making leather shoes) or assemble finished parts (e.g. car manufacturing). By processing, fabricating and assembling, manufacturing adds value to products.

- The **tertiary sector** is often used as a general term that covers all service activities. However, if we define a fourth employment sector (i.e. quaternary), then the tertiary sector includes public services such as education, healthcare and local government; public utilities such as electricity, water and gas; and retailing and wholesaling. The **quaternary sector** consists of producer services such as financial services, accounting, advertising, marketing etc. that serve other economic activities such as commerce and industry directly

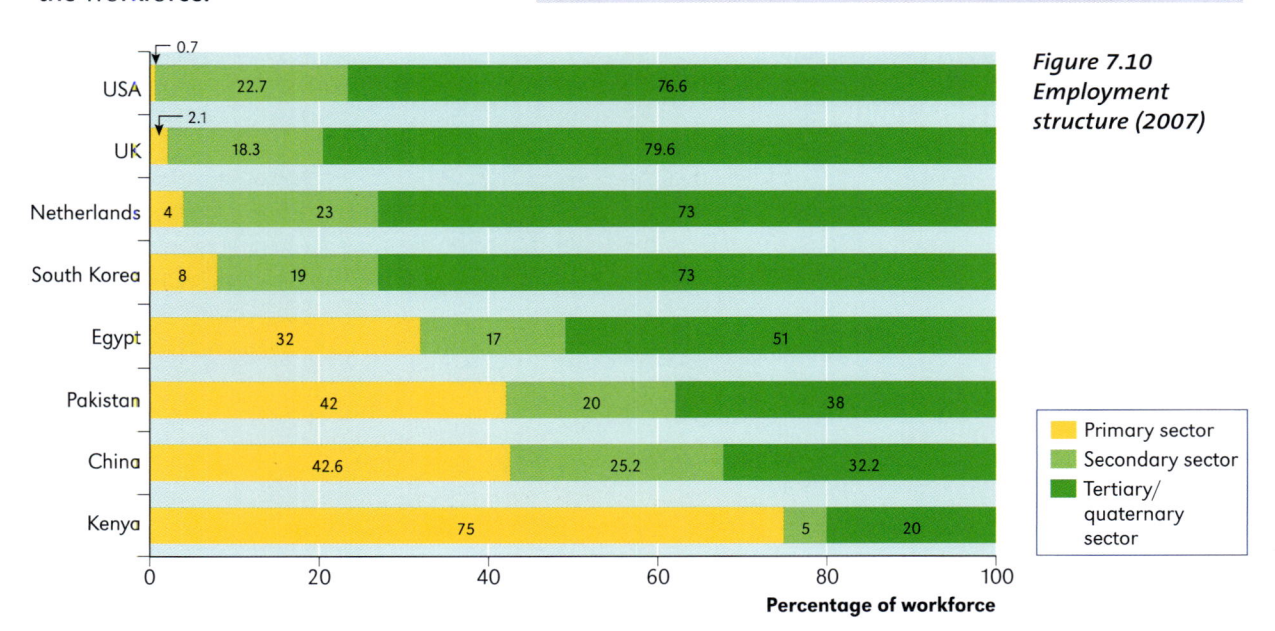

nearly 80% of employment in the UK is in the service sector, which employs just 32% of Chinese workers. At the global scale employment structure follows a predictable pattern:

- Primary activities (especially agriculture) dominate employment in the least developed countries.
- In MEDCs the service sector on average accounts for around 75% of the workforce.

*Figure 7.10 Employment structure (2007)*

| Country | Primary | Secondary | Tertiary/quaternary |
|---|---|---|---|
| USA | 0.7 | 22.7 | 76.6 |
| UK | 2.1 | 18.3 | 79.6 |
| Netherlands | 4 | 23 | 73 |
| South Korea | 8 | 19 | 73 |
| Egypt | 32 | 17 | 51 |
| Pakistan | 42 | 20 | 38 |
| China | 42.6 | 25.2 | 32.2 |
| Kenya | 75 | 5 | 20 |

Percentage of workforce

Economic development

# Chapter 7 Development and employment

- The secondary sector employs only a minority of the workforce in both the poorest and richest countries. Even in middle-income countries, such as the Czech Republic and Taiwan, secondary activities rarely account for more than 35% of the workforce.
- The secondary sector becomes relatively more important in industrialising (emerging) economies such as China and Brazil.

## Explaining global contrasts in employment

Economic development is the single most important influence on employment structure. There are three stages of development: **pre-industrial**, **industrial** and **post-industrial**. Each has its own employment structure (see Figure 7.11).

Countries yet to undergo economic development are in the pre-industrial phase. Agriculture dominates employment in the least developed countries. Most of these countries, which are the poorest in the world, are in sub-Saharan Africa and Asia.

The industrial stage includes countries currently experiencing rapid industrial growth. China is the most important of these countries. In the past 20 years, rapid industrialisation has transformed it into the 'workshop of the world'. China is not the only emerging economy in east Asia: others include Malaysia, Taiwan and Thailand.

MEDCs are in the post-industrial phase. In some countries, such as the USA and the UK, four fifths of the workforce is now in the service sector. This sector continues to grow as the manufacturing and farming sectors decline.

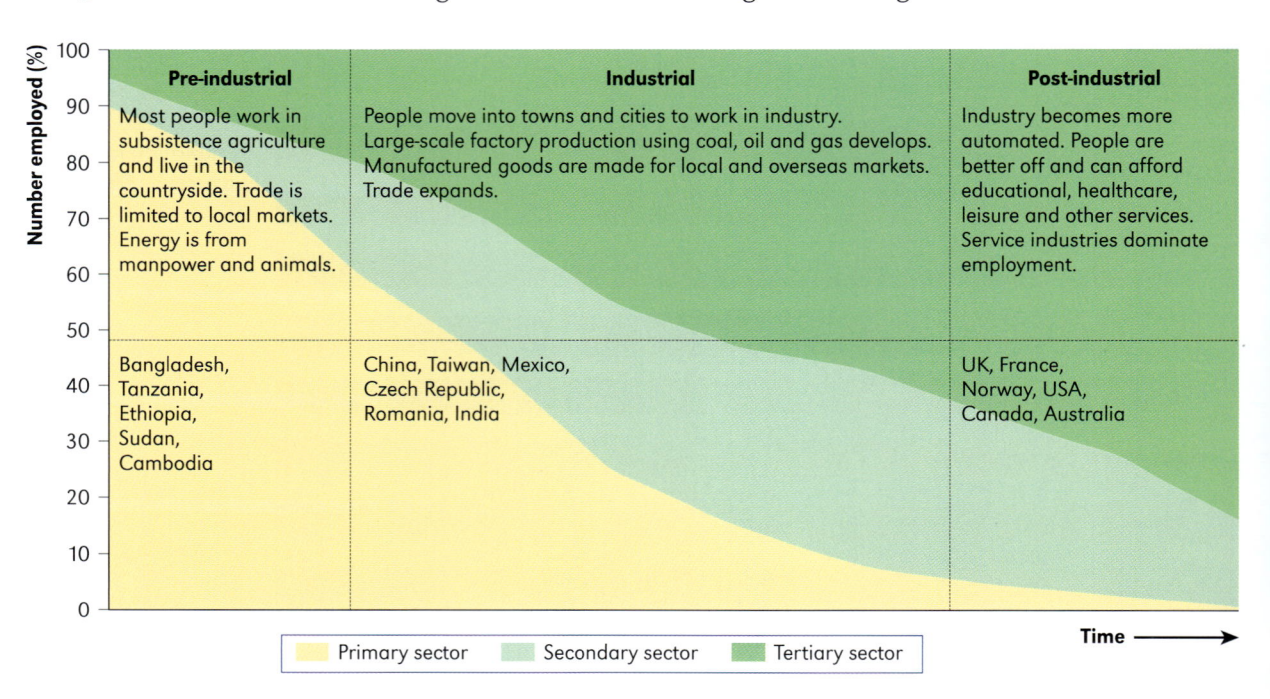

*Figure 7.11 Sectoral model of employment change*

| Pre-industrial | Industrial | Post-industrial |
|---|---|---|
| Most people work in subsistence agriculture and live in the countryside. Trade is limited to local markets. Energy is from manpower and animals. | People move into towns and cities to work in industry. Large-scale factory production using coal, oil and gas develops. Manufactured goods are made for local and overseas markets. Trade expands. | Industry becomes more automated. People are better off and can afford educational, healthcare, leisure and other services. Service industries dominate employment. |
| Bangladesh, Tanzania, Ethiopia, Sudan, Cambodia | China, Taiwan, Mexico, Czech Republic, Romania, India | UK, France, Norway, USA, Canada, Australia |

Primary sector — Secondary sector — Tertiary sector

# Changing employment structures

## UK

Figure 7.12 shows how the UK's employment structure has changed since 1840. Before the nineteenth century most people worked in agriculture and lived on the land. Yet by 1850 employment had undergone a dramatic change. The **Industrial Revolution** was in full swing and towns and cities were growing rapidly. At this time manufacturing employed over half of the working population, and for the next century industry dominated the UK's economy.

From the mid-twentieth century to the present day, employment in industry has been in decline. This process quickened in the 1980s — a period of rapid **deindustrialisation**. Many factory tasks became automated and thousands of workers lost their jobs. Although output from industry continued to increase, fewer workers were needed. Meanwhile, poorer countries in Asia and South America began to develop their own industries. It became cheaper to outsource production from the UK and import manufactured goods from these countries. As people in the UK became richer, the demand for services increased and more and more people found jobs in the service sector — in hotels, restaurants, financial services, shops, entertainment, travel, education and healthcare.

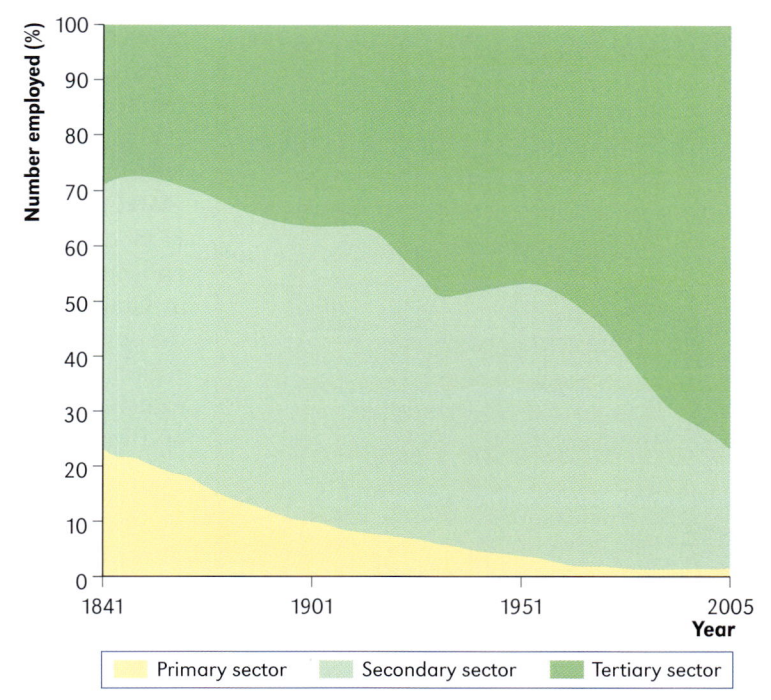

*Figure 7.12 Changing employment sectors in the UK, 1841–2005*

### Activity 7.7

Study Figure 7.12.

1 Describe the changes in the primary and secondary sectors between 1841 and 2005.

2 Suggest two reasons for the rapid growth of the tertiary sector after 1950.

## China

China is industrialising rapidly and, as you would expect, its employment structure is changing rapidly too (see Table 7.3). Economic change began in the late 1970s, when China's communist government relaxed its control over the economy. Small businesses and **light industries** were encouraged, and China was opened up to trade and foreign investment.

*Table 7.3 China's changing employment structure, 1978–2007 (%)*

|  | Primary sector | Secondary sector | Tertiary/quaternary sector |
|---|---|---|---|
| 1978 | 70.5 | 17.3 | 12.2 |
| 1990 | 60.1 | 22.4 | 18.5 |
| 2007 | 42.6 | 25.2 | 32.2 |

Economic development

# Chapter 7 Development and employment

> **Activity 7.8**
>
> Look at Figure 7.10, which shows the employment structures of several countries in 2007.
>
> **1** Define the terms primary, secondary, tertiary and quaternary activities.
>
> **2** Compare the employment structure of the USA (an MEDC) with that of Pakistan (an LEDC).
>
> **3** Suggest reasons for the differences between the employment structures of the two countries.
>
> **4** (a) Using the data in Table 7.3 draw an area chart (similar to Figure 7.12) to show China's changing employment structure between 1978 and 2007.
> (b) Describe the main changes in China's employment structure between 1978 and 2007.

Between 1978 and 2006 China's gross domestic product (GDP) quadrupled, and its economy became the second largest in the world. Today more than 160 million people work in China's manufacturing industries. Leading **multi-national corporations** (**MNCs**), such as General Motors, Siemens, Nike, Honda and Panasonic, have invested heavily in China, and new industrial regions, like the Pearl River Delta in Guangdong Province in southern China, have developed. Located on the coast, factories in this region can easily export goods such as clothing, footwear and electronics to markets in North America and Europe.

The Chinese government has attracted investment by lowering taxes and customs duties for foreign firms. But the main attraction for US, European and Japanese companies is China's low labour costs. For example, Chinese workers making cotton jeans are paid around 50p an hour — just one fortieth of wage rates in the USA.

# Theme 4 Economic development

# Chapter 8 Economic activity

## Part 1 The location of economic activities

### Types of economic activity

We saw in Chapter 7 (see Factfile 7.5) that economic activities can be grouped into primary, secondary, tertiary and quaternary sectors. A range of locational factors influence the geography of each activity (see Figure 8.1 and Table 8.1). Some activities, such as farming, energy generation and mining, are strongly influenced by physical or environmental factors. For manufacturing, economic considerations such as the cost of labour or the supply of materials and components are most important; while for service activities, in the tertiary and quaternary sectors, locations are often chosen that give good access to consumers and markets.

> **Key ideas**
>
> - A number of economic, social and environmental factors influence the location of primary, secondary, tertiary and quaternary economic activities.
> - The location of economic activities changes in response to changing economic, social and environmental factors.

**Labour**
Skills, cost, quantity

**Site**
Extent, cost of land

**Transport**
Access to ports, airports, motorways, railways to source materials/parts and send products to market

**Other firms**
Access to parts suppliers and assemblers of parts

**Government assistance**
Availability of grants, loans and other assistance from government

**Raw materials & energy**
Important to processing industries and industries needing own energy supplies, e.g. aluminium smelting

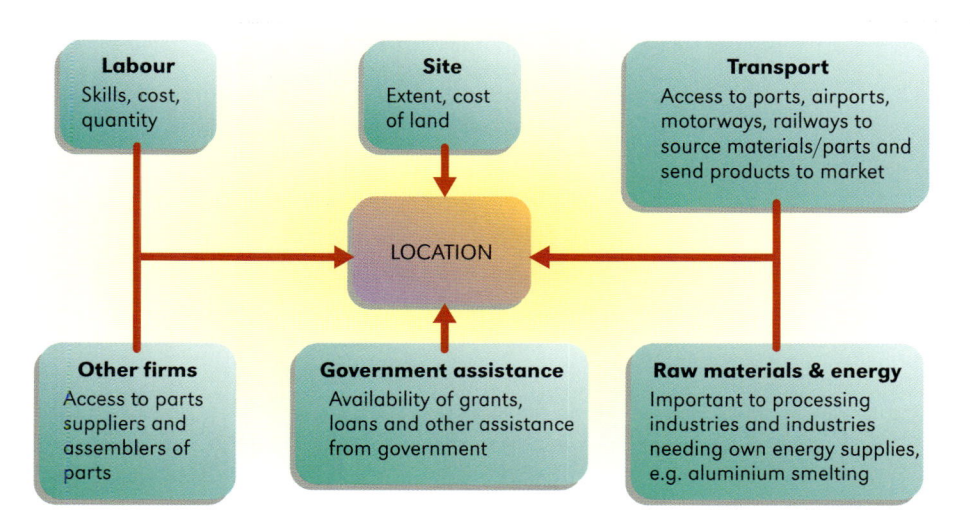

→ LOCATION

*Figure 8.1 Factors influencing the location of industry*

Economic development

161

# Chapter 8 Economic activity

Table 8.1 Factors influencing the location of some economic activities

| Sector | Industry | Environmental | Economic | Social, political |
|---|---|---|---|---|
| Primary | Farming, e.g. arable, hill, sheep | Relief, climate and soils set geographical limits on types of farming | | Government subsidies may make farming profitable in less favoured regions |
| | Mining and quarrying, e.g. coal, limestone | Location is fixed where energy and mineral resources are found. Environmental protection may prevent development in some areas | Production will depend on the costs of procurement and market prices | Government subsidies may encourage production for social reasons (e.g. to protect employment) |
| Secondary | Heavy processing industries, e.g. steel | Raw materials and energy supplies; locations that minimise the impact of environmental pollution | Labour costs and labour skills. Large, flat sites. Access to bulk transport by sea, road, rail | |
| | Light industries, e.g. electronics | Industrial estates and business parks, separate from housing areas | Access to parts/material suppliers. Labour costs and skills. Access to research and development. Access to motorways | |
| Tertiary | Retailing, e.g. supermarket | | Access to customers (i.e. shoppers). Large sites for parking and superstore buildings | |
| | Tourism | Environmental resources for tourism: climate, beaches, culture etc. | Infrastructure — airports, hotels, roads, budget airlines | Stable governments. Secure geopolitical region |
| Quaternary | Financial services, e.g. stockbrokers | | Access to IT and global telecommunications. Access to highly skilled workforce. Access to customers (i.e. companies) | |

OCR (B) GCSE Geography

# Theme 4

*Figure 8.2 Economic activities*

▼ **(a) Water supply**

▼ **(c) Shopping**

▼ **(b) Transport**

▲ **(e) Heavy industry**

▼ **(d) Tourism**

▶ **(f) Mining**

### Activity 8.1

Study Figure 8.2, which shows six different economic activities.

1. Identify the sector to which each activity belongs (i.e. primary, secondary or tertiary).
2. Explain how you chose the sector for each activity.

Economic development

# Chapter 8 Economic activity

## The changing location of economic activities

As the importance of individual locational factors changes, so there is a corresponding change in the location of economic activities. These locational changes affect the distribution of economic activities at global, national and local scales.

### Global changes

There has been a huge growth in manufacturing industry in the Far East, and in particular in China, since 1980 (see Figure 8.3). The scale of this growth is such that in 2009, China overtook the USA as the world's leading manufacturer. Today, China accounts for 17% of the value of world manufacturing output.

China and has attracted huge investments in manufacturing industries from multi-national corporations (MNCs) based in the USA, Japan and the EU countries, such as IBM, Hitachi, Siemens, Coca-Cola, Toyota and Nike. Many MNCs have transferred manufacturing operations from North America and Europe to China and the Far East — a process known as **offshoring**. This development is part of a wider trend that has affected the world economy in the past 30 years, called **globalisation** (see Factfile 8.1).

▼ Figure 8.3 Production of colour televisions and refrigerators in China

▼ Photograph 8.1 A textiles factory in China, where wages in the clothing industry are just US$1.40 per hour

### Activity 8.2

Visit either a clothing store like *GAP* or a household goods store such as *IKEA*.

1. Examine (discreetly and with permission) the labels of origin on clothing or furniture items, and make a list of the countries from which they were sourced.

2. Plot the origins of these items on a world map and comment on the geographical distribution. Does the distribution show the effects of globalisation?

Theme **4**

◀ *Photograph 8.2 Transport costs have fallen as ships have increased in size*

This global shift of manufacturing is mainly due to three factors: lower wages in LEDCs, improvements in transport and telecommunications, and the growth of **free trade**. Typical wages in the clothing industry in China are just US$1.40 per hour (see Photograph 8.1), compared with a minimum wage in the UK of US$11.20 per hour. Elsewhere in east Asia (e.g. Vietnam, Cambodia, Indonesia, Philippines) wages are even lower.

Improvements in transport and communications have also boosted offshoring and globalisation. As ships have increased in size, transport costs have fallen (see Photograph 8.2). Today, thanks to huge container ships, it costs just US$10 to transport a TV from China to the UK. Modern telecommunications allow factories located on the other side of the world to be managed by company headquarters (HQ) in the USA or EU. This is vital in controlling output, and transferring information between HQ, research and development (R&D) and production.

Free trade has also contributed to the global shift of manufacturing. The **World Trade Organization (WTO)** has, over the past 20 years, reduced trade barriers such as tariffs and quotas between countries. The result has been a big expansion of international trade, which has in turn helped to drive globalisation.

### National and local changes

In recent decades in MEDCs, the relative importance of manufacturing industry in large towns and cities has declined. Meanwhile, the proportion of manufacturing employment in small towns and rural areas has increased. We call this change the rural–urban shift of manufacturing.

**Factfile 8.1 Globalisation**

- Globalisation describes the increasing international flows of people, goods, services and money, in particular in the past 20 years or so.
- Globalisation has created closer economic ties between countries (interdependence) and a more integrated world economy.
- Globalisation has increased world trade and *vice versa*.
- Globalisation has meant that more manufactured goods are produced by MNCs, especially in locations in LEDCs.
- Globalisation has increased the importance of major world financial centres such as New York, London and Tokyo. These cities have become the command centres of the global economy.

Economic development

# Chapter 8 Economic activity

▶ Table 8.2 Reasons for the urban–rural shift of manufacturing industry in the UK

|  | Push factors (inner city) | Pull factors (small towns/rural areas) |
|---|---|---|
| Space | Inner city sites are cramped — not enough space for single-storey buildings, expansion and parking | Sites in small towns and rural areas are more spacious |
| Cost | High land and rent costs; high taxes | Cheaper land, rents and taxes |
| Access | Traffic congestion makes access difficult for trucks and workers | Good access, with locations close to motorways, by-passes and trunk roads |
| Buildings | Mainly old, multi-storey buildings, unsuitable for production lines | Factories are often purpose-built on small industrial estates and business parks |
| Environment | Often run-down and derelict; problems of crime | Attractive, purpose-built estates on greenfield sites; lower levels of crime |
| Labour | Inner cities have a disproportionate number of low-skilled workers | More highly skilled and qualified workers in commuter villages and small towns |

## Activity 8.3

Study Figure 8.4, which shows changes in employment in the Birmingham–Hoover metropolitan area, Alabama, USA, between 1998 and 2006.

1 Plot the data as a line chart and describe the geographical pattern of change.
2 Suggest possible reasons for the change.

▲ Figure 8.4 Changes in employment in the Birmingham–Hoover metropolitan area, 1998–2006

Jobs lost or gained
- −4,525
- +3,678
- +24,384

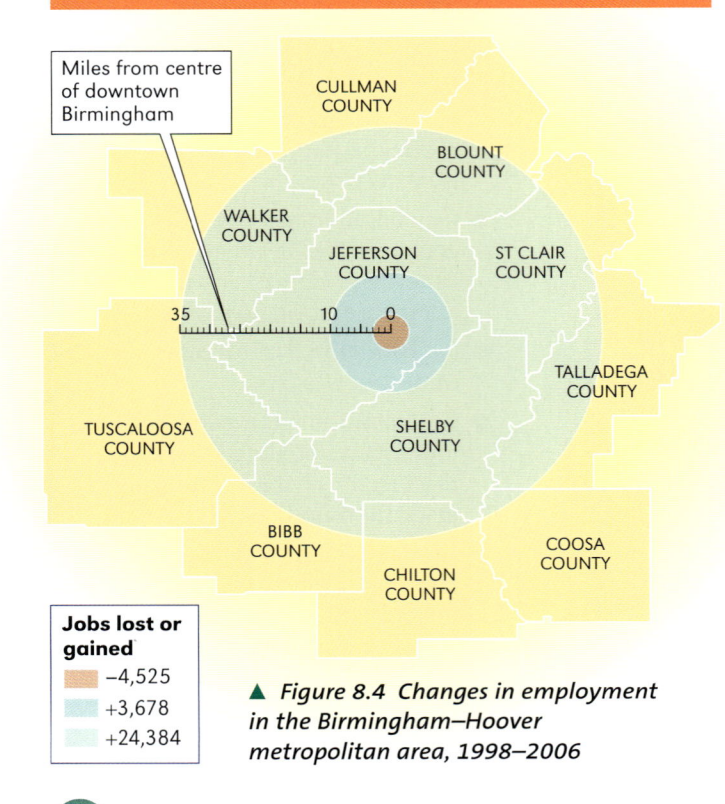

During the 1970s and 1980s, in the UK and other countries in the economically developed world, many factories in inner city locations closed down. New factories have increasingly opted for locations in small towns and rural areas. The reasons for the urban-rural shift are a combination of push and pull factors (see Table 8.2), which together make large urban areas unattractive locations for industry.

Within large urban areas in MEDCs, new investment by industrial and commercial enterprises has tended to favour the outer suburbs rather than inner urban areas. The reasons for this are similar to those that have driven the urban–rural shift. There are more spacious sites in the suburbs with purpose-built industrial estates and business parks. Suburban locations connect directly to motorways making it easier to access suppliers and distribute finished products to market. In addition, suburban locations are often closer to the bulk of the workforce and other businesses with which firms have links. In fact, the movement of industry to the outer suburbs is part of the suburbanisation that has occurred in the past three decades or so.

OCR (B) GCSE Geography

# Theme 4

## Case study: Steel making in the UK

Steel making is a heavy industry. Iron ore and limestone are placed in blast furnaces and smelted with coke to produce liquid iron. Iron is then refined to make steel. Finally, steel is shaped into finished products, such as beams, coil and plate (see Figure 8.5).

### Locational factors

The location of the iron and steel industry is dominated by the costs of raw materials and energy. The materials used to make steel — iron, limestone and coke — have a number of features in common:

- They are heavy and used in very large quantities.
- They lose weight in manufacturing.
- They are expensive to transport.

As a result, the iron and steel industry tends to locate where the cost of assembling the raw material and energy inputs are lowest.

### Changing location

In 1967 the UK iron and steel industry employed nearly a quarter of a million workers. In that year, steel output was around 25 million tonnes. By 2006 employment in the industry had fallen to 19,000, and production was down to just 13.2 million tonnes (see Figure 8.6). This contraction led to major geographical changes.

In 1967 there were 23 iron and steelworks in the UK (see Figure 8.7). Most were small, and the majority were located on coalfields in south Wales, Yorkshire, north Wales, northeast England and central Scotland. A few, such as Corby in the east Midlands and Scunthorpe, were on orefields. These locations, near to local coal and iron deposits, reduced the industry's transport costs.

By the 1970s local iron and coal deposits were either exhausted or becoming too expensive to extract. The steel industry depended increasingly on foreign supplies of ore and coking coal. The result was the

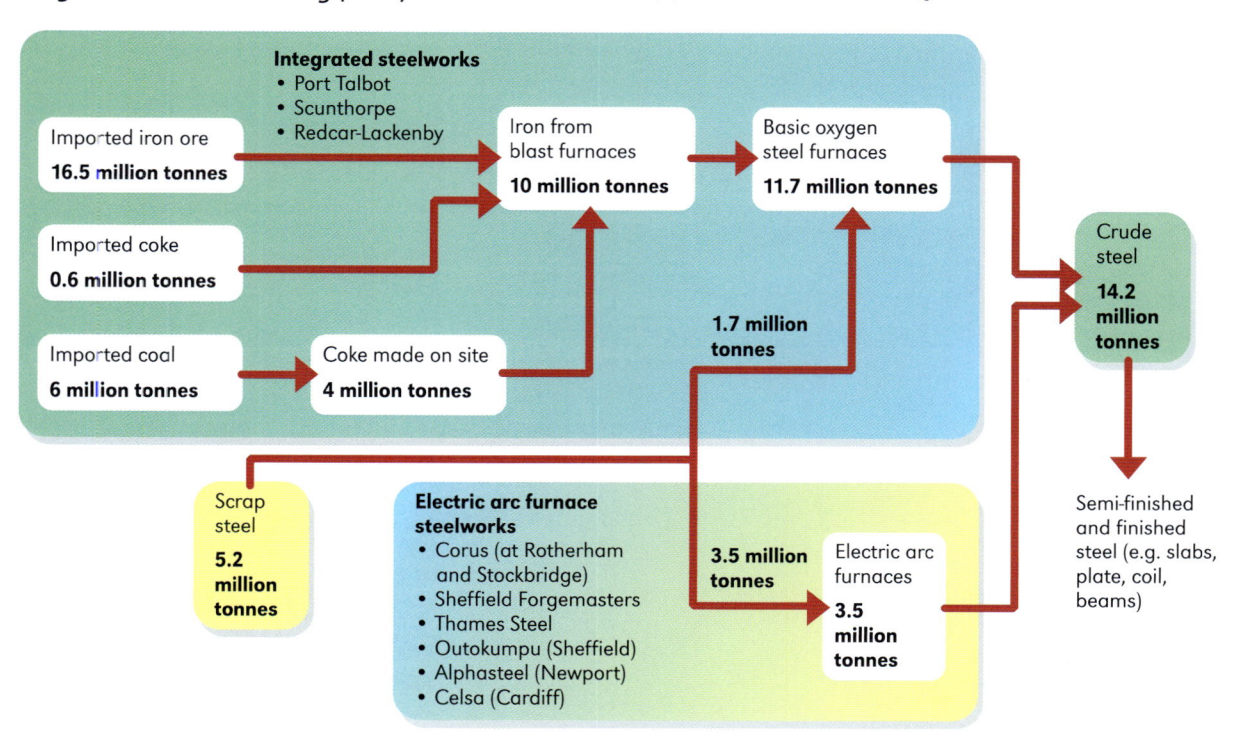

▼ *Figure 8.5 UK steel making (2004)*

Economic development

167

## Chapter 8 Economic activity

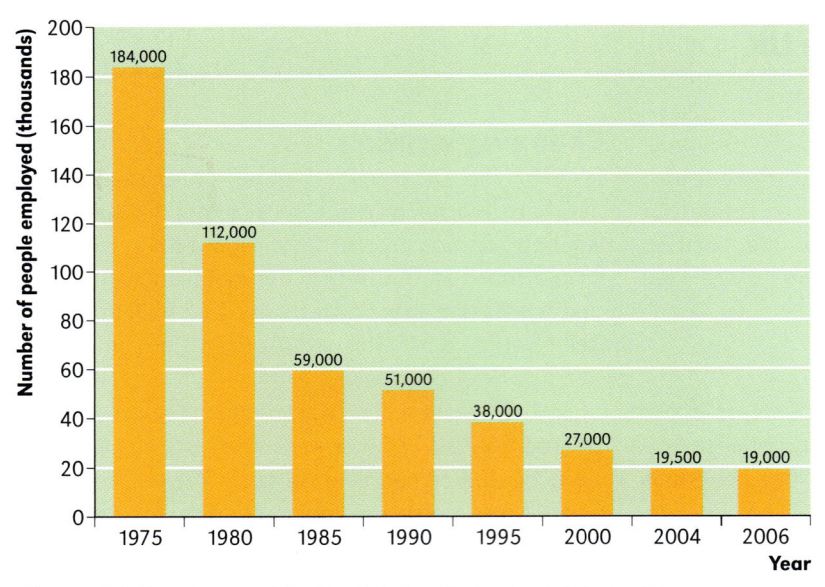

*Figure 8.6 Employment in the UK steel industry, 1975–2006*

concentration of production at **tidewater** (coastal) sites, where imported materials could be assembled cheaply. Meanwhile iron and steelworks at inland sites closed.

Today only three **integrated** iron and steelworks survive in the UK: Port Talbot near Swansea in south Wales; Scunthorpe in north Lincolnshire; and Redcar-Lackenby on Teesside in northeast England (see Figure 8.8). Steel is also produced at Rotherham, Sheffield and Stockbridge in South Yorkshire using electric arc furnaces, which rely on scrap steel rather than iron ore.

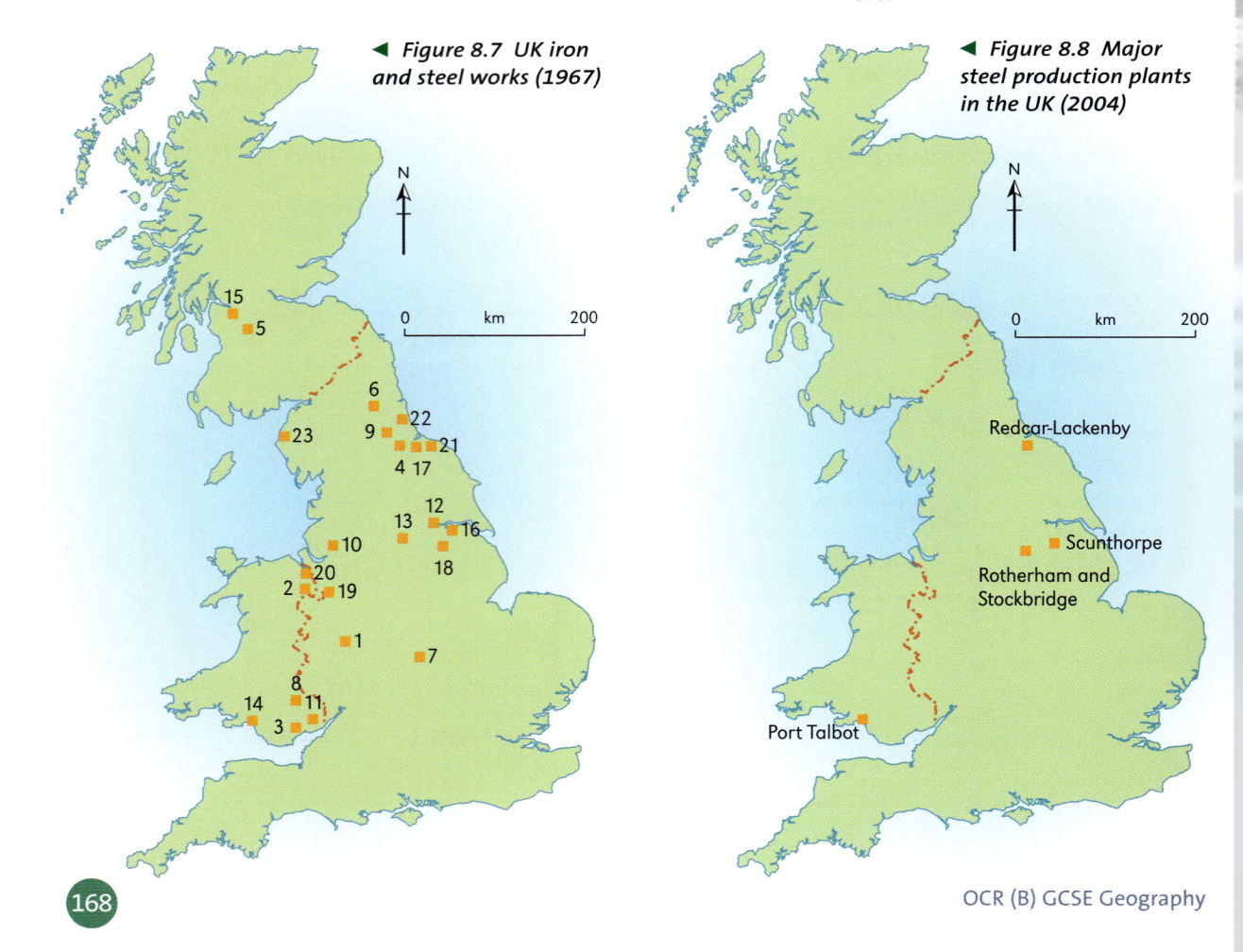

*◀ Figure 8.7 UK iron and steel works (1967)*

*◀ Figure 8.8 Major steel production plants in the UK (2004)*

OCR (B) GCSE Geography

# Theme 4

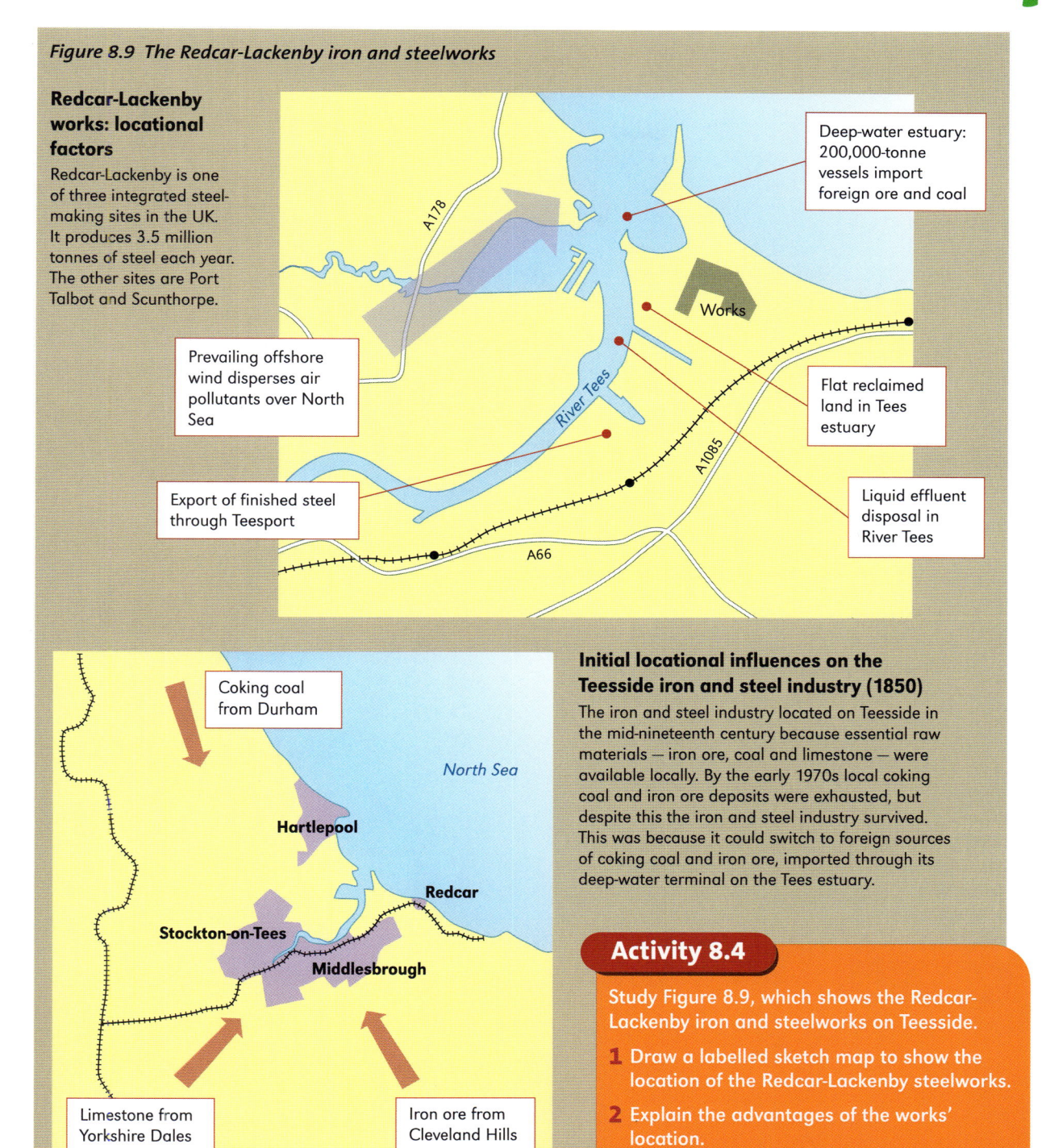

*Figure 8.9 The Redcar-Lackenby iron and steelworks*

## Redcar-Lackenby works: locational factors

Redcar-Lackenby is one of three integrated steel-making sites in the UK. It produces 3.5 million tonnes of steel each year. The other sites are Port Talbot and Scunthorpe.

Labels on map:
- Deep-water estuary: 200,000-tonne vessels import foreign ore and coal
- Prevailing offshore wind disperses air pollutants over North Sea
- Flat reclaimed land in Tees estuary
- Export of finished steel through Teesport
- Liquid effluent disposal in River Tees
- Works
- River Tees, A178, A1085, A66

Lower map labels:
- Coking coal from Durham
- Hartlepool
- North Sea
- Redcar
- Stockton-on-Tees
- Middlesbrough
- Limestone from Yorkshire Dales
- Iron ore from Cleveland Hills

## Initial locational influences on the Teesside iron and steel industry (1850)

The iron and steel industry located on Teesside in the mid-nineteenth century because essential raw materials — iron ore, coal and limestone — were available locally. By the early 1970s local coking coal and iron ore deposits were exhausted, but despite this the iron and steel industry survived. This was because it could switch to foreign sources of coking coal and iron ore, imported through its deep-water terminal on the Tees estuary.

### Activity 8.4

Study Figure 8.9, which shows the Redcar-Lackenby iron and steelworks on Teesside.

1. Draw a labelled sketch map to show the location of the Redcar-Lackenby steelworks.
2. Explain the advantages of the works' location.
3. Explain how this economic activity affects people in the local area.

Economic development

Chapter 8  Economic activity

*Figure 8.10  1:50,000 OS map extract of Port Talbot*

## Activity 8.5

Study Figure 8.10, which shows the Port Talbot area in south Wales.

1. What is the approximate size of the area occupied by the steelworks at Margam?
   (a) 2 km²  (d) 8 km²
   (b) 4 km²  (e) 10 km²
   (c) 6 km²

2. Using the evidence of the map, describe the transport links in and around the site of the steelworks.

3. Apart from transport, state two other advantages of the site of the steelworks.

4. Describe one advantage and one disadvantage of the steelworks for the residents of Margam.

OCR (B) GCSE Geography

# Theme 4

## Steel making and the environment

For many years air pollution from heavy industries, such as iron and steel making, has been linked to poor health and respiratory diseases like lung cancer and asthma. Concentrated in a small area at the mouth of the River Tees are 17 of the most polluting factories in the UK (see Figure 8.11). One of these factories is the Redcar-Lackenby steelworks.

Poor health, respiratory diseases and death rates are much higher than average in residential areas such as Grangetown, which is close to heavy polluting industries on Teesside. Rates of lung cancer among women on Teesside are four times the national average.

However, it is difficult to prove that poor health is caused solely by air pollution. People who live close to polluting industries are often poor and suffer ill health due to a number of other causes, such as unbalanced diets, smoking and poor housing. Air pollution is just one other disadvantage many poor people suffer, on top of high unemployment and neighbourhood crime.

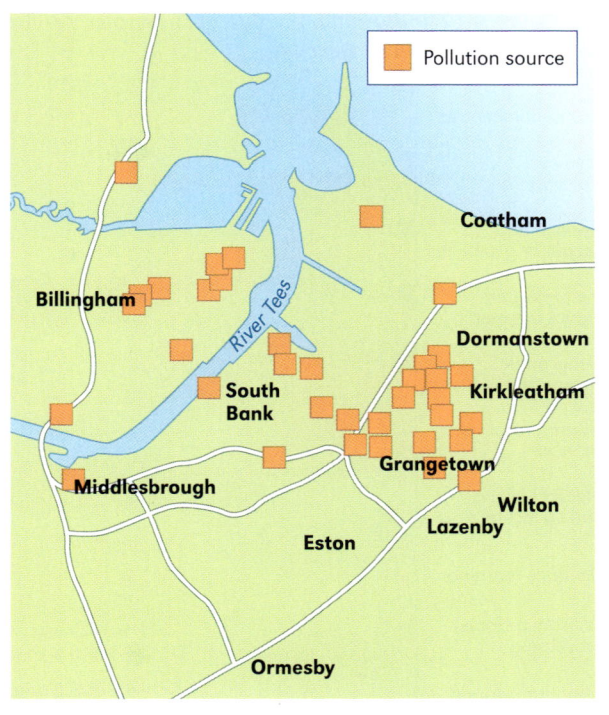

*Figure 8.11 Sources of air pollution on Teesside*

## Case study: Offshored service industries in India

Information and communications technology (ICT) is changing the geography of employment at a global scale and is a major factor behind globalisation. Today, information can be digitised and sent overseas for processing. Since the mid 1990s, hundreds of companies in the UK and the USA have transferred service-sector jobs to India. This process is known as **offshoring**.

The main locational factor driving the offshoring of service-sector jobs to India is labour. India has a large surplus of high-quality graduates who speak English; wage rates are only a fraction of those in the UK; and productivity is high. Initially, call centre jobs were outsourced to India from the UK and the USA. Examples included airline booking and internet banking. Hundreds of leading companies such as Dell, HSBC, British Airways, American Express and Tesco transferred so-called 'back-office' jobs which don't require direct contact with clients. By 2008, India had 4 million service jobs offshored by companies in North America and Europe, worth US$57 billion per year. Not only are these jobs relatively well paid, they also provide much-needed employment for Indian women.

However, offshoring is not just confined to low-level service activities. Increasingly, highly skilled operations, such as research, product design, product development and marketing are being moved offshore. ICT services now employ 1.5 million and account for 7% of India's GDP (see Figure 8.12). Bangalore in southern India is India's ICT capital (see Figure 8.13). In addition to its skilled workforce, Bangalore attracts foreign investment because of its established infrastructure. It has state-of-the-art business parks, modern innovation centres and direct flights to New York, London and Tokyo (see Photograph 8.3).

Economic development

# Chapter 8 Economic activity

▼ Figure 8.12 India calling: value of IT-enabled service exports from India to the USA

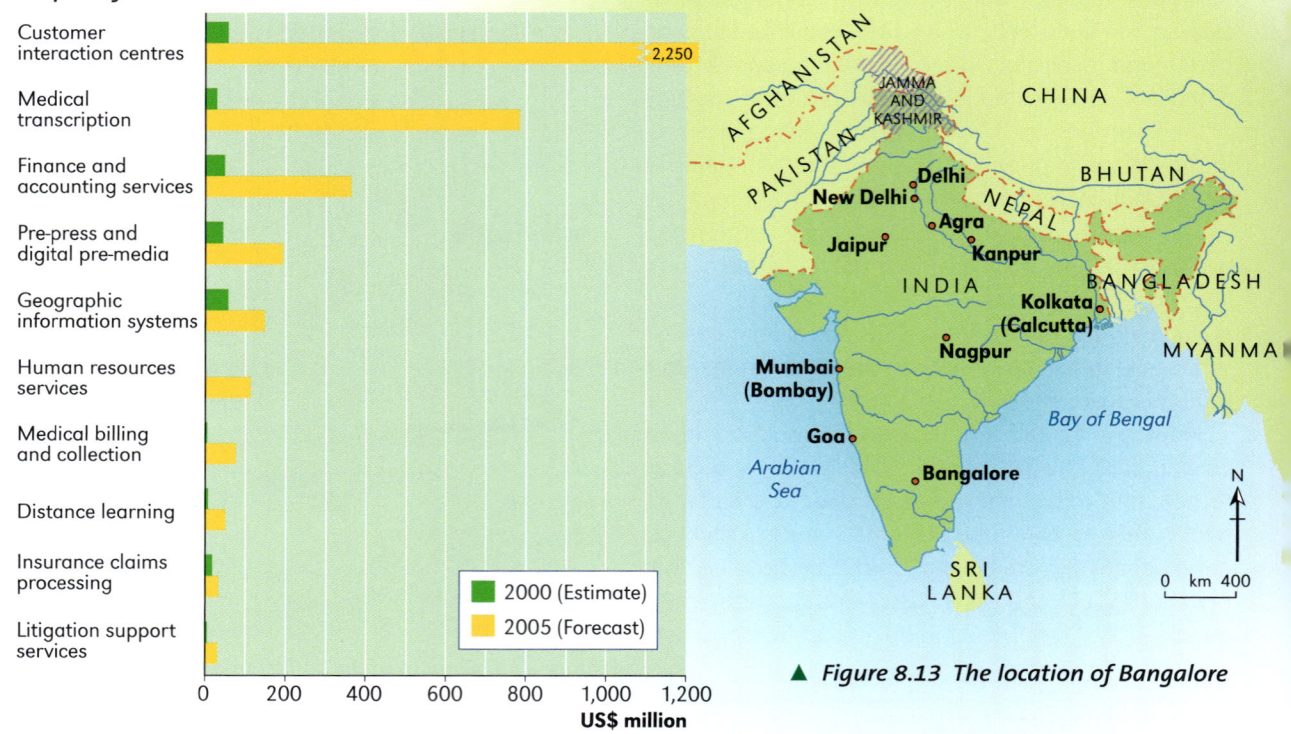

| Service | Value |
|---|---|
| Customer interaction centres | 2,250 |
| Medical transcription | |
| Finance and accounting services | |
| Pre-press and digital pre-media | |
| Geographic information systems | |
| Human resources services | |
| Medical billing and collection | |
| Distance learning | |
| Insurance claims processing | |
| Litigation support services | |

■ 2000 (Estimate)
■ 2005 (Forecast)

US$ million (0–1,200)

▲ Figure 8.13 The location of Bangalore

Photograph 8.3 The Millenia software and technology business park in Bangalore

### Activity 8.6

Offshoring jobs from the UK to LEDCs such as India is a controversial issue. Read the arguments in Figure 8.14 and write a paragraph expressing your own views on the issue of offshoring. Be prepared to defend your views in a class debate.

OCR (B) GCSE Geography

# Theme 4

- Offshoring creates new and well-paid jobs in LEDCs. This helps the world economy and promotes world trade, from which everyone can benefit.

- Offshoring means that countries such as the UK and the USA will lose jobs and wage levels will fall. MEDCs simply cannot compete with the low wages in LEDCs.

- Cheaper services provided abroad will help British people save money, which they can spend on personal services to create more jobs in the UK.

- Offshoring gives millions of poor people in LEDCs the chance to pull themselves out of poverty.

- Most service-sector jobs, such as those in shops, hotels and personal care, require face-to-face contact. They cannot be outsourced and so will remain in the UK.

- Offshoring is done to boost companies' profits and dividends for their shareholders. It is the workers in MEDCs who lose out.

- Losing jobs to cheap overseas labour is bad for workers, bad for families and bad for the economies of MEDCs.

- To survive, companies have no choice but to go wherever they can get things done most cheaply.

*Figure 8.14 Arguments about offshoring*

# Part 2 Multi-national corporations (MNCs) and development

Multi-national (or transnational) corporations are large companies that produce goods or deliver services on a global scale. Table 8.3 gives a list of the top 10 MNCs in 2008.

The list of top 500 MNCs is dominated by countries in the economically developed world. In 2008, nearly 80% of these MNCs were based in the USA, EU and Japan. Thirty-five per cent of the top 500 MNCs were

### Key ideas

- Multi-national corporations (MNCs) are large companies whose production of goods and/or services are organised on a global scale.
- MNCs have both positive and negative effects on employment opportunities and economic development in the areas they locate in.
- MNCs have an increasing influence on employment opportunities and economic development.
- Globalisation brings economic benefits to some groups, and disadvantages to others.

*Table 8.3 Top ten MNCs (by turnover) in 2008*

| Company | Nationality | Economic activity |
|---|---|---|
| Wal Mart | US | Retail |
| ExxonMobil | US | Oil |
| Royal Dutch Shell | Netherlands/UK | Oil |
| BP | UK | Oil |
| Toyota Motors | Japan | Automobiles |
| Chevron | US | Oil |
| ING group | Netherlands | Banking |
| Total | France | Oil |
| GM Motors | US | Automobiles |
| Conoco-Phillips | US | Oil |

Economic development

# Chapter 8 Economic activity

concentrated in just five world cities: Tokyo, Paris, London, Beijing and New York. Increasingly these cities are the control and command centres of the global economy.

Table 8.4 The positive and negative effects of MNCs on employment and development

| Positive effects | Negative effects |
| --- | --- |
| • Provide inward investment and create jobs for local people.<br>• Raise living standards and incomes among employees.<br>• Increase local spending that benefits other businesses (e.g. retail) and creates further employment.<br>• Help the national economy by boosting exports.<br>• Improve skill levels among the local workforce and introduce new technologies.<br>• Initial investment attracts further investment to create clusters of economic activity. | • Exploitation of workforce, especially in LEDCs, with low wages and poor working conditions.<br>• Environmental pollution, which may be tolerated by LEDC governments in order to attract investment.<br>• Little security: plants may be closed at short notice and transferred to other, lower-cost locations overseas.<br>• Most jobs are low-skilled in labour intensive industries, e.g. clothing, assembly.<br>• Greater competition for domestic firms, which could lead to their closure.<br>• In LEDCs, MNCs may increase economic inequalities between those who find work in the new factories and those working in the traditional economy. |

## The impact of MNCs on employment and development

MNCs exert a huge influence on the global economy. They are responsible for around one quarter of world output and two-thirds of the world's exports of goods and services. A large proportion of the goods and services traded by MNCs takes place either within or between MNCs.

While overseas investment by MNCs is generally welcomed by governments, MNCs can have negative as well as positive effects on employment and development. These effects are summarised in Table 8.4.

## Case study: General Motors: a multi-national corporation

General Motors (GM) is a leading MNC and the world's second largest motor vehicle manufacturer. As well as GM, the company owns brands such as Saab, Daewoo, Opel, Vauxhall and Chevrolet.

GM has its headquarters in Detroit in the USA, but it makes cars and trucks in 32 different countries (see Figure 8.15). Worldwide, the company employs 266,000 workers.

GM is typical of the companies that dominate the motor vehicle industry. The major players — such as Toyota, Ford, Chrysler, Volkswagen, and Nissan — are all, like GM, large, globalised companies. Why is this?

• Large companies have advantages over smaller companies. Their sheer size enables them to cut costs. They can spread the huge fixed costs of developing, designing and producing new models over millions of vehicles and can buy parts such as wheels, tyres, seats and even engines and gearboxes in bulk, which makes them cheaper.

• Making cars and trucks in many different countries has advantages. Take GM's car factories in Brazil as an example. Because of their location, the costs of transporting vehicles to customers in São Paulo or Rio de Janeiro are small. Since the cars are made in Brazil, there are no tariffs or import quotas to pay. In addition, labour costs in Brazil are only a fraction of those in the USA.

### GM in China

In 2005, GM opened a new car assembly plant at Liuzhou in southeast China. The plant is a joint venture with the Shanghai Automotive Industry Group and will make over 300,000 cars a year.

GM is not the only foreign MNC to set up production in China. European companies such as

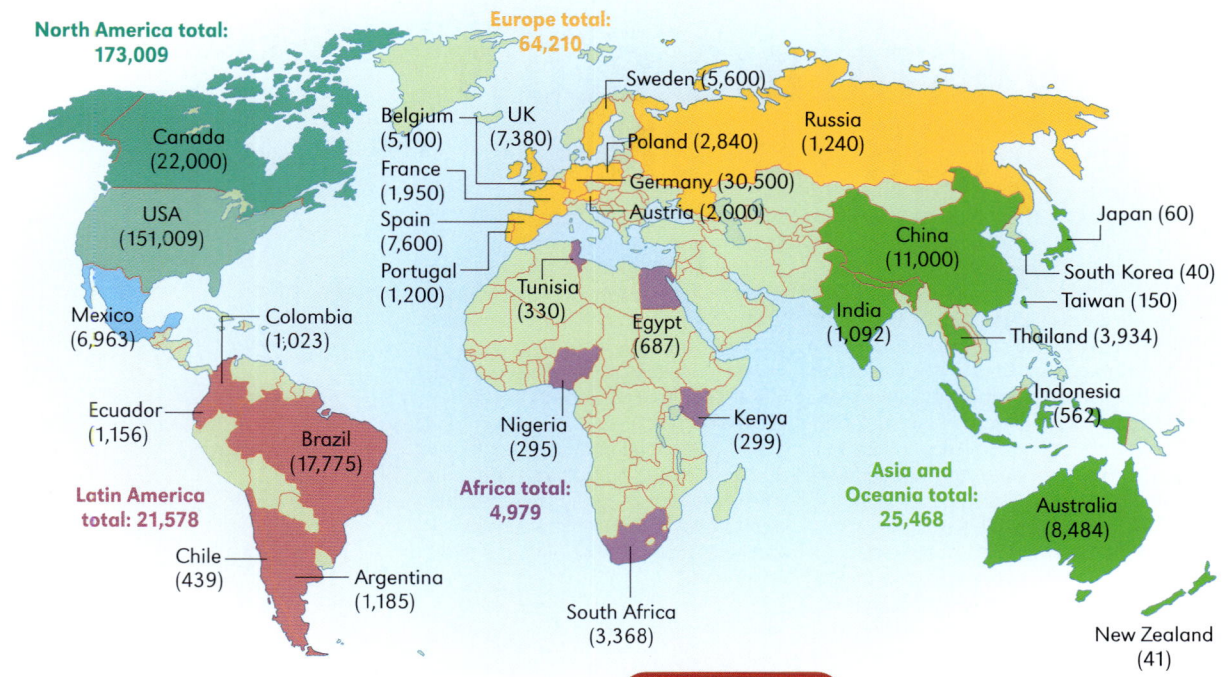

**North America total: 173,009**
- Canada (22,000)
- USA (151,009)
- Mexico (6,963)

**Europe total: 64,210**
- Sweden (5,600)
- Belgium (5,100)
- UK (7,380)
- Poland (2,840)
- Russia (1,240)
- France (1,950)
- Germany (30,500)
- Spain (7,600)
- Austria (2,000)
- Portugal (1,200)

**Africa total: 4,979**
- Tunisia (330)
- Egypt (687)
- Nigeria (295)
- Kenya (299)
- South Africa (3,368)

**Asia and Oceania total: 25,468**
- China (11,000)
- Japan (60)
- South Korea (40)
- Taiwan (150)
- India (1,092)
- Thailand (3,934)
- Indonesia (562)
- Australia (8,484)
- New Zealand (41)

**Latin America total: 21,578**
- Colombia (1,023)
- Ecuador (1,156)
- Brazil (17,775)
- Chile (439)
- Argentina (1,185)

▲ *Figure 8.15 Number of General Motors employees by country*

Volkswagen and BMW are already there. So too are the three top Japanese carmakers — Toyota, Nissan and Honda.

China is currently attracting large investments from foreign MNCs. The advantages of locating in China for GM are:
- China's huge potential market: it has a population of 1.3 billion — the largest in the world.
- China's rapid industrialisation, which increases demand for commercial vehicles; and its economic development, which means that more people can afford to buy cars.
- China's relatively low labour costs (wage rates are just 10% of those in the USA).
- The low-cost materials and parts, such as steel and electronic components, which are already made in China.

## Advantages and disadvantages of foreign MNCs

Most countries welcome MNCs like General Motors. Foreign investment brings social and economic advantages, such as employment, new skills and exports. However, MNCs also bring disadvantages (see Table 8.4). If profits fall they can easily close factories and transfer production overseas. This is not such a problem with national companies: they usually serve the local market, make decisions and have their headquarters in the country where production is based, and generally have a greater commitment to the home country.

In 2008 General Motors faced severe financial problems and had to depend on financial support

### Activity 8.7

Study Figure 8.15.

1. What is a multi-national corporation?
2. Draw a pie chart to show the proportion of GM's workforce employed in the USA, Canada, Mexico, Latin America, Africa, Europe, and Asia and Oceania.
3. Describe the global distribution of employment in GM's factories.
4. Suggest two reasons why GM has located factories in LEDCs. Explain your answer.

Economic development

Chapter 8 Economic activity

# DEVASTATING BLOW FOR LUTON

The closure of the Vauxhall (GM) plant at Luton will have devastating consequences for the area, say business experts. Vauxhall is the largest manufacturing company in the town and is at the heart of the local community.

Richard Lacey, Chief Executive of the Bedfordshire Chamber of Commerce, told BBC News Online: 'There are 2,000 people being made redundant…but when you consider the trickledown effect, it could end up being much more. You can double that figure if you include the immediate supply chain to the plant, and when you look at the service sector and support industries, the figure rises steeply again. The effect of closure is devastating. We think that anything from 35,000 to 50,000 people could be affected.'

General Motors is blaming the closure of the plant on what it calls 'changing market conditions' in Europe and overcapacity.

Jason Boniface, a forklift driver, said: 'What's going to become of this place? Vauxhall is Luton.'

The Trade and Industry Secretary Stephen Byers said that 'Vauxhall's announcement of job losses at Luton was a bitter blow for the individuals affected, their families and the local community.'

Source: http://news.bbc.co.uk, 12 December 2000

### Activity 8.8

1. Explain how the location of a new car assembly plant can bring economic benefits to a region.

Read Figure 8.16, which is about the closure of General Motors' car assembly plant in Luton.

2. What reason is given by General Motors for closing the car assembly plant at Luton?

3. Describe the economic and social effects the loss of jobs at the Vauxhall factory might have had on the Luton area.

◀ *Figure 8.16*

from the US government. Future closures of some assembly plants, both in the US and overseas, now seem inevitable. The knock-on effects on parts suppliers, local businesses and employment in the USA and in many other countries will be considerable.

Globalisation, led by MNCs, has brought undeniable economic advantages through increased trade, employment and growth. However, the new interdependence of the global economy means that during an economic downturn, the negative effects are greater than ever before. As demand falls, MNCs like General Motors will cut back on production, plants will close and many thousands of people in the automotive industries and related activities will lose their jobs.

The overall impact of globalisation is very variable (Table 8.5). While it is clear that some groups

*Table 8.5 Globalisation: winners and losers*

| Winners | Losers |
| --- | --- |
| • Well educated young workers in LEDCs who are an attractive potential workforce for MNCs.<br>• Workers fortunate enough to get a job with an MNC.<br>• Women. MNCs and the global economy offer job opportunities to women, who in traditional societies often have very limited work prospects.<br>• Young workers who are mobile and willing to emigrate to find jobs. | • Poorly educated people working in the traditional sector such as farming. These people have few skills relevant to the global economy.<br>• Workers in industries and companies unable to survive competition in the global economy from foreign MNCs. These workers will lose their jobs.<br>• Workers in agriculture in LEDCs, exposed to free trade. Cheap imports of food, subsidised by exporters, may cause the collapse of local agriculture.<br>• Workers in factories owned by foreign MNCs who are made redundant when the MNC decides to transfer operations to a lower-cost location overseas. |

in India, such as ICT workers and well-educated graduates, do benefit, millions of others will gain few advantages and could even be worse off. One thing is certain: globalisation will increase, not decrease, global inequalities as well as the gap between rich and poor.

## Part 3 Economic activities and the physical environment

### Economic activity and the physical environment

Most economic activities, whether they are farming, fishing or tourism, have harmful effects on the physical environment. These effects often degrade aspects of the physical environment such as rivers, soils and landscapes, reducing their quality and their value as resources.

> **Key ideas**
> - Different economic activities affect the physical environment in a range of ways.
> - Conflicts arise between responsibilities for the physical environment and the need for development.
> - GIS, new technologies and satellite images can be used to analyse economic activity and environmental conflict.
> - There is a need to balance environmental concerns and economic development and manage conflicts sustainably.
> - The causes, effects and responses to global climate change occur at a variety of scales.

> **Activity 8.9**
> 1. Which economic activities in Table 8.6 appear to have the most widespread impact on the physical environment?
> 2. Which aspects of the physical environment appear to be most sensitive to change caused by economic activities?
> 3. For one economic activity in Table 8.6, explain how it could impact adversely on one or more components of the physical environment.

▼ Table 8.6 The impact of economic activities on the physical environment

| ECONOMIC ACTIVITIES | PHYSICAL ENVIRONMENT | | | | | |
|---|---|---|---|---|---|---|
| | Atmosphere | Rivers, lakes, groundwater | Seas and oceans | Soil | Wildlife and ecosystems | Landscapes |
| Agriculture | | ✓ | | ✓ | ✓ | ✓ |
| Mining minerals and energy | | ✓ | ✓ | ✓ | ✓ | ✓ |
| Fishing | | | ✓ | | ✓ | |
| Manufacturing | ✓ | ✓ | | | ✓ | ✓ |
| Energy generation | ✓ | ✓ | | | ✓ | ✓ |
| Tourism | | | ✓ | | ✓ | ✓ |

Economic development

## Chapter 8 Economic activity

In extreme cases, economic activities like mining and logging can destroy entire landscapes and **ecosystems**. The environmental impact of economic activities can be deliberate or unintentional; and can vary in scale from local areas, to entire ecosystems and, ultimately, the planet.

Degradation and destruction may result from:
(a) overexploitation of resources
(b) pollution — routine discharges of waste material into the environment, which pollute water, soil and air
(c) deliberate changes in land use

## Using satellite images to analyse conflicts between economic activities and the physical environment

### Deforestation in Amazonia

Deforestation in the Amazon basin in South America is both a local and global environmental problem. It destroys the forest ecosystem, disrupts the local hydrological cycle and climate stability, and increases the threat of global warming. A number of economic activities are responsible for deforestation, including farming, logging and mining. Farming causes most damage. Vast areas

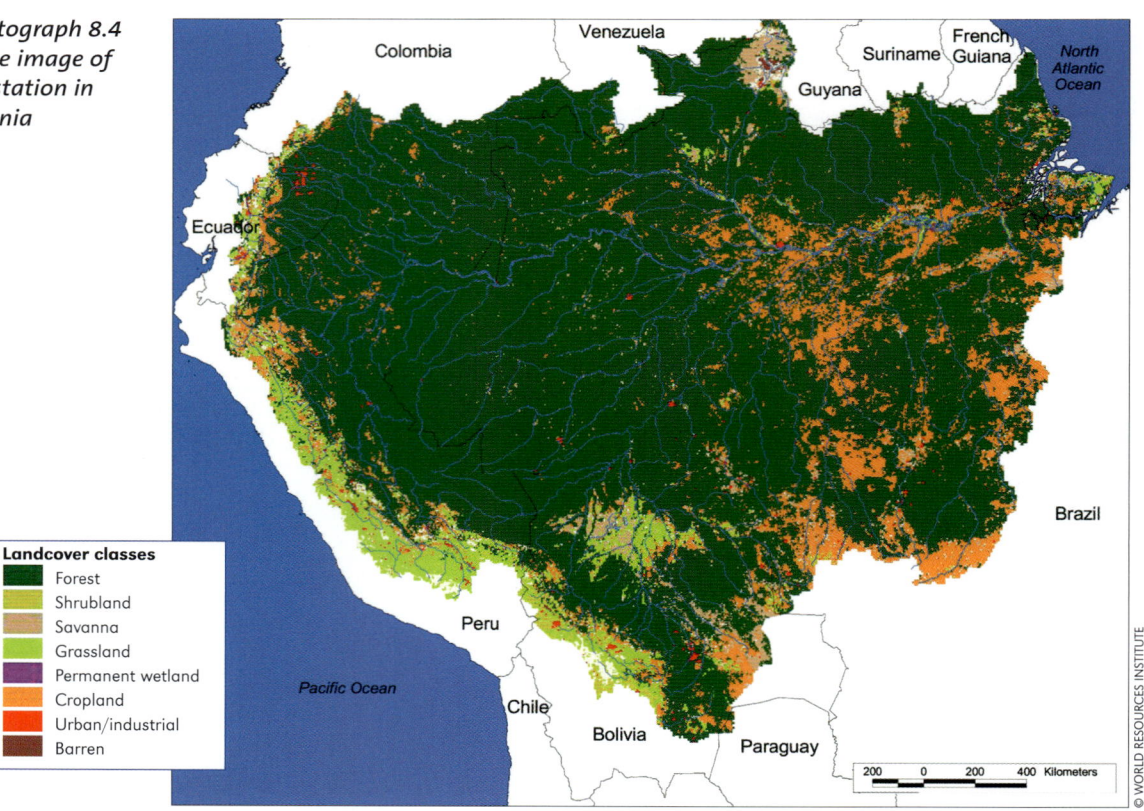

▶ *Photograph 8.4 Satellite image of deforestation in Amazonia*

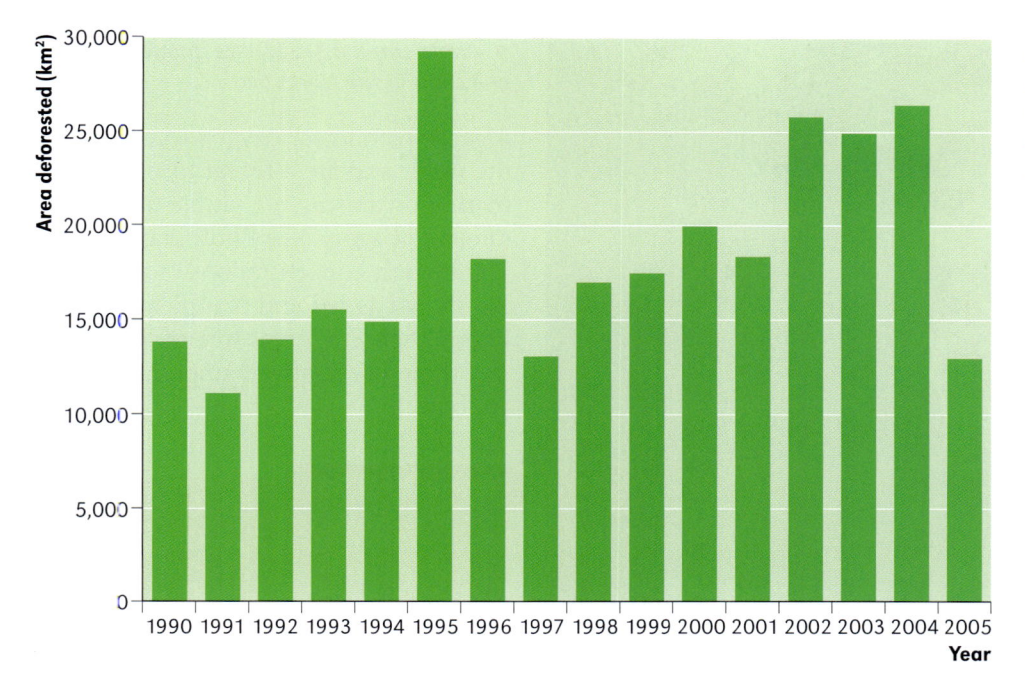

*Figure 8.17 Annual deforestation in Amazonia, 1990–2005*

of rainforest have been cleared and replaced by pasture for cattle and soybean cultivation (see Figure 8.17). Satellite images allow us to monitor the progress and extent of deforestation. Often deforestation begins with the building of roads and highways. This opens up the forest. Clearings are made by subsistence farmers at right angles to the road, forming a herringbone pattern when viewed from space.

The area of deforestation can be measured from satellite images (see Photograph 8.4). Since 1990, annual deforestation has averaged around 16,000 km² a year, peaking at nearly 30,000 km² in 1995. In Photograph 8.4 the forest areas are shown in dark green and deforested land in orange and red.

### Activity 8.10

Study the satellite image of Amazonia (see Photograph 8.4).

1. Describe the geographical pattern of deforestation in Amazonia (i.e. assume areas of cropland and urban/industrial land were formerly rainforest).
2. Estimate the proportion of Amazonian rainforest that has been cleared.
3. Outline possible conflicts that might arise between economic activity and the environment in areas of deforestation.

### Pollution in the North Sea

The North Sea is a shallow, enclosed basin, surrounded by several of the world's most industrialised countries. Pollution is caused by wastes produced by agriculture, industry and domestic sources, which pour into the southern North Sea from the Thames, Rhine, Elbe and other major rivers. GIS and satellite imaging help us to monitor the quality of the water and the health of the North Sea ecosystem.

Because much of the effluent reaching the North Sea is nutrient-rich, it produces high concentrations of algae, particularly during the summer months.

Economic development

Chapter 8 Economic activity

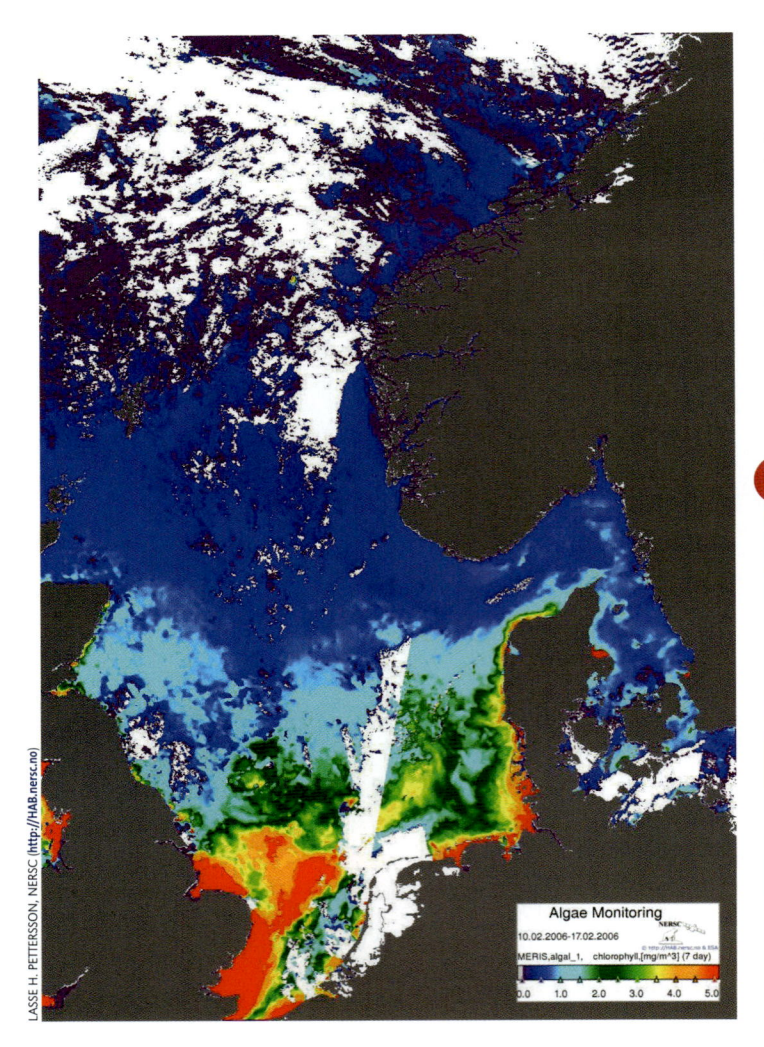

◀ **Photograph 8.5** Satellite image of pollution in the North Sea

Algae, which lower oxygen levels in the water and are a threat to other marine organisms, are visible from satellite imagery (see Photograph 8.5). The highest concentrations of algae are shown as red and orange in Photograph 8.5. Areas free of algae, and therefore relatively unpolluted, are blue.

### Activity 8.11

Study the satellite image of the North Sea (Photograph 8.5).

1. Refer to an atlas map of northern Europe and describe the geographical pattern of pollution in the North Sea.

2. Again, refer to an atlas, and assess the extent to which the pollution can be blamed on the distribution of rivers that drain into the North Sea from densely populated and highly urbanised catchments.

3. Outline possible conflicts that might arise between economic activity and the environment in the most polluted parts of the North Sea.

## Global climate change

There is mounting evidence of **global warming** and disruption to the world's weather and climate. Average global temperatures rose by 0.6°C in the twentieth century. Scientists forecast a further rise of 1.5–6.0°C by the end of the twenty-first century. Worryingly, rates of global warming appear to be accelerating (see Figure 8.18): 1998 was the warmest year on record, 2005 was the second warmest and 2003 was the third warmest. The rise in temperature between 1976 and 2003 was three times greater than in the whole of the previous 100 years.

### Causes of global warming

Most scientists now believe that human activities are forcing global **climate change**. The culprits are the so-called greenhouse gases, especially carbon dioxide. Rapid population growth, together with massive **urbanisation** and

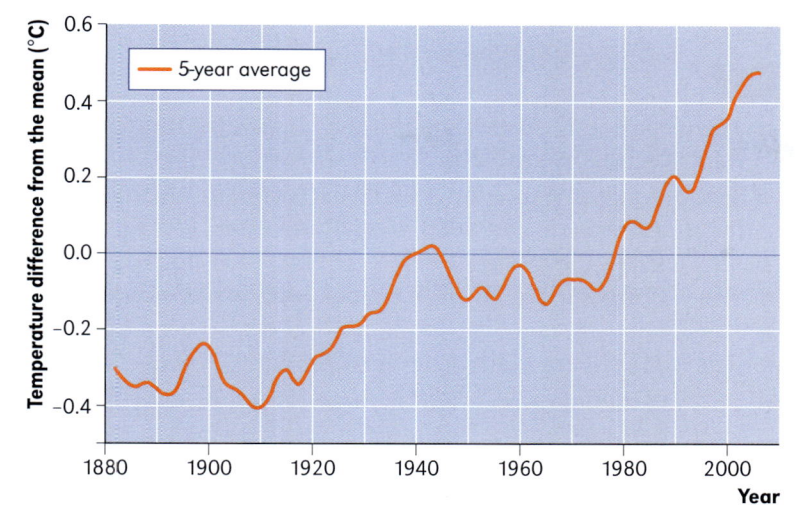

▲ Figure 8.18 Graph showing global temperature difference from the global mean, 1880–2006

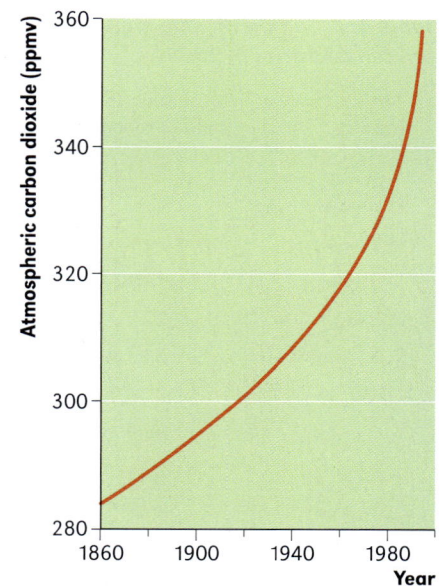

## Factfile  8.2 Global warming

- Human activities are forcing climate change on a global level.
- The highest average annual global temperatures on record all occurred between 1997 and 2008.
- Average global temperatures could increase by up to 6°C by the end of twenty-first century.
- The 'enhanced **greenhouse effect**' caused by rising levels of carbon dioxide is thought to be responsible for global warming.
- Increasing levels of carbon dioxide are due to human activities, principally the burning of **fossil fuels**.
- Global warming will cause major disruption to the world's weather and climate.
- Changes in rainfall patterns, storms and temperature, along with rising sea levels, could be disastrous for people and ecosystems in many parts of the world.
- Poor countries will be less able to cope with climate change than rich countries.

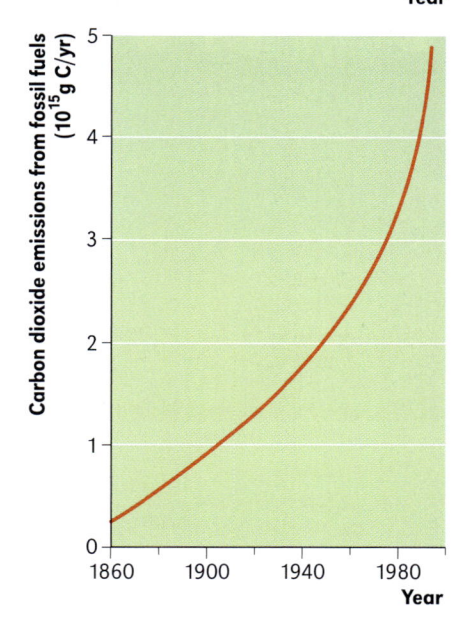

▲ Figure 8.19 Increases in the levels of atmospheric carbon dioxide and emissions from fossil fuels, 1860–2000

**industrialisation**, have led to increases in demand for oil, coal and gas. Burning these fossil fuels releases carbon dioxide into the atmosphere. Today, atmospheric carbon dioxide levels are higher than at any time in the past 600,000 years (see Figure 8.19).

## Chapter 8 Economic activity

*Table 8.7 Carbon dioxide emissions: top ten countries in 2005*

| Country | Total emissions (million tonnes) |
|---|---|
| (1) USA | 6.09 |
| (2) China | 4.30 |
| (3) Russia | 1.74 |
| (4) Japan | 1.29 |
| (5) India | 1.20 |
| (6) Germany | 0.87 |
| (7) UK | 0.56 |
| (8) Canada | 0.58 |
| (9) Italy | 0.49 |
| (10) Mexico | 0.42 |
| **World total** | **28.1** |

### Factfile 8.3 The greenhouse effect

- The greenhouse effect is the process responsible for global warming (see Figure 8.20).
- Sunlight passes through the Earth's atmosphere, unaffected by carbon dioxide and other greenhouse gases, and warms the Earth's surface.
- The warmed surface gives off heat as **long-wave radiation**.
- Carbon dioxide in the atmosphere traps some of this long-wave radiation and re-radiates it to Earth.
- The build-up of carbon dioxide means that less energy leaves the atmosphere. The result is rising temperatures and global warming.

### Activity 8.12

1. Plot the emissions of carbon dioxide by country in Table 8.7 as a horizontal bar chart.
2. What proportion of the world's total carbon dioxide emissions is produced by:
   (a) the top ten countries?
   (b) the USA?
3. Explain how the following factors might influence levels of carbon dioxide emission:
   (a) size of economy
   (b) standard of living
   (c) population size
   (d) energy resources found within each country

▼ *Figure 8.20 The greenhouse effect*

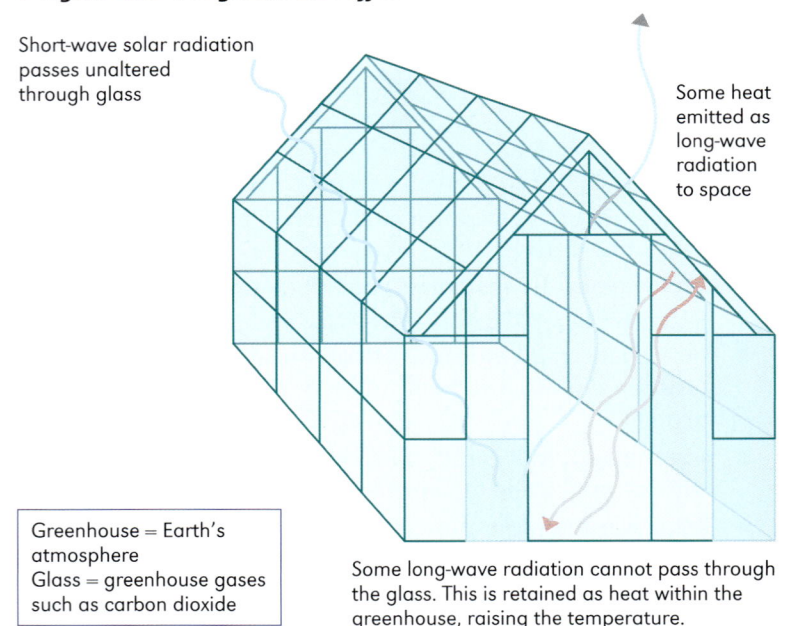

Short-wave solar radiation passes unaltered through glass

Some heat emitted as long-wave radiation to space

Greenhouse = Earth's atmosphere
Glass = greenhouse gases such as carbon dioxide

Some long-wave radiation cannot pass through the glass. This is retained as heat within the greenhouse, raising the temperature.

## Changes to the world's weather and climate

The effect of global warming on weather and climate is likely to vary from place to place. Some places will get warmer and drier; others will get warmer and wetter; and a few could even get cooler.

In the UK, global warming is likely to bring warmer and drier summers to southern Britain and higher rainfall to northern areas. Throughout the country, winters will be milder and stormier than in the past. These higher temperatures will bring some benefits: they should give the UK tourism industry a boost, and farmers will have a longer growing season, enabling them to grow a wider range of crops. Vines and maize, for example, may become important crops.

On the other hand, drier summers will create problems (see Photograph 8.6). Droughts will occur more often and milder winters will increase the threat to crops from pests and diseases. In Scotland, milder winters will mean less snow and the end of the skiing industry. Higher rainfall will result in more frequent river floods, and stormier winters will increase coastal floods and coastal erosion. Overall, our weather will become less predictable with more heatwaves, droughts and flash floods.

Rising temperatures will also affect wildlife. Many arctic and sub-arctic plants and animals, which have survived in Britain since the ice age, could disappear altogether. However, such losses could be balanced by invasions of new species from southern Europe.

In other parts of the world the effects are likely to be more serious. Any decrease in rainfall in dryland regions such as the Sahel in Africa, the Great Plains of the USA and southern Spain could make farming impossible. Some areas might be abandoned altogether and turn to desert. Indeed, in much of the Mediterranean basin farming without irrigation would become impossible.

*Photograph 8.6 Water levels drop in the Weir Wood Reservoir, southeast England, 2005*

## Chapter 8 Economic activity

*Photograph 8.7 Glaciers are threatened by climate change*

*Figure 8.21 Rising sea levels*

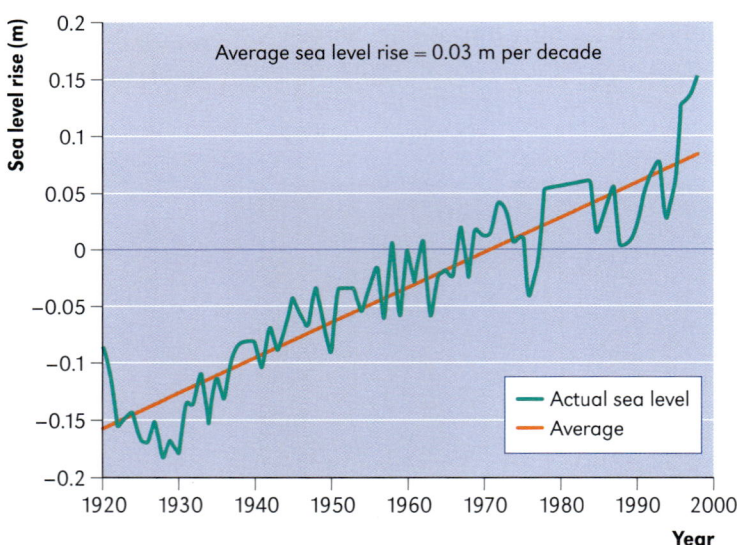

*Table 8.8 World's largest cities (population more than 8 million people)*

| | | | |
|---|---|---|---|
| Bangalore | Istanbul | Manila | Rio de Janeiro |
| Bangkok | Jakarta | Mexico City | São Paulo |
| Beijing | Karachi | Moscow | Seoul |
| Buenos Aires | Kolkata | Mumbai | Shanghai |
| Cairo | Lagos | New York | Tehran |
| Delhi | Lima | Osaka | Tianjin |
| Dhaka | Los Angeles | Paris | Tokyo |

### Rising sea levels

As the Earth's climate warms, **glaciers** and **ice sheets** are shrinking, releasing huge volumes of meltwater into the oceans (see Photograph 8.7). With more water in the oceans, sea levels rise. However, there is also another reason for rising sea levels: global warming heats the oceans, causing them to expand.

During the past 100 years, sea levels have risen by 10–25 cm (see Figure 8.21). But much larger rises are forecast for the future. Current estimates suggest a rise of 1.5 m by the end of the century. However, if giant glaciers in Antarctica were to become unstable and slide into the ocean, sea levels could rise by as much as 6 m in just a few decades.

### The impact of rising sea levels

A 1 m rise in sea levels could be disastrous. First, a large part of the world's population, and most of the world's major cities, are located on or near the coast. Second, most of these

OCR (B) GCSE Geography

people and cities are in poor countries with few resources to protect themselves.

Even modest sea level rises spell doom for several island states. The Maldives in the Indian Ocean, which are just 1 or 2 metres above sea level, could disappear altogether. Bangladesh, one of the world's poorest and most densely populated countries, is at particular risk. Most of the country is a delta just a few metres above sea level. Already floods from rivers and from **tropical cyclones** in the Bay of Bengal affect two thirds of the country for half the year. Rising sea levels can only make matters worse. Any large rise in sea level will make large parts of Bangladesh, which is home to over 150 million people, uninhabitable (see Figure 8.22).

### Activity 8.13

1. Use an atlas to find:
   (a) the location of the 28 cities in Table 8.8
   (b) the countries in which they are found

2. How many of the world's largest 28 cities have coastal locations?

3. How many of the world's largest 28 cities are in LEDCs? To find out, log on to the UN Development Report website:
   http://hdr.undp.org/en/statistics/

   Find the human development index (HDI) tables and the HDI index scores for the countries represented in Table 8.8. The HDI is a measure of a country's development. Its values range from 0 (least developed) to 1 (most developed). Use the UN's own classification to divide the countries into three groups: high human development (over 0.915), medium human development (0.695–0.914) and low human development (less than 0.695).

4. Write a paragraph to summarise the findings of your investigation.

▼ *Figure 8.22 Potential impact of rising sea levels on Bangladesh*

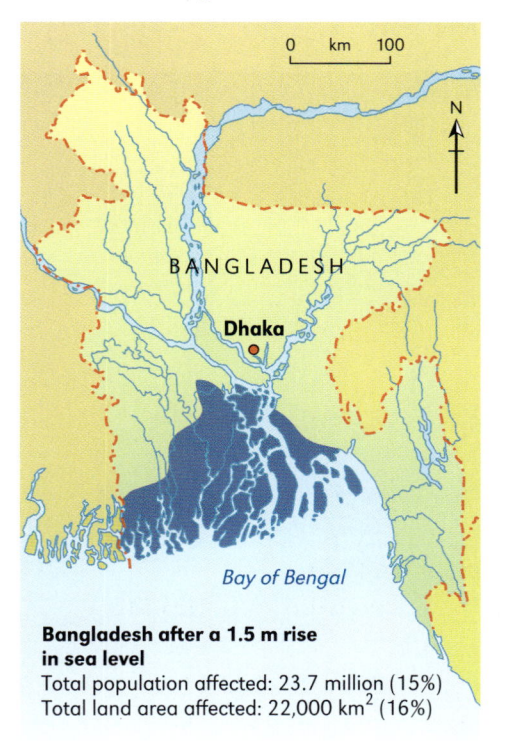

**Bangladesh in 2009**
Total population: 158 million
Total land area: 134,000 km²

**Bangladesh after a 1.5 m rise in sea level**
Total population affected: 23.7 million (15%)
Total land area affected: 22,000 km² (16%)

Economic development

## Chapter 8 Economic activity

> ### Activity 8.14
>
> Study Figure 8.18 on page 181, which shows global temperature changes between 1880 and 2006.
>
> 1. Describe how average global temperatures changed between 1880 and 2006.
> 2. Outline the probable cause of global warming.
> 3. Describe and explain three ways in which global warming could affect weather and climate.
> 4. Suggest ways in which people and organisations could help reduce global warming.

It would be wrong to assume that only poorer countries need to take rising sea levels seriously. Rich countries will be affected too. For example, a 2 m rise in sea level would flood most large cities like New York and Boston on the east coast of the USA. Nearly one quarter of the land in the Netherlands lies below sea level; this vulnerable area is densely populated and includes Amsterdam and Rotterdam, the country's two largest cities.

Rising sea levels and stormier weather will increase coastal erosion. In the future it will be too costly to maintain all of the UK's sea defences. Already there are plans to abandon some stretches of coast in eastern England to the sea. London, however, will be protected at all costs. In London 150 km$^2$ of land lies below the high tide level. These areas house 750,000 people, as well as parliament, the stock exchange and many commercial organisations. A major flood in London could cost the UK £20 billion. This would cripple the country's economy and threaten London's position as the world's leading financial centre. Flood protection up to 2030 is provided by the Thames flood barrier (Photograph 8.8). Since its completion in 1982, the Thames barrier has been raised to provide flood protection on 88 separate occasions. It is rather worrying that the barrier has had to be raised more often in the past few years.

*Photograph 8.8 The Thames flood barrier*

*Photograph 8.9
A wind farm in Scotland*

## Responses to global warming

Tackling global warming is possibly the greatest environmental challenge faced by humankind. The challenge is particularly daunting because global warming is an international problem. This means that a solution requires the agreement and cooperation of all the world's largest economies.

There are four main approaches to tackling global warming: international treaties to limit carbon dioxide (and other greenhouse gas (GHG)) emissions; investing in **alternative energy** such as wind and nuclear power; developing new energy technologies; and carbon trading.

### The Kyoto Treaty

The Kyoto Treaty is the first attempt to control carbon dioxide emissions through international law. So far, 161 countries have signed the treaty. The treaty sets targets for individual countries to reduce their emissions of carbon dioxide and other GHGs. Most MEDCs have to cut their GHG emissions by 5% below 1990 levels by 2012. But up to 2009, several major polluters, including the USA, had not signed the treaty. Moreover, China and India and other industrialising LEDCs are exempt and free to carry on polluting.

### Alternative energies

Individual countries may opt to meet their obligations under Kyoto by investing in alternative forms of energy. The UK, for example, is committed to expanding wind power and producing 20% of its electricity from renewable sources by 2020 (see Photograph 8.9). In addition, the UK government has decided to invest heavily in nuclear power.

Economic development

## Chapter 8 Economic activity

### New technologies
New technologies could provide a low-carbon fuel substitue for oil. One possibility is to use hydrogen as a transport fuel. However, this clean technology could take decades to perfect. Carbon capture offers another solution. It involves capturing carbon dioxide released by power stations and storing it underground in old mine workings and oil and gas fields.

### Carbon trading
Under this system governments set a limit on the amount of carbon dioxide emitted by a company or an organisation. The polluters gets allowances or credits giving them a right to emit a specific amount of carbon dioxide a year. If the pollution limit is exceeded, the polluter must buy credits from those companies that pollute less. This transfer of credits is called carbon trading. The system provides a money incentive to reduce pollution.

The value of carbon traded in 2008 was nearly US$60 billion, with London already established as the carbon trading capital of the world.

## Case study: Economic/environmental conflict — Whinash wind farm

Whinash in Cumbria is the site of a proposed giant **wind farm**. It is one of several wind farms planned to meet government targets to expand **alternative energy** and reduce carbon dioxide emissions. These farms are controversial for two reasons. First, they are much larger than earlier wind farms. Second, many are in environmentally sensitive areas.

Whinash will occupy an 8 km stretch of moorland between the Lake District and Yorkshire Dales National Parks (see Figure 8.23 and Photograph 8.10). Twenty-seven giant wind turbines, each 120 m tall, are planned for the site (see Figure 8.24).

*Figure 8.23 Proposed location of Whinash wind farm*

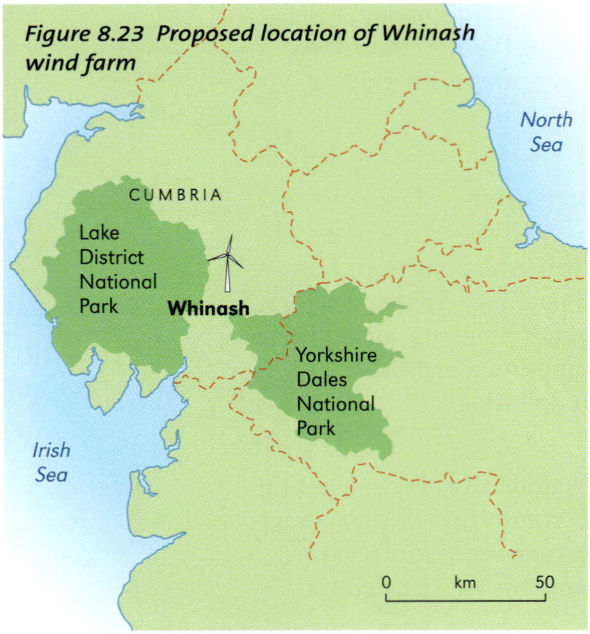

### Factfile 8.4 The Whinash wind farm

- The UK agreed under the 1997 Kyoto Treaty to reduce its carbon dioxide emissions by 12% (from the 1999–2000 levels) before 2010.
- Whinash wind farm in Cumbria will help reduce the UK's carbon dioxide emissions by 178,000 tonnes a year.
- It will produce enough electricity to power 47,000 homes, or a population of 110,000.
- Cumbria is one of the windiest parts of the UK, but the most suitable sites for building wind farms (e.g. in the Lake District National Park) are unavailable.

Theme 4

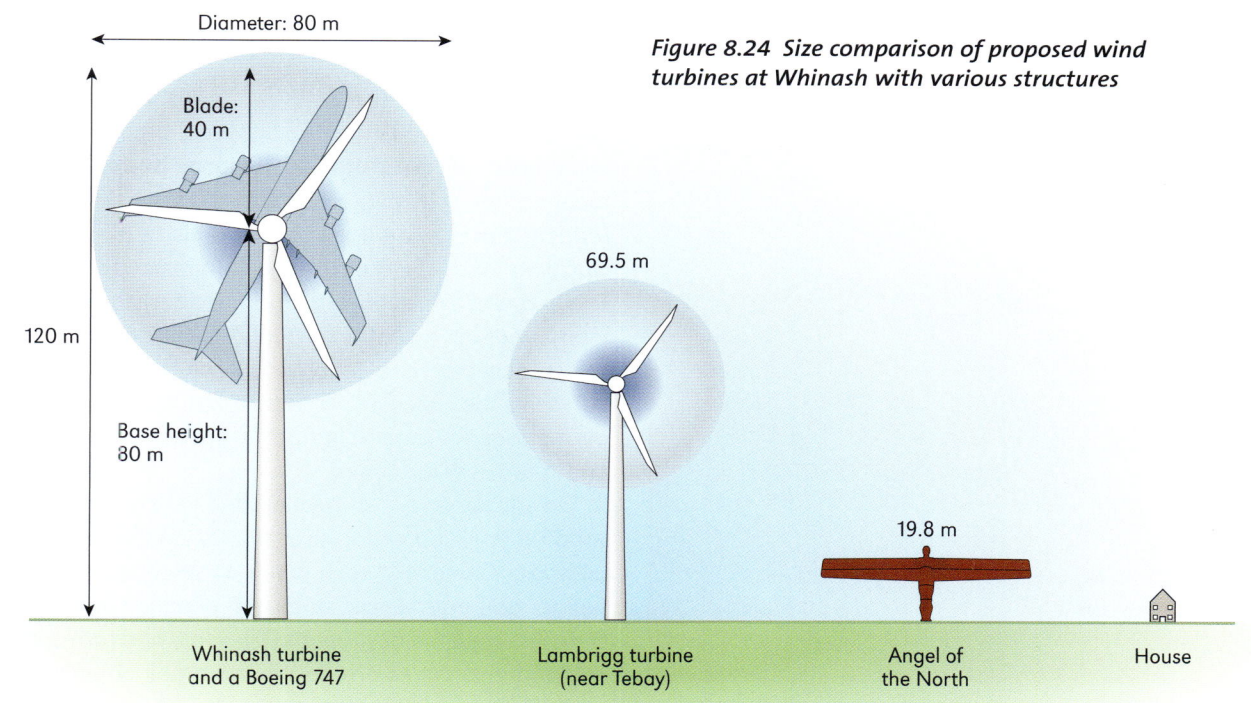

**Photograph 8.10** The Whinash landscape

*Figure 8.24 Size comparison of proposed wind turbines at Whinash with various structures*

Diameter: 80 m
Blade: 40 m
120 m
Base height: 80 m
69.5 m
19.8 m

Whinash turbine and a Boeing 747 | Lambrigg turbine (near Tebay) | Angel of the North | House

Economic development

## Chapter 8 Economic activity

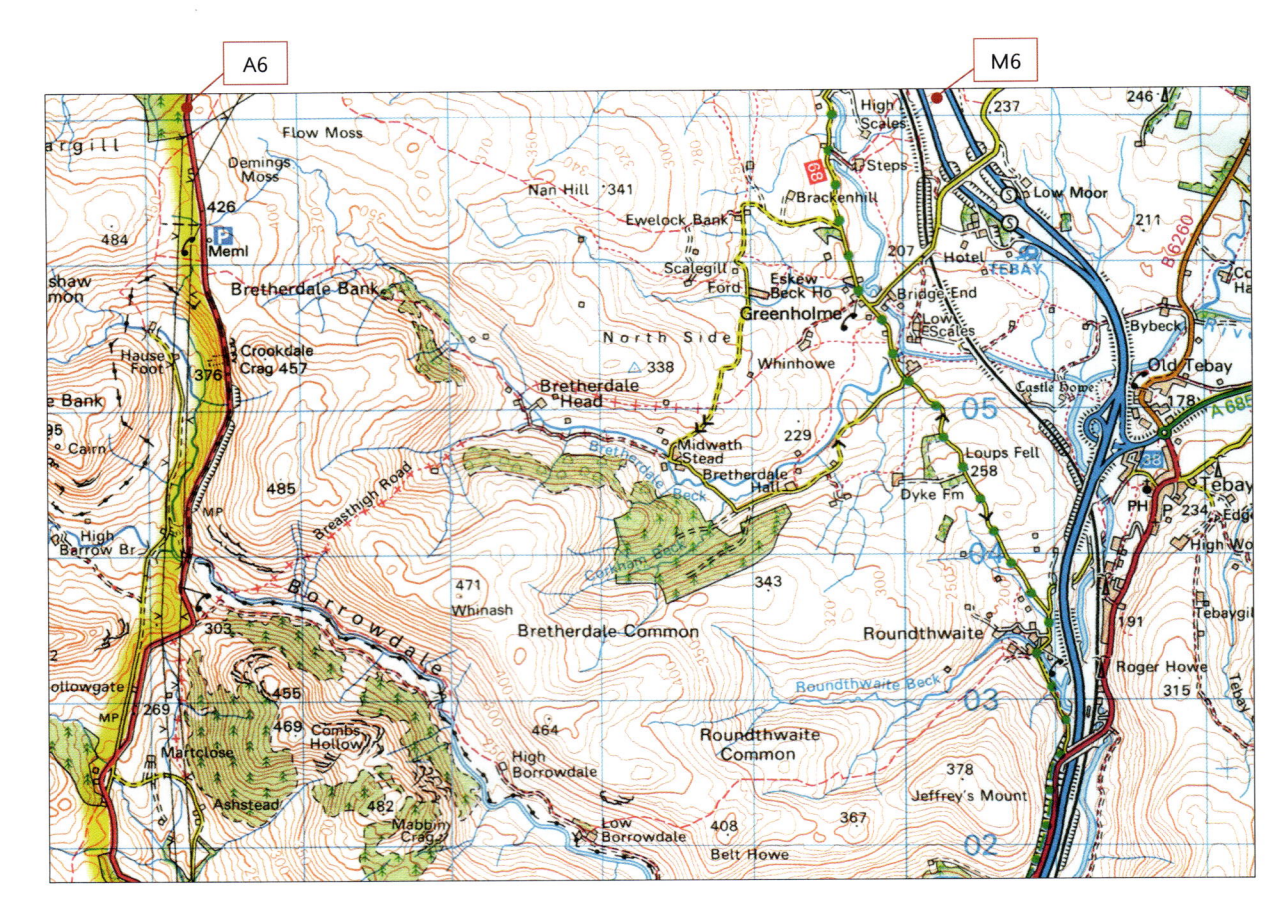

▲ *Figure 8.25 1:50,000 OS map extract of the area surrounding the proposed Whinash wind farm; the site occupies the upland north of Borrowdale between the M6 and the A6*

### Activity 8.15

Study Figure 8.25 and Photograph 8.10.

1. Describe the relief, drainage and landscape of the area between the M6 and the A6.
2. Using the evidence in Figure 8.25, state and explain three possible reasons why the area of land between the A6 and the M6 was chosen as the site for a large wind farm.
3. Using the evidence in Figure 8.25, suggest reasons why many people and interest groups oppose the Whinash scheme.

## The conflict at Whinash

The conflict at Whinash is between protecting a local **area of outstanding natural beauty** and meeting the UK's international commitments to reduce GHG emissions responsible for global warming and climate change. National parks in England and Wales have the primary duty to protect landscapes of exceptional quality against inappropriate development. In other words, the national parks like the Lake District and Yorkshire Dales must be managed sustainably for the benefit of present and future generations.

On the other hand, inland sites with significant wind energy potential are mainly found in the uplands. Whinash is such a site and has the potential to generate large amounts of clean energy. Unfortunately the best upland sites for wind farms in England and Wales are also in the areas of highest

# Theme 4

## Views against

When...some of the finest landscape in the country is under threat it is necessary for the agency to intervene.
*Richard Honey, The Countryside Agency*

Our reasons for opposing the farm have nothing to do with **nimbyism** ['not in my back yard']. The fact is this wind farm will not deliver what the public is led to believe it will.
*Kyle Blue, No Whinash Wind Farm Group*

If this project proceeds it will expose the finest windy countryside to similar developments… for insignificant benefit to the nation.
*Kyle Blue*

Giant wind turbines cause visual pollution, destroy jobs in tourism and only work a third of the time.
*David MacClean, Conservative candidate for Penrith and the Borders*

This is a wonderful piece of landscape that is being considered for classification as a National Park. This project would be absolutely catastrophic for the area.
*Ian Brodie, Friends of the Lake District*

The giant turbines would be visible from the M6 and would damage tourism worth millions of pounds a year.
*Cumbria Tourist Board*

## Views in favour

Local opposition is partly nimbyism and partly arguments that don't add up. For example they claim that the turbines kill birds but there is no evidence to show that.
*Jill Perry, Friends of the Earth*

The project will help meet government targets on **renewable energy** and most of the objections are from private interest groups.
*Andrew Newcombe, CWP*

It is very important that we build wind farms to solve the problems (of pollution) we have created in the past.
*Jill Perry*

Whinash is the most appropriate location in northwest England… a quarter of England is covered by National Parks or Areas of Outstanding Natural Beauty. We have to pick up the scraps that are left.
*Stephen Molloy, project manager for Chalmerston Wind Power (CWP)*

The presence of the M6 has already degraded the landscape visually and by generating noise and air pollution.
*Environmental campaigner*

It's time something was done to tackle climate change. I'm still waiting to return to my house after the January floods.
*Margaret Sanders, Carlisle resident whose home was flooded in January 2005*

I have rented out holiday accommodation for a number of years and I'm totally in favour of the scheme. Many people who come to the Lake District are walkers and outdoor types who are interested in green lifestyles — they're not going to be put off by wind turbines.
*Anita Stirzaker, local business woman*

Clean energy alternatives such as the Whinash wind farm are crucial if we are to avoid the worst effects of climate change.
*Jim Footner, Greenpeace*

*Figure 8.26 What people and interest groups say about Whinash*

### Activity 8.16

1. Study Figure 8.26 together with the rest of the information in this case study and summarise the case for and against the Whinash wind farm.
2. State your view on the proposal. Present your argument to a public enquiry, either from the viewpoint of a resident living in Tebay (see Figure 8.26) opposed to the scheme or as an environmentalist from Greenpeace or Friends of the Earth who supports the development.

Economic development

# Chapter 8 Economic activity

landscape quality, and are already protected by government legislation.

The Whinash scheme was so controversial that it went to a public enquiry in 2005. An unusual feature of the enquiry was that environmental groups took opposite sides. Greenpeace and Friends of the Earth supported the scheme because it would reduce the carbon dioxide emissions that cause climate change and global warming. The Countryside Agency and Lake District National Park Authority opposed Whinash. They argued that the wind farm would ruin the landscape and destroy important habitats for moorland birds. Most local people were strongly opposed to the scheme.

## Case study: Over-fishing in the North Sea

Current levels of fishing in the North Sea are unsustainable. Stocks of cod, hake, whiting and plaice are on the verge of collapse (see Figure 8.27). This situation is mainly due to over-fishing, though pollution and climate change (causing a gradual warming of the North Sea) have also played a part.

Fish are a common resource and sea fishing is difficult to regulate. This is because:
- fish are migratory, moving freely between national boundaries in the North Sea
- managing fish stocks sustainably requires the agreement of all countries bordering the North Sea
- the livelihoods of people in many coastal communities in eastern Scotland and eastern England depend almost entirely on fish-catching and fish-processing industries

Over-fishing and the collapse of fish stocks is nothing new. It happened to the herring fishery in the North Sea in the 1960s and 1970s. It also happened to the cod fisheries on the Grand Banks of Newfoundland, eastern Canada, in the 1980s. Worryingly, this fishery has never recovered.

### The impact of over-fishing
#### Social and economic effects
As fish stocks decline, fishermen lose their jobs and the fishing fleet is reduced. Lower catches mean that fish processing factories (often located in the fishing ports) close, which further increases unemployment and has negative effects on local businesses.

Northeast Scotland is the leading centre of the UK's fishing effort in the North Sea. Declining fish stocks have hit this region hard. Between 1993 and 2007, the number of fishermen in northeast Scotland fell by nearly 60%, from 3,826 to 1,470 (see Figure 8.28). Employment in fish processing, such as jobs in filleting and packaging, fell by 6.5% between 2000 and 2004. For a fishing port like Fraserburgh, where one in three jobs is in the fishing sector, this decline has been a severe blow.

### Factfile 8.5 The North Sea

- The North Sea is part of a **continental shelf** — a low-lying area on the European continent flooded by the sea.
- The North Sea has a surface area of 1,010 km$^2$, approximately four times the land area of the UK.
- The North Sea occupies a shallow basin. Water depth averages just 30 m in the southern North Sea. This increases to 200 m in the north between Scotland and Norway (see Figure 8.29).
- There are 185 million people living in the catchments of rivers that drain into the North Sea.
- Most of the North Sea's catchment is highly urbanised. It includes major urban areas such as London, the Randstad agglomeration in the Netherlands and the Rhine-Ruhr area in Germany.

Figure 8.27 Environmental impact of fishing in the North Sea

Bottlenose dolphins

Sand eels

◀ Over-fishing of sand eels in the North Sea is partly to blame for disastrous breeding seasons for common seabirds in the past 10 years. Sand eels are at the base of the food chain that supports seabirds such as razorbills, puffins, guillemots, kittiwakes and terns.

▲ Bottlenose dolphins and harbour porpoises are caught by accident in nets in the North Sea. The practice of pair trawling by two boats using a huge net is particularly damaging.

A hake catch

◀ The hake stock in the southern North Sea is barely 10,000 tonnes, compared with a minimum recommended level of 35,000 tonnes. Before over-fishing, hake was a common species.

Plaice

◀ The current stock of plaice in the North Sea is 190,000 tonnes — below the minimum level of 240,000 tonnes. The level of fishing must be reduced by 55% to allow stocks to recover.

A shoal of cod

A fishing trawler

▲ Cod has been so over-fished that it has almost disappeared from the North Sea. In the North Sea the minimum recommended stock size is 150,000 tonnes. It is now just 46,000 tonnes.

◀ Bottom trawling ploughs up the sea bed, destroying fragile corals and important fish nurseries.

Economic development

# Chapter 8 Economic activity

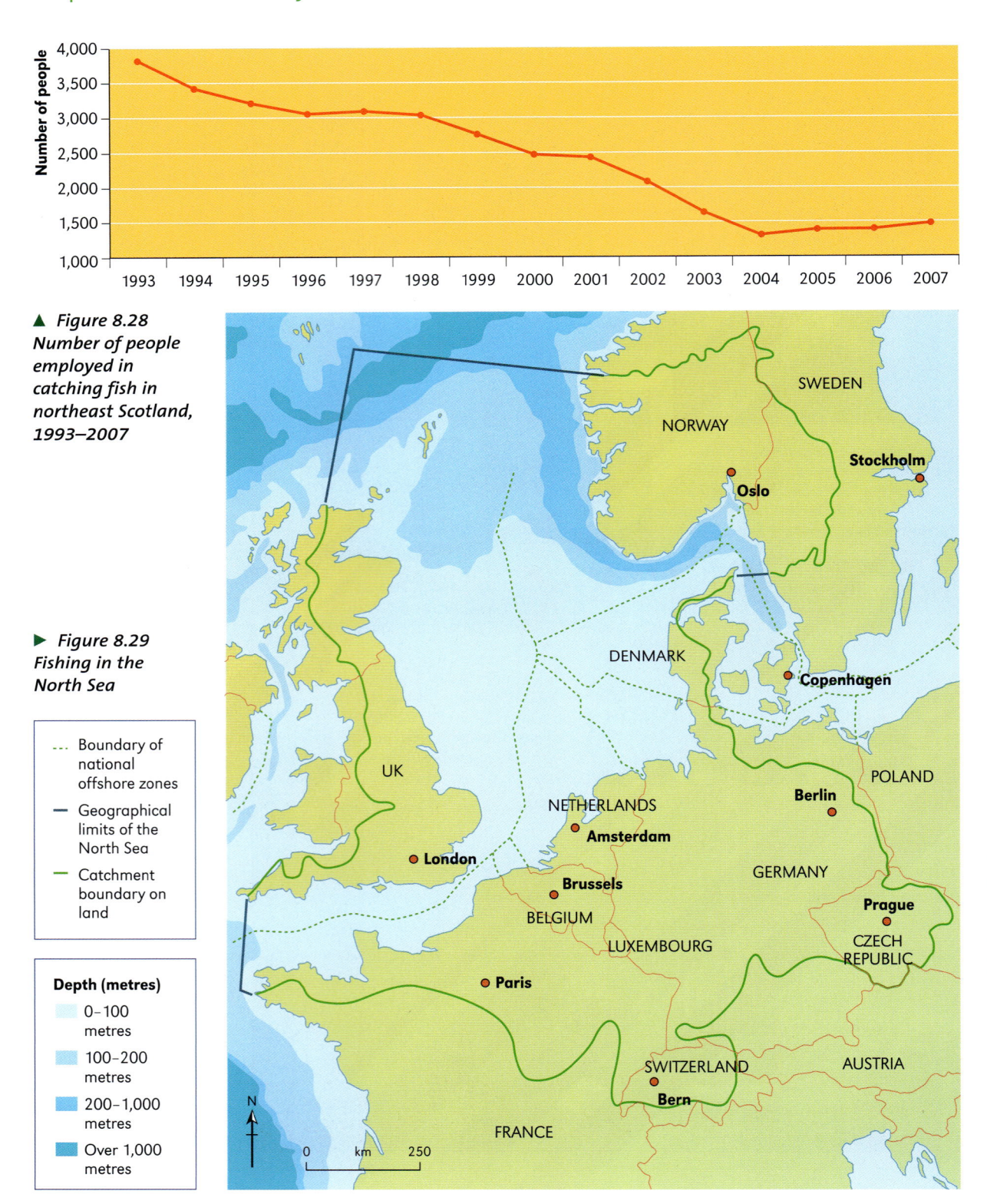

▲ Figure 8.28 Number of people employed in catching fish in northeast Scotland, 1993–2007

▶ Figure 8.29 Fishing in the North Sea

**Legend:**
- ····· Boundary of national offshore zones
- ─── Geographical limits of the North Sea
- ─── Catchment boundary on land

**Depth (metres)**
- 0–100 metres
- 100–200 metres
- 200–1,000 metres
- Over 1,000 metres

OCR (B) GCSE Geography

# Theme 4

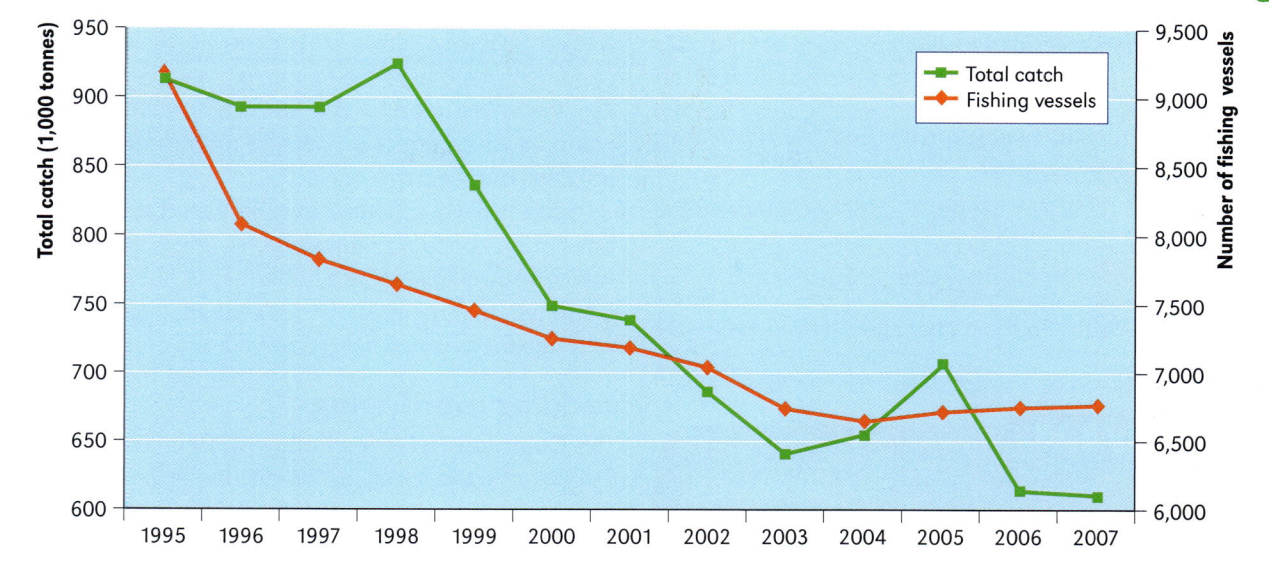

▲ Figure 8.30 Total UK fishing catch and number of fishing vessels, 1995–2007

## Activity 8.17

1. Look at Figure 8.29. Which countries:
   (a) lie within the North Sea's drainage basin?
   (b) have a coastline on the North Sea?
2. Explain why fishing is a primary economic activity.
3. Look at Figure 8.30. What was the total UK fish catch in:
   (a) 1995?
   (b) 2007?

### Environmental effects of unsustainable fishing

The North Sea is a complex ecosystem. At the base of the food chain are tiny organisms called plankton. Sand eels and other small fish eat the plankton, and they are eaten in turn by larger predatory fish such as cod and haddock. Healthy fish stocks are essential to the survival of creatures further along the food chain, such as seabirds, dolphins, porpoises and seals.

As stocks of predatory fish such as cod and whiting have declined, fishermen have turned to smaller species, especially sand eels. In 2005 sand eels accounted for around 40% by weight of the entire North Sea catch. Most of the catch is used for

## Factfile 8.6 The Common Fisheries Policy

Since 1983, the EU regulates fishing in the North Sea through its **Common Fisheries Policy (CFP)**. The aim of the policy is to create a sustainable fishery, where the annual catch of fish and other sea creatures does not exceed natural replacement. The CFP does this in a number of ways:

- It defines the total allowable catch per year (TAC) of each commercial fish species. If there is evidence of over-fishing these quotas are reduced. In extreme conditions the fishery might be closed completely.
- It reduces fishing by:
  (a) compensating fishing boat owners who agree to scrap their vessels
  (b) deciding the number of days each year that boats are allowed to fish
- It determines the mesh size of nets to allow immature fish to escape.
- It provides hard-pressed communities, hit by the decline of fishing, with money for new employment, retraining and education.

Economic development

fertiliser and animal feed. It is now believed that this industrial fishing is having disastrous effects on

Table 8.9 Total allowable catches from the North Sea: 2005 and 2007 (tonnes)

|         | 2005   | 2007   |
|---------|--------|--------|
| Plaice  | 57,370 | 49,000 |
| Whiting | 19,800 | 17,850 |
| Haddock | 51,321 | 46,444 |
| Cod     | 22,659 | 22,152 |

### Activity 8.18

1. Using information in Figure 8.27 and Table 8.9 draw bar charts to show the total allowable catches for plaice, whiting, haddock and cod from the North Sea.
2. Outline the evidence in Figure 8.27 and Table 8.9 that suggests that North Sea fishing remains unsustainable.

wildlife. Seabird colonies around the North Sea, which depend on sand eels, are failing to breed. Fewer sand eels mean less food for predatory fish, which in turn has a knock-on effect on marine mammals such as dolphins and seals.

Huge trawlers catch juvenile fish before they have the chance to reproduce, so there are fewer fish to spawn subsequent generations. Trawling has ploughed up large areas of the seabed, destroying a vital habitat for small fish, spawning and crustaceans.

## Tackling over-fishing

The **Common Fisheries Policy (CFP)** is used by the EU to tackle the social, economic and environmental problems caused by over-fishing (see Factfile 8.6). Although the CFP has existed since 1983, it has failed to protect fish stocks in the North Sea. In fact, the CFP is accused of encouraging over-fishing. Subsidies are paid to trawlers that may otherwise be uneconomic and quotas are not set at sustainable levels.

# Geographical enquiry

# Chapter 9 Fieldwork investigation in geography

You must submit a 1,200 word fieldwork enquiry based on a question or hypothesis from one of three key themes in the specification (Rivers and Coasts, Population and Settlement, and Economic Development). Theme 3: Natural hazards is not included here for obvious reasons! The fieldwork enquiry is based on **primary data** that you (or a group of students) have collected through fieldwork.

The structure of the enquiry falls into four parts:
1 Setting the scene
2 Methods of data collection
3 Data presentation and analysis
4 Evaluation and conclusion

## Possible topics for GCSE fieldwork investigations

### Theme 1: Rivers and Coasts
- How does channel efficiency change downstream?
- How does channel width and depth change downstream?
- How does sediment shape change downstream?
- How does sediment size change downstream?
- What effect does a river confluence have on sediment size/shape or channel size/efficiency or channel shape in/of the main channel?
- How does discharge change downstream?
- What are the differences in cross-section between meandering and straight channels?
- How does channel slope vary with channel width/efficiency?
- How are sediments sorted on a point bar?
- How do different groups perceive river and coastal flood hazards?
- How do shingle beaches and sand beaches vary in profile?
- How does wave period influence beach profiles?
- How do groynes affect beach width?

Geographical enquiry

# Chapter 9 Fieldwork investigation in geography

### Theme 2: Population and Settlement
- How often do people move house and how far do they move?
- How does rural population change affect service provision and the environment in rural areas?
- To what extent is there inequality in access to services in rural/urban areas?
- How and why are there differences in service provision between settlements of similar population size?
- How does distance travelled by shoppers affect the purchase of different goods and services?
- How do the trade areas of two market towns differ?
- What is the geographical pattern of shopping in the CBD of a town or city?
- How have the number and types of shop in a town or city centre changed in the past 20 years?
- How do pedestrian flows in a town or city centre influence types of shop?
- What is the geographical pattern of spending by shoppers in a town or city centre?
- To what extent is land use in a town or city organised into zones, sectors and areas?

### Theme 4: Economic Development
- What are the main differences in the use of two contrasting recreational areas by visitors, e.g. country park, national park?
- What are the harmful environmental effects of a factory in a large urban area?
- What are the economic, social and environmental impacts of a new supermarket/by-pass/housing estate, etc. on a local area?
- How do journeys to work differ between residents in contrasting housing areas?
- How does shopping behaviour differ between the customers of two supermarkets, e.g. Tesco and Netto?

# Part 1 Setting the scene

## Aim

The first stage is to state the aim or target of your enquiry. This needs to be specific and not too wide ranging. Remember that your enquiry must not exceed 1,200 words. Your focus will be either a question or a hypothesis. For example, if you decided to investigate the characteristics of a stream or small river, your question might be:

> How does the size of sediment change with distance downstream?

On the other hand you may prefer to present your aim more scientifically as a hypothesis. A hypothesis is a statement whose accuracy we can test. So in this example, we might replace our question with the following hypothesis:

*Sediments get smaller with increasing distance downstream.*

## Expected outcomes

Having presented a question or hypothesis you will need to give the reasoning behind it. This is an opportunity for you to demonstrate your knowledge and understanding of a topic that you have studied in class as part of the specification. Let us consider the hypothesis that sediment gets smaller downstream. We have to explain how this happens. This will involve referring back to your notes and textbook and describing how bedload is eroded by abrasion and attrition. Of course, you have to remember that rarely in the natural world are explanations as simple as that. This is because other factors influence sediments in rivers. These other factors include: inputs of sediments from tributary streams; sediments released into the stream channel by erosion of the banks and valley side; the effects of reservoirs, weirs etc. However, this discussion can be deferred until your conclusion and evaluation.

## Explaining how the question or hypothesis links to the specification

The topic you have chosen must be part of the GCSE specification. You should, therefore, already have a solid background of understanding. This part of your enquiry gives you the opportunity to place it in its context.

If you were testing the hypothesis that river sediments get smaller downstream, then in this section you might want to describe, briefly, how rivers transport sediment. For example, you could say how, when the river has sufficient energy (due to its gradient and discharge), it is able to move large sediments such as gravels and cobbles along the channel; that these sediments are known as the bedload; and that the process of transport is called traction. As the bedload is transferred downstream, erosion by abrasion and attrition occurs, causing the sediments to become smaller and rounder. A diagram to explain these processes might be helpful.

In order to put in context a study that aims to show how the number of shoppers in a market centre falls with distance, an outline of the factors that influence shopping behaviour is needed. This would cover the following areas: the influence of competing service centres; the increasing transport and time costs involved in shopping trips over greater distance; the attraction of lower-order service centres for the purchase of convenience goods and services; the lower density of population living in the rural areas around market centres.

> **Activity 9.1**
>
> Choose 10 enquiry questions from the lists on pages 197–98 and re-write them as hypotheses.

> **Activity 9.2**
>
> Give the explanations and logic behind the following hypotheses:
> - Shoppers travel to their nearest centre to purchase the goods and services they need.
> - People normally move house over relatively short distances.
> - Settlements with larger populations normally have more shops than settlements with smaller populations.
> - River discharge increases downstream.

Geographical enquiry

Chapter 9 Fieldwork investigation in geography

## Geographical background of places/features chosen for the investigation

Your enquiry is also placed in its relevant geographical context. This means providing a description of the geography of the area or feature that you are investigating. In a river study you will want to describe the main features of the drainage basin. This would include its size, shape, rock types, relief, vegetation, land use and the influence of human activities. You might also research **secondary data** on the local climate, including temperatures, rainfall and evaporation. A sketch map of the drainage basin, based on either a 1:25,000 or 1:10,000 scale would be essential.

An enquiry based on shopping in a market centre would include background information on the centre's population, its main functions (e.g. service centre, industry, commuting, tourism etc.), its transport connections with the surrounding area and recent changes in population and economic activity. A sketch map, showing the situation of the town, other competing centres and the main road and rail network would also be needed (see Figure 9.1).

For both studies, satellite images (from Google maps or Google Earth) and ground photos would add important information to the geographical context of the enquiry.

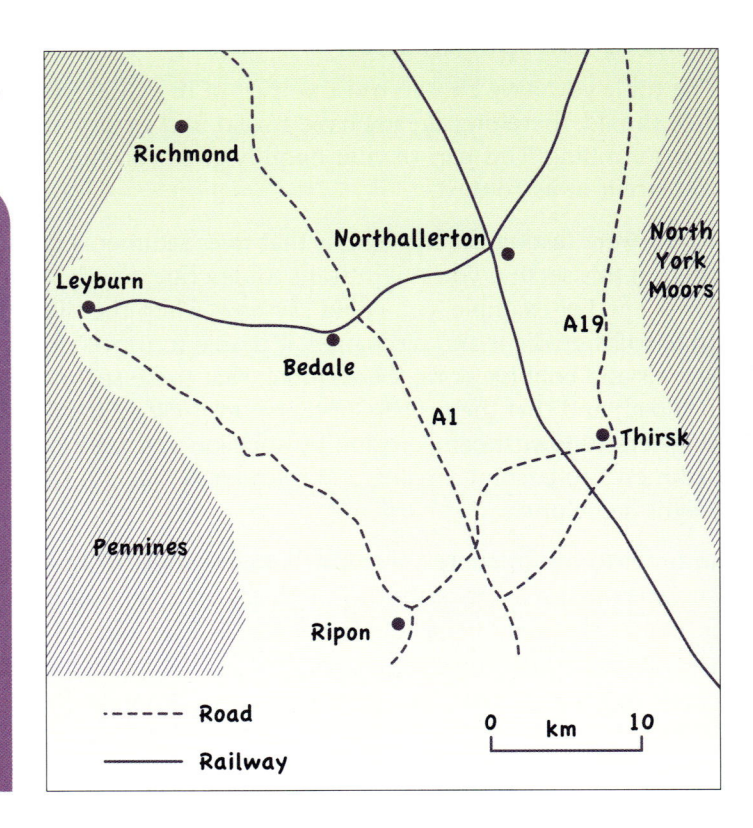

▶ Figure 9.1 Sketch map showing location of Northallerton

### Enquiry tips

- Choose a topic for which the data are readily available and easy to collect.

- A topic that involves a comparison (e.g. is A different from B) often provides a successful study. An alternative is to investigate how A is related to B.

- Try to avoid relying exclusively on scanned OS maps or downloaded Google maps in your enquiry. Drawing a sketch is often a better alternative and demonstrates a worthwhile skill (see Figures 9.1 and 9.2). OS maps provide a clutter of information, most of which will have little relevance to your enquiry. A sketch map on the other hand provides selective information, which is focused and relevant.

OCR (B) GCSE Geography

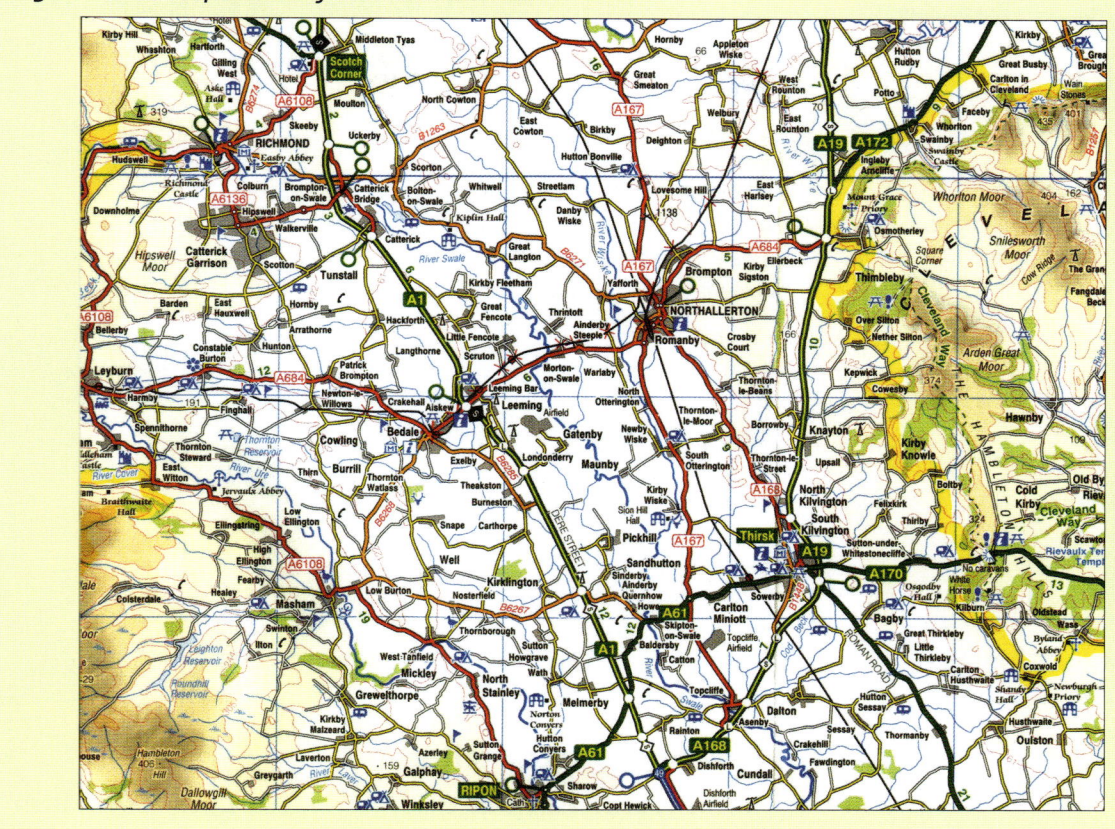

*Figure 9.2 OS map extract of Northallerton area*

# Part 2: Method of data collection

This section includes:
- a description of the methods used in primary data collection
- an explanation of why these methods are used
- a description of the problems encountered in the collection of data

## Data and data sources

There are two types of data: primary and secondary. Primary data are new data, which have not previously been collected or processed. Any data collected through fieldwork, by measurement, observation and interview, are primary data. Secondary data are not quite so easy to define. However, all secondary data are in documentary form, and include textbooks, articles, magazines, websites and maps. Essentially, secondary data have already been processed and analysed before publication.

Geographical enquiry

# Chapter 9 Fieldwork investigation in geography

*Table 9.1 Some important sources of secondary data*

| Data source | Description | Location of data |
|---|---|---|
| Census of population for England & Wales | Provides a wealth of information on population and socio-economic features at local scales. Published at 10 year intervals since 1801. | www.statistics.gov.uk/ Search for neighbourhood statistics |
| National Water Archive | Provides flow data for larger rivers in the UK. Also provides land use, relief and climate information for individual drainage basins. | www.nwl.ac.uk/ih/nwa/index.htm |
| Up my street | Postcode units (using full postcodes) are classified into 55 demographic/social and economic housing areas (ACORN classification). The site includes a map showing the location of postcode units. | www.upmystreet.com |
| Store locator | Distances of postcode areas from supermarkets. Useful in calculating distances of shoppers from supermarkets and town centres. | www.multimap.com/clients/places.cgi?client=asda_sf This example is for Asda stores; try other major supermarket chains |
| Google Earth | Satellite images. High resolution in urban areas, showing housing types and land use. | http://earth.google.com/ |
| Google Maps | Maps showing settlements, street names, roads etc. at a variety of scales | http://google.maps.com |
| Multimap | Similar maps to Google. Shows location of postcode units and features such as cash points, parking etc. | http://www.multimap.com/ |
| OS maps | Small map extracts at 1:250,000, 1:50,000, 1:25,000, 1:10,000 | www.ordnancesurvey.co.uk/oswebsite/ |

## Methods of primary data collection

There are three methods of primary data collection: measurement, observation and interviews. Both river and coastal enquiries will depend to some degree on measurement. Gravel and shingle are measured with a ruler or pair of callipers; river channel gradients and beach gradients are measured with tapes, clinometers and ranging poles; river channels in cross-section are measured with tapes and metre rulers and so on (Photograph 9.1).

▶ Photograph 9.1 Primary data collection

Enquiries in human geography often depend on observation. Examples of data sourced by observation include land use, shop types, house types, traffic flows and pedestrian flows. Figure 9.3 shows a retailer classification sheet used to record types of retailer in town centres.

*Figure 9.3 Retailer classification sheet*

**Product retailers**

*Convenience outlets:*
Baker
Butcher
Chemist
Confectioner
Tobacconist/newsagent
Delicatessen/health food
Frozen food
General store
Greengrocer/fishmonger
Off licence
Petrol station
Supermarket
Superstore (mainly food)
Others

*Comparison outlets:*
Clothing and footwear
Bridal wear
Boys' wear
Clothes — general
Children's wear
Costumier/fancy dress
Footwear
Girls' wear
Jeans
Ladies' wear
Lingerie/hosiery
Men's wear
Millinery
Rainwear
Ties/socks
Others

*Carpet/furniture/household goods:*
Bathroom equipment
Bedding
Carpets/floor covering
China/glassware/fancy goods
Furniture
Glazier

*Electrical goods:*
Audio–visual equipment
Computer equipment
Electrical goods (white goods)
Electronic equipment
Mobile phones

*Miscellaneous:*
Antiques
Artists' materials
Books/stationery
Cards/posters/gifts
Cameras/photo equipment
Camping/government surplus
Car accessories
Cars/motor cycles
Catalogue shop (e.g. Argos)
Charity shop/second hand
Cosmetics/toiletries
Cycles
Department store (e.g. House of Fraser)
Variety store
Discount store (non-food)
DIY superstore
Fabrics/wool
Florist
Garden centre
Handbags
Haberdashery
Hobby/craft
Ironmongery/hardware
Jewellers/watchmakers
Leather goods
Musical instruments
Nursery goods
Pet shop/pet food
Picture framing
Videos/CDs/DVDs
Sewing machines
Sports equipment
Telephones (e.g. BT)
Toys/games
Umbrellas

**Service retailers**

*Household services:*
Estate agent
Solicitor

*Financial services:*
Accountant
Bank
Building society
Insurer/broker

*Health care services:*
Optician
Chiropodist

*Business/government services:*
Consumer advice centre
Employment agency
Job centre
Printing/copying

*Leisure services:*
Amusement arcade
Bowling alley
Café
Cinema
Betting office
Fast food
Fish and chips
Guest house/bed and breakfast
Gym
Hotel
Ice rink
Pub
Restaurant
Snooker/bingo
Swimming pool
Take-away food
Theatre
Wine bar

*Personal consumer services:*
Hairdresser/beautician
Solarium/health salon

*Miscellaneous services:*
Photographer
Shoe repair
Tool hire
Travel agent
Television/video rental
Video hire
Others

*Vacant premises:*
Vacant outlets
Outlets under construction

Geographical enquiry

# Chapter 9 Fieldwork investigation in geography

Photograph 9.2 Students with questionnaires

▼ *Figure 9.4 Checklist for compiling questionnaires*

- Make clear the target population, e.g. people who live in the survey village, regular shoppers etc.
- Keep the number of questions to a minimum and the maximum time for completion to less than 2 minutes.
- Make the questions clear and unambiguous and avoid using jargon and technical terms.
- Construct the questions from the hypotheses you are testing in your enquiry.
- Make most of the questions 'closed', i.e. respondents choose from a list of possible answers.
- Plan the layout so that the early questions focus on behaviour (e.g. length of journey to work, frequency of shopping etc.) and leave any questions that may be sensitive or personal to the end (e.g. postcode).
- Minimise the number of questions that are personal and intrusive, e.g. income, age, employment. If in doubt avoid them altogether.
- Never ask for the detailed address of the respondent — the name of a settlement or suburb is usually sufficient.
- Avoid questions that require simple 'yes'/'no' responses.
- Avoid questions that have political, racist, sexist or religious connotations.
- Plan the questionnaire so that it fits on a single side of A4.

## *Questionnaires*

Sometimes we require information about people's attitudes, opinions, actions and movements. This kind of information relies on questionnaire surveys. Questionnaires can be done either by interview or by post. Most student questionnaires are done by interview in public places (see Photograph 9.2). The success of any questionnaire survey depends, in large part, on the quality of the questions. Figure 9.4 provides a checklist of good practice in compiling questionnaires and Figure 9.5 is an exemplar questionnaire used for a village survey.

## Sampling

Most data collection in geography relies of sampling. A sample is a sub-set of items chosen from the wider population. For example, you might select a sample of 100 pebbles on a beach in order to investigate the size, shape and rock type of all the pebbles. Clearly, with thousands of pebbles, it would be impossible to measure every one (i.e. the population). Nor would it be necessary: if our sample is selected objectively, using scientific method, we can probably learn all that we need to know about the population from a small sample.

The crucial thing about sampling is that the sample should, as far as possible, *represent* the population accurately. If it fails to do this, then we can have little confidence in the results of our enquiry.

## *Sampling strategies*

There are three main strategies we can use to increase sample accuracy:

- random
- systematic
- stratified

If you select a sample of items randomly it means using random numbers. You can use your calculator to generate random numbers and then select your sample. Suppose you were doing a random postal survey of noise pollution

## Village survey questionnaire

| | | |
|---|---|---|
| **1** How many years have you lived in this village? | >20 ☐  10–20 ☐  5–9 ☐  <5 ☐ | Tick boxes for all possible responses |
| **2** If you have lived in this village for no more than 20 years, where did you live previously? (name of village or town) | | Geographical scale specified |
| **3** Does your household have access to a car for private transport? | No ☐  1 car ☐  2 cars ☐  >2 cars ☐ | Provides more information then simple yes/no |
| **4** How many members of your household: | Are retired ☐<br>Commute to work ☐<br>Work in the village ☐<br>Work from home ☐<br>Work in the home ☐ | Questionnaire is brief — should be completed within 2 minutes |
| **5** If members of your household commute, in which town or village do they work? | | |
| **6** Where do you normally shop for food and clothes? (name of settlement or online) | Food<br>Clothes | Minimal use of jargon |
| **7** How have the following village services changed in the past 5 years? |       Better  Worse  No change<br>Shops ☐ ☐ ☐<br>Transport ☐ ☐ ☐<br>Schools ☐ ☐ ☐<br>Doctors ☐ ☐ ☐ | Closed response needed — giving standardised data which are easier to process |
| **8** What is your full postcode? (e.g. PR5 0DP) | | This information could be regarded as confidential therefore it is best to leave until the end of the questionnaire |

▲ Figure 9.5 Village survey questionnaire

in a busy residential street with 100 households, and you decided on a 20% sample. First you would number the houses from 1 to 100. Then you would generate 20 random numbers between one and 100 on your calculator. These numbers would give you a **random sample** of households.

A simpler strategy is to collect a systematic sample. With a 20% sample we would select every fifth household and deliver our postal questionnaire. With a 50% sample we would deliver questionnaires to every other household. **Systematic sampling** is the simplest and most practical sampling method for conducting street interviews. You simply select a random number between say 2 and 9 (e.g. 4) and then attempt to interview every fourth person.

Unfortunately most populations are not uniform but consist of sub-groups. For example, the impact of noise pollution on a street might vary according to the house type occupied by residents. Households occupying terraced housing, which fronts directly onto the street, are likely to suffer more noise than households in semi-detached houses, set back from the road by gardens. Households in first floor apartments might be worse affected than those in ground floor apartments. Thus, in order to get the most accurate picture of

Geographical enquiry

Chapter 9 Fieldwork investigation in geography

▲ *Photograph 9.3 Housing types*

### Sampling tips

- Remember that your enquiry is only as good as the data on which it is based.
- A good sample will represent the population accurately.
- You must have an objective strategy for selecting your sample, i.e. either random, systematic or stratified.
- A good sample, as well as being accurate, is easy to collect.
- Generally the larger the sample, the more confidence you can have in your results.
- The size of your sample will reflect a balance between the need for accuracy and the limits imposed by time and other resources.

the noise problem, we could **stratify** our sample by house type. If the 100 households in the street occupied 50 semi-detached houses, 30 terraces, and 20 apartments, then our 20% sample would comprise 10 semi-detached households, 6 terraces and 4 apartments. The households chosen for our sample would still be selected either randomly or systematically.

### Activity 9.3

Study Photograph 9.3, which is a satellite image of a mixed housing area, comprising semi-detached and terraced housing. Assume that you want to investigate the supermarket preferences of residents in this area based on a 20% sample of households.

1. Make a traced copy (with three photocopies) to show the housing units in Photograph 9.3, and colour them according to the type of housing.
2. Select (a) a 20% random sample, (b) a 20% systematic sample and (c) a 20% stratified systematic sample. Locate each on the photocopied maps.

OCR (B) GCSE Geography

## Sample size

Normally, the larger the sample the more confidence you can have in your results. Collecting data in groups is an obvious way of boosting sample size, and may be essential where data collection is time-consuming, as in questionnaire surveys. In contrast, it is relatively easy to collect large samples of sediments from a stream or beach, or rock particles from a scree slope. In the end, sample size is often a compromise between the desire for accuracy and the limited time available for data collection.

## Spatial sampling

Spatial sampling is used where location is an important feature of the items being studied. In geography fieldwork, samples are usually selected either from areas (**quadrats**) or from lines (transects) using random, systematic and stratified methods.

Area sampling is done using quadrats. A quadrat is a metal frame (typically 1 m × 1 m), sub-divided into smaller squares. In quadrat sampling the first step is to locate the quadrat, either randomly or systematically. Then use the smaller squares within the quadrat to count items such as sediment types and plant species. Quadrats can also be used to record the presence or absence of items, or to estimate their areal cover.

Photograph 9.4 shows an exposure of boulder clay left by a glacier. It consists of a matrix of fine material, interspersed with larger rock particles. A quadrat,

◀ *Photograph 9.4 Quadrat sampling of larger rock particles in boulder clay*

Geographical enquiry

# Chapter 9 Fieldwork investigation in geography

▶ *Photograph 9.5 A line of transect down a scree slope with particles measured at regular intervals*

located randomly, is used to select a sample of rock particles. The particles chosen are those located at the intersection of the cross-wires. Each particle in the sample can then be measured, weighed and identified according to rock type.

Many geographical enquiries use samples derived from lines or transects. Transects are especially useful when they cross areas of contrasting slope, geology, soils and vegetation. Like quadrats, transects are located randomly, and samples are collected at systematic or random intervals along the line of transect (often using quadrats). In Photograph 9.5 a line of transect has been established along a scree slope. Sample points are located at regular intervals where scree particles will be selected and measured.

## Common problems encountered in data collection

When you write up your fieldwork enquiry, you must provide a detailed account of data collection methods, and comment on the problems you encountered and on the accuracy of your data. You should also say what steps you took, if any, to overcome these problems. Table 9.2 lists a number of common problems in data collection and possible responses to them.

## Risk assessment

Geographical fieldwork, whether in urban or rural environments, always includes an element of risk. Before undertaking fieldwork you must complete a risk assessment. This involves three stages:

◀ Table 9.2 Some common problems of data collection

| Problem | Possible response |
|---|---|
| Insufficient data collected | Pre-empt this problem by liaising closely with your teacher, and having a clear target for sample size. Return to the field and collect more data; share data with students doing similar enquiries. Make sure that you have enough students in your group to complete the fieldwork. Rivers and coasts fieldwork usually needs a minimum of three students. |
| High refusal rate for street interviews | Choose locations that are less busy, or where people have time to respond, e.g. bus stops, taxi ranks, car parks. Make a greater effort to explain to potential respondents what you are doing, emphasising the brevity of the interview, and engaging in the politest terms. |
| Too few people to interview in a town centre or village | Choose a Saturday or a market day when there is more business. For village surveys choose a weekend, when people are more likely to be at home. |
| Access to fieldwork sites | Surveys in supermarket premises will require the prior permission of the manager. The approval of landowners will be needed for physical geography fieldwork on private land. |
| Complaints from shops regarding questionnaires | You should circulate throughout the central area of a town and avoid standing outside shop doorways, and in front of specific shops for more than a few minutes. You should interview respondents individually and not in groups. If a large group of students is interviewing, the interviews should be staggered so that no more than half-a-dozen are interviewing at any one time. |
| Scale | The scale may be too large to be practical, e.g. land use survey in the CBD of a major city such as Manchester or Birmingham; channel and sediment studies on a river rather than a stream. The scale may also be too small, e.g. downstream changes in channel characteristics and sediments may only be evident over 20–30 km. Think carefully about the scale of your enquiry before attempting data collection; opt for fewer samples. |
| Adverse weather | River studies must not be attempted when discharge is above average: return when water levels have subsided. Shopping surveys in town centres may be done in arcades, covered shopping centres, supermarket foyers etc. but permission will be needed. |
| Recording data | Date, time and the precise location should be recorded on a pre-prepared recording schedule. Data should be recorded consistently and legibly. Contingencies should be made for wet weather (e.g. use of pencil, plastic covers on recording schedule). |

- identifying the potential hazards — awareness of possible hazards is vital
- assessing the level of risk posed by each hazard
- devising a strategy to minimise the hazard to yourself and other members of the fieldwork party

We often formalise this process by completing a risk assessment sheet (see Figure 9.6), which is submitted for approval to your teacher.

A number of safety guidelines common to all geographical fieldwork should always be followed. These are as follows:
1. Work in groups. Ideally, groups should comprise at least three people. If an accident occurs resulting in injury, one member of the group can get help while the other remains with the injured person.

2 Carry a mobile phone. Leave your phone switched on for the duration of the fieldwork and make sure that you have exchanged phone numbers with your teacher or supervisor.
3 Wear (or carry in a rucksack) suitable outdoor clothing. This includes waterproofs (jacket and trousers) and several layers of clothing. For river studies wellies or waders are essential, and for work on slopes or in rough terrain, wear walking boots that provide good grip and protect your ankles.
4 If you are working in a remote rural area you should carry a torch, a survival bag, a whistle and emergency rations.
5 Carry a small first aid kit at all times.
6 Carry a map at the appropriate scale.
7 Leave details of your itinerary with your teacher, including your times of departure and return.

*Figure 9.6 A risk assessment form*

### Risk assessment

| Location | | | | | Date | | | |
|---|---|---|---|---|---|---|---|---|
| **Potential hazards** | Risk present/ Absent | Level of risk | | | Depart time | | Return time | |
| | | High | Medium | Low | | | | |
| *Urban hazards* | | | | | Action taken | | | |
| Roads/traffic | | | | | | | | |
| Threats from public | | | | | | | | |
| Getting lost | | | | | | | | |
| Toxic wastes | | | | | | | | |
| Others | | | | | | | | |
| *Rural hazards* | | | | | | | | |
| Rivers | | | | | | | | |
| Rockfalls | | | | | | | | |
| Toxic wastes | | | | | | | | |
| Fieldwork equipment | | | | | | | | |
| Tides | | | | | | | | |
| Waves | | | | | | | | |
| Cliffs | | | | | | | | |
| Steep slopes | | | | | | | | |
| Animals | | | | | | | | |
| Exposure to weather | | | | | | | | |
| Getting lost | | | | | | | | |
| Others | | | | | | | | |
| Signed (Student) | | | | | Date | | | |
| Signed (Teacher) | | | | | Date | | | |

# Part 3 Data presentation and analysis

In this section we shall look at ways of presenting fieldwork data in charts and maps, and at the analysis of data to determine our key findings.

## Types of chart

Charts are used to store data and to reveal the trends and patterns in data sets.

### Histograms

A histogram is a type of bar chart that shows a frequency distribution (see Figure 9.7). Individual values in a data set (e.g. slope angles) are grouped into classes, with each class represented by a bar in the histogram. Two decisions are made when drawing a histogram: (a) the number of classes required; (b) the interval between classes. As a rough guide, we determine the number of classes

### Data analysis tips

- Before writing up the data presentation and analysis section of your enquiry, you should first draw all of the relevant charts and maps.
- The charts and maps you use should be the ones that are most appropriate for the data.
- You should try to use a range of different chart and map types.
- Do not present the same data in more than one chart or map form.
- You might prefer to draw all of your charts on the computer. All the charts described in this section can be drawn using Microsoft Excel.

▼ Figure 9.7 Histogram of Norber limestone pedestals

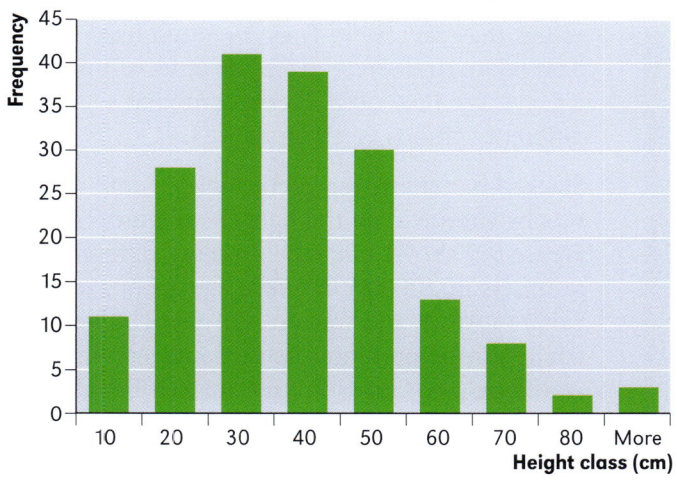

▼ Table 9.3 Scree particle sizes on a slope in North Yorkshire (median axes of particles in cm)

| | | | | |
|---|---|---|---|---|
| 10.5 | 13 | 7 | 5 | 2.5 |
| 12 | 12 | 9 | 4.5 | 2.5 |
| 5.5 | 14 | 6 | 2.5 | 5 |
| 7 | 11.5 | 10.5 | 3 | 4 |
| 9 | 17 | 8.5 | 7 | 4 |
| 15 | 23 | 9 | 8 | 2 |
| 17 | 10 | 11 | 2.5 | 1 |
| 9 | 8.5 | 15 | 4.5 | 5 |
| 6 | 9 | 15 | 2 | 2 |
| 9.5 | 8 | 8 | 7.5 | 2.5 |
| 29 | 12 | 12 | 3.5 | 4 |
| 11 | 13 | 5 | 2.5 | 3 |
| 6 | 14 | 10.5 | 4.5 | 2.5 |
| 8.5 | 26 | 9 | 3 | 6.5 |
| 10 | 12.5 | 6 | 3 | 4 |
| 18 | 13 | 16.5 | 3.5 | 3 |
| 8.5 | 10 | 11 | 1.5 | 5 |
| 9 | 12 | 12 | 15 | 5 |
| 6 | 14 | 11 | 3 | 3 |
| 8 | 20 | 10.5 | 4 | 5 |
| 11 | 17 | 8 | 2 | 1 |
| 13 | 11 | 8.5 | 5.5 | 1 |
| 9 | 14 | 9 | 4 | 2 |
| 10.5 | 12 | 9.5 | 3 | 2 |

Geographical enquiry

# Chapter 9 Fieldwork investigation in geography

*Photograph 9.6 Austwick screes, North Yorkshire*

### Activity 9.4

Present the data on scree particle sizes on a scree slope in North Yorkshire (see Table 9.3 and Photograph 9.6) as a histogram. Start by deciding the number of classes and then the interval between classes.

▼ *Figure 9.8 Downstream changes in discharge on the River Thames*

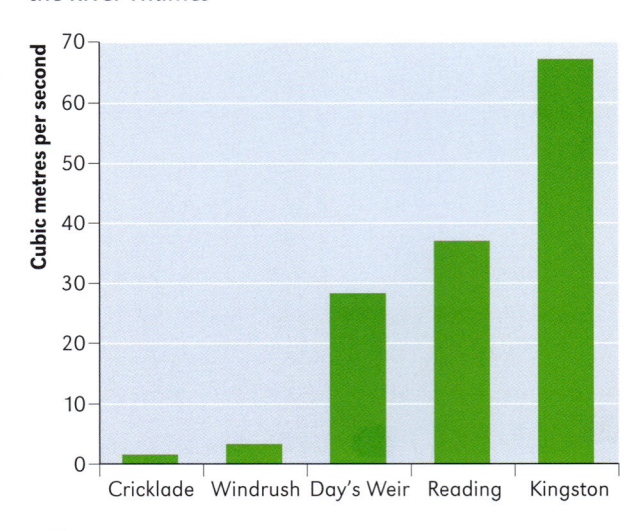

by taking the square root of the number of values. Too few classes and the histogram is excessively generalised: too many and any patterns and trends are lost. Class intervals are obtained by dividing the range of values by the number of classes.

## Bar charts

Bar charts consist of a series of rectangles — arranged either vertically or horizontally — which are proportional in length and area to the values they represent. They are often used where data relate to discrete places or units of time, e.g. average flow on a river recorded at several different stations (see Figure 9.8).

Stacked bar charts represent two or more data sets by sub-dividing the bars (see Figure 9.9). Figure 9.9 shows both the absolute difference in numbers in 2009 in different age groups in sub-Saharan Africa and western Europe. The data could also be presented as percentages, which would help comparison. In a stacked bar chart based on percentages, both bars would be the same height.

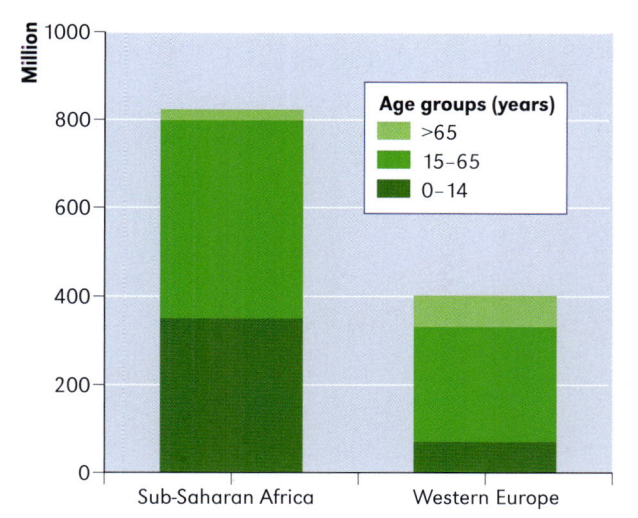

▲ Figure 9.9 Stacked bar chart: age structure of sub-Saharan Africa and western Europe, 2009

## Pie charts

Pie charts are a type of circular graph divided into segments to show the importance of sub-groups in the population (see Figure 9.10). Normally, the first segment in the chart starts at 12 o'clock. Pie charts are a quick and easy way of representing values as proportions. However, the number of sub-groups in the chart should be limited: with more than seven or eight it is difficult to differentiate segmental shading.

## Line charts

Line charts are used to plot variables that change continuously, such as temperature, or land values with distance from city centres (see Figure 9.11). Line charts differ from trend lines because they show actual patterns, rather than general trends.

## Scatter charts

Scatter charts are used when we want to plot two variables, *x* and *y* (see Figure 9.12). Variable *x* (always plotted on the horizontal axis) is known as the **independent variable**, and variable *y* (on the vertical axis) is the **dependent variable**. We assume that the independent variable causes change in the dependent variable. In Figure 9.12 the air speed of a 757 jet airliner on a flight between Manchester and

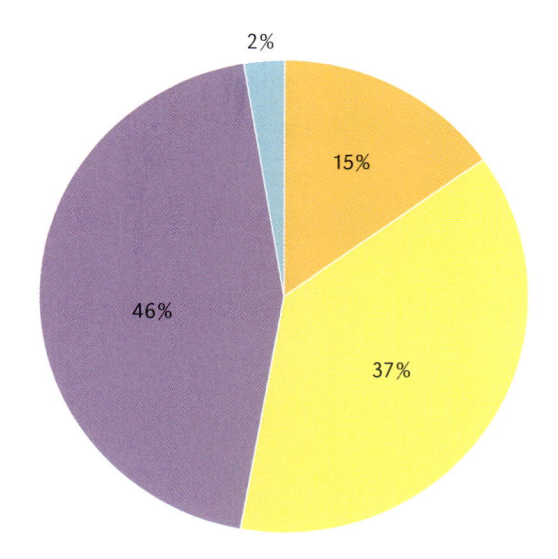

▲ Figure 9.10 Pie chart: retail units in Wetherby

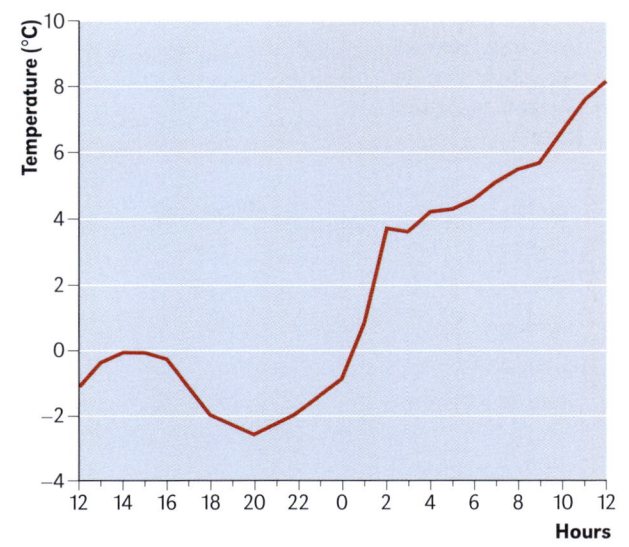

▲ Figure 9.11 Temperature change at hourly intervals in Portsmouth

Geographical enquiry

# Chapter 9 Fieldwork investigation in geography

*Figure 9.12 Scatter chart: 757 jet airliner speed and headwind strength: Manchester to New York*

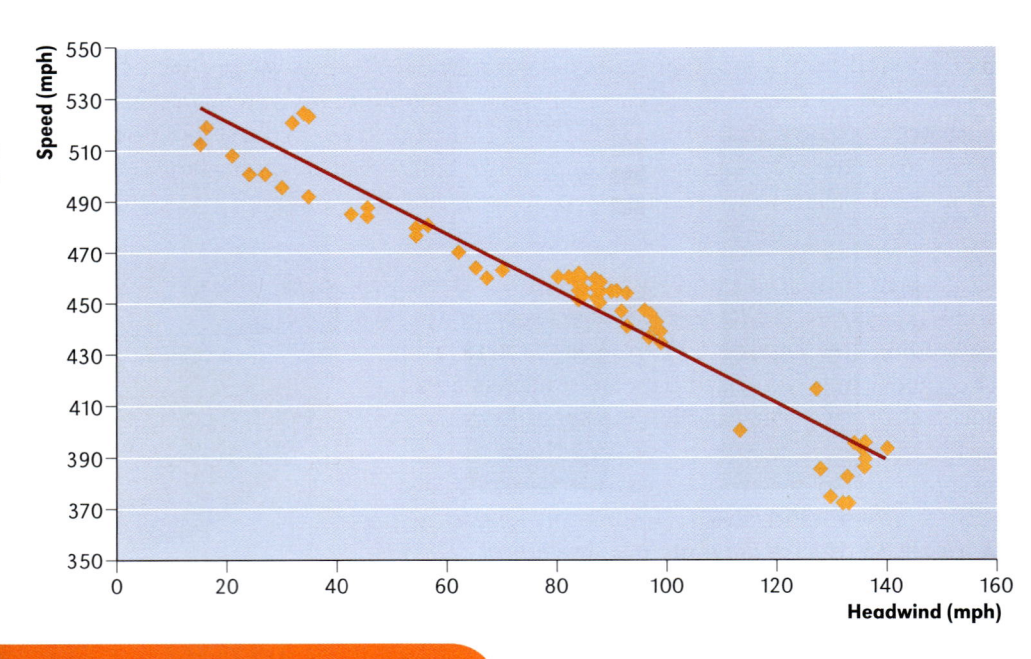

## Activity 9.5

Draw a chart to represent the data in (a) Table 9.4 and (b) Table 9.5.

Explain your choice of chart for each data set.

▼ *Table 9.5 Altitude and mean annual rainfall of climate stations in eastern Britain*

▼ *Table 9.4 Types of goods and services purchased by shoppers in Thirsk, North Yorkshire*

| | Number of shoppers |
|---|---|
| Food and household consumables | 259 |
| Durable goods | 119 |
| Financial and legal services | 145 |
| Other services | 146 |

| Station | Altitude (m) | Mean annual rainfall (mm) |
|---|---|---|
| Braemar | 339 | 913 |
| Cambridge | 26 | 554 |
| Durham | 102 | 643 |
| Greenwich | 7 | 584 |
| High Mowthorpe | 175 | 729 |
| Oxford | 63 | 642 |
| Rothamsted | 128 | 698 |
| Sheffield | 131 | 825 |
| Sutton Bonnington | 48 | 606 |

New York has been plotted against the strength of the headwind (jet stream). In this example, the air speed of the plane is influenced by the headwind. Therefore, headwind is the independent variable (*x*), and airspeed is the dependent variable (*y*). The pattern of points on the chart almost follows a straight line. This suggests a strong relationship. In this instance we have an inverse or negative relationship, with an increase in headwind (*x*) causing a decrease in air speed (*y*).

When the point pattern on a scatter chart is close to a straight line, it is reasonable to summarise the relationship by drawing an average trend line through the points (as in Figure 9.12).

## Types of map

Maps are the single most important means of presenting geographical information. They show spatial patterns and trends more effectively than charts, and are important stores of information. In your fieldwork enquiry you should look for opportunities to map both primary and secondary data. In this section we shall consider only those maps that you are most likely to include in your fieldwork enquiry: **choropleth** maps, **proportional symbol** maps and **flow maps**.

## Choropleth maps

Choropleth maps, also known as proportional shading maps, show geographical differences in classes of values by colour or shading (see Figure 9.13). In order to draw a choropleth map you need data for statistical areas such as census units, parishes, wards, and health districts, and a base map that shows their boundaries. Because the size of each statistical area is likely to influence the magnitude of the data, we normally construct choropleth maps from standardised values. So, instead of drawing a map to show the total population of each statistical area, we would map population density. Similarly, rather than plot the absolute change of population over time within each unit, we would plot the percentage population change. Other examples include cropland, which would be shown as the percentage area devoted to crops such as wheat and oilseed; and unemployment, which would be shown as a percentage.

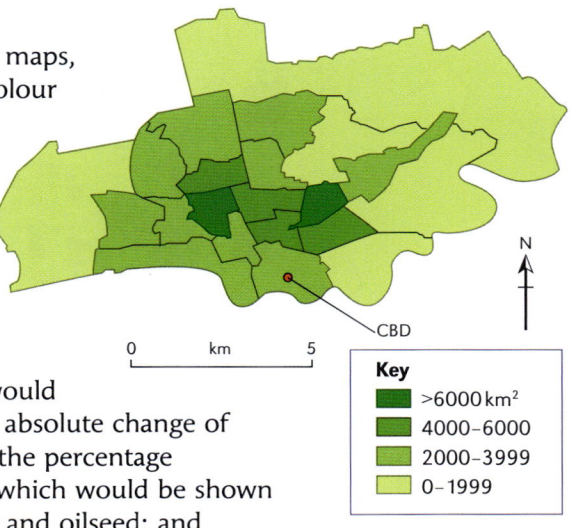

▲ *Figure 9.13 Choropleth map showing population density by ward in Preston*

Drawing choropleth maps requires you to make several decisions:
- The number of classes of values — five or six classes are usually sufficient
- The class intervals — we normally divide the range of values by the number of classes.
- The type of shading or colouring scheme — with black and white maps, the denser the shading the greater the value; with colour maps the higher value classes are shaded with more striking colours from the extreme ends of the spectrum (e.g. red, violet) and the lower value classes with softer colours from the middle part of the spectrum (e.g. yellow, green).

As with all maps, you must include a title, scale, directional symbol and where appropriate, a key.

## Proportional symbol maps

Proportional symbols can be used to represent absolute values on a map (see Figure 9.14). The basic principle is that the area of the symbol is proportional to the quantity represented. Circles and squares are the symbols most often used. Proportional symbol maps show absolute rather than standardised values, e.g. total population, total crop area. The symbols are usually placed in the centre of each statistical unit, and can overlap each other, providing it is possible to estimate the radius of each circle, or the side of each square. Proportional symbol maps based on squares are easier to draw than circles because the side

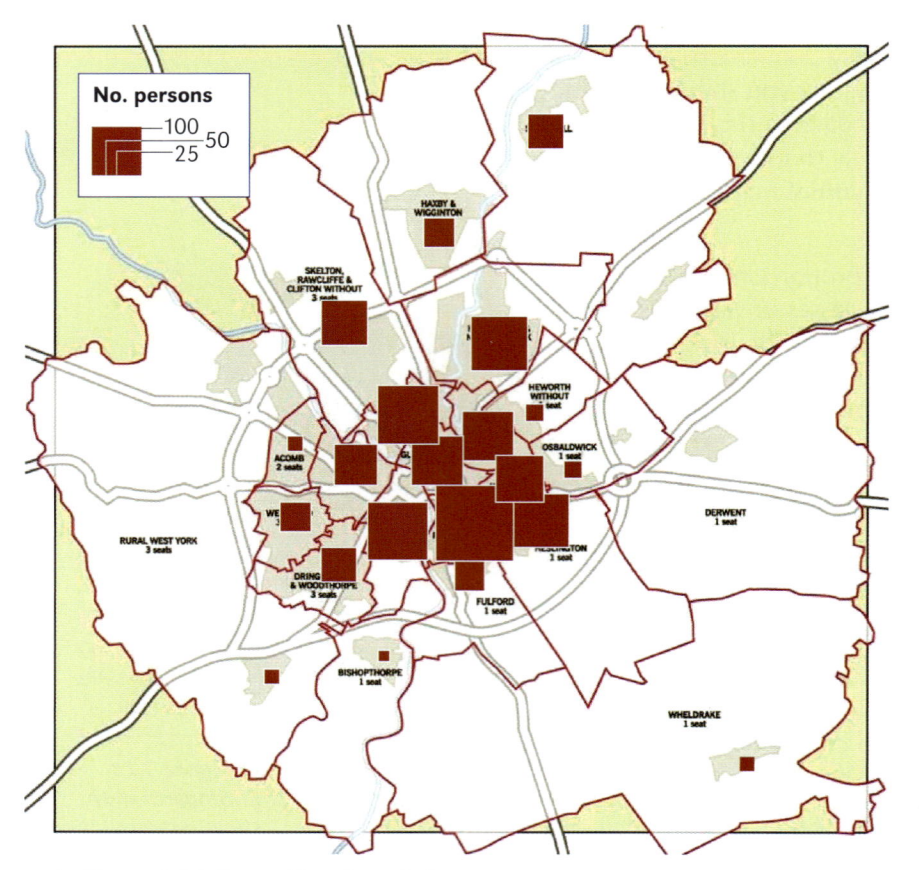

## Chapter 9 Fieldwork investigation in geography

▲ *Figure 9.14 Proportional symbol map*

▼ *Figure 9.15 Flow map: River Tees (m³/s)*

of the square is simply the square root of the value represented. Circles have the advantage that they can be sub-divided (like pie charts) to show additional information. For example, the total population of a unit could be represented by the area of a circle, and the proportion of males and females by subdividing the circle into two segments.

### Flow maps

Flow maps are used to show the movement of people, traffic, freight, information and so on between places. These movements are represented as lines, proportional in width to the volume of flow (see Figure 9.15). Flow paths can either follow routes (e.g. roads, railways, river channels,

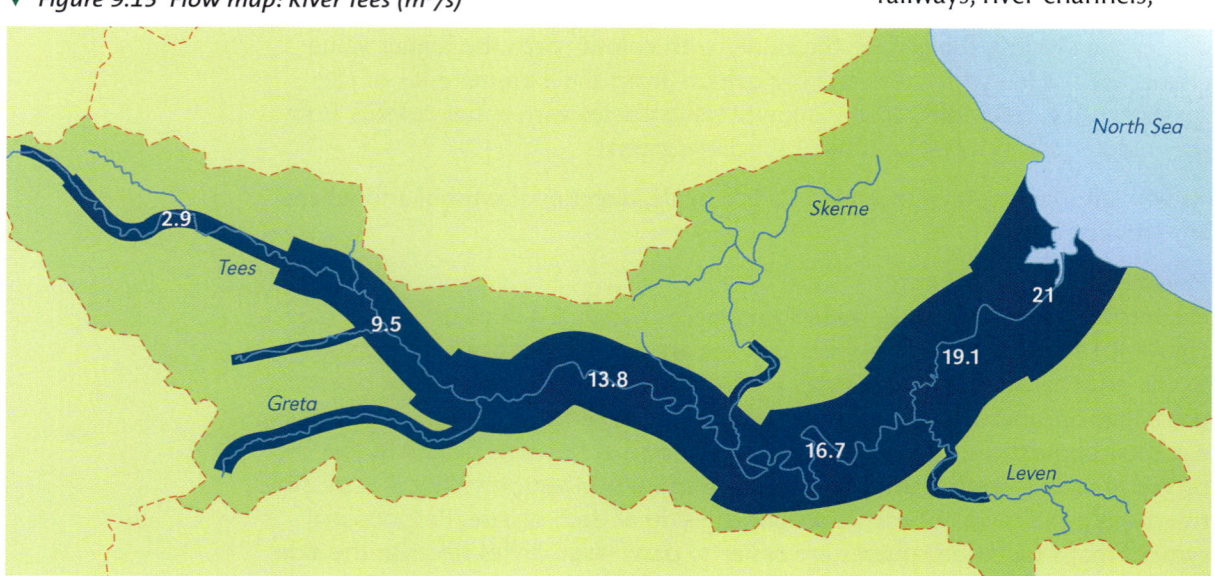

OCR (B) GCSE Geography

Theme 4

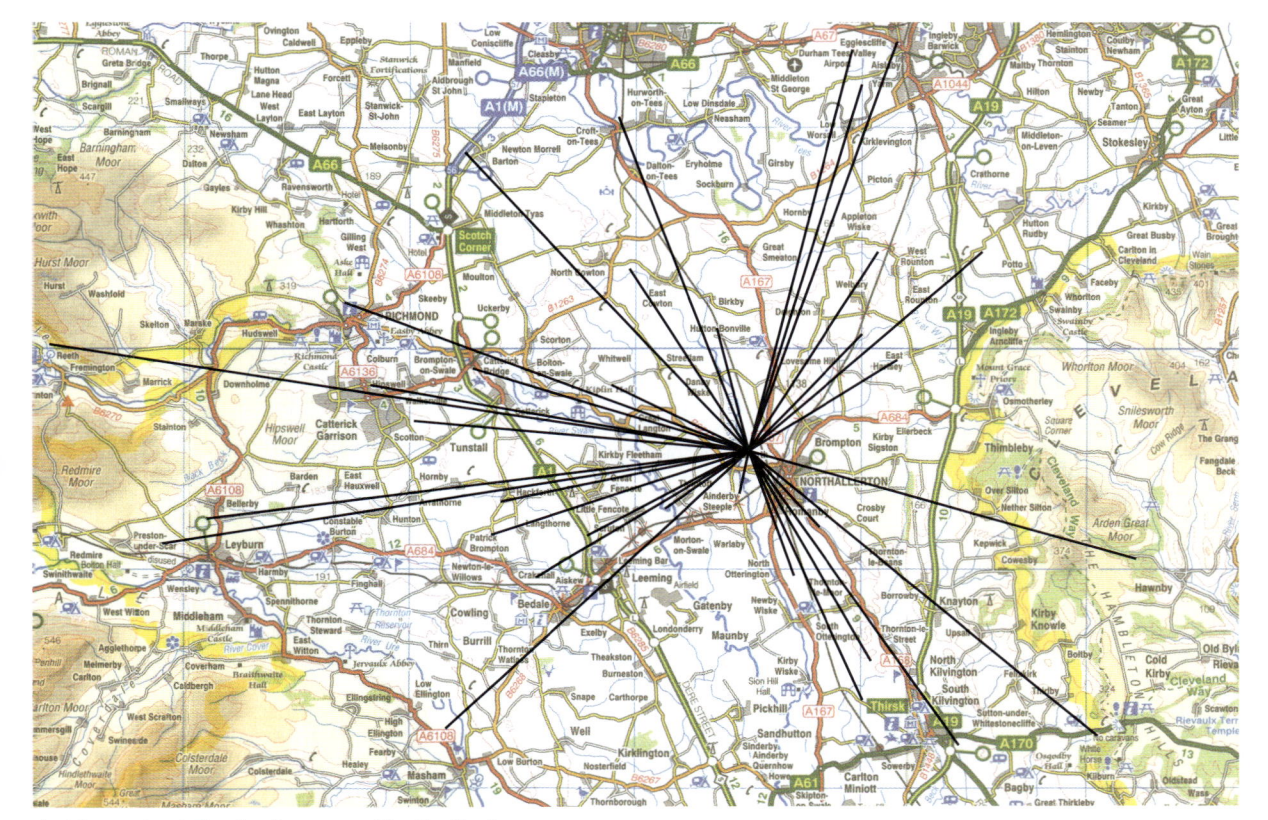

▲ Figure 9.16 Desire line map: Northallerton

pipelines) or straight lines. A **desire line map** is type of flow map that is particularly useful in fieldwork enquiries. Desire line maps show the origin and destination of movements as straight lines, but do not include information on flow volumes. They are often used to show the trade area or field of interaction around market centres and service functions (see Figure 9.16).

### Activity 9.6

Study the data in Table 9.6. Using the outline map (Figure 9.17) of ward boundaries, draw a map that you think best represents the data.

Explain why the map you chose is preferable to other map types.

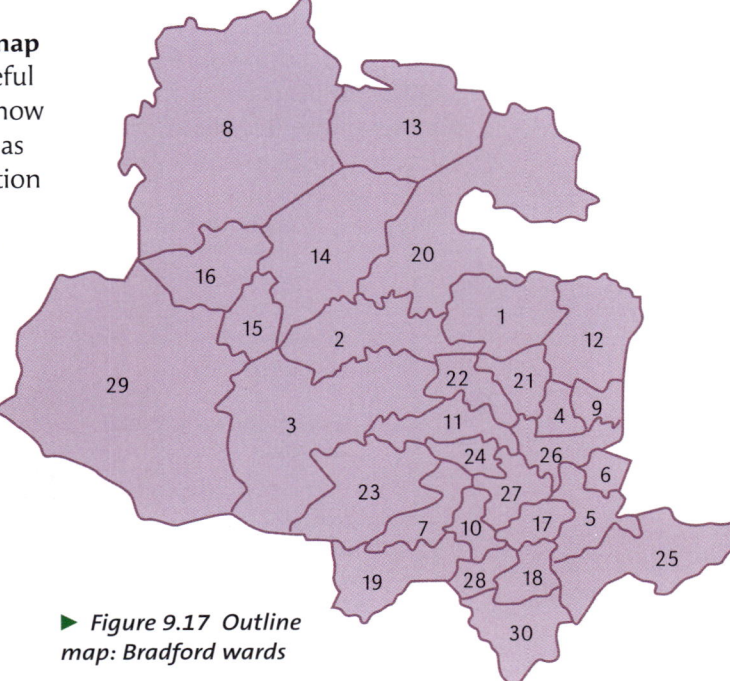

▶ Figure 9.17 Outline map: Bradford wards

Geographical enquiry

217

# Chapter 9 Fieldwork investigation in geography

*Table 9.6 Bradford wards*

| No. Ward | Total pop. | Asian pop. | % Asian | No. Ward | Total pop. | Asian pop. | % Asian |
|---|---|---|---|---|---|---|---|
| 1 Baildon | 15,569 | 164 | 1.05 | 16 Keighley West | 16,281 | 2,318 | 14.24 |
| 2 Bingley | 13,675 | 150 | 1.10 | 17 Little Horton | 16,431 | 6,563 | 39.94 |
| 3 Bingley Rural | 15,142 | 190 | 1.25 | 18 Odsal | 16,454 | 2,966 | 18.03 |
| 4 Bolton | 13,762 | 1,593 | 11.58 | 19 Queensbury | 17,573 | 595 | 3.39 |
| 5 Bowling | 17,722 | 1,593 | 1.25 | 20 Rombalds | 16,043 | 119 | 0.74 |
| 6 Bradford Moor | 17,497 | 11,609 | 66.35 | 21 Shipley East | 13,455 | 309 | 2.03 |
| 7 Clayton | 14,491 | 1,717 | 11.85 | 22 Shipley West | 15,032 | 2,606 | 17.34 |
| 8 Craven | 15,876 | 171 | 1.08 | 23 Thornton | 12,959 | 395 | 3.05 |
| 9 Eccleshill | 13,278 | 213 | 1.06 | 24 Toller | 18,951 | 13,185 | 69.57 |
| 10 Great Horton | 16,019 | 4,778 | 29.83 | 25 Tong | 13,823 | 388 | 2.81 |
| 11 Heaton | 16,913 | 6,368 | 37.65 | 26 Undercliffe | 14,732 | 4,314 | 29.28 |
| 12 Idle | 15,985 | 314 | 1.96 | 27 University | 22,640 | 15,406 | 68.05 |
| 13 Ilkley | 13,828 | 100 | 0.72 | 28 Wibsey | 13,447 | 428 | 3.18 |
| 14 Keighley North | 15,465 | 4,099 | 26.51 | 29 Worth Valley | 15,545 | 201 | 1.29 |
| 15 Keighley South | 13,181 | 1,608 | 12.20 | 30 Wyke | 15,898 | 282 | 1.77 |

## Field Sketches

Field sketching is a traditional geographical skill that can add valuable information to a fieldwork enquiry (see Figure 9.18). Most field sketches focus on landscapes and physical features. The main elements of the physical landscape such as slopes, valleys, coastlines and settlement sites are sketched in broad outline. Sketches are simple and require no great artistic skills. Details can be included, but most important is to label the features on the sketch, and add annotations, explaining the features, forms and processes. Compared with a photograph, a field sketch is selective and shows only what is relevant. It is a valuable type of primary data.

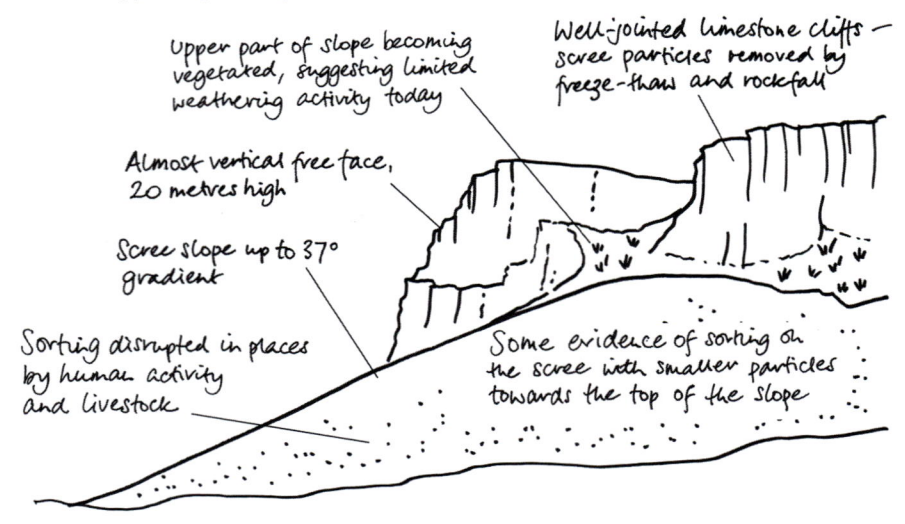

▶ Figure 9.18 Field sketch of a scree slope at Norber Scar

*Table 9.7 Data description and analysis: the key findings*

| Stage | Method and content |
|---|---|
| 1 | State the question or hypothesis and underline or embolden it. |
| 2 | Give a brief explanation or justification for the question or hypothesis. |
| 3 | Describe in detail the data in tables, charts and maps. First describe the main patterns and trends. Illustrate these by referring to specific values that support the patterns and trends. Then describe any data that are anomalous, and appear not to fit the expected pattern and trends. |
| 4 | Conclude by assessing the extent to which the data provide an answer to your question, or support your hypothesis. State your confidence in the results. |

Often it is not possible to say with certainty that you have a conclusive answer to your question or that you have verified your hypothesis. However, this does not mean that your enquiry has been a failure. Your task is to suggest reasons why your enquiry did not work out exactly as you expected. You might point out that reality is much more complicated than simple textbook explanations; that human behaviour if often unpredictable; and that many factors operate together to produce a given outcome, and that your investigation considered only one or two. It may be that your methodology was flawed. Sample data sets in fieldwork enquiries are often too small to give conclusive results; representative samples are extremely difficult to achieve, especially in questionnaire surveys; and measurements may have been (unavoidably) inaccurate.

## Describing and explaining the key findings

In this section you aim to answer the question or hypothesis you posed at the outset of your enquiry. You do this by describing and analysing the data you have presented as tables, charts or maps. Table 9.7 provides a breakdown of how to do this.

### Data analysis tips

- Don't assume that because your findings fail to answer your question positively or verify your hypothesis that your enquiry has failed.
- A negative outcome is itself an important finding.
- Negative outcomes provide scope for explaining why the outcome was different from what you expected.
- Explanations of these findings usually focus on the methodology of the enquiry (e.g. sample size, sampling strategy) and the sheer complexity of geography in the real world.
- Remember that the main purpose of your enquiry is to show that you can investigate a topic systematically, using scientific methods.

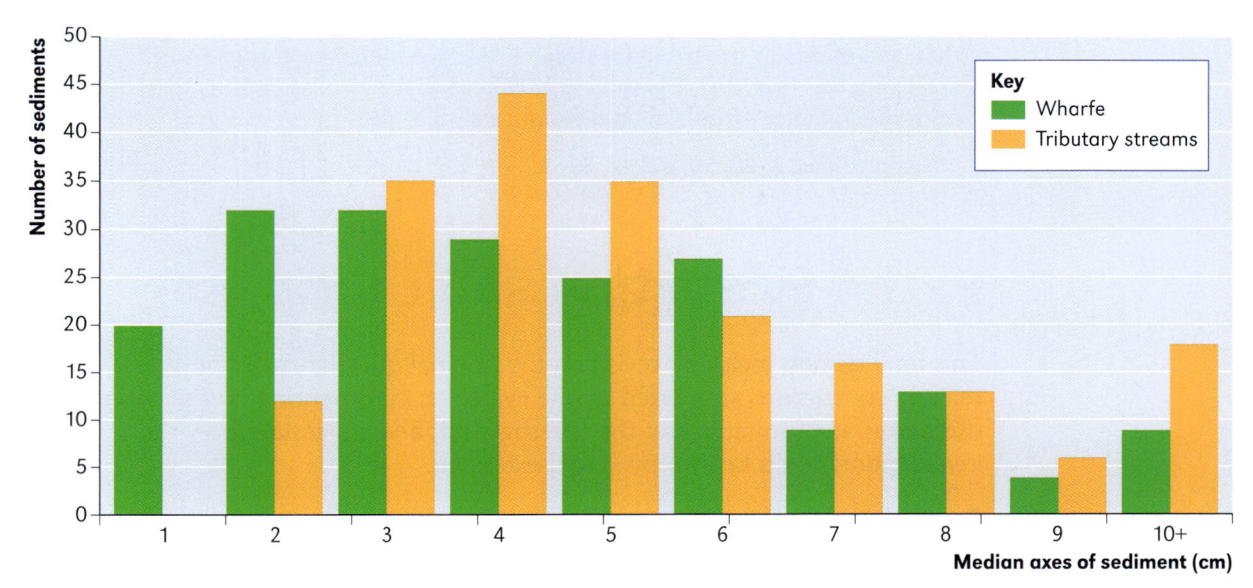

▲ Figure 9.19 Frequency of sediment size: River Wharf and tributaries

# Chapter 9 Fieldwork investigation in geography

### Activity 9.7
On the right is an example of how to describe and analyse data presented in a chart (see Figure 9.19). Read through this section and with reference to Figure 9.18 complete the description and analysis that follows.

## Hypothesis
**Sediments input to the River Wharfe by three small tributaries are coarser than those in the main river.**

### Justification
Sediments in the main river have been transported further and for a longer time than sedments in the shorter tributaries. As a result, the effects of attrition and abrasion are greater, making the sediments in the main river finer than sediments in the tributaries.

### Data description and analysis
Figure 9.19 shows the distribution of a sample of bedload particles in the River Wharfe and three small tributaries, close to their confluence with the main river. The sample is grouped into size classes from 1 cm to 10 cm and over.

Particles in the River Wharfe are more evenly spread across the size classes than in the tributaries. The Wharfe classes with the greatest frequency are …… cm and …… cm. Each contains …… particles. Particles between 4 cm and 6 cm also occur frequently. However, the frequency of particles that are 7 cm or larger decreases rapidly in the main river. In total, the classes covering 7 cm to 9 cm have only …… particles.

The size distribution of the tributary particles is very different. There are no fine particles of 1 cm and less, compared with ..… in the River Wharfe. The most common size of particle is 4 cm, which is 1 cm to 2 cm larger than the particles that occur most frequently in the Wharfe. Above 4 cm, tributary particles are dominant or equal in 5 of the 6 classes. In the size classes 1 cm and 2 cm there are only …… tributary particles, compared with …… in the main river.

Although the two distributions show considerable overlap, there is strong evidence to suggest that sediments in the River Wharfe are, on average, finer than sediments in the tributary streams. We are therefore confident in accepting the hypothesis as valid and believe that a similar enquiry, based on a much larger sample, would produce similar results.

**Missing values: 2, 26, 20, 52, 12, 32, 3**

## Part 4 Evaluation and conclusion

This final section includes: revisiting the original question/hypothesis and making conclusions supported by the evidence; commenting on the success, usefulness and limitations of the investigation; and suggesting how the investigation could be improved and extended.

### Summary of findings
Your conclusion should begin by listing the main findings of your enquiry. Remember that negative findings are just as valuable as positive ones. For

example, an enquiry may show that sediments do not get smaller downstream, or that shoppers do not necessarily shop at their nearest supermarket. Your findings should be backed up with some evidence: sediments may have increased in size by 5% between the first and last sites in a river study; or only a third of shoppers chose their nearest supermarket for their main weekly shop.

## Success of the enquiry

It is important to look back at your enquiry's original aims and objectives, and assess the extent to which they have been achieved. For most enquiries, the aims and objectives will be limited to investigating systematically one or more questions or hypotheses, using primary fieldwork data. If this has been done, and the enquiry has come to a firm conclusion, it must be judged a success. You should understand that success is not measured by outcomes, i.e. answering a question in the affirmative or verifying a hypothesis.

Every enquiry will have limitations and you should review these critically and in detail. Possible limitations include:
- a database that is too small to give confidence in the results
- inaccurate sample data, that are not fully representative of the population. This may be due to factors beyond your control (e.g. people refusing interviews, lack of time) or to a poorly designed questionnaire or inadequate sampling strategy.
- problems of sourcing secondary data such as rents, land values, local climate statistics, soil maps, land use maps, large scale maps etc.
- a topic that was too narrow or too ambitious in scope
- inappropriate timing of data collection (e.g. shopping surveys are more successful on market days or Saturdays; rural land-use surveys should be conducted in summer)
- poorly constructed and self-evident hypotheses (e.g. most shopping trips to supermarkets are by car)

## Improving and extending the enquiry

Having outlined the limitations of your enquiry, the final task is to say how, with hindsight, it could be improved. This needs to go further than simply stating that you would collect more data, although the main improvements will probably be to your sampling strategy. In the light of your results, you may suggest modifications to your original hypotheses or questions. For instance, an original enquiry on the size and shape of river sediments might have been based on a random sample of 50 sediments at several sites. However, you may have observed that the sediments consisted of both sandstone and limestone. As these rock types are likely to erode at different rates, you could suggest that a more accurate investigation would focus exclusively on sandstone *or* limestone. You could also suggest extending the enquiry by comparing the size and shape of sandstone and limestone sediments, and analysing how they change downstream.

# Glossary

**Affordable housing** Cheap housing for families on relatively low incomes.
**Age dependency** The ratio of the non-employed population (i.e. children and old people) to the working population.
**Ageing population** An increase in the average age of a population due to natural change, migration or both.
**Agribusiness** Large-scale, capital-intensive farming based on business and scientific principles.
**Alluvium** Sediments (clay, silt, sand, gravel) deposited by rivers.
**Alternative energy** An energy resource that is renewable and therefore sustainable, e.g. wind power, solar power.
**Andesite** A type of igneous rock (and magma) produced by explosive volcanoes.
**Anticyclone** Area of high atmospheric pressure associated with light winds, dry weather, and variable sunshine and cloud.
**Area of Outstanding Natural Beauty** Area of exceptional landscape quality (mainly upland) in England and Wales protected by planning controls.
**Attrition** Erosion of rock particles transported by rivers and waves.
**Backwash** The return flow of water from a beach to the sea, following the wave swash.
**Balance of trade** The difference between the values of a country's imports and exports.
**Basalt** A type of igneous rock or magma which is runny and associated with quiet, non-explosive eruptions.
**Base flow** The flow of water into streams and rivers from stores such as permeable rocks, peat and wetlands.
**Beach** Accumulation of sand and shingle on the coast in the inter-tidal zone.
**Bedding plane** A surface separating two layers of rock.

**Bedload** Coarse rock particles transported at high flow by rolling and sliding along a stream bed.
**Bilateral aid** Aid given directly by one country to another.
**Biological weathering** The physical and chemical breakdown of rocks by the action of plants, animals and other organisms.
**Birth rate** (see crude birth rate)
**Blow hole** A vertical shaft on a coastal cliff top that is joined to a sea cave.
**Brandt Line** An imaginary line that separates the rich, more developed countries of the northern hemisphere, from the poor, less developed countries of the southern hemisphere.
**Brownfield land** Land available for development that has been used previously for urban and/or industrial purposes.
**Catchment area** Area provided with goods and services by a shopping centre (also known as a trade area).
**Central business district (CBD)** The central area of a town or city, dominated by shops and offices.
**Choropleth map** A type of map that represents values by area. Variations in values between areas are shown by differences in the density of shading or colour.
**Climate change** Impact of global warming on temperatures and rainfall patterns.
**Common Fisheries Policy (CFP)** The European Union's policy for creating a sustainable fishing industry among its member states.
**Commuter zone** Residential area where commuters live, beyond the suburbs of a town or city.
**Comparison goods/services** Goods and services that are purchased infrequently, are relatively expensive and have high thresholds, e.g. electronic equipment and air travel.
**Conservative plate boundary** A tectonic plate margin where two plates shear (horizontally) past

each other. Associated with earthquakes but with no volcanic activity.

**Constructive plate boundary** A tectonic plate margin, located in mid-ocean, where volcanic activity creates new crust and lithosphere.

**Convenience goods/services** Everyday goods and services that are purchased frequently, are relatively low cost and have low thresholds, e.g. food and banking.

**Counterurbanisation** The migration of people in MEDCs from cities to small towns and rural areas, increasing the proportion of the population living in these places.

**Crude birth rate** Number of births in a year per 1,000 of the population.

**Crude death rate** Number of deaths in a year per 1,000 of the population.

**Crust** The thin, rocky, outermost layer of the Earth. There are two types: continental crust (mainly granite) and oceanic crust (mainly basalt).

**Death rate** (see crude death rate)

**Deforestation** Decline in forest cover usually caused by deliberate clearance and/or overgrazing of livestock.

**Deindustrialisation** Large-scale decline of manufacturing industries in a country or region.

**Demographic transition** The changes that occur in birth rates, death rates and natural population growth as a result of economic development.

**Dependent variable** A factor that is influenced by change in another (independent) factor. For example, temperature (dependent variable) is influenced by a change in altitude (independent variable).

**Depopulation** Population decline in a country or region resulting from either natural decrease, net migration loss or both.

**Deposition** Sediments laid down by rivers, waves, glaciers and the wind, which no longer have the energy to transport them.

**Desire line map** A type of flow map that shows the movement of people, goods and information between origins and destination. The flows are represented by straight lines.

**Destructive plate boundary** A type of plate margin where an oceanic plate, descends beneath a less dense oceanic or continental plate into the mantle. This process, known as subduction, destroys the descending plate and causes volcanic activity and earthquakes.

**Dormitory settlement** A commuter settlement dominated by residential land use and with relatively few local economic activities.

**Drought** Prolonged period without appreciable rainfall.

**Dunes** Low hills of sand formed by the wind in coastal and hot desert environments.

**Economic development** A rise in income and living standards in a country or region due to the growth of production.

**Ecosystem** Community of plants and animals that interact with each other and with their physical environment.

**Emerging economy** A country currently undergoing rapid industrialisation and economic development, e.g. China. Also referred to as a newly industrialising country.

**Emigrant** An international migrant leaving a country.

**Employment structure** Proportion of a workforce, country or region engaged in the three main economic sectors (primary, secondary, tertiary).

**Epicentre** The location on the Earth's surface directly above the focus of an earthquake.

**Erosion** Wearing away of the land surface by natural agents such as rivers, waves, glaciers and winds.

**Exurbs** Settlements that rely on a large town or city for services and employment, but which, unlike the suburbs, are not joined physically to the urban area.

**Fault** A crack or fissure that normally runs at a steep angle across several rock layers and along which movement has occurred.

**Flash flood** Sudden flood event usually caused by an intense thunderstorm.

**Flood embankment** Raised earthen bank or levée built to protect a valley floor or lowland coast from flooding.

**Floodplain** Flat land at the sides of a river, built from silt deposited every time the river floods.
**Flow map** A type of map that shows the volume of movement of people, goods and information between places.
**Focus** The place of origin of an earthquake within the Earth's crust.
**Fold mountain** A mountain chain formed at a destructive plate boundary (or collision zone) by the convergent movement of tectonic plates.
**Formal sector** The part of a country's economy that is controlled and regulated, e.g. workers pay taxes and have contracts with employers, and employers contribute to workers' benefits such as pensions.
**Fossil fuel** Non-renewable form of energy, such as oil, coal, gas and peat formed by the decomposition of prehistoric organisms.
**Free trade** The unrestricted movement of goods between countries without the hindrance of trade barriers (e.g. tariffs, quotas).
**GDP (gross domestic product) per person** The total value of goods and services produced by a nation divided by its population. It does not include goods and services produced overseas. GDP per person is often used as a measure of wealth and development.
**Glacier** A large body of ice showing evidence of movement, such as crevasses and flow lines.
**Global warming** The increase in average global temperature that has occurred in the past century, particularly in the past 40 years.
**Globalisation** Worldwide production of goods and services to supply a global market.
**Gorge** A deep, narrow river valley with almost vertical sides cut into solid rock.
**Greenhouse effect** The warming of the Earth's climate due to the absorption of long-wave radiation (emitted from the Earth) by gases such as carbon dioxide, methane and water vapour in the atmosphere.
**Groundwater flow** The slow movement of water through underground permeable rocks.
**Groynes** Wooden and concrete barriers built at right angles to the shore to interrupt the longshore drift of sediment. Groynes encourage the formation of beaches, which protect the coastline from erosion.
**Hazard** (see natural hazard)
**Hierarchy** An ordering of service centres and settlements according to some measure of their size and importance, e.g. number of shops, retail floorspace.
**Human development** Improvements in people's quality of life through the provision of essential services and amenities.
**Human development index (HDI)** UN-devised measure of human wellbeing based on both social and economic criteria.
**Hurricane** Powerful tropical storm associated with violent winds, torrential rain and flooding in the Atlantic and Caribbean region.
**Hydraulic action** The erosive action of water in rivers and waves.
**Hydrological cycle** The continuous circulation of water between continents, oceans and atmosphere.
**Ice sheet** Large, stable glacier that can survive prolonged periods of warming, e.g. East Antarctic ice sheet.
**Immigrants** International migrants entering a country.
**Impermeable rock** Rock that does not absorb water, e.g. granite.
**Independent variable** A factor that causes change in another factor (dependent variable). For example, carbon dioxide is thought to be the independent variable forcing global climate change.
**Industrial Revolution** The development of large-scale, factory-based production, based on supplies of cheap energy and machinery.
**Industrialisation** Rapid growth of manufacturing industry in a country or region.
**Infiltration** Downward movement of water into soil.
**Informal sector** Economic activities in LEDCs (especially employment) unregulated by governments.
**Infrastructure** The transport networks and public utilities (e.g. water, electricity, gas) that support economic activities.
**Inner city** The zone of housing and industry in UK cities, dating from the late nineteenth and early twentieth centuries, within 1–3 km of the CBD.

**Integrated plant** Large iron and steelworks where iron, steel and finished products are all made on the same site.
**Interception** Precipitation that is temporarily stored on the surfaces of plant leaves, stems and branches.
**Interlocking spur** Area of higher ground that projects into upland river valleys. Interlocking spurs occur on alternate sides of the valley.
**International aid** Donations (and loans) of money, goods, services and skills from MEDCs to LEDCs.
**International migration** The permanent movement of people from one country to another.
**Irrigation** Artificial watering of crops.
**Isobar** An isoline on a weather chart joining places of equal pressure.
**Lag time** The time interval on a hydrograph between maximum precipitation and peak flow.
**Land degradation** Decline in the agricultural potential of an area due to overgrazing, over-cultivation, soil erosion and deforestation.
**Lateral erosion** River erosion on the outer (cut) bank of a meander. Lateral erosion causes the river channel to shift across a floodplain and widen the valley.
**Less economically developed country (LEDC)** One of the world's poorer countries. LEDCs have an economic profile that includes low GDP per capita, low value of trade per capita and over-dependence on agriculture and the export of primary products (e.g. mineral ores, coffee, bananas).
**Levée** Alternative name for a flood embankment.
**Light industry** An industry that makes consumer products which have relatively high value in relation to their bulk or weight, e.g. food processing.
**Lithosphere** The collective name given to the Earth's crust and the uppermost layer of the mantle. Tectonic plates are slabs of lithosphere.
**Load** Sediment transported by a river.
**Longshore current** Sea current that moves parallel to the coast and just offshore. It is caused when waves strike the coast obliquely.
**Longshore drift** Movement of sediment along a beach and parallel to the coast offshore. It occurs when waves strike the coast obliquely.

**Long-wave radiation** Radiation (or heat) emitted by the Earth (also known as infrared radiation).
**Magma** Molten rock that forms in the upper part of the mantle and is sometimes erupted as lava by a volcano.
**Malnutrition** An inadequate diet, often lacking in protein and vitamins, and its harmful effects on human health.
**Managed realignment** A sustainable coastal management policy that no longer seeks to protect some stretches of lowland coast from flooding.
**Managed retreat** A less fashionable term for managed realignment.
**Meander** Bend in a river, usually along its middle or lower course.
**Mega city** A city with 10 million or more inhabitants.
**Mid-ocean ridge** A submarine mountain range in mid-ocean which follows a constructive plate boundary.
**Migration** The permanent movement of people from one place to another.
**More economically developed country (MEDC)** One of the world's richer countries, with high GDP per person, high value of trade per person, and a dependence on service activities.
**Multilateral aid** Aid given to poor countries by organisations such as the World Bank, the UN and NGOs.
**Multi-national corporation** (see **transnational corporation**).
**National Park** Large area of exceptional landscape and/or ecological value given special protection status by a government.
**Natural decrease** An excess of deaths over births.
**Natural disaster** A natural hazard that causes major economic loss and/or loss of life.
**Natural hazard** Natural events such as earthquakes, hurricanes and drought that have harmful effects on people and society.
**Natural increase** An excess of births over deaths.
**Natural population change** The annual difference between births and deaths (excluding migration) which may result in population growth, population decline or no change.

Glossary

**Non-governmental organisation (NGO)** Independent organisation, such as a charity, which gives aid to LEDCs.

**Ocean trench** A deep and narrow depression on the ocean floor caused by subduction.

**Offshoring** Manufacturing and services jobs in MEDCs transferred overseas (usually to LEDCs) where costs (especially labour costs) are lower.

**Overpopulation** An excess of people over resources in a country or region, which may result in a lower standard of living and damage to the environment.

**Ox-bow lake** (or cut-off) An abandoned meander (temporarily filled with water), formed when a river flowing across a floodplain, straightens its course.

**Peak flow** Maximum discharge of a river following rainfall.

**Percolation** The vertical movement of water from the surface into permeable rocks.

**Permeable rock** Rock that can be penetrated by water, e.g. limestone.

**Population density** The number of people living in a unit area, usually 1 km$^2$ or 1 hectare.

**Population growth** Increase in population over time.

**Porous rock** Rock such as chalk, which contains tiny air spaces (pores) that absorb water.

**Post-industrial** Describes the economy of an MEDC that, in terms of employment and output, is dominated by service activities.

**Pre-industrial** Describes the economy of a country before industrialisation, when it is dominated by primary industries, especially agriculture.

**Primary data** Original data collected through fieldwork.

**Primary hazard** The direct hazards resulting from natural events, e.g. ground shaking in earthquakes, high winds associated with hurricanes, lava flows from volcanoes.

**Primary sector** Economic activities such as mining and farming, and the production of raw materials, energy and food.

**Proportional symbol map** A type of map that shows the absolute values of variables by symbols such as circles and squares. The areas of the symbols are proportional to the values represented.

**Pull factors** The advantages of a migrant's place of destination, e.g. better job prospects, better services.

**Push factors** The disadvantages of a migrant's place of residence, which may cause them to move away, e.g. lack of jobs, civil war.

**Quadrat** In field studies, a metre (or half metre) square frame, sub-divided into smaller squares and used to select samples of plants, sediments etc.

**Quality of life** The level of satisfaction, happiness and wellbeing of an individual or family.

**Quaternary sector** The fourth employment sector comprising producer services sold directly to businesses such as accounting, advertising, marketing, investment banking etc.

**Random sampling** A type of sampling based on random numbers, where every item in a population has an equal probability of inclusion in the sample.

**Raw material** An unprocessed commodity such as mineral ore or timber.

**Regional centre** A large, suburban shopping area which ranks second in the urban shopping hierarchy within a town or city.

**Regional shopping centre** A large purpose-built shopping mall situated close to a large town or city. The number and range of shops are similar to those found in a CBD.

**Relief channel** Artificial river channel that diverts water from the main channel to reduce the risk of flooding.

**Renewable resource** An energy resource that cannot run out, such as inexhaustible energy (e.g. solar power), or energy that follows a natural physical cycle (e.g. hydroelectric power).

**Revetments** Slatted, wooden fences, running parallel to the coastline, that absorb wave energy and protect the coast from erosion.

**Rift valley** A valley formed by downfaulting between parallel faults. Rift valleys are most often found at constructive plate boundaries.

**Rock armour** Boulders of rock and concrete used to protect vulnerable coastlines from erosion.

**Runoff** Water that runs over the land and enters streams.

**Rural–urban migration** The permanent movement of people from the countryside to towns and cities.

**Salt marsh** Vegetated coastal mudflats, situated above the mean high tide level.

**Salt weathering** Rock breakdown caused by the growth of salt crystals from solution inside porous rocks. A common process on the coast associated with salt spray.

**Sea floor spreading** The lateral and divergent movement of tectonic plates away from a constructive plate boundary.

**Sea wall** A stone or concrete wall or embankment built parallel to the shoreline, designed to stop coastal erosion and flooding.

**Second home** A home occupied for only a small part of the year and usually situated in an area of high scenic and recreational value, e.g. south Lakeland, north Wales.

**Secondary data** Data in books, articles, maps, websites etc. which have already been processed and published.

**Secondary hazard** Natural hazards that are the indirect result of earthquakes, volcanic eruptions, hurricanes and so on. Landlides and floods are common secondary hazards.

**Secondary sector** Manufacturing industries, e.g. car making, electronics.

**Sediment load** The volume of rock particles transported by a river.

**Sediment** Rock particles transported by rivers, waves and tidal currents.

**Seepage** Groundwater emerging at the surface and forming an extensive boggy area.

**Settlement hierarchy** (see **hierarchy**)

**Shanty town** An unplanned, illegal settlement found in cities in LEDCs. Houses are makeshift constructions and initially have few essential services such as piped water and sanitation. Also called squatter settlements.

**Shield volcano** A large, shallow-sided volcano which erupts gently and produces thin, runny basalt lava.

**Shingle** Coarse rounded sediments (e.g. pebbles) in coastal environments.

**Slow flood** Floods that develop slowly, often over several days. They are often caused by steady but continuous rain.

**Sluice gate** A floodgate housed on a riverbed and raised during flood alerts. The sluice gate holds floodwaters back, allowing storage on the floodplain immediately upstream.

**Slum** Area of low-quality housing.

**Social development** Progress in improving the quality of life of an individual or group, e.g. free healthcare, provision of primary and secondary education.

**Soil erosion** The destruction of soil by either heavy rain or wind. Soil erosion is usually caused by human activities and mismanagement.

**Solution load** Dissolved minerals transported by streams and rivers.

**Solution** The process by which minerals in rocks (e.g. calcium carbonate) are dissolved by acidic water.

**Spit** A type of beach joined to the land at one end. Formed by longshore drift, the seaward end of a spit is usually hooked or recurved.

**Spring** Groundwater emerging at the surface and flowing in a single channel.

**Squatter settlement** An alternative name for a shanty town.

**Standard of living** Amount and quality of goods and services purchased/owned by an individual or family; largely determined by income.

**Storm flow** That part of a river's flow derived from recent rainfall.

**Storm surge** Wall of water, up to 8 m high, moving on-shore and caused by violent winds and low pressure. Storm surges are associated with hurricanes and mid-latitude depressions.

**Strato-volcano** A steep-sided, cone-shaped volcano which often erupts violently.

**Subduction zone** A destructive plate boundary where an oceanic plate slowly descends into the upper mantle and is destroyed.

**Suburbanisation** Expansion of the suburbs due to the growth of housing, businesses and services.

**Suburbs** The outer, mainly residential areas of a town or city, which form a zone beyond the inner city.

**Suspended load** Tiny particles of silt and clay entrained in a river's flow.

**Sustainable** An activity that is not harmful to the environment and can continue indefinitely.

**Swash** Movement of water up a beach that follows a breaking wave.

**Systematic sampling** A method of sampling where individuals in a population are selected at regular intervals. The interval is determined by random numbers.

**Tectonic plate** A large slab of the Earth's crust and lithosphere, e.g. the South American plate.

**Tertiary sector** Service industries that deal directly with individual consumers (rather than businesses and coporations), e.g. tourism, shops, restaurants, public transport.

**Threshold** The minimum number of people or spending needed to support a retail service.

**Throughflow** Water moving horizontally through soil.

**Tidewater** Industrial sites on the coast close to deep-water terminals, where bulk raw materials can be imported cheaply.

**Transnational corporation (TNC)** A large company that operates globally and has factories or offices in several countries, e.g. General Motors, Coca-Cola, HSBC.

**Transpiration** Evaporation from leaf surfaces of the water taken up by plants.

**Tropical cyclone** Alternative name for a hurricane in south Asia.

**Typhoon** Alternative name for a hurricane in east Asia and northern Australia.

**Unsustainable** Describes human activities and actions that either cause long-term damage to the environment, or which because of costs cannot be continued indefinitely.

**Urban shopping hierarchy** The ordering of shopping centres within cities from local centres at the bottom to the CBD at the top. Several new types of centre have appeared in the past 40 years, including retail parks and regional shopping centres.

**Urbanisation** An increase in the proportion of urban dwellers in a country or region.

**Vertical erosion** Downward erosion by a river which deepens its channel and valley. Vertical erosion is most effective in the uplands where rivers have steep gradients.

**Volcanic island arc** A line of volcanoes that form a chain of islands (e.g. Lesser Antilles). They develop close to destructive plate boundaries where oceanic plates converge and subduction takes place.

**V-shaped valley** Upland river valley that is typically steep-sided and has a narrow floor.

**Water table** The upper surface of saturation in permeable rocks or in the soil.

**Water transfer scheme** The large-scale movement of water between drainage basins using aqueducts and rivers.

**Waterfall** A landform where water in a river drops vertically.

**Wave crest** The highest point of a wave.

**Wave** Undulating movement of water particles as energy is transferred from the wind to the ocean surface.

**Weathering** Breakdown of rocks exposed at or near to the Earth's surface by the weather.

**Wetland** Area of saturated ground where the water table is at the surface.

**Wildfire** A fire that burns out of control in an area of forest, grassland or moorland.

**Wind farm** A cluster of wind turbines.

**World Bank** An organisation funded by the richest countries that provides loans, advice and research etc. to LEDCs to promote economic development.

**World Trade Organization (WTO)** International agency that promotes trade between member nations, administers global trade agreements and resolves trade disputes.

# Index

## A

acid rain 112, 113
affordable housing 73, 84
afforestation 10
Africa, sub-Saharan
    colonial history 149
    drought in 136
age and gender of population
    Japan 43
    Nigeria 43
age dependency 55-7
ageing crisis in MEDCs 56-7
ageing population 66
agribusiness in Spain 141
agricultural employment
    sub-Saharan Africa 158
agriculture, unsustainable 66
aid
    bilateral 150
    multilateral 150
air pollution, South Africa 92
Alexandra Renewal Project
    quality of life improvement 92
Alexandra township, Johannesburg 88-92
    apartheid 89
    life of residents, newspaper cutting 90
    map 90
    photograph 91
    quality of life 89
algae in North Sea
    threat to marine organisms 179-80
alluvium 25
Almeria, southern Spain
    monthly precipitation 142
alternative energies 187, 188
Altiplano, Bolivia 65
America, central, levels of development 138
andesite magma 112
anticyclones 131
apartheid, South Africa 89
arch formation, natural 28, 34
    Flamborough 34
Areas of Outstanding Natural Beauty
    protection for 84
armour blocks 38
ashfalls 112-13
Atlantic hurricanes, worst 139
atmosphere 1
Austin, Texas
    land use change 82-3
    population change 81
Austwick screes, North Yorkshire 212

## B

backwash 29
Bangalore, India
    Millennia business park 172
Bangladesh
    effects of overpopulation 52-5
    risk from sea rising 185
bar charts 212
Bay of Bengal, map 52
beaches 28, 35
beach renewal 40
bedding planes 34
bedload 18, 20
bilateral aid 151
    market for exports of donor country 151
birth rates 43
Blakeney Point, Norfolk
    bird and seal protection at 37
blow holes 34
Bolivia, case study
    over-cultivated land 66
    poverty in rural areas 65
    urbanisation 64-8
border security in US/Mexican border 62
Boscastle floods 11-13

bottom trawling, sea fishing 193
Bradford
    central business district (CBD) 75
    dormitory settlements 79
    housing types 77
    inner city 78
    land use areas 75
    map 77
Brandt line
    patterns of development 145
Briggate, Leeds,
    pedestrianisation 96
brownfield sites for building 84
    regions 87
Buckden Beck 22
    Upper Wharfedale 21
building codes, strict
    for earthquakes 118
building collapse 118
building on floodplain, Boscastle 12

## C

California, population 119
Campaign Against Stevenage Expansion (CASE)
    pressure group 85
carbon capture
    new technology 188
carbon dioxide
    emissions 182
    limitation 187
carbon trading 188
catchment area 94
cave formation 28, 34
central business district (CBD) 74
    Alexandra township, Johannesburg 88
    Bradford 75
chalk 33, 34
channel straightening 11
char (silt islands) in Bangladesh 53
children in population
    list of countries 47
China 115
    General Motors (GM), advantages of
      location 175

    low labour costs 160
    mineral wealth, Democratic Republic
      of Congo (DRC) 151
    rapid industrialisation, employment
      structure 159, 160
cholera, South Africa 92
choropleth maps 215
Christian Aid
    aid, multilateral 151
city centre living
    Leeds 97
city centres, decline of 96
cliffs 33
climate change 9
    in UK 136
closures of village services 101–2
Coastal Concern Action Group (CCAG)
    North Norfolk District Council 40
coastal defences, engineering structures
    armour blocks 38
    gabions 38
    groynes 38
    revetments 38
    sea walls 38
coastal erosion
    from stormier weather 186
    grants for protection against 40
coastal management 37–42
coastal processes and landforms 27–42
coastal protection 37
coasts 27–42
cod stocks declining in North Sea 193
colonial history of countries
    and their development 149
colour televisions
    production in China 164
Common Fisheries Policy (CFP) 195
    failure to protect fishstocks 196
commuter zone (exurbs)
    Bradford 78
comparison goods and services, retail provision
    higher thresholds 93
comparison shops 94
competition from supermarkets

small shops, decline 97
condensation 1, 2
conservative plate boundaries 108
constructive plate boundaries 105-6
continental shelf, North Sea 192
contraception, lack of
    Bangladesh 54-5
convenience goods 94
convenience goods and services
    lower thresholds 93
Cornwall, Boscastle
    floods 11-13
counterurbanisation 63
    in MEDCs 70-73, 79
    in UK, urban exodus 70
crude birth rate (CBR) 45-6
    Bolivia, case study, urbanisation 64
    declining 57
    influencing factors 51
    selected countries 49
    Sweden 48, 49
crude death rate (CDR) 45, 46
    Bolivia, case study, urbanisation 64
    influencing factors 51
    selected countries 49
    Sweden 48, 49
crust of earth 103
    Cuba 145-7
        educational standards 147
        infant mortality rate 147
        life expectancy 147
cumulus clouds 7
cut-off (oxbow) 24
cyclones 123-30

## D

dams 11
data
    collection method 201
    presentation and analysis 211
death rates 43
    from hurricanes 126
decentralisation of shopping 96
deforestation 66, 135
    Amazon basin 1990-2005 179
    causing hurricanes 139
    farming as main cause of 179
    local and global problem 178
deindustrialisation in UK 159
demographic transition 49
    Sweden 48
depopulation, Witherslack, Cumbria 100
deposition of sediment 16, 18
desertification 135
desire line maps 217
destructive plate boundaries 106, 107
development
    economic well-being 143-60
    measuring 143-9
development aid, sustainable 151-2
    and international aid 150-54
disaster planning, negative
    Hurricane Mitch 139-40
displacement of people by flooding 153
dormitory settlement
    Alexandra township, Johannesburg 88
drainage basins 6, 8
drought 4, 130-6
    causes in UK 131, 132, 136
    hazards 134-6
    risk areas, global distribution 130
dunes, 27

## E

earthquake-resistant building, design 120
earthquakes 103-5, 107, 109
    active regions, California 118
    global distribution 104
    hazard map, Los Angeles 121
    impacts 116-18
    major, since 1990 117
economic activities
    physical environment 177
economic activity 161-96
    changing locations 164-7
    primary, secondary and tertiary 161
economic development
    industrial 158

post-industrial 158
pre-industrial 158
educational standards
   Cuba 147
El Alto, Bolivia
   population pyramids 67
   shanty town 66–8
El Niño 132
embankments 11
emerging economy, China 115
employment
   quality of life 143–60
employment in LEDCs
   formal and informal sectors 70
employment structures
   changing patterns 159
   primary, secondary and tertiary 156–8
England, Northern, population change 72
environmental damage
   Nam Theun 2 Dam Project, Laos 153
environmental degradation
   symptom of overpopulation 52
erosion 9, 16
   abrasion 28
   attrition 28
   hydraulic action 28
   protection from 37
erosional landforms 32
erosion cycle of cliffs, Happisburgh, Norfolk 39–41
evaluation and conclusion 220
evaporation 1, 2

## F

family planning clinics
   Bangladesh 54–5
farming 162
   intensive in Bangladesh 53
faults 33
field sketches 218
fieldwork investigation in geography 197–221
   economic development 198
   population and settlement 198
   rivers and coasts 197

financial incentives to have children 56
fires 119
fishing in North Sea
   bottlenose dolphins/
     porpoises accidental killings 193
   overfishing 192
   unsustainable environmental
     effects of 193–6
Flamborough Head 31–5
flood basins 11
flood disaster responses
   Koshi river floods 15
flood embankments
   levées 9
floodplains 9, 24–5
floods, 9–16
   control through engineering 11
   hazards 9
   management 10, 13
   protection strategies 10, 37, 186
   risk 5
   warnings 10
flow maps 216
fluvial landform in lowlands 16–26
fluvial landform in uplands
   River Wharfe case study 18
focus of earthquakes 109
forest destruction 16
forest fires 135
forests, replacement of 9
fossil fuel burning
   causes of global warming 181
free trade 165
freezing of water 1

## G

gabions 38
Ganges-Brahmaputra-Meghna delta 53
GDP per capita 143–5
   list of countries' GDP 47
GDP per person in Ghana 155
General Motors (GM), case study 174
   in China 175

General Motors, Luton, closure 176
geographical factors, influence 148
    Geographical Information Systems, (GIS) 79
    New Delhi, India 81
geology
    influence of 16
    of Yorkshire coast 32
Ghana
    case study 155
    infant mortality rate 155
    life expectancy 155
    water supply improvement 156
glaciers 1
    threat to, from climate change 184
globalisation 164-5
    winners and losers 176-7
global warming 9, 180-81
    international problem 187
    threat by deforestation 178
gold in Johannesburg 88
gorge 22
governments, corruption of 149
granite reefs, Sea Palling
    erosion cause 40
green-belt land 85
    destruction 84
greenfield land 85
greenhouse gases (GHG) 181-2
    causes of global warming 180
    limitation 187
gross national income (GNI) 150-51
ground shaking 119, 121
    Sichuan earthquake, China, 2008 115
groundwater flow 1, 2, 6, 7
groynes 28, 38

# H

hake stocks declining in North Sea 193
Happisburgh
    arguments for/against defending from
        coastal erosion 42
    cliff-top houses 41
    coastal protection, case study 37-42

hard defences, lack of 40
harmful effects of economic activities
    physical environment 177
Hayeswater 3
headland erosion
stacks and stumps 28
headlands 32
headwaters of Wharfe 19-20
health and heavy industries 171
health clinics, Bangladesh 55
heavy industry 163
Hertfordshire County Council 85
Hertfordshire, densely populated 87
hierarchy of shopping centres
    Leeds 93, 94
High Cup Nick, Cumbria 5
Himalayas, snow melt 13
Hispanic population in USA
    distribution 61
Holderness 35-7
Honduras 137-8
houses, self-built 68
housing areas
    Bradford 75, 78
housing shortage
    London and southeast England 84
housing types 206
human development, China 115
Human Development Index (HDI) 143-5
human population growth 50
human resources 148
Humber Estuary 31-6
Hurricane Charley, Florida, 2004
    deaths 130
Hurricane Georges, Caribbean 1998
    deaths 130
Hurricane Katrina 127-8
Hurricane Mitch, 1998, central America
    case study 137-40
hurricanes 123-30
hydrograph
    River Lambourn, Thames tributary 4
    River Ock, Thames tributary 4

hydrographs 3
    peak flow 4
    stream flow 4
hydrological cycle 1–3
hydrology 1–26
hypothesis 220

## I

illegal immigration 60, 62
immigration of young adults 56
impermeable rocks 7
independent stores, decline of 96
Indian Ocean earthquake, 2004 111
industrial employment
    China as emerging economy 158
industrialisation
    causes of global warming 181
    Sweden 48
Industrial Revolution, UK 159
industries responsible for deforestation 178
industry location, factors influencing
    primary, secondary and tertiary 161–2
infant mortality
    Ghana 155
    reduction in Cuba 146
infiltration of water 7
information and communication technology (ICT)
    globalisation 171
infrastructure 15
    Alexandra township, Johannesburg 89
inner city 74
instability of slopes without trees 139
interlocking spurs 16, 18, 22
international aid 151
    and development 150–54
international migration
    management 57
International Monetary Fund (IMF) 151
    aid, multilateral 150
iron and steel works, integrated 168
irrigated agriculture
    destruction of wildlife, Spain 141
irrigation 3
IT-enabled service from India 172

## J

Japan, MEDC 44–7
    birth rates 45
    death rates 45
    older population 45
    population structure
    ratio of men to women 45
Johannesburg, unsustainable urban growth
    case study 88–92

## K

Koshi River floods
    Bihar, India, 13–16
    map 15
    satellite image 14
    tributary of Ganges 13
Kosi *see* Koshi, Bihar, India
Kyoto Treaty
    China and India exempt 187
    USA not signed 187

## L

Lagos, Nigeria, slums 44
lag times 5
lahars 112
Lake District National Park, UK 100–2
lakes 1
land degradation 66
    from drought, Niger 135
landlocked countries
    and their development 148
landslide damage in Honduras
    Hurricane Mitch 139
landslides 110–13, 119
    Sichuan earthquake, China, 2008 115–16
land use patterns, cities 74–102
    changing patterns 79
La Paz, Bolivia 65
lateral erosion 23
lava flows 112–13
LEDC *see* less economically developed country
Leeds, White Rose Shopping Centre 98–9
less economically developed country
    (LEDC) 129, 145

levées in Koshi river 13
    cause of Koshi floods 15
life expectancy
    Cuba 147
    Ghana 155
light industries in China 159
limestone rocks, Yorkshire 17
line charts 213
line of transects 208
lithosphere 103
livelihoods, destruction of
    Nam Theun 2 Dam Project, Laos 153
Lleyn Peninsula 31
location of economic activities
    factors influencing 161–2
London and southeast England
    urban change, case study 84
longshore current 30
longshore drift 30, 36
longshore transport 30
Lyon, France
    rapid runoff in cities 5

## M

magma 106
Maine, New England, storm waves 29
Maldives, Indian ocean
    threat from sea rising 185
malnutrition, South Africa 92
managed realignment 37, 40
marriage age raising
    Bangladesh 54
Mauna Loa, Hawaii
    shield volcano 112
meanders 23–24, 26
MEDC *see* more economically developed country
medical services and the elderly 56
mega cities 63–4
melting of ice 1
Mexican migration to USA, case study 60–62
    border patrol 62
    illegal migration 62
    wooden shack in Mexico (photo) 58
mid-ocean ridges 103

migration 57–62
    economic causes 60
    facts 59
    managing 61
    positive and negative consequences 61
mining 162, 163
monsoon rains 13
more economically developed country (MEDC) 129, 145
    post-industrial 158
Mount Rainier, Washington state, USA 114
Mount St Helens 113
Mount Teide, Tenerife,
    strato-volcano 111
mudflats 28
mudflow in Philippines 128
multilateral aid 151
mult-national corporations (MNCs) 173
    advantages and disadvantages 175
    impact on employment and development 174
    investment in China 160, 164
murder rate, South Africa 92

## N

Nam Theun 2 Dam Project, Laos 153
    arguments for and against 154
    case study 152
    economic impact 153
    environmental impact 153
    funded by World Bank 152
    social impact 153
National Park 100–2
natural decrease and natural increase 45
natural disasters 109
natural hazards 103–42, 109
natural population change 45–6
natural resources 148
Nepal, satellite image 14
New Delhi, India
    land use change 79
    slums 80
    urban growth 80
Nicaragua 137

Nigeria, population structure
    LEDC 44–7
Niger, map of 134
nitrate contamination of water
    Spain 141
non-governmental organisations (NGOs) 118
    aid, multilateral 151
North Atlantic Oscillation (NAO) 132
Northridge, California, earthquake
    case study 118–22
    freeway damage 119
    impact 120
North Sea fishing, map 194
North Sea, over-fishing, case study 192
nuclear power 187

## O

ocean currents 125
oceans 1
    with tropical storms 124
ocean trenches 108
offshoring 164, 171, 172
Organisation for Economic Cooperation and
    Development (OECD) 152
overcrowding in Alexandra 91
overfishing, impact of 192–6
    decline in fish stocks 192
    decline in sea birds 193
    unemployment 192
overgrazing 135
overpopulation
    Bihar, Nepal 16
    Asia and Africa 52
oxbow lake, development of 24
Oxfam
    aid, multilateral 151

## P

Pacific Ring of Fire 106
peak flow 5
Pearl River Delta, Guangdong Province, China 160
Pennines, UK 18–21
    rainfall in 20
percolation of water 7

permeable rocks 7
Persimmon
    development company 85
pie charts 213
plaice stocks declining in North Sea 193
plastic greenhouses in Spain
    irrigated agriculture 141
polar ice 1
political migrants 58
pollution
    in Alexandra, South Africa 91
    by economic activity 178
    in North Sea
    wastes from major rivers 179
population 43–62
    change in Witherslack, Cumbria 100
    development 148
    densities 52
        Alexandra, South Africa 91
    exposure to hurricanes 127
population growth
    Bradford, UK 75
    limitation strategies, Bangladesh 54
    London and southeast England 84
    rapid, causing global warming 180
population scatter plot
    Nigeria and Japan 46–7
population structures 43, 50
    and economic development 46
porous rocks 1, 3
Port Talbot steelworks, UK 170
potholes in River Wharfe 21
poverty
    Bangladesh 53
    El Alto, Bolivia 68
    Hurricane Mitch 138, 139
    symptom of overpopulation 52
    widespread
precipitation 1, 2
    evaporation 6
primary data collection
    river 202
primary hazards 109–13, 119, 126
    droughts 134

proportional symbol maps 215-16
pub closures 101
puddling of water 7
push and pull factors 58-9
    migration 57
    urban-rural migrants 72
push factors 66
pyroclastic flows 112

## Q

quake lakes
    Sichuan earthquake, China, 2008 116
quality of life 145
    Bolivia 66
quarrying 162

## R

rain 126
    Boscastle floods 12
rainfall
    decrease and desertification 183
    heavy 128
rainforest damage
    destruction of rainforest by flooding 153
    Nam Theun 2 Dam Project, Laos 153
rainwater on oak leaves 7
raw materials, consumers 83
Red Crescent
    aid, multilateral 151
Red Cross 15
refrigerators
    production in China 164
regional centres 93
    multiples 94
regional shopping centres, England 97-8
relief channels 9, 11
relief effort, Koshi flood 15
renewable resources 152
reservoirs 1, 2
    building 136
residential development and tourist industry,
    Spain 142
retail change, economic and social
  impact 96-9

retail provision 162
    Leeds urban settlement, case study 93-6
    rural and urban settlements 93
retirement, raising age of 56
revetments 37, 38
rice planting in Bangladesh 53
Richter scale, earthquake measure 111
rift valley 106
risk assessment 208-10
river basins 1, 6
    rock type 5
    slopes 5
    woodland 5
river cliffs
    Cow Beck 26
river engineering
    cause of Koshi floods 15
river erosion
    abrasion 17
    attrition 17
    hydraulic action 17
river floods 10
rivers 1, 2
River Skirfare floodplain
    meander 24, 25
rock armour 37
rocks, weathering of 27
runoff 1, 6
rural population change in UK 71
rural-urban migration 63, 70-73
    Bolivia 65
rural-urban shift of manufacturing 165

## S

Sahel region of Africa
    droughts 132
    land degradation 135
    rainy season 133
salt marshes 27
salt weathering 27
sampling 204
San Andreas fault
    Los Angeles 118-19
    southern California 108

sand dredging, Great Yarmouth
    erosion cause 40
sand dunes, coastal protection 37
sand eel fishing
    disastrous effects on sea wildlife 193-6
Sandton, white suburb, South Africa
    quality of life 89
San Francisco
    earthquake -proof construction 120
scatter charts 213-14
scenic areas, retirement in 73
sea defences, cost of 40
sea floor spreading 106
sea level rises
    threat to all countries 186
    world threat 184, 185
seasonal rainfall distribution 131
sea surface temperatures (SSTs) 126
sea walls 38
    erosion cause 40
secondary data sources 202
secondary hazards, 109-13, 119, 126
    droughts 134
second homes, Witherslack, Cumbria 101
sediment 1, 24, 26
    load 17
    Koshi river 13
    transfers in river basins 9
    transport 28
Selwick's Bay, shore platform 33
service industries in India, offshored
    case study 171-2
services decline in Witherslack, Cumbria 101
services in Alexandra 91, 92
settlement 63-103
settlement hierarchy 93
shanty town 138
    El Alto 66
shield volcanoes 111
shingle 28
shopping 163
    changing patterns 93-6
    decline in central business district (CBD) 96
    decline in small shops 97

shopping centres, hierarchy in cities 95
    Leeds 93, 94
shops in settlements 93
shore platforms 34
Sichuan earthquake, China, 2008 111, 114, 116
    case study 115
    newspaper article 117
site-and-service schemes 68
Sites of Special Scientific Interest 40
sluice gates 9, 11
slums 68
    El Alto, Bolivia 66
social development 145
society, changes in
    London and southeast England 84
soil erosion 135
    from deforestation 66
    cause of Koshi floods 15
soils 1
solution load 18
Spain
    low reservoir 134
    southern, drought 2005
    case study 140-2
spatial sampling 207
spit 36
Spurn Head 35-7
squatter settlements
    *barrios*
        Bolivia 66
        Mexico 68
    *favelas,* Brazil 68
    hazards of 70
    Nairobi 69
    *townships,* South Africa 68
stacks and stumps 34
standard of living 52
steel making
    and pollution 171
    UK, case study 167-9
Stevenage
    green belt 85
    map 85
    proposed development site 88

storage time for water molecules
   atmosphere 3
   glaciers 3
   groundwater 3
   lakes 3
   puddles 3
   snow cover 3
   soils 3
   vegetation surfaces 3
storm hydrograph 1, 3
   base flow 4
   storm flow 4
storm surges 53, 126–7
storm waves 29
strato-volcano 111
subduction zones 106
suburbanisation
   Bradford 78
suburbs 74
sulphur dioxide 112
supermarket chains, growth 96
   disadvantages 97
surface runoff 2
suspended load 18
swash 29
Sweden
   population changes 1800-2009 48–9
   population pyramids 49

# T

Tagus-Murcia water transfer scheme 141–2
tax raising 56
Taylor Woodrow
   development company 85
tectonic hazards 103–22
tectonic plate boundaries 105–8
tectonic plates 103–9
   boundaries, destructive plate 106–8
   global distribution 105
Teesside iron and steel industry
   UK 169
temperatures rising 183
Thailand 153
   surplus electricity capacity 154

Thames flood barrier 186
Thingvellir rift valley, Iceland 106
threshold spending 93
throughflow 2, 6, 7
tidewater 168
Tokyo, affluence in Japan 45
tourism 162, 163
   southern Spain 140–42
transects 208
transnational corporations
   formal sector 70
transpiration 1, 2
   stream flow 6
transport 16, 163
   and telecommunications improvements 165
trawling on sea bottom
   destruction of fish stocks and corals 193, 196
tropical cyclones
   Bay of Bengal 185
tropical storms 123–30
   aircraft 129
   causes 124
   radar 129
   radiosondes 129
   satellites 129
   ships and buoys 129
tropical storms, protection
   Cuba 129
   USA 129
tsunamis 110
Tucson, Arizona, business centre buildings 59
typhoons 123–30

# U

United Kingdom
   deindustrialisation 159
   Industrial Revolution 159
United Nations (UN) 151
   aid, multilateral 150
   human development index (HDI) 145
urban and rural populations 63–102
urban change
   London and southeast England, case study 84
urban growth, New Delhi, India 81

urbanisation 9, 63
  in Bolivia 66
  in LEDCs 68
  massive
    cause of global warming 181
urban land use 74–102
urban management in MEDCs 84
urban planning, sustainable
  features 83
urban-rural migration 71
  demographic effect 73
  economic effect 73
  environmental effect 73
  social effect 73
urban-rural shift in USA
  Birmingham, Alabama 166
urban-rural shift of manufacturing
  reasons for, in UK 166
urban shopping hierarchy 94

# V

Valency River, Boscastle, drainage basin 12
vertical erosion 22
village survey questionnaire 205
volcanic blasts 112
volcanic hazards 111–12
volcanic island arcs 108
volcanoes 103–14
V-shaped valleys 18
  formation 22

# W

wages, lower in LEDCs 165
water 1, 2
  for golf courses in Spain 142
*Water Aid* (NGO), British charity 136, 156
water contamination in Ghana 155–6
water cycle 2
  drinking, 3
  electricity generating 3
  irrigation 3
  manufacturing 3
  sanitation 3
water demand reduction 136

waterfalls 18, 20
  formation 22
water grid 136
water meters 136
water 'recycling' 136
water shortage 134
water supply 163
water tables, falling 134
water transfers in river basins 6–9
wave crest 29
wave erosion 33
waves 27
  and currents 28–9
  high-energy and low-energy 29
  transport by 29
wealth of country
  GDP per capita 143
weather and climate changes
  benefits and problems 182, 183
weather changes in UK
weathering
  biological 27
  chemical
  solution 16–18
  physical 16
weathering processes 16
West Stevenage Development Project 85
  green belt conflict 85–8
  people's views 86
wetlands 9
  draining 16
Wharfe, river in Yorkshire Dales
  map 18–21
Whinash, Cumbria
  Area of Outstanding Natural Beauty 190
  conflict 190
  controversial scheme, public enquiry, 2005 192
  map of proposed site 190
  opinions for and against 191
  site of proposed wind farm 188, 189
wind farm in Scotland 187–8
wind power 187
winds 126–7
wind turbines, diagram 189

Witherslack, Cumbria
    rural service provision 100-2
World Bank 151
    aid, multilateral 150
    on Bangladeshi poverty 53
    world population 63

world population growth 50, 51
World Trade Organization (WTO) 165

## Y
Yorkshire coast 31-7
youthful population in LEDCs 56-7